Ian Mackersey is a New Zealand writer and documentary film maker whose programmes since 1977 have won 24 awards internationally. He learnt to fly after the Second World War on a small open cockpit bi-plane in Jean Batten's home town, Rotorua, and later flew with the RAFVR in England. He has worked as a journalist in New Zealand, Hong Kong, London, and Central Africa where he began making television documentaries in the mid-1960s. Before returning to New Zealand in 1983 he was for many years head of film and television production at British Airways in London. He and his wife Caroline, a former BBC Television researcher, make documentaries from a large old wooden house in the Auckland suburb of Mount Eden where they live with their daughter, a Danish au-pair, and two Burmese cats.

G000088513

By the same author

IAN MACKERSEY

Jean Batten:
The Garbo of the Skies

WARNER BOOKS

A *Warner* Book

First published in Great Britain in 1990
by Macdonald & Co (Publishers) Ltd
Reprinted 1990
This edition published by Warner Books in 1992
Reprinted 1999

Copyright © Ian Mackersey 1990

The moral right of the author has been asserted.

A CIP catalogue record for this book is
available from the British Library.

ISBN 0 7088 3019 0

Printed and bound in Great Britain by
Mackays of Chatham plc, Chatham, Kent

Warner Books
A Division of
Little, Brown and Company (UK)
Brettenham House
Lancaster Place
London WC2E 7EN

CONTENTS

To Caroline

who discovered what
happened to Jean

PREFACE

Except briefly, as a shy child observer, I was never privileged to meet Jean Batten. The views of her that emerge in this biography, therefore, come largely, and in surprising consensus, from many of the people who did know her: from the days of her New Zealand childhood, through the years of her enormous fame, to the months of her tragic final loneliness in a corner of Spain. To these people, in many countries, for their generosity in long discussions, telephone conversations and in hundreds of valuable letters, I am deeply indebted. Their helpfulness and patience has made possible for the first time a portrayal not only of the fairy princess figure that was the creation of the media but also of the often sadly troubled, intensely private person.

First and foremost I owe thanks to the Batten family for their generous co-operation and support throughout a complex and frequently bewildering research task that began with the unusual dilemma that the whereabouts and fate of my subject were shrouded in mystery. For the willingness and patience with which they allowed their lives to be so regularly disrupted by my research demands, I am particularly grateful to Jean's New Zealand relatives: her nephew Rick and his wife Margaret, Rick's brother Jim and his wife Rhoda, Jean's niece, Isobel Scott Davidson and Rick's daughter, Kathie. In England I am indebted to Jean's niece, Penny Messer, and to her father, Jean's brother, John, for his willingness to discuss some painful and, for him, personally distressing episodes in his relationship with his famous sister. The Batten family, who entered my life as an obviously vital source of biographical information, soon became warm and permanent friends.

I am specially grateful, too, for the extensive co-operation and kindness shown me by Bob and Lyn Pooley and for much hospitality at their home at Felden in Hertfordshire where Jean had frequently been their guest. I owe further thanks to Bob, for allowing me to quote from his company Airlife Publishing's *Alone in the Sky*, a 1979 reprint of Jean's book, *My Life*, first published in 1938.

For the deeply professional interest they took in Jean's complex personality, for the time they devoted to studying her writing and the events of her life, and for their patience in attempting explanations of her unique style and character, I owe enormous gratitude to two Auckland psychologists, Yvonne and Michael Edwards.

In my search for greater understanding of what it must have been like to fly alone in a small, fragile aeroplane through the violence of tropical storms, I was greatly helped by Gordon Thompson of Air New Zealand, who has done it (and been frightened by the experience) many times.

Beyond the reminiscences of the people who knew her, the principal sources of Jean's quotations used in this biography – but not always necessarily identified as such – are *My Life*, her first book *Solo Flight*, published in 1934, and her unpublished memoirs, *Luck and the Record Breaker*. For permission to quote from the latter I must thank Jean's next-of-kin, Rick Batten, and the executors of her estate, Barclays Bank Trust Company. The memoirs contained numerous misspellings and a tendency towards repetition. Here and there in the interests of clarity I have taken the liberty of correcting these lapses.

I am indebted to the Batten family in New Zealand, particularly to Isobel Scott Davidson, for their kindness in making available to me the family archive of newspaper cuttings, photographs and correspondence collected by Jean's father, Fred. For access to the much larger archive assembled by Jean, and lodged with the Royal Air Force Museum at Hendon in London, I owe very great thanks to the museum's Keeper of Aviation Records, Peter Murton, whose consistent helpfulness over many months significantly helped unlock some of the carefully guarded secrets of Jean's private life.

My research was materially helped by the fact that it was also contributing to a television documentary programme. For their faith in the film project, and the provision of funds for it, I must thank Energy Source Television Ltd in Wellington and, for his encouragement and enthusiasm, the company's former commissioning editor, Peter Sainsbury. For much of the international travel involved, I am grateful for the generous assistance of Air New Zealand.

My special thanks and gratitude are due to Sir Peter Masefield, who knew Jean both in her golden years and in the more desperate decade of her comeback; not only did he contribute much valuable insight into her disturbingly complex character but, through his kindness in agreeing to read the complete manuscript, gave me the added benefit of his incomparable historical knowledge of the 1930s' British aviation scene, and of its celebrated and colourful characters, many of whom he knew personally.

The final task of committing the book to the word processor, and helping me collate and select the illustrations from around three thousand photographs collected across the world, owes thanks to four people: my daughters Paula and Kiri, Marianne Mouritzen from Denmark, and my wife, Caroline. To the latter also must go my biggest tribute of all. Not only did her dedication and perseverance help reveal much of Jean's hitherto carefully concealed private world — her secret places and her even more secret relationships — it was responsible for the triumph of detective work that, late in the day, was to solve the seemingly insoluble mystery of her fate.

Ian Mackersey
Auckland
New Zealand

August 1989

PROLOGUE

In what must have been the winter of 1934 I remember, as a very small boy, going with my mother to visit her sister in another part of New Zealand's North Island. We travelled overnight, from our home in Wellington, several hundred miles north in the sleeping car of a steam train to a place called Frankton Junction. Here, next morning, we boarded another train for the slow and grimy journey over forested hills to Rotorua, the tourist town in the centre of New Zealand's thermal region.

The first-class open-plan carriage had only one other occupant, a strikingly attractive dark-haired woman in her mid-twenties wearing, I can still remember, a hat with a feather and a large fur coat. I don't think I would have given her a second thought but for two things. She was accompanied by a small black kitten which piddled under the seats and upset the saucer of milk a solicitous guard had supplied from the station café. But more memorable was the woman's response to the conventional civility of my mother's greeting.

New Zealand in those days was a friendly, informal country of less than a million-and-a-half people. Passengers on long train journeys were gregarious and friendly. But this beautiful woman was different. She ignored my mother's cheerful 'good morning', cutting her dead with a haughty glance. My mother, a formidable person of Edwardian correctness who placed high importance on good manners, was affronted. She had immediately recognised the other woman. And as the train rumbled off I can still vividly remember her, in her tailored brown tweed suit, seething with indignation at the snub.

'Who does she think she is?' she hissed.

The woman was clearly someone of importance. The guard made a huge fuss of her, treating her with excessive respect,

1

regularly mopping up after the kitten and replenishing its milk
from wayside refreshment stations. She addressed him in the
superior manner of someone accustomed to giving instructions,
and with an affected accent which in itself commanded a degree
of awe. My mother made no further attempt at conversation
and the woman never spoke to us.

In the late afternoon we pulled into Rotorua. The normally
deserted platform was thronged with people. They surged
forward, jostling and cheering, towards our carriage. It was clear
that our fellow passenger was the object of a major civic
welcome.

'Who is that lady?' I remember asking my mother.

'Jean Batten,' she snorted. Years later at school I learnt that
the young woman who'd upset my mother that day was one of
my country's very few national heroes. Indeed she was an
international celebrity made famous by a series of spectacular
record-breaking flights across the world in small primitive aeroplanes in the mid-1930s. She was New Zealand's Amy Johnson.
But more beautiful and, as a pilot, rather more capable. She
was, I now know, one of the greatest women aviators of this
century.

Her flights became legends of epic quality in the years of the
great world depression when the public needed adventurous
heroes, preferably female and beautiful, as an antidote to the
gloom of the times. It was an era in which long-distance solo
record flying became an epidemic, encouraged by newspapers,
radio and cinema newsreels in the days before television when
great crowds would create traffic jams, converging on airports to
see and touch the flying celebrities in their moments of triumph.
It began in the late 1920s and, by the mid-1930s, as war clouds
loomed, it was all over. It made overnight celebrities of Charles
Lindbergh, Bert Hinkler, Amy Johnson, Jim Mollison, Amelia
Earhart, Charles Kingsford Smith, Beryl Markham, and scores
of colourful personalities whose exploits briefly captured public
interest. Although they claimed to be pioneering airline routes,
most were doing it for egos fed by phenomenal public adulation.
But they were undoubtedly brave, were constantly frightened,
and shared a short life expectancy. The unsophisticated
daughter of an impoverished dentist from the bottom of the

world, Jean Batten stepped into the big league of this élite community of aviation heroes.

She leapt to fame when, in 1934, she flew alone in a tiny wood-and-fabric Gipsy Moth from England to Australia in just under fifteen days, knocking four days off Amy Johnson's hugely publicised 1930 record. Then, not only had she flown back again, she had gone on, in a small cabin plane, to fly the South Atlantic and, later, to become the first person ever to fly from England to New Zealand.

Throughout the mid-thirties her flights made front-page news in Fleet Street. The billboards needed only to refer to her as 'Jean'. She became an aviation megastar, treated like royalty. But the determined young woman from the colonial world of New Zealand took it all in her stride.

Yet one thing was always to distinguish her from her famous colleagues whose affairs and private lives frequently became sordid public property. She was a loner. Around herself she built an impenetrable wall. Not a word of scandal was breathed about this woman so remarkable for her beauty and modest charm. Few people were ever to know that her dazzling public façade concealed a darker personality in which fame and adulation had bred deceit and ruthlessness. Or that the forces that drove her to fulfil what she saw as her destiny were controlled from behind the scenes by the shadowy figure of her mother, with whom she had become emotionally fused in a symbiotic relationship of astonishing psychological intensity.

It is difficult today, sitting in the comfort of a 747 crossing the world at ten miles a minute, far above the weather, to appreciate the courage and endurance of the pioneer aviators. They flew at low level through the violently destructive turbulence and darkness of tropical storms too large to be avoided. They did it alone, without radio, in small, relatively fragile machines, with the most rudimentary of flight instruments.

It is equally difficult to comprehend the fever of excitement and sense of pride in achievement for King and Empire that these flights created. I can remember my father, at our home in Wellington, crouched over our primitive crystal wireless set, earphones clamped on his head, twiddling the 'cat's whisker' control for a signal bringing news of Jean Batten's progress. Stations would interrupt their programmes to report that she had safely arrived in Singapore, or Darwin, or passed overhead some outback Australian settlement. When she arrived in places like Sydney and Auckland thousands would stop work and rush to the airports to cheer her. They were far bigger, more emotional greetings than ever awaited the astronauts of over thirty years later.

As a young newspaper reporter in the years after the Second World War I went back to Rotorua, this time to live and work. I learnt that it was Jean's birthplace. But there were no memorials, no streets named in her honour and no one seemed to know in which house the town's famous daughter had been born in 1909.

During my year there I learnt to fly myself, qualifying as a pilot on an Avro Avian, a small open cockpit biplane similar to the Moth in which Jean made her first headlines. But at the flying club there was nothing to remind us of the local heroine. No pictures, no trophies, no press cuttings of her great flights in the years when she had walked the world stage making front-page news, been fêted by the crowned heads of Europe, mobbed by huge crowds. It was as if her name had been expunged from local history.*

Nor was it only from her home town that memories of her exploits had faded. Elsewhere in New Zealand at that time – apart from a tiny Auckland city sidestreet – there was little to remind the country of its pre-war heroine.

The reason, I was to discover, was that when, in 1939, she'd hung up her flying helmet for the last time, after just four brief years of fame, she had never returned to her homeland. She and her mother, obsessed with the need for privacy, had gone into such fiercely guarded seclusion that very few people, including their family, had known in which country they were actually living.

It caused great astonishment, therefore, when in the late

---

*A Rotorua street was belatedly to be named after her in 1955. Insignificant and less than 100 yards long, it was called, perhaps somewhat brusquely, Batten Street.

1960s, Jean suddenly reappeared. Now approaching sixty, but remarkably well preserved and still strikingly beautiful, she startled the world by emerging in a mini-skirt, her hair dyed jet black and looking not a day over forty. For the first time in thirty years she offered herself for media interviews and, although no longer an active pilot, immediately began to re-involve herself in aviation causes. Where had she been and where had she sprung from?

It transpired that she had been living the life of a recluse. On the details she was vague and not immediately forthcoming. And so long had she been out of sight many people now had never even heard of her. 'Don't they know who I am?' she would ask bewilderedly. Sadly few did.

During the years of her triumphant emergence from oblivion I was living out of New Zealand, making films in London. I did not hear her name again until my wife Caroline and I decided to return to Auckland early in 1983 to set up a small documentary production company. Somehow I had assumed that Jean Batten was dead, that she had long since joined her illustrious contemporaries in some aviation Valhalla. It was with mild surprise, therefore, that early in 1986, I saw her name one morning in a headline in an Auckland newspaper. She was missing.

In late 1982, at the age of seventy-three, she had apparently gone to the Spanish Mediterranean island of Majorca to look for a new home. Soon after arriving there she had written a letter to her publisher in England. It was just a routine note. But it was the last anyone had heard from her. Curiously there did not seem to be much concern for her welfare or whereabouts. The most persistent theory was that she had merely gone to ground – something she had apparently often done for long periods.

But, as the months became years, she did not reappear. When, by the middle of 1986, my interest as a pilot and film maker was beginning to stir, Jean Batten had become the centre of a deepening mystery that had taken on an international dimension.

It was around this time that Caroline came home one day with a book called *Alone in the Sky*.* She had found it tucked

*Airlife Publishing, Shrewsbury, England, 1979

away as a remaindered edition on the dusty back shelves of an Auckland bookshop. It was a book Jean had written in 1938 about her flying adventures. Originally published under the somewhat immodest title *My Life*,* its reissue had apparently not been a great success.

I settled down with keen interest to read it. It was a narrative of her great flights and much preoccupied with the rich and famous people, particularly the English aristocracy, in whose society she had found herself. It was an extraordinarily self-centred book. As a pilot it failed to tell me many of the things I wanted to know about her flights. Of her childhood, her family, and private life out of the headlines, the ebb and flow of her emotions and feelings, it revealed virtually nothing.

Yet my fascination was aroused. Here was one of the most publicised and publicly honoured people in New Zealand's history. Somewhere there must exist, I assumed, a biography or perhaps a documentary film that would illuminate her life and describe the real person she was. It didn't take long to discover that there was neither. A year later this was no longer to surprise me, but at the time it seemed hard to credit.

In the New Zealand winter of 1986 public interest in the mystery of her whereabouts began to grow. The London and Australian newspapers had by now picked up the story. But bafflingly the reports soon began to recycle the slender available information. Not only was Jean's life, beyond her flying adventures, virtually a closed book, the mystery of her whereabouts since she had posted her last letter from Majorca was proving highly resistant to investigation.

Here, it occurred to me, was a story with all the ingredients of classic documentary; a life surrounded by secrecy, and the public drama of her disappearance. In September 1986 Caroline and I decided to make a one-hour programme about her for world-wide television distribution.

It was obviously important to establish quickly if she was alive and willing to co-operate. Equally urgent was the need to learn a great deal more about her. In October 1986 we started on both fronts. It was to prove a formidable research challenge. It

*George Harrap, London, 1938

was to take us round the world four times. It was to thrust us personally into the headlines.

Of all the documentaries Caroline, as a former BBC Television researcher, and I had worked on, together and separately, over twenty years, the Jean Batten programme was quite unique in that comprehensive information about the subject simply did not exist. It was a long time before we were to discover the reason – that she had gone to elaborate lengths to ensure that it didn't. And that, where she had been prepared to reveal details of her private life, she had often been singularly economical with the truth – especially where it conflicted with the perfectionist image she had so successfully created for herself.

When we began our research the most extensive biographies we could find were brief single-paragraph entries in various *Who's Who*s and aviation directories. The longest ran to twenty-five lines. Unbelievable as it seemed, these cryptic summaries listed only her flying records and made no reference to her life after 1937. It was as if, at the age of twenty-nine, she had ceased to exist.

Our search began in the files of Auckland's two daily newspapers. In both quarters the national aviation heroine, who had come to be known as the Garbo of the Skies, did not appear to be regarded with much importance. The reference library of one had kept only two cuttings of the thousands of stories it had once carried about her exploits. The other held none. But both papers had kept cuttings of the interviews she gave when, in the 1970s, she had unexpectedly emerged from her long retreat.

Mellowing with age she had become more forthcoming about some of the more innocent private details of her earlier life. For the first time she began to describe the childhood she wanted to remember. In one interview she recalled how it all began: in a humble wooden cottage in Rotorua in the Edwardian New Zealand of 1909 – to the strains of La Paloma.

CHAPTER 1

The Dentist's Daughter (1909–1913)

Towards the end of 1986 I went down to Rotorua to find Jean's birthplace. I had wanted to make the journey by train to revive memories of my childhood encounter with her fifty years earlier, but it was only a freight railway now. So I drove to the lakeside spa town, today a tourist metropolis, strongly North American in character, sprawling with neon-lit motels among sulphur-smelling clouds of steam.

But of the little house in Amohia Street there was no trace. It had long ago disappeared under a multi-storey car park. Beneath the concrete ramps it was hard to imagine the little house with its corrugated iron roof, circular rainwater tank, and front verandah, in which Jean Batten had been born in the evening of 15 September, 1909. While her mother Ellen lay in labour, attended by the local midwife, her father Fred and two of his friends, who formed a small instrumental group, gathered in the next room for their weekly musical evening. In her unpublished memoirs Jean describes how Fred, who played the flute, 'tiptoed into the bedroom to ask mother if she would prefer them not to play. But her reply was that music was what she needed. They therefore played, very quietly, selections from

8

their repertoire and I enjoyed one of my first meals, albeit a liquid one, to the strains of La Paloma and Schubert's Trout Quintet.'

The secrecy that was to become characteristic of Jean's, and her mother's, life had already taken root. 'Mother had not told anyone that I was expected and, in fact, went to a ball only two nights before my arrival.' Reflecting on this nearly seventy years later, Jean wrote: 'I like to think that privacy was such an integral part of life in those days and the mystery and wonder of creation preserved as a very special thing.'

Ellen and Fred had not been slow to explore these mysteries, for their first child, Harold, had been born only eight and a half months after their marriage in the town of Wanganui on 3 September, 1900. Fred was training to be a dentist. His father, James William Batten, a surveyor, was English – from Reading in Berkshire. He married Jane Gardner Rigden, the daughter of a wealthy shipowner, and they emigrated to New Zealand, arriving in Wellington on the sailing ship *Loch Cree* in August, 1879, with their daughters Ida, Isabella and Helen. Fred, the fourth of their six children, was born in Wellington two months later, by which time his father James's profession, as declared on the birth certificate, had changed from surveyor to 'gentleman'. However, for whatever reason, a few years later he ceased to be around – leaving his wife to bring up the six children from her income as a professional music teacher. From these small earnings she helped not only Fred, but his brother Edgar, to qualify as dentists.

Ellen's father also came from the United Kingdom to become a first generation New Zealander. John Blackmore, born around 1835, had served as a soldier in South Africa before coming to New Zealand where he arrived in 1869. In interviews Jean spoke with pride of her grandfather as an army officer who came out with his regiment, the Staffordshire Light Infantry, to fight in the Maori Land Wars. With the help of New Zealand Army records and the Military Historical Society I tried to trace him – but was surprised to be told that no Staffordshire regiment had fought in the wars and that the campaigns involving Imperial troops were long over when Blackmore arrived in 1869.

The truth would appear to be that he came as a civilian

immigrant having been discharged from the British Army after service as a sergeant-major drill instructor. This theory was partly confirmed by the street directories of the day for the South Island town of Invercargill in which he settled and where his profession was shown as drill instructor and his address as the local garrison hall. If indeed he ever served in the Maori Wars he could only have done so as a volunteer in the local militia. However, the New Zealand Historical Society could find no record of that either and wrote: 'Most probably he was employed at the garrison hall as a caretaker and was used as a drill instructor for the Volunteers.'

Jean obviously promoted him from his former NCO rank to commissioned officer and created the glamorous fiction that he had come to fight in the Wars because it sounded more impressive than the humble truth.

John Blackmore, whom Jean claimed was related to R.D. Blackmore, the author of *Lorna Doone*, came from Devon. The sailing ship which took him to New Zealand was six months on the voyage. According to Jean, it ran aground off the coast of Brazil, was dismasted near Cape Horn, and the captain died of drink and was buried at sea. John Blackmore brought with him his seventeen-year-old Scottish bride of a few weeks, Mary Anne Shaw, who produced nine children in Invercargill where she was permanently consumed by homesickness.

Describing her grandfather's drill instructor background Jean once said: 'Mother used to tell us of her father handing out broomsticks to the nine and putting them through infantry drill. He used to say to them, "If you want to get on, walk well and talk well."'

Ellen was born in October 1876. Little information survives about her early life in Invercargill, in those days a bleak settlement in the cool far south of New Zealand. According to Jean's memoirs, she was a creative person, fond of poetry and sufficiently talented as a painter to become an art teacher. Strongly drawn to the stage, she devoted much of her time as a young woman to amateur dramatics. Several people were to tell me that she was a thwarted actress. She was also said to have been a high-spirited young woman who once created a minor stir in late Victorian Invercargill by peddling in serge bloomers down the main street on a man's bicycle. One of her brothers is quoted as saying: 'There was a great commotion with much laughter, clapping and shouts of bravo. Can you imagine how amazed and ashamed I felt when I recognised the girl as my own sister – riding *my* bicycle.'

After their marriage Fred and Ellen – she was then calling herself 'Nellie' – went to live in Auckland where he joined the practice of the London Dental Institute in Queen Street. A couple of years later they moved to Wellington. By 1903 they had two sons, Harold, and a new arrival, John. (A third son was to die in infancy.)

In 1904 Fred, by now a qualified dentist, seized an opportunity to go north and join the local branch of the London Dental Institute in Rotorua. It was a small town of about two thousand people in those days, looking not unlike a pioneer settlement of the American mid-west with wide, dusty, unpaved streets, iron-roofed wooden weatherboard buildings and hitching rails. Contemporary photographs reflect its colonial Edwardian atmosphere with horsedrawn coaches and women in ankle-length dresses riding sidesaddle.

But most of the population was then Maori – unlike today most of them full-bloodedly dark-skinned. They lived in villages beside the lake, and around the white silica terraces of the hot springs, their presence heightening the sense of a frontier society. To take the recuperative mineral waters and view the spectacular geothermal activity, tourists even then came to Rotorua from all over the world.

This was the environment, with the permanent tang of sulphur in the air, in which Jean spent her first four years. She had been christened Jane Gardner Batten after her grandmother, but the name Jane didn't survive long after an uncle taught her to say in a Scots accent: 'I'm bonny Jean fra Aberdeen.'

Ellen was already actively involved in local amateur drama, much of it then expressing itself in elaborately costumed and silently acted tableaux. Contemporary newspaper cuttings and faded pictures in the Batten family album recapture a little of the Rotorua social scene of 1910 in which Ellen was prominent. The pictures show her as a tall, elegant, and strikingly attractive dark-haired woman in her mid-thirties, always smartly dressed and, as often as not, in fancy dress. It is not difficult to believe that she was a highly extrovert personality, a woman who knew her own mind, a force to be reckoned with. She was a tireless organiser, sitting on numerous committees on which, one suspects, she would have been a dominating influence. On horseback she was a familiar sight about town. 'We three children were immensely proud of her for she looked so lovely on that white mare, riding sidesaddle and wearing a flowing habit and a tiny hat with a feather. She often lifted me up onto the saddle in front of her where I clung to the pommel as she cantered along.'

Ellen's versatility was daunting. She played Mary Queen of Scots and Juliet to praise from the local newspaper critics. She organised rollerskating competitions. 'Mrs Batten, the moving spirit in the carnival, was much admired in her butterfly dance ... her movements were particularly graceful.' She helped organise the annual military ball of the local Territorial company. 'The ball was opened with a grand march, led by Surgeon-Captain Buckhill and Mrs Batten.' Her sweet peas won prizes for the champion bloom in the flower show. She was captain of the women's rowing club.

But the social and sporting outlets which life in Rotorua provided were not wholly satisfying to Ellen. Privately she sought more demanding adventures – to do some of the things that only men then did. A few weeks before Jean was born, Blériot became the first person to fly the English Channel. On the wall beside Jean's cot she carefully pinned a newspaper picture of the French pilot and his famous aeroplane. It was as if she was saying to her newborn daughter that the next generation of women would themselves be making history with achievements like this.

Fred Batten was a ruggedly goodlooking man, highly attractive to women – which was said to have been very helpful to the success of his dental practice. But he was more prominent in sport than in the social whirl. As a captain in the Territorial Army he commanded the town's cadet force and, like Ellen, won prizes for rowing. He also excelled as an amateur boxer and at rugby. He was exceedingly popular among the men of the town and was an ardent freemason.

One gets the feeling that these early days of the marriage were relatively happy. From the house in Amohia Street there frequently came the sound in the evenings of Fred's neighbourhood orchestra in which Ellen played the piano and the guitar and they all sang numbers from Gilbert and Sullivan, sea shanties, and American Civil War songs like 'Dixieland'. On long weekends they would go camping, taking their gear by pony-and-trap down the narrow, sandy, volcanic pumice road, fifty miles south to Lake Taupo; here they would sail in the family boat and Jean, at the age of three, was helped to land her first trout – which Ellen cooked on the camp fire.

In the long summer holiday at Christmas they would go north to Mt Maunganui on the warm Bay of Plenty coast to stay in a cottage by the sea to sunbathe and swim in the surf. Jean wrote about this phase of her life in idyllic terms in her unpublished manuscript: 'There seemed to be so much fun and laughter in those days and my childhood was an exceptionally happy one, possibly because I was really wanted by my parents and from the moment I was born, loved and treasured by the whole family.'

Her brother John, when I was later, with some difficulty, to track him down, at the age of eighty-four, in England, confirmed this. 'Jean was a very tiny and frail baby. She was so delicate that she needed special rearing and, after weaning, special feeding. All this led to the whole family making a special fuss of her. And I think it must have been right from that moment that the unusually close relationship between Jean and mother began. Back in the Rotorua days there was no doubt, Jean was the favourite, worshipped by both parents.' But despite all the special nurturing she enjoyed, Jean remained a sickly child, her susceptibility to illness a constant concern. It resulted in her excessive over-protection by the whole family.

It is clear from her unpublished recollections that Ellen assumed a powerful role in the philosophy of treatment of her ailments. Her methods were startlingly basic old wives' cures. 'If I had an earache mother would cure it with a few drops of warm oil in the ear – then a hot potato, baked in its jacket and wrapped in a piece of flannel, held against it. For a cold in the head one had to sit with the feet soaking in a very hot mustard bath while sucking a lump of sugar with drops of oil of eucalyptus on it.

'Illness was something I was taught to avoid at all costs and mother believed that the mind played a great part in this. A clean healthy mind meant a clean healthy body. There were few ailments that could not be cured or avoided by adequate fresh air, fresh food and fresh water coupled with exercise and a genuine desire for cleanliness in mind and body. In this I think that I agree with her.' This elementary doctrine was, seventy years later, to contribute directly to Jean's death.

At nearly 1,000 feet above sea level the winters are cold and frosty in Roturua. Life in the Batten home centred on the kitchen, kept permanently warm by a large coal stove from which Ellen produced, for that time, unusually well planned meals. Diet was important to her. She had studied nutrition long before it was fashionable, and Jean was to acquire a deep concern for the importance of food values and an antipathy for the dishes considered harmful. Writing about it years later Jean said: 'I can remember others staring in uncomprehending amazement when she talked of proteins and carbohydrates. All highly spiced foods, savouries, curries and pickles were taboo for they were thought to make children mature too soon. I was urged to eat plenty of lettuce because it contained laudanum to make me sleep well. Spinach for the iron to make me strong. Cabbage to prevent rheumatism. Cream for the nerves. Milk for the skin. Fruit for the bowels.'

Ellen also stressed upon Jean the importance of good health for the persuasive reason that they couldn't afford doctors' bills. The children's pets were never allowed inside the house, there were always festoons of sticky fly papers hanging from the ceilings and the milk and sugar bowls were covered with cotton net circles weighed down with dangling blue beads. And when spring cleaning took place the house was turned upside down. The linoleum and carpets were rolled up and taken outside to be washed and beaten and the wooden floorboards scrubbed with sandsoap and swabbed with disinfectant. Ellen was obsessed with cleanliness. Looking back at her dedication to the family's wellbeing Jean was to say: 'I did not realise at the time how lucky I was to have a mother who considered being a housewife a career. The fact that she did is a tribute to her self-sacrifice and sense of duty. For I now know that she was a rebel at heart and the role of housewife must have been terribly restricting for a woman of her talents and outlook.'

But although she was a highly organised and efficient mother Ellen was a cold person who showed her children little overt affection. And even though she was to develop an excessively close relationship with Jean, she denied her, as she did her sons, any great warmth of physical contact. It was a pattern that was to repeat itself in Jean's adult life and, at times, in her highly ambivalent relations with men. John commented: 'I never thought mother ever actually loved me.'

But in intellectual areas Jean flourished. She developed as a highly intelligent child, demanding – from the stimulus of a house full of books and endless storytelling by Ellen – to be taught to read, she claims, at the age of three. This prompted one of her aunts, Jean recounted, to say to Ellen: ' "You should not push Jeannie too much or she will burn herself out," to which mother replied, "Jean has a will of her own and I would not dream of damping her joyous zest for life." '

One of the few necessarily second hand observations of Ellen at this time, around eighty years ago, came from an elderly Auckland woman, Lucy Goodison. Her aunt, Millicent Bridle, was then a teacher in Rotorua and knew Ellen well. 'I can remember her telling me,' Miss Goodison said, 'what a very domineering, possessive person she was. She wanted everything her way; she wanted to "own" people. My aunt was convinced the marriage was foundering.' The reason, almost certainly, was that Fred had begun to take more than a passing interest in other women.

Money, one suspects, was always short in the Batten household and an awareness of its importance was one of Jean's earliest memories. Long before she went to school: 'I was able to count and knew the relative value of coins, for the importance of thrift had been impressed on me at an early age. I was often allowed to tender money for a purchase after which I would count the change carefully, helped by my mother and an amused shop assistant.' This preoccupation with thrift was to remain with Jean throughout her life.

She developed, too, as a headstrong child who liked to get her own way. And quite early she showed a tendency to wanderlust and fearlessness — two of the qualities that were to take her to fame. In her memoirs she describes how her mother helped her to become a brave and stoical little girl who rarely cried: 'I was certainly not pampered for I always went to bed in the dark so that I would never be frightened of it. This no doubt made me independent and self-reliant but, alas, with these characteristics came a strong desire to wander. One day when I was missing and my worried parents searched frantically they discovered me sitting calmly on the floor of a stable, stroking the silky leg of one of the coach horses. My father approached stealthily, and as he later told me, made a grab before I saw him or the horse moved.'

John Batten remembered another incident from the Rotorua days. 'There was this violent thunderstorm raging over the town and we were all inside waiting for it to pass. Then we discovered that Jean, who would have been about three, was outside, exposed to the weather, watching it with fascination and shouting with glee. I thought: gosh how terrifying, and rushed out to get her. There, bathed in the lightning flashes, she insisted on staying to watch "the pretty lights". It remains one of my abiding memories of her as a child.'

Jean wrote about the perils of growing up in a town that had scalding unfenced pools steaming and bubbling in craters in almost every street. From time to time people fell into them late at night and were boiled alive. The Battens fitted a latch high up on their front gate but Jean quickly learnt to climb up and open it. Her father tried to dissuade her, Jean wrote, by saying, ' "Do you know what will happen one day if you go out the gate alone? The suffragettes will get you and take you away from us." In answer to my query he added, "They are tall thin women dressed in black and they carry umbrellas with which to whack naughty little girls." ' But Mrs Batten, herself an outspoken feminist, said later: 'You need not have put Jean off suffragettes for they are doing a lot for women and she will benefit from their efforts.'

Ellen was a staunch believer in the right of women to do as

they wished, free of the restrictions and conventions shaped for them by men. It was sometimes to bring her into conflict with Fred. On one occasion she and some women friends went without telling their husbands to a personal appearance of a famous muscleman called Sandow. Describing the incident Jean says her father, who prided himself on the excellence of his physique, was 'jealous and shocked' when he heard about it, 'even though Sandow wore cotton tights and a small loin cloth of tigerskin and had removed the hair from his chest in order not to offend the ladies in the audience'.

Meanwhile three-year-old Jean was busy exercising her own free will and her determination to explore, despite her father's threats. She continued to escape into town, regularly to be returned by delivery men, among whom she became well known. 'On one occasion I arrived home in the milk float which resembled a small chariot and was drawn by a piebald horse which the milkman whipped up to give me a special thrill. We raced down the street, the tall churns rattling and the whip cracking, then pulled up with such a resounding clatter of hooves and metal-rimmed wheels that mother, who hadn't missed me, ran onto the long wooden verandah to see what was happening. Next time it was the butcher boy who brought me home, perched in front of him on the saddle of his spirited black mare. Yet mother never scolded me.'

In one of the Rotorua chapters of her memoirs Jean wrote of her early longings for adventure, how she 'felt impelled by instinct to follow where it led, without either conscious thought or plan'. She described at length an incident when she was four which she regarded as one of the milestones of her life. Taken by her father and an uncle to listen to a military band playing in the municipal gardens, she hijacked a tricycle from a small boy and pedalled off at high speed. 'Up and down the paths I raced in an ecstasy of delight pursued by the owner and his father.' After a lengthy chase and much shouting she was cornered by father and uncle. To dodge them she left the path and suddenly was heading for a concealed boiling pool. 'My father was only able to stop the bike with a flying rugger tackle just before it reached the wispy columns of steam.'

With bleeding nose, and torn and blackened dress, she was

plucked by Fred out of the warm mud. 'I laid my hot little face on his shoulder and sobbed as if my heart would break.' At home Ellen bathed her wounds and tried to comfort her. But Jean was much more concerned, as she was to be throughout the years of fame, with her mother's approval. 'That night when I said my prayers at her knee and came to the line "please forgive me my sins and make me a good girl from now on", I opened one eye a little to peep up at her face to see if she was very disappointed in me. To my great surprise she was deep in thought and smiling. I felt puzzled and wondered why. Years later I learnt that she, too, had once fallen in love with a bicycle.'

In 1913, with war in Europe only a year away, the idyllic, leisurely Rotorua days came to an end. The Battens moved to the relative bustle of Auckland where Fred rejoined the city practice of the London Dental Institute. For the family it was the end of an era. Although few people were to notice, because they went to extraordinary lengths to cover up the cracks, the marriage was beginning to falter. Life was never to be the same again for any of them.

CHAPTER 2

Parting of the Ways (1913–1930)

After the gentle pulse of life in Rotorua, Auckland in 1913, with its population of nearly 120,000, its electric trams, its noisy motor cars, and harbour bustling with steam ferries, must have appeared to the Battens a bewildering and frenetic place. Unable to afford their own house they moved into a private hotel at the upper end of Queen Street, the city's broad main thoroughfare in which the London Dental Institute was situated. Ellen, much given to elevating status, was now referring to Fred as a 'surgeon dentist'. A few months later the family moved to Parnell, an attractive suburb on a ridge overlooking the harbour. Here, at 35 St George's Bay Road, they rented the first of many Auckland houses. Fred and Ellen joined the local rowing club where Ellen trained the women's team and Harold and John became coxswains. They were now at local state schools, but Jean, still the darling of the family, was sent to a private one, Melmerley College. She went at the age of five, early in 1915.

I found only one person who remembers Jean at Melmerley. Ruth Flashoff, now living at Havelock North in Hawkes Bay, New Zealand, was a fellow pupil. She used to go to Jean's house after school to play with her dolls. She had vivid memories of Ellen. 'I was afraid of her, she spoke so sharply. She was a bossy woman, always jumping on us. I remember Jean did exactly as she was told. She seemed afraid to defy her mother who utterly dominated her.'

Two years after Jean started at Melmerley, by which time the Battens had moved to another rented house in Richmond Avenue, Grey Lynn, their life was to be turned upside down. The First World War was consuming men at a prodigious rate and Fred, as a Territorial Army captain, joined up with the New Zealand Expeditionary Force. As a married man of nearly thirty-eight with three children, he didn't have to go. But, in 1917, he chose to volunteer and in July that year sailed from Auckland with the 28th Reinforcements in the troopship *Waitemata*.

'Tightly clasping mother's hand I stood on the quay. The ship with its khaki-clad figures became blurred as I strove to keep my tears back. But mother looked at me with her large dark eyes and reminded me that brave girls never cried.' It was a self-control she was to observe for most of her life.

Jean missed her father badly. She was later to write that he was her 'first hero'. One day a letter came for her from France where, from December 1917, Fred served for seven months on the Western Front with the New Zealand forces. It was a bunch of violets he had specially picked for her in some woods on the Somme.

As the war dragged on Ellen began to feel the pinch. With the dental practice closed money was short and life became increasingly tough for the family. For a time Ellen put John into a private school, Kings College, but within a few months couldn't afford the fees and removed him. Even the rent of their Grey Lynn house became a strain. They had to give it up and Jean had to leave Melmerley College whose fees, also, Ellen could no longer afford. In the first of a succession of even more down-at-heel rented homes their shabby-genteel existence took them to a house on the unfashionable south side of Remuera where Jean had her first taste of a state school.

A younger fellow pupil, Keith Watson, retains one vivid memory of her. Jean had been deputed to escort him to school every day and had been instructed to hold his hand. When

Keith refused to be seen hand-in-hand with a girl in public she stamped her feet and burst into tears.

As with much of Jean's life it is difficult in the absence of any surviving witnesses to recreate a picture of her First World War years in Auckland with any accuracy. She devotes only a few lines in her memoirs to this period of obvious difficulty for Ellen and would have been too young to have recognised the symptoms of undoubted stress on her mother. But what is clear is that during this period the family established a style of nomadic living, their chronically distressed circumstances driving them from one drab lodging to another. This rolling-stone pattern was to become a permanent feature of Jean's life. I tried to trace their movements around Auckland from the contemporary street directories, but as all their homes were rented their name never appeared.

Whatever unsettling influences were affecting Jean as she grew from eight to ten years old, it is clear that Ellen gave her welfare and development a very high priority. Where she was never able, despite her competence as a mother, according to John, to show the boys much affection, Jean was to get an abundance of it.

She was also during these formative years to have instilled in her constantly by Ellen the potential she had to compete with men, to become an achiever in a masculine world. It is significant that Ellen went out of her way to take Jean down to the harbour at Kohimarama to watch the flying boats of New Zealand's first flying school, then training pilots for service with the Royal Flying Corps in France. One cannot escape the feeling that, as with the picture of Blériot she had pinned on the wall, it was principally her own subconscious frustrations and intense personal fascination that drew Ellen to the launching ramp on the beach. Whatever the motive, there is no doubt of the effect it was to have on her eight-year-old daughter. Jean claims in her memoirs that it was there and then that she was first seized with the ambition one day to fly: 'The little seaplane would skim across the water throwing up a curtain of spray and rise like a seabird up into the blue sky. At such moments as I watched spellbound and the plane turned to fly back and circle the bay with the sunlight glistening on its silver wings, I experienced such a surge of exhilaration that I felt quite sick with longing to be up there in it.'

One afternoon Jean went down to the flying school with Harold and John. A pilot invited the brothers to look inside one of the planes. 'They hurried forward and easily swung themselves up to the cockpit while I was left standing alone trying hard not to cry with sheer disappointment.' But then the pilot spotted Jean. ' "Does the little girl want to look inside too?" There was no need to wait for the answer when he saw the smile that lit up my face. I ran forward eagerly and he swung me up onto his shoulder.

'From this vantage point I was able to peer into the dim recesses of the cockpit. At the deep metal seat, the rudder bar, the control column and the pale round dials of the few instruments. Had I but known it I was looking at the pattern of my own future.'

Meanwhile Jean's fascination with flight was satisfied by fantasy. In the garden of their rented house was a pepper tree in which her brothers had fixed a swing. 'I used to pretend it was the seaplane and strive to go higher and higher up into the cool green shade where the soft fern-like leaves brushed my face, then out into the sunlight and the blue sky.'

To try and make ends meet, Ellen turned to gambling on horses. There is no record of how successful she was. On one occasion she took Jean to the races and, against her better judgement, allowed her to invest ten shillings on a rank outsider, a chestnut gelding called Uncle Ned. The favourite on which Ellen had put her money stumbled on the final straight and Uncle Ned won. Jean went home with a wad of pound notes to contribute to the housekeeping.

In Fred's absence during her formative years, Jean forgot what it was like to have a father around and the emotional bonding to Ellen became deeply established. With her emancipated views Ellen discouraged traditional role modelling, encouraging Jean to follow conventionally male pursuits and interests. To John's annoyance she began to creep into the sacred preserve of his bedroom to borrow his scout manual — which she hid on her own bookshelf behind her copy of *Arabian Nights* — and taught herself the semaphore code.

Her library, carefully chosen by Ellen, had a strong bias towards travel and biographies of heroes and explorers: Drake, Colombus, Stanley, Cook and Buffalo Bill. And when she found the stories of Florence Nightingale and Joan of Arc she read them again and again. Beside her bed she kept a notebook. Ellen had instructed her to copy into it and memorise a catalogue of moral platitudes: Honesty is the best policy ... What's worth doing is worth doing well ... The devil finds work for idle hands.

In August 1918 Fred was pulled out of active service in France and repatriated to New Zealand. In London that month he wrote the only letter of his to Ellen that has survived. It is a warm and affectionate note that suggests he had been missing her badly:

August 1st 1918

My dearest Nell,
I'm in London at present and will be leaving here for NZ about the 12th inst. so should arrive HOME about October. I can hardly believe the good tidings. I am getting a transfer into the Dental Corps and will probably obtain my discharge in NZ ... I'm too excited to write any more Dear so will tell you all the news when I arrive.
Goodbye Dearest
From your loving husband

Fred

Sadly the fourteen months' absence that had made Fred's heart grow fonder was to prove to have been too long. But the cracks in the marriage were initially concealed by the joy of reunion. He arrived back in Auckland a month before the Armistice, and early in 1919 resumed his former existence as a dentist. Ellen and the children were then in a tacky flat in Devonport on the north side of the harbour, but Fred soon brought them back to a rented house at 5 Bracken Avenue in the more desirable suburb of Epsom on the tram route into the city. To help get the practice back on its feet Ellen assisted Fred as his nurse and receptionist for a time.

The months immediately following her father's return, as Jean recalls them in her memoirs, were for her initially happy ones. There was the excitement of helping him unpack his trunk and handling its military treasures, his manuals, maps and compass. Jean demanded to be shown how to use the compass so Fred, who had bought a motorbike, took her on the pillion out into the Waitakere Ranges to the west of Auckland. 'Through him I first discovered the intoxicating effect that speed had on me. When he accelerated and shouted back at me, "I'm going to try her flat out, are you all right?" I would gasp, "Yes, yes", with the wind tearing at my hair and the breath blown back into my nostrils, experiencing a wonderful feeling of exhilaration.'

Out on the mud tracks of the Waitakeres, where the forested ridges ran down to the black iron sands of the creaming surf beaches of the Tasman Sea, Jean, now ten years old, had her first navigation lessons using Fred's prismatic compass and maps. '"Where are we, little Mit, you tell me how to get home." And when I hesitated he would say, "Have a go. Try and pinpoint our position. Never be afraid to try. There's no harm done if you make a mistake." Then he would add, with his handsome head thrown back and wide shoulders heaving with laughter, "You know we are in the North Island at the narrowest part, so take the map and line up the compass." After much trial and error I became quite proficient. One day when we arrived home I overheard him say to mother, "She's really got a flair for map reading and a sense of direction – almost a sixth sense."'

Her interest in navigation and flying was again stimulated when Ellen showed her, later in 1919, the newspaper stories of the first nonstop crossing of the Atlantic by Alcock and Brown. They had flown in a Vickers Vimy twin-engined biplane bomber from Newfoundland to Ireland in sixteen and a half hours. And a few months later she learnt of another historic aviation event, the first flight from England to Australia, also in a Vimy, by the Australian brothers Ross and Keith Smith. It had taken them nearly a month and they received a £10,000 prize and a knighthood each. But Jean's growing interest in the infant aviation industry was now overshadowed by mounting domestic drama. Her parents' marriage finally broke up.

The war had changed Fred. In France he had known the company of French women. The memory of their generous warmth made it more difficult to accept Ellen's physical coldness. He found, too, that his former unquestioned role as head of the house was now challenged by Ellen who had grown used to taking the major decisions. The quarrels became more bitter and they began to grow apart.

A former patient of Fred's, Willow Macky, who lives in Auckland, said: 'I don't think Mrs Batten was very keen on the physical side of married life. She had a block where that was concerned. She kept a very tight rein on her emotions and couldn't demonstrate affection for her children or her husband.'

The details of how, and precisely when, Fred and Ellen split up no one seems to know. They did not divorce, but formally separated. One of the few people still living in Auckland who did know was Ramai Hawyard, the widow of the late Rudall Hawyard, New Zealand's most prominent feature-film maker between the wars. Ramai's knowledge of the Batten family came from her warm friendship with Jean's brother, John. She said: 'Yes, I do know what broke the marriage up, but I think you should get it from John.'

When, later, in England, I asked him, he said: 'The idea that mother was frigid is absolutely ludicrous. She was, as the Americans put it, a "one-man woman". When she realised that she had not married a "one-woman man" her love and pride were shattered. She turned against the male sex and, when Jean arrived, poured all her love and devotion and pent-up emotion onto her. It's as simple as that.'

John went on to say that there was a fundamental incompatibility between Fred and Ellen. 'Mother was a bit of a gypsy in spirit – a very beautiful, very thwarted woman who should have been an actress – she was definitely theatrical in temperament. Dad, on the other hand, was this goodlooking, good physique, phlegmatic, easygoing man married to a temperamental woman with a much stronger personality. She was always striving to do something with her life – things that women just didn't do in those days. Which was why, I believe, she eventually had to live out her hopes and ambitions through Jean.'

Ramai Hayward, however, did confirm that it was Ellen who had left Fred. One of the reasons, obviously, was Fred's infidelity. 'He was very attractive to women, but discreet with his affairs. I suppose it was inevitable, once she got drawn into the Higher Thought Temple where she abandoned the needs of the flesh for those of the spirit. However, when she did discover what he was up to it's true to say she came to hate him. It was very much a case of hell having no fury like a woman scorned. She was a possessive woman, used to being on a pedestal in her husband's life. When that ended she reacted very bitterly.'

Ramai likened the Battens to the couple in Ibsen's *Doll's House*: a strong, intelligent woman increasingly desperate to break free of the chains that made her no more than a wife and mother. Jean was to draw a permanent veil over the separation, maintaining until the end of her life the extraordinary pretence that it had never happened. Indeed she was to go to great lengths to insist in public interviews, and in private conversations with friends, that her parents' marriage had been uniquely blissful. In the only published interview she ever gave in which she attempted to trace the main events of her life, she told an Auckland *Star* reporter, Robert Gilmore, in 1977: 'I was lucky with my parents ... My parents were fun.' And in her unpublished memoirs she says emphatically: 'My childhood was a happy one' and later, of a period when her parents had long ceased to live together, she refers astonishingly to 'the warm cocoon of family life.' When the cocoon exploded, probably around 1920, she would have been ten or eleven. The stress level in the home had by then reached an intensity which had begun seriously to affect her health. As a result Fred arranged for her to go away for a holiday with friends in the country. She first went to a farm on the outskirts of Auckland, and then to the Brook family who had an eleven-acre orchard and dairy farmlet at Birkdale on the north side of Auckland harbour. Julian Brook was headmaster of Birkdale School and his daughter, Alice, took Jean under her wing. Recalling the occasion sixty-seven years later, Alice, now Alice Carrick-Robertson, said: 'Jean had been very ill. She arrived looking thin and pale and extremely unhappy. We used to play together and I eventually broke through her great reserve a little. But it was hard to draw her out, she was so remote and she never ever mentioned her brothers or her parents. Not once. I thought she was an only child.

'We had this favourite hedge we used to sit under and talk. She told me and my brothers with deadly seriousness that one day she was going to be very famous. We asked how and she said she didn't know but it would be doing something important. But the thing I remember most clearly was her insistence that never, ever, would she get married. When I asked why she said, "Because grown-ups when they get married fight and argue and shout at each other all the time." I didn't know until years later that her parents' marriage was falling apart before her eyes.'

When Ellen walked out of the Epsom home for the last time, she took Jean, now eleven, with her. Fred also moved out. He now had his own dental practice and rented space in rooms next to the surgery on the first floor of a building above a Queen Street shoe shop in down-town Auckland. He and John went to live there; Harold had already left home. But the arrangement didn't last long. Sometime in 1921 Fred gave his sons fifty gold sovereigns each and they both sailed to Australia, Harold to farm and John on his way to an acting career in England and America.

Ellen, meanwhile, had taken Jean to live out of Auckland, to the small nearby township of Howick. Snaps in the family album for this period, when Ellen had reached her mid-forties, show her as a still highly attractive woman with much of the extraordinary beauty her daughter had inherited. In Howick she sent Jean as a day girl to a Catholic convent called the Star of the Sea. Jean makes no reference to it in her memoirs, nor to her abrupt move to the country. Connie Foubister, who was at the convent with Jean, remembers her as a particularly well-behaved girl, with a long black plait down her back, who never put a foot wrong. 'She was always very determined, but a rather delicate child, small for her age.'

The Howick phase was shortlived. Ellen became ill and came back to Auckland to go into hospital after which, in the summer

vacation of early 1922, she went to Australia for a holiday,
taking Jean with her. On their return to Auckland they moved
into a boarding-house and Jean, now thirteen, was sent to board
at an exclusive and expensive private girls' school in the smart
suburb of Remuera. Fred, whose dental practice was building up
again and who had now moved into a flat, paid the fees. An
early voluntary arrangement for maintenance was apparently
not satisfactory to Ellen and she later went to court and got an
order under which Fred was required to pay her £3 a week plus
some arrears. For many years it was to be her only source of
income.

Ladies College, where Jean arrived sometime in 1922, was an
elegant place with the atmosphere of a baronial hall. Its castle-
like building stood in spacious parkland with its own dairy cows,
horse paddocks, tennis courts and croquet lawns. Set on the
exclusive Remuera ridge overlooking Auckland harbour, the
school still prided itself, in the early 1920s, on the traditions of
Victorian society it instilled. Its main aim was the preparation of
the girls for marriage in a society in which it was assumed they
would never work, devoting their lives to entertaining and the
management of servants. According to a school history, 'great
stress was laid on pure English refined speech, deportment and
drawing-room manners'. It was almost certainly under this
influence that Jean began to lose her flat nasal New Zealand
accent and to acquire the slightly affected, carefully over-
enunciated speech that was to remain with her permanently.
The school also undoubtedly sowed the seeds of the snobbery
that was to make rank, position and wealth important to her in
later years.

To prevent girls from probing into her unhappy background
Jean drew a wall around herself. She rarely spoke about her
family and was too ashamed to reveal to anyone that her
parents had separated. The few old girls we were able to trace
remembered her as a highly intelligent, rather solitary person
with whom they had difficulty communicating. Laurel Stewart,
now Lady Armstrong, living at Henley-on-Thames in England,
shared a bedroom with Jean, but never really got to know her. 'I
remember her as rather a loner who did not make any particular
friend,' she said.

Gwen Blott, president of the Ladies College Old Girls'
Association, who lives in Auckland, also used the word loner.
'She was an aloof girl, not very outgoing and didn't seem to
have many friends at school. She was not one of those people
one remembers – she didn't stand out in any way because, I
think, she just didn't want to be particularly friendly with
anyone.'

Clare Howden (today Mrs Clare Higham, who divides her
time between New Zealand and Raratonga) remembers Ellen
arriving on parents' visiting day every Thursday. 'All the other
girls used to await the event with awe and curiosity because she
was far and away the most conspicuous of mothers.' She was,
according to Clare, 'flighty' by which, she explained, she meant
she was dressed to attract attention. 'She was always under a
dramatically fashionable and eye-catching hat and, most
unusual for the 1920s, she wore make-up – the only mother
who ever dared appear with lipstick. Her arrival, as she strode
in, always created a ripple of fascination among us.' Jean lists
the highlights of her boarding-school days as throwing the
winning goal in a basketball match and of playing the piano for
the hymns at morning prayers. She was beginning to reveal
talent as a pianist, a painter and as a dancer.

Photographs of her in a bathing costume in her last year at
the age of fifteen show a highly attractive young woman posing
with care to reveal her fine legs and startlingly well-developed
figure. In all the pictures she has arranged herself prominently
in front of the others, flaunting her sexuality quite erotically and
deliberately allowing her wet swimsuit to leave little to the
imagination. Deeply aware of her blossoming nubility Ellen
who, in the wake of a heightened postwar public awareness of
the subject, appears to have become haunted by the spectre of
venereal disease, decided that her daughter's sex education
should include some shock treatment. She took her to a film
called *Damaged Goods*. Although by today's standards the film is
boringly inexplicit it was considered in the early 1920s to be
searing and shocking. Its message was blunt. 'Clean living' was
the only true safeguard against venereal disease. The film's
images were intended to shock, illustrating the incurability of
syphilis and the congenitally blind and shrunken babies it

created. People, almost exclusively men, went to see it secretly out of prurient curiosity, ashamed to admit they had been. It was considered altogether inappropriate for women.

In her memoirs Jean describes at some length the row between her parents when Ellen told Fred of her intentions. Although they were living separate lives it is clear that they met from time to time to discuss matters of mutual concern.

'The film caused an uproar in Auckland and many leading citizens tried to stop it being shown. My father was a good-natured, easygoing man and I had never before seen him so upset as when mother insisted on taking me. "I don't think it's fair for you to disillusion Jean about men," he said. "I always thought you were an idealist." But mother was adamant: "It's not right for a girl to go out into the world knowing so little of life." She was far too kind and diplomatic to add, "especially as she is your daughter and in many ways very like you"' – a reference to what she would certainly have called Fred's 'weakness' for women. If she suspected he was still having affairs with other women she would have been right. But with one conspicuous exception he was always discreet.

Damaged Goods was to have a profound effect on Jean's attitude to men and sex. 'We saw it together, shown to our seats by an embarrassed attendant among an almost entirely male audience who stared boldly at us during the interval when I felt too sick to eat an icecream. The film made a lasting impression on me, although I cannot even remember the plot, only the dreadful sight of a syphilitic baby covered with suppurating sores and blind – a direct result of promiscuity. Long afterwards I realised how lucky I was to have seen that film at such an impressionable age. I now think that although she found it distasteful mother felt impelled to let me see it to counteract the theories being propounded at the time by people who considered their views very modern. Mother considered that emancipation should not be confused with the advocacy of licentiousness. True freedom could only be attained by training the mind to master the emotions. To be governed by the body was to enslave oneself.' Jean was already replicating her mother's prudery and distrust of men. However, she was, when it suited her, to modify these views – while managing to retain a deceptive reputation for chastity.

At the end of 1924, soon after her fifteenth birthday, Jean left Ladies College. In her memoirs she attempts to rationalise this unhappy decision by saying that she had arrived as one of the youngest girls in the top form. But the top form was the sixth and she was only in the fourth. Although she had gained high marks in her exams, and won prizes for scripture, English, music, history and botany, it was a premature end to her formal education at a time when the daughters of professional families normally stayed at school at least a year longer and most until they were seventeen.

Mrs Puti Kingdon, who was then working in the school office, said she remembered Jean having to leave at short notice. 'She was suddenly taken away in a great hurry. There was some family reason behind it. I do remember they were a very odd family.'

In her memoirs Jean describes it differently. When the schools were re-opened early in 1925 after a longer than usual summer holiday because of a polio epidemic, she says: 'I was reluctant to give up my new-found freedom and refused to go back.' She says she persuaded her parents that she could devote more time to the musical career they envisaged for her if she left school. Ellen was opposed for she saw higher education as a liberating force, but Fred was less insistent. There was also another factor, Jean claims, that influenced Fred: 'our close companionship during that long summer vacation and which my father was as reluctant to terminate as I was.' It is not clear where she was living during what she calls 'that golden summer', for her memoirs at this point carefully avoid all clues to the location of her parents' separate homes. But wherever Ellen was it is certain that Jean and Fred spent a lot of time together on sailing trips up the Hauraki Gulf. They are recorded in photographs of Fred and his sister Ida, her husband, and girlfriends of Jean's enjoying themselves on boats and beaches. Always Jean is the most prominent, carefully adopting poses that draw attention. In one snap of them all draped over a rock she has positioned herself in a siren-like attitude on top, like a model posing for a men's magazine.

Through 1925 her life was preoccupied with mastering shorthand and typing and studying the piano and ballet with a view to becoming a professional in both. A fellow piano pupil was Mary Nathan who, today, is one of New Zealand's leading music teachers. Since much publicity was later to be given to Jean's abandonment for flying of what was said to be a highly promising music career, I asked her for a professional assessment of her abilities.

'She played in a showy, spectacular way but I think music was too dull, not exciting enough for her,' Mary recalled. 'Her playing had a kind of brilliance about it, but she lacked that essential emotional quality to reduce people to tears. I somehow doubt if she would have made it to the top.'

Mary Nathan remembers Jean as an extraordinarily determined young woman. 'Once at a big concert in Auckland she left the audience and, without asking anyone, went up and sat on the stage. There was this solitary figure sitting there – until they moved her back. And what a job they had. It took three ushers over half an hour to prise her off that stage she was so stubborn. I was not surprised a few years later to hear that she had done something really spectacular.'

Another former pupil still living in Auckland, Eleanor Spragg, confirmed Mary Nathan's opinion. 'She was older than the others and much more proficient. But somehow there was no real emotional depth to her playing.

'If I am truthful I don't think she was very well liked. She refused to conform and this used to upset her teacher Alice Law. Alice would go to a lot of trouble at recitals to colour co-ordinate the dresses the girls were wearing. All the mothers co-operated, except Mrs Batten. She just didn't care. She was the outsider in the group and we were all frightened of her – the way she kept Jean tightly under her thumb. They were certainly powerful figures. You could feel their presence there.

'Looking back,' said Eleanor Spragg, 'I think that what put them on the outside was their poverty. They behaved as if they were people set apart.' Eleanor used to observe Jean at the piano classes with fascination. 'She always reminded me of a beautiful china doll – pretty but quite expressionless. She would wear this slightly bland look, never really looking directly at you, her eyes roving restlessly, darting about like a bird's. It was as if she was alone in the world, as if there was no one else around to be considered. She was remote. A sort of, how can I describe it, not-there feeling about her.'

Another fascinated observer of the Batten family in mid-1920s Auckland was Julia Yates, now in her eighties, who, with her sister, ran a millinery shop in Queen Street. Their hats were for the upper strata of local society. Ellen was one of her clients. 'I'll never forget the way she used to come into the shop,' she said. 'She had the physique of Queen Mary, without the massive bosom, and a regal manner in the way she stood and looked down on people. She was also extremely masculine. I really do think she was a lesbian. Although I was too young to recognise the characteristics at the time I've become so familiar with them since that, looking back now, I'm sure she was in love with her daughter. We all thought it was a totally un-natural relationship. It wouldn't surprise me at all to learn that they might actually have shared a double bed.* It's not difficult to understand why Fred Batten turned to other women.'

During the teenage years immediately after leaving school Jean appears to have been more preoccupied with the performing arts than with aviation. She attended a ballet school run by Valerie Scott, a former dancer in Diaghilev's company in Europe, who called herself Madame Valeska. Before long Jean was playing the piano for her and had become her assistant teacher on a small salary.

Over sixty years later it was difficult to find people who remembered Jean at the ballet school. One of the few, Connie Parker, said: 'Valeska told me that when she began she was the clumsiest pupil she ever had. The other girls used to laugh at her. But Valeska always claimed there was talent there. While the rest of us would be standing around talking, waiting for the

---

*There is no evidence, despite suspicions raised among some observers by their abnormally close relationship, and the years they spent in close proximity in one-roomed apartments, that Ellen and Jean ever had a physical lesbian relationship. Psychologists in London and New Zealand with whom this was discussed pointed out that, between mother and daughter, it was extremely rare. The probability is – and with this members of the Batten family in New Zealand tend to agree – that the union did not extend beyond an unnaturally deep emotional one.

class to begin, Jean would never join us. She would always be over in the corner, one hand on the bar, practising.' But Jean persevered with such determination that Valeska chose her as the soloist at the school's annual public performance on the town hall stage.

Another former protégée of Madame Valeska, Freda Stark, told us that she used to feel sorry for Jean. She sometimes walked home with her to Elizabeth O'Dea's boarding house at 33 Symonds Street on the ridge above central city. 'She and her mother were sharing a small room there. I don't think she ever had a proper home — just a succession of boarding houses and one-roomed apartments. That was just how she was to live all her life.'

Trying to piece together the fragments of the Batten family's lives through the 1920s proved hopeless. The information prompted by my appeals in newspapers and on radio talk-back shows was always insubstantial — like handfuls of sand, always flowing through one's fingers. People remembered Fred best. He emerges as a sociable person, a warm and likeable man, much laid back and with a reputation, in the days of ferociously painful slow-speed drilling, as one of the gentlest dentists in Auckland.

Tracing people who were more than mere acquaintances of Ellen and Jean was also difficult. They appear to have chosen the isolation of each other's company, discouraging intrusion into their space. They were clearly an intimidating pair: the formidable, dominating mother rarely seen in public and the beautiful daughter, aloof and unapproachable, her emotions frozen behind a psychological wall. But there is evidence that, deep inside Jean, there was already another persona: smouldering, frustrated, fiercely ambitious, determined to escape from the hateful claustrophobia of it all — from the poverty trap and from the colonial parochialism of New Zealand. And possibly, although she would not have consciously admitted it, from her mother.

For Ellen was now confirming the popular view of her unconventional spirit: flirtations with the wilder shores of religion had led her into a fringe sect in Auckland known as the Higher Thought Temple. It was concerned with the occult. Its followers spoke in terms of destiny and fulfilment, of things being preordained and immutable. It helped Ellen face her disillusionment and frustration. But Jean's memoirs make no mention of the temple in Cook Street with its astrologically decorated stained-glass windows or the lonely people who trooped in there. In her memoirs Jean describes Ellen 'as something of a mystic – she had the gift of remarkable intuition and dreams which often heralded future events with great clarity. She once told me that she could sense immediately on entering a room full of people whether they were positive or negative by their aura and the degree of magnetism each possessed.' Years later, during the biggest personal crisis of her life, Jean was to go to the writings of the mystics for solace.

But there is no evidence that she ever went with Ellen to the Higher Thought Temple. In fact at this time she appears to have been involved in more earthy pursuits. Once a week at Madame Valeska's there was a ballroom dancing class to which large numbers of young men from the university came to learn the foxtrot, the tango and the Charleston. Jean played the piano and partnered them through their awkward beginners' steps to 'Yes we have no Bananas' and 'Moonlight and Roses'.

Jean's beauty and sensuous figure made her a magnetic centre of attraction. 'I was a well-developed girl for my age and able to pass myself off as seventeen at dances when I thought it great fun to be in demand as a partner,' she wrote. 'A number of the university boys imagined they were in love with me and I even received a few poems.' One of the boys was a dedicated rugby player whom Jean in her memoirs calls Les. She began to go out with him. 'To please him I would sit shivering in the cold watching him play.

'But I found it impossible to raise any enthusiasm for a game that always seemed to be played on cold raining days and during which Les always seemed to be injured.' However, she adds significantly, 'Rugby does develop the team spirit which seems to be so lacking in my own character.'

At a dance one evening Les surprised Jean by asking her to marry him. It was her first proposal. She turned him down. But Les did not give up easily. He went next day to see Ellen to plead his case. 'I remember going home after class and on entering the house saw him, with his handsome head on mother's shoulder, sobbing while she smoothed his fair curly hair, trying to console him. I hastily withdrew before he saw me, ran round the house and hid, appropriately enough, in the passionfruit vine, until he had gone. When I later saw mother she said to me: "You have hurt poor Les, you should not have encouraged him. I suppose you're just too attractive to the opposite sex like your father — with the same smiling eyes and charm." '

I tried to trace Les. Jean adopted the convention throughout her memoirs of giving only first names to those men she was prepared partly to reveal. Where the names were capable of being checked they turned out always to be correct. Auckland University records showed that thirty-one students called Les had enrolled during the relevant period. One, Les Colgan, had been a prominent member of the rugby club. But a phone call to his home established that he had very recently died. His widow said that he had never spoken of Jean — but he had been a very good dancer. Whether or not he was Jean Batten's first boyfriend will probably remain a mystery.

In May 1927, when Jean was seventeen, the world was stirred by the first of a series of dramatic aviation events which were to herald an era of hugely publicised long-distance record-breaking flights. An American airmail pilot, Charles Lindbergh, flying a Ryan single-engined monoplane, *The Spirit of St Louis*, made the first nonstop solo crossing of the Atlantic, flying the 3,500 miles from New York to Paris in one leap of 33½ hours. His flight created an international sensation, making him an instant hero and a wealthy man. Reading about it, Jean's secret ambition to fly, inspired by the Walsh Brothers' flying boats, was revived. 'In my vivid imagination I saw myself winging my way across the lonely skies in an aeroplane,' she wrote. And the following year, 1928, a vintage one for the history of aviation, there was another spectacular flight to grip her imagination. A small, modest Australian, Bert Hinkler, who used to fly in crumpled double-breasted suits, made the first solo flight from England to Australia. He did it in 15½ days in a fragile wood-and-fabric Avro Avian biplane powered by a small four-cylinder engine.

Three months later another Australian hit the headlines with a flight that still ranks as one of aviation's epics. With three companions, Charles Kingsford-Smith captained a lumbering, 90-miles-an-hour, three-engined Fokker cabin monoplane, the *Southern Cross*, on the first ever flight across the Pacific. They flew from San Francisco to Brisbane in three big hops, the second of which, from Hawaii to Fiji, through a succession of violent storms, took an incredible 35 hours.

Over the years Jean, in interviews, was to date her first serious determination to become a flying hero from these 1928 flights. But the pilot who influenced her most directly was Kingsford Smith, the cocky, broad-grinning, Royal Flying Corps veteran and former Hollywood stunt pilot. 'Smithy', who was to be described as 'the greatest trans-world flier of them all', was already on his way to becoming a legend when, in September 1928, in the first ever flight across the Tasman Sea, he brought the *Southern Cross* to New Zealand and to a welcome by 30,000 at Wigram aerodrome in Christchurch. For a month he and his Pacific flight co-pilot, Charles Ulm, and the other two members of their crew, were fêted in a nonstop round of receptions throughout the country. At one of these, a dinner in Auckland, Fred Batten was a guest. To her great delight and excitement he took Jean along.

After the dinner and speeches were over Smithy moved about the dining room chatting and joking with the guests. At Fred's table Jean was thrilled to be introduced to him. To her father's utter astonishment she told the great Australian aviator, 'I'm going to learn to fly.' Much amused Smithy turned to Fred and said, 'Your little girl going to fly! Upon my word. Let's give her a toast.' Whereupon he filled everyone's glasses, bowed deeply to Jean, who sat po-faced, flushed with embarrassment and anger, and declared: 'To the day when Jean gets her licence.' And everyone at the table got to their feet and cheered. But there was more laughter than cheers, for Smithy had intended it as a joke. Jean was consumed with inner misery and resentment. Later, back at the boarding house, she poured it all out to Ellen.

Recounting the incident to the London *Evening News* six years later, Mrs Batten described how Jean had come home that evening sobbing. ' "Mother," she said, "none of them took me

seriously. But just let them wait. I'm going to fly. They'll see." '
And Ellen added, 'Of course, I was the only one in on her
secret.'

Ellen was frequently to admit with a measure of pride her role
in the conspiracy they now began secretly to engineer to fulfil
Jean's dream behind Fred's back. The following year it began to
take shape.

On another holiday in Sydney with Ellen, Jean went for a
flight with Kingsford Smith. She was too much in awe of the
god-figure to approach him directly so she got Ellen to phone
him and fix the trip in the 'Old Bus' – Smithy's *Southern Cross*.
It was a short flight from the Royal Australian Air Force aerodrome at Richmond outside Sydney but Jean – as she had done
at the sight of the seaplane cockpit years before – was to claim it
as a turning point in her life. 'I knew it as soon as we took off.
Cruising about high above the Blue Mountains I felt completely
at home in the air and decided that here indeed was my
element. I was even more determined to fly myself.'

Among the likely circle of Jean's friends at the time, former
Ladies College old girls and ex-ballet and piano pupils of
Madame Valeska and Alice Law, I tried to find someone in
whom she may have confided her exotic new career plans. But
it appeared that then, as later, there weren't any close friends,
only a few acquaintances, and none of those could suggest
anyone with whom Jean might have shared the secret.

Back in Auckland in the months following the excitement of
her Sydney flight Jean found herself at loggerheads with her
father for the first time. On a lunchtime walk with him around
the Auckland docks, she revealed that she intended to abandon
both the piano and ballet and become a professional pilot. But
much more than that she wanted to achieve something really
spectacular, something that hadn't ever been done before. She
wanted to do for New Zealand what Kingsford Smith had done
for Australia. She wanted to prove that women could do these
things. And she stunned Fred by announcing that she intended
to be the first person, man or woman, to fly from England to
New Zealand.

'I have never forgotten the incredulous look he gave me of
astonishment and almost awe – for he knew that I was abso-

lutely in earnest.' And then she asked him outright if he would
pay for her to learn to fly at the Auckland Aero Club.

Fred was deeply shocked. He regarded the whole notion as
preposterous. 'It's far too dangerous,' he said, recalling many
flying accidents he had witnessed on the Western Front. 'The
aeroplane isn't safe yet. And it's very expensive.' Even if he
could afford it he wouldn't give her a penny to invest in such a
crazy venture, he declared. Flying was not an occupation for
women. She should stick to her dancing.

It was the beginning of hard feelings towards her father that
Jean was never to forget or forgive. She went back to the
boarding house to tell Ellen. Together they hatched a plot. The
conspiracy was to become enshrined in the elaborate folklore
that was to grow up around her. It began with a simple deceit.
Jean would sell her piano and they would go to England, telling
Fred that Jean was going to study for her licentiate at the Royal
College of Music. In fact the only purpose of the trip was for
Jean to learn to fly out of Fred's sight.

How they planned to fund this expensive venture on their
slender resources is not clear. Certainly the piano, in the late
1920s, would have fetched anything from £50 to £80 –
probably enough to pay for their one-way boat fares of around
£30 each to England. But with flying lessons then costing £2 10
shillings an hour they would soon have needed more than
Ellen's £3-a-week maintenance from Fred. In an interview with
the London *Evening News* a few years later Ellen admitted: 'I'm
afraid I encouraged her because she was so keen. So eventually I
sold a little property of my own and saved the money to bring
her to England for the express purpose of learning to fly.'

Whether Ellen's nest-egg property ever existed was impossible to discover. Jean's brother John, however, was to admit
that, to his knowledge, their mother never owned any property.
If the story is a fiction then the most likely explanation for
Ellen's invention of it would have been as a smokescreen to
conceal other major sources of money which were soon to come
Jean's way but which they were too ashamed of to reveal
publicly.

Early in 1930 Jean and Ellen put their plan into action. Fred
apparently didn't smell a rat when the piano – wherever it then

resided – was sold on the grounds of financing Jean's overseas education in music. Ellen arranged for an auctioneer to put it under the hammer. With the proceeds she booked two passages on a ship to England. Early in 1930 she and Jean sailed out of Auckland. They were never permanently to live in New Zealand again.

CHAPTER 3

Wings over London (1930)

Jean and Ellen made the voyage to England in two stages. They took a ship to Sydney where, in February 1930, they joined a P & O liner, the *Otranto*, for the six-week journey to London.

She was an elderly, slow and uncomfortable ship, crowded with Australians and New Zealanders bound for the sophistication and excitement of Europe. The decks and saloons buzzed with social activity, shipboard romances and endless gossip. But Mrs Batten, conspicuous by her grim and proud demeanour, made sure that her beautiful daughter, who was quickly turning many heads, would not be exposed to the temptations of shipboard life as the tropical warmth of the Indian Ocean began to melt inhibitions. Convinced that Jean's innocence was threatened by some of the more obvious seducers on board, she virtually confined her to her cabin. Mary Martin (today Mrs Lee-Richards) a professional musician, who lives in Greenhithe in Auckland, was on the *Otranto* en route to London with her parents to study at the Royal College of Music. She took pity on Jean and tried unsuccessfully to befriend her.

'I was about eighteen at the time and looking round for someone of my own age to team up with. When I first saw her I thought, what a beautiful creature. But she didn't respond. All I managed to learn was that her father was a dentist and she was going to study music. A few years later when her face was on the front pages I realised it was a lie. I'd never before met anyone so unfriendly. You could almost see the wall she had erected around herself.'

Mary still recalls vividly the intimidating Mrs Batten. 'She struck me as a really quite frightening figure. I remember she had dark flashing eyes and a prominent nose with hair growing beautifully back from her forehead and coiled round the back. And these winged eyebrows. She was immediately the most prominent personality on the ship. She sort of coruscated, if you know what I mean: radiated immensely powerful vibes, yet in a very controlled austere way. It was eerie. Somehow she reminded me of an eagle with her wings spread out to protect her daughter. It was as if she was saying to everyone, hands off her.

'She treated Jean like a small child. I'd sometimes go down to her cabin and she'd be lying on the top bunk reading. I'd try and persuade her to come up on deck but the response was always: "I'm not allowed to". She wasn't bitter or resentful. She had this total calm uncomplaining acceptance and she always carried a little half-smile. We really felt sorry for her – she was virtually a prisoner.'

The Battens, according to Mary, exuded poverty. 'One had the impression they'd only just scraped up the money for the boat fare and there was nothing left over. At the various ports they never went ashore. They never joined in anything that cost money. I don't think Jean could even afford the hairdresser – her hair just stayed the way it was for the whole voyage: little round curls all over her head like a halo. And she seemed to have only one dress. It was a very pretty green silk frock which must have been all she owned because whenever Mrs Batten washed it out Jean had to get into her bunk and wait until it was dry and ironed again. When it came to the big event of the fancy dress ball we all thought Mrs Batten would relent. To our surprise she herself went in Spanish costume. But Jean had to stay in her cabin. In fact, looking back, the only time she was allowed out was to practise the piano, a big Steinway in the saloon. She used to play Chopin's Revolutionary Prelude but usually she'd only play the first ten bars before getting up and walking off.'

In her memoirs, Jean's cursory treatment of that historic voyage through India and the Suez Canal suggests that she had few happy memories of it. Whenever her manuscript dealt with her travels she invariably wrote lengthy descriptions. But of this event all she said, without much enthusiasm, was: 'The highlight of the long voyage of six weeks to England was, to me, the thrill of crossing the Equator and seeing the North Star for the first time.' The only other surviving record of the voyage is a small sepia photograph of Ellen with the team of substantially built women she led to victory in a tug-of-war competition.

In London, which must have seemed a bewildering place after the gentle provincialism of New Zealand, Jean and Ellen were briefly reunited that spring of 1930 with John Batten. He had arrived there having worked successfully as an actor in Australia, Hollywood, and now in a major film *Under the Greenwood Tree* at Elstree in which he had the lead role. John, who was earning again after the loss of most of his Hollywood savings in the 1929 Wall Street crash, had a flat over a fish shop in St John's Wood. But Ellen and Jean wanted to be independent. They didn't want to see too much of John in case he discovered the true purpose of their trip and wrote and told Fred.

They rented a room in a large house in James Street, a few minutes' walk from Oxford Street in the heart of the West End, and made no attempt to get in touch with the Royal College of Music. Instead, within a week of arriving, they were on an underground train heading out through the endless suburbia of north-west London to Burnt Oak station from where they walked to nearby Stag Lane aerodrome. It lay in open farmland at the northern fringe of the city's sprawl in the southern part of Edgware, only ten miles from Piccadilly Circus. It no longer exists and today the site of the grass airfield is quite difficult to find in what has become a characterless suburb of brick and pebble-dash semi-detached houses. But, for the nostalgic, there are rewarding clues here and there in streets with such famous names as Mollison Way, de Havilland Road, Cody Close. And on the eastern side there still stand the construction hangars and brick buildings of the once famous de Havilland Aircraft Company which its founder, Geoffrey de Havilland, set up there in 1920.

The aerodrome ('a large paddock at the end of Edgware Road', one former club member said), was the home both of the London Aeroplane Club and the de Havilland company whose factory was pouring out its sturdy little two-seat open cockpit Gipsy Moth biplanes, the aeroplane that had just begun to set the company on the road to huge prosperity. Nearby was the humble wooden hut that was the club's headquarters, outside which stood its modest fleet of seven or eight Moths all painted bright yellow. There was a small hangar presided over by the club's chief ground engineer, the legendary Jack Humphreys, who was later to fly to Japan with Amy Johnson as her mechanic. And close by were the long rows of lock-up garages in which, with wings folded back, members' privately owned Moths were kept. The club was subsidised by the government as a policy to encourage flying and create a pool of trained pilots for use in the event of war. But it was still expensive. At a time when many English families were supporting themselves on around £5 a week, dual instruction cost £2 10 shillings and solo flying £1 10 shillings an hour.*

The club had a reputation for its aristocratic membership. One former member recalled Edward, Prince of Wales, coming out for flying lessons late in 1930 – 'arriving in his Bentley with fabulous birds'. But although it was remarkable for its rich and titled members and the preponderance of public-school accents, male and female, it was, like aero clubs the world over, a friendly place that put flying above the divisions of class and prided itself on egalitarian spirit and absence of snobbery. One of the foundation members, Norman Jones, still flying at the age of eighty-two, whom, in 1987, I tracked down at one of his homes at Rye in Sussex, said: 'It had a quite remarkable atmosphere about it. All social differences disappeared in the common binding interest of flying. You could walk in there and find in

*For a period in the early 1930s this was reduced to £1.10 shillings and £1 respectively.

the same group a duchess and a London bus driver chatting away over a cup of tea round the fire. The only judgement that counted was how good a pilot you were.' However, although the clubhouse was an outwardly welcoming place, unspoken social barriers were firmly established. An Australian woman pilot, who joined in the mid-1930s, said: 'Mateship stopped at the aerodrome. You never got invited into anyone's home.'

Into this community of casually well-to-do people, conspicuous by their arrival on foot, and the traces of colonial accent with its slow New Zealand diction in their speech, came one afternoon the elegant tweedy figure of Mrs Batten and her pretty daughter clad, a photograph shows, in a too-large suit, probably cut down from one of Ellen's. They met the club secretary and, within a few minutes, Jean had been signed up as a member. Because she was under twenty-one Ellen had to give her written consent. To Jean's huge relief it wasn't necessary for her father to give his permission – he most certainly would not have done. They paid the entrance fee of 3 guineas plus a year's subscription, also 3 guineas – and booked her first lesson for the following morning. She planned to pay for that with the help of the £2-a-week allowance Fred was sending in the belief that she was now immersed in her music studies.

There was nothing specially remarkable in 1930 about a woman learning to fly. They had been making news since 1912 when America's first woman pilot, Harriet Quimby, a woman as beautiful as Jean Batten, had flown solo across the English Channel. In America the exploits of a tousle-haired tomboyish-looking social worker, Amelia Earhart, had become well known to millions. So too, imminently, were to be the historic journeys of a young typist from Yorkshire, Amy Johnson.

In fact the London Aeroplane Club had a large membership of women, the list of whom read like the pages of *Debrett*. One member, Lady Heath, was a tireless champion of women's rights in aviation and had successfully campaigned to remove an international requirement that women could not be commercial pilots because the male establishment believed that menstruation threatened their competence. Lady Heath personally demonstrated that it didn't. She and another titled Irish woman, Lady Mary Bailey, had become celebrated for their solo flights through Africa. But most awesome of them all was the legendary Duchess of Bedford who had learnt to fly in her sixties and flew about the world in her own large Fokker cabin plane, flown by her personal pilot, while she stretched out on a deck-chair in the back admiring the view and knitting.

Other women pilots were emerging for their sheer professional competence: Winifred Spooner, Winifred Brown, Pauline Gower, Dorothy Spicer were already well known in Britain. These were the women, most of them confident, highly educated, and sophisticated, whose society Jean had joined. But none of them was ever really to get to know her.

There are two versions of the ease with which Jean became a pilot in the summer of 1930. In her memoirs she says: 'I learnt to fly fairly quickly and found, as I had long suspected, that I had a natural aptitude for it.' Years later in New Zealand she told the Auckland *Star*: 'Have you ever seen a penguin enter the water at speed? I took to the air like a penguin to water.' But a rather different view was taken by an anonymous fellow New Zealander who was learning to fly at the London Aeroplane Club at the same time. In a letter to the Auckland correspondent of the *New Zealand Freelance* he wrote: 'I'm learning to fly here at Stag Lane. There's a rather nice little girl here from Auckland too. She says that some day she is going to fly from England to New Zealand. But it doesn't look much that way yet for she is having such terrific trouble with her landings. This morning she crashed into a fence; fortunately she wasn't hurt, just a little bruised, but the pluck of the girl is astounding. She lives in your road in Auckland; do you know her? Her name is Jean Batten.'

A former member who was at Stag Lane when Jean was learning to fly was Bill Oliver, a retired airline pilot who today lives in Hawaii. On a visit to New Zealand in 1988 he said that, not only did he remember Jean well, he had actually fallen in love with her. However, he added, he had been too shy and unsure of himself to declare it. 'I was seventeen and she would have been twenty. She was an absolute knock-out in those days – really quite spectacularly beautiful. And yes she did have some trouble learning to fly. I don't think it was quite like a penguin taking to water. I don't know what precise problems the instructors had with her but she was so uniquely attractive that we were all fascinated by her progress and the club was buzzing with rumours about how she was doing, because even then, she was talking preposterously about flying alone to New Zealand. None of us took her seriously and we teased her mercilessly. She was one of the very slow learners and there was a story going around that two instructors had given up on her. That may not have been true because each instructor wasn't there every day, but she certainly went through three of them — Matthews, Sparks and finally the chief flying instructor, Travers.'

Confirmation that Jean was a determined but exceedingly slow learner came from another fellow student, Tom Hollinrake, a New Zealand engineer and boat builder who now lives in Australia. He got his A licence in seven weeks at the club on a visit to England in 1930 and Jean was already there when he arrived. 'I think she was far from being a natural pilot,' he said. He remembered her crash well. Flying solo she had overshot on landing; her aircraft had hit a wire fence and overturned, but she had 'emerged unscathed'. Tom, as a fellow New Zealander, was asked to help comfort her and restore her shattered confidence. 'She was very upset and Herbert Travers suggested I take her somewhere to get her mind off it. So I took her to see Louis Armstrong and his band at a theatre at Marble Arch. But it didn't help. She cried all afternoon and was very depressed. She didn't think she would ever become a good pilot. I eventually took her home to Mum.' Deeply ashamed of her crash, Jean was never to mention it to a soul.

Known to his pupils as 'Major Travers', Herbert Travers had been one of Amy Johnson's instructors the previous year. She, too, had gone through three of them but, unlike Jean, who was to develop into a highly competent pilot, Amy never acquired the gift, the harmony of co-ordination and sensitivity of touch, that marks the true pilot.

Travers, who had seen action with the Royal Naval Air Service in the First World War, had been a test pilot. He was sometimes referred to by some of the more impatient younger pupils as 'a nice old boy', and by others as 'an old woman'. But these were affectionate comments on his concern to keep his pupils alive. By temperament both serious people, he and Jean hit it off immediately.

Travers died in 1958. His daughter, Mrs Eva Fitzpatrick, at her home at Sittingbourne in Kent, said that, as a child, she vividly remembered hearing her father discussing his attractive student from New Zealand. 'He used to come home in the evening and tell us all about his pupils. He didn't often wax eloquent about them but I'll never forget the day in 1930 we first heard about Jean Batten. He was so deeply impressed he couldn't stop talking about her. He said here was a remarkable woman with great vision who one day would be famous. He was quite knocked out by her. She was totally unknown but I recall him saying, "She's got the dream of the century. She'll open up the air routes." And later, when she was famous, he likened her to Francis Drake. He saw the same determination and ruthlessness in pursuit of money and ambition. It's true to say he was genuinely inspired by her.'

Some amateur 1930s film footage, acquired for my documentary programme, shows Herbert Travers and Jean beside a Gipsy Moth at Stag Lane. Dressed for the cockpit in the English custom of the thirties in a heavy tweed suit, collar and tie and plus-fours, he was an exceedingly goodlooking man, in his late thirties, balding prematurely and exuding boyish charm. To Jean he was a father figure about whom she was to contribute some flattering comments in a note to Eva Fitzpatrick for her father's biography. 'A born instructor with the rare gift of divine patience,' she wrote in 1966. 'He was a very practical man. "Don't forget the three Cs", he used to say to anyone setting off on a first cross-country flight: "Clock, Compass – and Commonsense." His pupils used to wait for their lessons sitting on a bench outside the tiny office. If it were fine and we could see the church spire on Harrow Hill all was well and he would take off with the first pupil. If the mist was thickening or snowflakes starting Travers would say: "Today no see, no fly" and we all made a dash for the small clubhouse where Ben would have a roaring fire and steaming cups of tea and ham sandwiches for the cold, hungry pupils.'

Sometime in the early autumn of 1930 Jean made her first solo. In the absence of her personal pilot's logbook there is no record of the number of hours of dual instruction she needed to achieve this milestone, but the evidence suggests that, because she was a slow and plodding learner, she would not have soloed quickly.

It did, however, give a tremendous boost to her self-confidence. She had never doubted her ability to become a pilot. But a recent event had given added urgency to her ambitions and her need to qualify. A few months earlier her fellow club pilot, Amy Johnson, had made her historic flight in a Gipsy Moth from England to Australia. She had taken 19½ days (5-24 May, 1930). Her flight had created an explosion of rejoicing and adulation; overnight a penniless typist had become a legend. It wasn't a particularly remarkable flight since the route had been flown eight times before. It wasn't the first solo. It wasn't the fastest. Its immense importance was that a woman had done it alone. And that woman had suddenly acquired immortality in aviation history. More badly than ever Jean wanted to fly that same route. She wanted to fly it faster than Amy. But most of all her heart was set on fame itself.

She spent the remaining months of 1930 having more lessons with Travers and building up her solo hours for her licence for which the requirements were minimal compared with today. The private pilot's licence, then known as an A licence, required only the incredibly small number of three hours' solo experience.

But funding her flying from her dwindling resources Jean could only afford two or three short trips a week and the hours were slow to accumulate. At the club she made no friends and rarely socialised. She and Ellen had now moved out of central London, resuming their itinerant way of life that was never to cease during all their years in the city. They took a room for a while in Goldhurst Terrace in South Hampstead before moving out to lodgings near the aerodrome, probably in the Hendon area. Jean used the club purely as a flying school for she could not afford to indulge in friendships that involved the need for reciprocal entertainment.

To minimise the risk she and Ellen gave their address to no one. They insisted that all their mail, including letters from Fred, be sent care of Thomas Cook and Son in Berkeley Street,

London. It was a practice they were to follow for the rest of their lives.

The few survivors of those Stag Lane days who knew Jean all described her in identical terms: a beautiful young woman, unfailingly well-mannered, who studiously kept herself to herself. 'She was a very quiet girl — quiet and determined,' said Norman Jones. 'We admired her.'

Bill Oliver, who was later to become an Imperial Airways co-pilot flying HP42 biplane airliners out of Croydon, doesn't ever recall seeing Jean mixing with other members after flying or having a drink at the bar. But the day he got his A licence he, Herbert Travers and Jean went up to London to celebrate. 'Travers and I belted back a few beers, but Jean never drank — she was on orange juice. I remember she didn't smoke either which was unusual for a woman in those circles in the thirties.

'I can only describe her as a thoroughly agreeable young woman whom everyone liked. She was in pretty hot competition for attention in those days with people like Amy Johnson and two glamorous women pilots, Pauline Gower and Dorothy Spicer, who also became legends. While they'd all be socialising in the bar Jean would have gone home to Ma I suppose. I never remember seeing Mrs Batten at the club.'

Then fresh out of school, Bill Oliver admits he was consumed with puppy love for Jean and secretly lusted for her in hopeless fantasies, knowing she was out of his league, older and un-attainable. Because he had this 'tremendous crush on her' he was sensitive to the attentions she got from older men in the club and he recalls listening with fascination and awe to vastly more experienced theories about Jean advanced around the bar by those who had failed to date her. 'The general conclusion always seemed to be — and she was so obviously desirable everyone seemed to have tried — that she just wasn't interested in men. She apparently never responded to any of the overtures. No one ever got to first base that I remember — indeed ever made one inch of headway. I recall very clearly some of the chaps discussing the possibility that she might actually be lesbian.'

One of the young pilots who tried to date her was Tom Hollinrake who was eighteen at the time and hoped that, as a fellow New Zealander, he might just succeed where all others had failed. 'She was a goodlooking girl with a trim figure, and in those days I noticed such things,' he said. 'But as far as I was concerned she had no sex appeal whatsoever. I made a couple of attempts to take her out, but gave up. I'm sure that she didn't go out on dates with anybody. She was singleminded, almost to the point of obsession, about flying to the exclusion of all else. She was most certainly not one of the crowd.'

Jean got her A licence on 5 December, 1930. She would have had less than twenty hours in her logbook, but she was now permitted to fly away from the airfield and begin her cross-country navigation training. But before she could start it the worst she had always feared happened. Fred at last discovered the true purpose of her trip to London. He was so angry he cut off her allowance forthwith.

In her memoirs Jean blames her aunt Ida, Fred's sister, who was now living in England and whom she and Ellen had visited. They had foolishly entrusted her with the secret believing it to be safe with someone they knew to hold forthright views on women's emancipation. But it is possible that Ida had taken Fred's side in the break-up of the marriage and did it to spite Ellen. 'It was a fearful setback to my plans,' Jean wrote, 'and meant that when the time came for mother to leave, I had to go back to New Zealand with her – which was just what my father had intended me to do.'

However, despite her minuscule number of flying hours, Jean was tempted to try and defeat Fred's ultimatum and have a go at an Australia flight without any further ado. 'Fortunately I had not quite exhausted my savings and thought that I might even be able to find someone to finance a long-distance flight,' she wrote optimistically. The notion, to put it mildly, was ludicrous and suggests that Jean was seriously lacking in self-awareness and out of touch with reality. But her belief in her own destiny was so total she took herself off to New Zealand House, then in the Strand, to try and persuade someone to finance a flight. Ellen went with her. The first person she bumped into was the father of Mary Martin, her shipboard friend. Having spent most of the voyage in her cabin Jean scarcely knew Mr Martin. He was, therefore, considerably taken aback when, without beating about the bush, she asked him if he would lend her £300. As that was more than a lot of professional people earned in a year, he thought at first she wasn't serious. But quickly he realised to his embarrassment she really meant it. 'She wasn't joking,' Mary told us. 'She told Dad she wanted to buy a plane to fly to New Zealand. Why she thought he had that sort of money I don't know. She must have known he was retired and trying to manage on a tiny pension. We were all really very hard up which made it quite ridiculous. The whole family fell about laughing but Dad said: "I wouldn't underestimate her. She's a very determined young lady."'

There is no record of any further attempts Jean may have made to raise money in London in 1930. She appears quite quickly to have accepted the hopelessness of the prospect for, according to a Colombo (Sri Lanka) stamp in her passport, she was, by January 1931, on her way with Ellen back to New Zealand.

On this voyage it appears that Ellen allowed her rather more personal freedom than on the trip to England for, in Bombay, she met and was permitted to develop a friendship with a twenty-nine-year-old Royal Air Force pilot, Flying Officer Fred Truman. Tanned by the Indian sun, with prematurely receding wavy brown hair and a fit, athletic figure, he was a New Zealander serving with No. 31 Squadron of the Royal Air Force at Quetta on the Northwest Frontier; he was going home on leave to see his family in Auckland. On the voyage of nearly a month a warm friendship, aided by their common interest in flying and closely monitored by Ellen, sprang up between them. Fred Truman, described as 'an outgoing sort of person, easy and comfortable to be with', was soon to make a major contribution to the fulfilment of Jean's dreams.

Back in Auckland in the late New Zealand summer of 1931 Jean was not relishing the post mortem with her father. She and Ellen moved into a flat and although there is no record of her father and mother meeting at this time Jean went to see Fred and was relieved that most of his anger had faded. 'I was only concerned for your safety,' he was reported to have told her. Any lingering resentment at the flying he probably now blamed on Ellen. In fact so pleased was he to see Jean again he began to lend her his car to drive to the aerodrome at Mangere where, temporarily, she joined the Auckland Aero Club to continue training.

Then Fred made an even more generous gesture. He paid for her to have instruction in navigation at the Richmond Navigation School, a local marine enterprise. Now that he had lost the battle to prevent her flying he wanted to help her to do it safely, he said.

Out at the small grass airfield, set among mangrove swamps beside Auckland's Manukau harbour, Jean obtained her licence endorsement to permit her to carry passengers and marked the event, 'within two minutes', she said, by taking Ellen for a flight. She began also to learn some of the more exciting things that could be done with a Gipsy Moth — exuberantly slow rolling, looping and stall turning in the sky over Mangere. 'Although my father had not known I was learning to fly he was very pleased when he saw me give a display of aerobatics at the local club,' she wrote proudly in *My Life*.

But not everyone was as pleased as Fred. One of the club's engineers was Doug Wood who is still living in Auckland. He recalled that the instructors found her wilful and slightly arrogant. 'I'll never forget one occasion when she came out,' he said. 'It was really nasty and stormy with huge black clouds and high winds off the Tasman driving drenching squalls across the aerodrome. She told (Squadron Leader) Dave Allen, the chief flying instructor, she wanted to go up and fly in that. He wasn't very happy because she had only a few hours' experience, but in the end he agreed on condition she just did some circuits and bumps and under no circumstances try to land during a squall. Well, off she went and presently I looked out of the hangar to see an enormous black cloud mass approaching and, right in the middle of it, blow me down if that silly little girl wasn't trying to land. The rain was bucketing down and there wasn't time to run so I jumped on my motorbike and roared out — the Moth was such a frail thing and I just managed to grab the wings before the squall could tip it over. I said to Jean: "You shouldn't have done that. You could have got yourself into a lot of difficulty." And instead of attempting to justify it by saying she needed bad weather practice for some long-distance flight she just said curtly: "I'll do what I like." Later Dave Allen tore a strip off her and I'll never forget her reply. She looked at him hard and said: "I'll do what I want when I want." '

One of Jean's hopes in returning to New Zealand had been that she might find someone willing to pay for her England–New Zealand attempt. There was no one. The country was in one of the deepest recessions in its history and her appeals were greeted with incredulity and cynicism. She was briefly tempted by an offer from Madame Valeska to join her in partnership at the dance studio, but, as she wrote determinedly in her memoirs, 'at this particular period in my life I felt that there was no going back and I must press forward impelled by an ambition which had to be gratified'.

By the middle of 1931 she had arrived at a new plan. To increase potential sponsors' confidence in her flying skill she decided she would have to become a professional pilot and get herself a commercial licence. There was only one problem: it required a minimum of 100 hours' flying experience. As she still had less than 30 hours in her logbook that was going to cost a lot of money she didn't have.

But Jean was beginning to acquire considerable skill in procuring money from other people with the philosophy that she was not only a deserving cause, but someone rather special in whom the world should feel privileged to invest. She had an almost messianic faith in herself, and an unshakeable conviction that she had a significant role to play in putting New Zealand womankind on the map. It stemmed from what seemed to many an almost unbelievable naivety but, increasingly, it was to be associated with a strand of ruthlessness in which her sexuality was to play a prominent part. It was already in operation in her friendship with Fred Truman of whom she saw a great deal during the four months he spent in Auckland in 1931. He took her frequently to the cinema, to dances and out to expensive meals. They also flew together at the Auckland Aero Club. He now regarded her as his girlfriend and was even daring to hope that she might marry him. But before he could persuade her he had to return to his Bristol fighter squadron in India. And shortly afterwards she sailed back to England in the *Rotorua* to study for her B licence at the London Aeroplane Club.

There is a conflict of evidence as to how she paid her fare this time, since the proceeds from the piano had undoubtedly been spent. Fred's dental practice had fallen on hard times; many of his patients were out of work and he was treating them for free. There wasn't even enough money for Ellen to go with Jean, who wrote in her memoirs: 'I was just able, with mother's help, to scrape enough money together for the fare to England and it almost broke my heart to leave her behind.'

However, John Batten told me what actually happened. 'I paid her fare,' he said. 'I was back in New Zealand briefly in 1931 looking for work between films in England. I was quite astonished when Dad told me that Jean was learning to fly; all that time in London and I'd thought she was studying music. The problem was she didn't have her fare back. So, although actually I was going through a very lean time myself and couldn't really afford it, I paid it rather than let Dad, who was getting practically no money from his patients, stump up. I also offered to put her up in my London flat.'

Jean was never to acknowledge her brother's gesture, nor ever attempt to repay him. As she was soon to do with many other men, she took the money for granted.

Arriving back in London in July 1931 she embarked almost immediately on training for her B licence. She teamed up with Major Travers again and set out to accumulate the seventy or so hours she now needed. How she funded this in the light of her family's financial crisis and in the absence of her father's allowance – he couldn't afford now to reinstate it even had he wished to – there is no record. In *My Life*, and in the unpublished manuscript, she does not refer to her means of support during this expensive phase of her career; for, unlike many young people who learnt to fly then and since, she always refused to take a part-time job. In the memoirs she says: 'But for the help of my mother, I could not have flown at all.' It is possible that Ellen was sending her a small portion of her £3-a-week maintenance. But if so, that was only part of the truth. The rest of the money, and quite a lot of it, came from Fred Truman in India.

Jean was never to admit the existence of Fred Truman. She never mentioned him to friends in later life, never spoke of him when recounting, in media interviews, the story of how she trained as a pilot, and totally ignored him in her two published books and her unpublished memoirs — in which all the other significant men in her life were cautiously identified by their first names. Yet without doubt she owed her subsequent success more directly to Fred Truman than to any other person.

I stumbled on his role in her life by chance while preparing to shoot the documentary toward the end of 1987. I had gone to the North Island town of Palmerston North to see a vintage aeroplane, hoping it might serve as one of Jean's aircraft in some flying reconstructions. When he heard the subject of our programme the plane's owner said quite casually: 'Someone you ought to talk to here in Palmerston is Rose Truman, Fred Truman's widow. She's in her early eighties. Fred was a flying instructor here just before the war. He died in the late 1940s, but I think the family can tell you quite a lot of things you should know about Jean. Apart from anything else, Fred was once in love with her.'

It was several months before I was able to meet Rose Truman. Sadly by then she was seriously ill in hospital, but her daughter, Shirley Anne, told me that although her mother was dying she was insistent on meeting me. She was concerned, before she went, to 'put the record straight' about Jean Batten.

Shirley Anne met me at the airport and drove me to the hospital. It was a poignant interlude, made more sombre by a day of scudding low black cloud and driving rain. Rose was very ill indeed. When I first saw her, grey faced and at death's door, I was convinced she was too frail to communicate and offered to leave. But, slowly realising who I was, she began to respond and made it clear that she wanted me to stay. I sat at her bedside and her voice was so weak I had to bend my head to catch the whispered words. Here is a summary of what she said:

'I can't really remember, but I think I met Fred in Auckland around 1933. I was working in a women's hat shop in Epsom and he'd just come back to live in New Zealand after five years overseas flying with the RAF. We started going out together but we were both involved with other people. I was engaged to a young farmer whom my father didn't much approve of. And Fred had been going around with this young woman pilot, Jean

Batten, but nobody had heard of her then, of course. The trouble was that she'd recently tried to break it off, but Fred was still in love with her. However, eventually, he said to me: "If you agree to give up your farmer bloke I promise to give up Jean Batten." I'll always remember him saying that. Well I broke it off with my fiancé and he said he would forget Jean. But I don't think he ever did. Not only was he still fond of her but she actually owed him a huge heap of money. When his five years with the RAF was up he was paid a gratuity of £500. I just couldn't believe it when he told me had given the whole lot to Jean – every blooming penny of it – to help pay for her flying. It was supposed to be a loan. What a joke that was. Because she wouldn't pay it back, and Fred and I needed it to get married and set up a home. Do you know, she kept him waiting for that money for years. Long after she had lots of her own. We couldn't afford to get married until 1937 because of her. I know she became very famous and everyone worshipped her and thought she was perfect. But if you're making a film and writing a book about her I think people should know there was another side to her. In my opinion she was a little gold digger.'

This did not coincide with the popular image of the Jean I had so far read about in the copious family cuttings from the newspapers of the day, so I tried to check Rose's story. I discovered that a younger brother of Fred's, Reg Truman, was living in Papakura, a town on Auckland's southern outskirts. Soon after Rose died, late in 1987, I went to meet him. A warm outgoing man in his late sixties, who now spent much of his time as a sailplane instructor, he had a sharp memory and was careful with the truth.

'Flying was really Fred's whole life,' he said. 'He worked as a counter assistant in a store in Gisborne in the mid-twenties to save his boat fare to England to join the RAF and learn to fly. When he met Jean on that 1931 leave trip he told me he just fell head over heels in love with her. He was really smitten and he wanted desperately to marry her. He proposed and there's no doubt at all that she accepted. They didn't become formally engaged but there was quite positively an understanding between them. And it was this that led Fred to lavish so much hospitality and money upon her. There wasn't much to spend his pay on in India and he was a careful saver so the money was available. And assuming she was going to marry him he was naturally a lot more generous than he would otherwise have been.'

Reg said that Jean's first request for a loan came when she got back to London in 1931 and needed money for her B licence flying at Stag Lane. She wrote to Fred in Quetta and he sent some immediately. It was the first of a series of loans which preceded the final gesture when Fred poured his entire £500 terminal gratuity – effectively his life savings – into Jean's flying account at the London Aeroplane Club.

'He did this around the end of 1932 when he left the RAF and, instead of coming back to New Zealand, went to London intending to marry her,' said Reg. 'Fred decided that it would be a good idea if he got himself a civil B licence, too, so he and Jean teamed up and studied for the exams together. It didn't cost him very much because he already had all the hours he needed from his RAF flying.'

With his military flying expertise Fred often flew with Jean at Stag Lane and helped her polish her airmanship and navigation – saving her the extra £1 an hour cost of a club instructor. And in the process he came to admire her skills which were rapidly gaining in confidence and precision. In an interview with the New Zealand Herald in 1934, long after Jean had walked out of his life, Fred was quoted as saying, generously: 'She is a born flier. She has those first essentials – air sense and air touch, particularly the latter, which I think is exceptional.'

Whether Fred and Jean ever became lovers is not certain. Discreet argument used to be conducted among many of the people who knew her throughout her life as to whether she ever had a physical affair. The consensus veered strongly towards the belief that she remained a lifelong virgin, keeping herself for the marriage that was to elude her. But Reg believes that Fred and Jean did consummate their relationship. 'He hired a car and drove her all over England on holiday. He was a very physical person. I don't think there's any doubt about it.' There probably wasn't. For, although Jean preferred never to speak or write of the intimate details of her relationships, those who convinced themselves of her permanent celibacy were mistaken.

The £500 which Fred invested in Jean in the early 1930s does not sound like a lot of money today. But when a London suburban semi-detached house could be had for £375, a new Austin 7 car sold for £118 and a ready-to-wear man's suit cost only £5, it represented a small fortune – in the inflated values of 1990 money in the region of £11,000. It guaranteed the B licence, issued to Jean in December 1932. It helped turn her into a competent pilot. Given a lot more money, and even more luck, she now had the basic skills to fly an aeroplane across the world.

Writing about this latest triumph in *My Life*, she expresses something of the singlemindedness which allowed her to cripple Fred Truman financially, apparently without a pang of conscience. 'Once my mind was set on anything,' she declared, 'it was quite useless to attempt to swerve me from my purpose or dampen my enthusiasm in any way.' Indeed, it is clear that so compulsively obsessed was she with the need for a resounding public achievement, that everything, and everybody – except Ellen, who fuelled the obsession – were now totally subordinated to this one consuming objective.

So, her immediate goal achieved, Jean now began to edge Fred Truman out of her life. Whatever the true relationship had been it is unlikely that she ever entertained the serious thought of marrying him. 'She led him right up the garden path,' said Reg. 'He was just another of the many stepping stones she walked over on her road to success.'

Jean didn't have the courage, Reg Truman claims, to end it all while Fred was still in London acting as her devoted tutor and chauffeur, passionately involved in imparting to her every trick and professional technique he knew, undoubtedly contributing, since his ever-willing services were free, a great deal more than Travers. 'She waited until he got back to Auckland, early in 1933, before ditching him. He got this very final letter which, of course, he never showed to me, but we knew in the family from the immediate effect it had on him what it must have said.'

Unable to contain or conceal his distress and now virtually penniless, Fred Truman went through a bad reactive patch. He began to drink heavily. 'He was very, very bitter,' Reg said, 'and he went into a mild depression which lasted several months. It didn't quite drive him to drink but he certainly drowned his sorrows for quite a while. He was an easygoing guy who didn't react aggressively but when he was in these depressive drinking bouts he got very talkative and resentful about the way he'd been treated. He would say: "She's taken so much from me, and left me with nothing." All he had in the world at the end of the whole episode were some Persian carpets he'd brought back from India. And even these he had to sell to tide himself over.'

Resigned to the fact that he'd been used in a way totally beyond his experience, Fred Truman began to rebuild his life. He took a job as a paint salesman and later returned to flying as a club instructor. But, as Reg told me, 'He never really got Jean out of his system. She haunted him for the rest of his life.' The haunting, however, was not one-sided.

What Fred Truman was never to know was that throughout the cold, foggy months of that English autumn and early winter of 1932, when he dedicated much of his time to Jean's advanced flying training, she was already involved with another man. A great deal more prosperous than Fred, he was a potential source of much greater wealth to back a flight to the other side of the world. But, before she could begin to tap his family's extensive resources, there was a crisis in her life. It involved her brother John.

CHAPTER 4

A Woman of Destiny (1931–1933)

Jean accepted John's offer and moved into his flat in St John's Wood on her return to London in the middle of 1931. He paid 30 shillings a week for it. John obligingly moved out of the only bedroom to make room for Jean and slept in the sitting room. He was now starring in another film, *Men Like These*, the dramatisation of a submarine disaster, and spent his days waist-deep in a water tank out at Elstree studios. 'There was a piano and we often had musical friends in for dinner after which I would accompany John, who had a rather nice baritone voice,' Jean wrote. 'He would sing Schubert Lieder and songs from Noel Coward's musical *Bitter Sweet*, then playing in London.' But these jolly evenings and her amiable relationship with John were soon to come to an abrupt and unhappy end. They had a fierce row and Jean walked out.

She describes it briefly in her memoirs. 'Unfortunately he was rather temperamental and, as my father had written asking him to try and stop me flying, feelings were at times rather strained. At last we had a fearful quarrel when he objected to my inviting a young flight lieutenant in to tea after he had given me a lift home from the aerodrome. A harmless enough gesture in itself, but with far reaching consequences, for I took him at his word and, a few days later, packed my bags and left the apartment.' The reference to her father's attempts to have John try and stop her flying were puzzling since by then, she had been home to New Zealand and Fred, far from maintaining his opposition, had indeed encouraged her by paying for navigation lessons. Presumably it was an allusion to her determination to make a hazardous long-distance flight. However, the memoirs were written around forty-five years later and it is likely that Jean had either forgotten the true cause of the row, or preferred not to recall it because she may not have been proud of her part in it. The 'flight lieutenant' I at first assumed to be Fred Truman but when I put this to his brother, Reg, he said that Fred would then still have been with his squadron in India.

John Batten was horrified at the mere suggestion of a row. He became visibly upset and overcome with emotion when I read him the passage in Jean's manuscript. 'There was quite definitely no quarrel,' he said. 'I don't know what she could have been talking about.' He pondered for a while, searching his memory, and then said: 'But what about mother? She was living there too.' If Jean's memoirs are to be relied upon Ellen was still in New Zealand unable to afford the boat fare to London. However John was quite emphatic that Ellen was there, saying he clearly remembered buying a bed for her. Moreover, he said, it was while his mother and sister were staying at that time that he had actually used his reputation as a prominent actor to try and find a flight sponsor for Jean.

'When I had completed Men Like These at Elstree I went on another visit to Australia and New Zealand and used the opportunity to try and persuade some of the newspapers out there to back her flight. Well, I had no luck at all. They all said it was a scatterbrained idea and, in any case, Amy Johnson had already done it and it wasn't a story any more. But what sticks in my mind is the memory of the day I left London to do that trip. Jean and mother were both there and they came down and stood on the pavement outside the fish shop to say goodbye when my taxi left. I remember it very clearly for one reason. Although I met mother, I think twice subsequently, it was the last time Jean and I ever spoke to each other. It's a very long time ago now and I can't be absolutely sure of the date, but it would have been around late 1931 or early 1932.'

Startled by this disclosure I said to John, 'Do you really mean *ever*? Not since the early thirties?' And he said, 'Yes, ever to speak to. I did see her once many years later. But we didn't actually speak then.'

I was never able to unravel satisfactorily the sequence of events that surrounded the last-ever contact between them. Undoubtedly something happened between Jean and John which he preferred to draw a veil over. His nephews and niece in New Zealand confirmed that there had been a rift but they didn't know the precise cause. Before I met John they had recalled that, during Jean's stay in his flat, he had for some reason objected to her bringing home men friends. But there was another theory that, at that time, Jean wasn't hitting it off with Madeleine Murat, the extremely pretty, passionate and strong-willed young writer whom John was shortly to marry.

This permanent parting of the ways with her brother, which neither was ever to attempt to repair, was a matter that Jean always regarded as too private to disclose, even to the handful of people who believed they enjoyed her confidence. And in her memoirs she never refers to John again. He is written out of her life as peremptorily and decisively as she dropped Fred Truman.

Towards the middle of 1989, when this book was nearing completion, John wrote to me with some further possible explanation of Jean's allegation of a row between them. 'I can only surmise', he said, 'that she cooked it up as an explanation to friends who may have wondered if John Batten, the film star, was any relation, and to account for the fact that she had no contact with me.'

John then went on to describe for the first time how, from the early 1930s onwards, he had been spurned also by Ellen. 'She definitely did not want any contact with me once Jean had begun to fulfil her flying ambitions,' he said. He also referred to his mother's rejection of him in relation to comments I had put to him from people who had said that Ellen 'tried to own people'. Poignantly, he wrote: 'Personally I would have loved to have been "owned" by her.'

Jean moved from John's flat to lodgings somewhere between Edgware and Hendon, close to the aerodrome – 'a small room in the house of a motherly woman and for which, I now find it difficult to believe, I paid only seven shillings and sixpence a week.' The room was in a semi-detached house, identifiable from one of her logbooks as 109 Stag Lane. Here she lived frugally. 'I made porridge on the little gas ring before I left in the mornings. In the evenings I usually cooked scrambled eggs on toast which I ate while reading the *Manual of Air Pilotage* propped up in front of me on the table. How could the lady and her family know that both camping and the pioneering instinct were in my blood.'

It was from her Stag Lane room that Jean worked for her B licence throughout 1932 and it was here, probably late that year, that she was joined by Ellen who (if one accepts Jean's version of the facts) would have hurried to London on hearing of the row with John, anxious that her daughter was now unchaperoned.

Over at the de Havilland Technical School, in a large unheated hangar, Jean prepared herself for long-distance flying by taking an evening course in aircraft and engine maintenance. And, when she had learnt the oily practicalities of keeping a Gipsy engine running sweetly, she tried at every opportunity to build up her flying hours by giving joyrides or delivering aeroplanes. While flying a Gipsy Moth to its new owner in Bournemouth one Sunday morning, she demonstrated for the first time something of the cool-headedness that was to characterise her handling of the many emergencies she was to face in her career.

'As I set course I could see all the landmarks I now knew so well and by which fledgling pilots were taught to recognise and locate their home aerodrome. There was the tall green gasometer near Northolt and to the south the one at Heston, grey and squat, shining in the early morning sunshine. Harrow-on-the-Hill with the delicate spire of St Mary's Church. The Welsh Harp reservoir, our best landmark, for even in fog one could usually locate it as a dark irregular blur. "When you pick it up", I was once told, "just follow the Edgware Road at roof-top height, turn left at the bank on the corner of Stag Lane, then throttle back and feel your way down to the aerodrome."*

'Flying at 2,000 feet I passed Sunningdale and Bagshot and was over fairly wooded country when suddenly, without any warning, the engine gave a loud bang, followed by a rumbling which sounded as if it was disintegrating. I immediately switched off to avoid any further damage and looking round for a suitable place to make a forced landing. But there seemed to be nothing but a carpet of trees beneath the aeroplane. However, at that moment, just to the west of my route, I saw what looked like a small clearing with a large building on one side of it where I thought I might be able to land.

'I lost a considerable amount of height as I glided towards it — and then, to my horror, I saw two tall trees straight ahead. There was no alternative but to glide between them and the only way to avoid having both wings torn off was to do so with an almost vertical bank. Deep shadows engulfed the cockpit as the Moth slid between the two great trees as through the eye of a large needle. I glimpsed an ornamental pool flash past beneath the wingtip as I side-slipped onto the ground. The Moth came to rest in front of a wide flight of steps which led up to a large brick building with an imposing clock tower. A man came running over. "By Jove," he called out, "that was pretty smart." Although I did not say so I certainly agreed with him as I climbed out of the cockpit. "And you're only a little girl," he added, smiling down at me. "My word the boys will be sorry to have missed this."

'"What boys?" I asked looking up at the imposing building. "What place is this?"

'"Don't you know?" he replied with an air of incredulity.

---

*Tom Hollinrake (who had taken Jean to see Louis Armstrong after her training crash) came home up the Edgware Road one afternoon. 'There were very few regulations and flying was great fun in those days,' he said. 'My biggest thrill was to get above the clouds and fly around among the cumulous peaks. It was fantastic. But getting through the clouds was a bit dicey — there were no blind flying instruments, of course, and I would invariably spin out a few times getting up there. One day I came spinning out of a cloud about 3,000 feet right above Oxford Circus. To find my way home I flew along Oxford Street and up the Edgware Road. The low-flying did get me into a bit of trouble.'

"Why this is Sandhurst Military Academy and you've landed on our parade ground. I'm the caretaker. All the cadets are away on vacation."

'I walked round to the front of the plane and removed the nose cowling. It didn't take long to locate the trouble, for one of the pushrods was missing; it must have snapped and fallen out.'

Jean claims that she happened to be carrying a spare pushrod in the luggage locker and that she quickly fitted it, watched by 'a small admiring crowd who had now gathered'. Commanding two of them to hold the wing-tips, she swung the propeller, climbed back into the cockpit and took off in a hair-raising steep turn, clearing the Sandhurst clocktower by just a few feet.

When later she landed at Bournemouth she was horrified to learn from its owner that the Moth was not insured. But she had acquitted herself with the panache of a much more experienced pilot. Her handling of the emergency was to establish the coolness of her style in the air – her ability never to panic, to respond with reason, never with fear or emotion.

There are, however, grounds for believing that the cause of the sudden engine problems may not have been precisely as she recorded. A Gipsy Moth owner who read her account was highly sceptical. 'It is inconceivable,' he said, 'that a valve pushrod would ever break – they just aren't subjected to those sort of loads. And, if by some remote chance it had fractured, it certainly couldn't have fallen out; it would have been contained within the engine cowling. I think she must have been dramatising the incident a little bit. It sounds as if the rod had just become disconnected. To slip it back would take her only a few minutes. And, incidentally, when it happened in the air she needn't have switched off; she could have used the power of the remaining three cylinders to help clear those trees. However, it was still a very cool performance.'

Another pilot who flew Gipsy Moths in the 1930s, and who knew Sandhurst well, agreed. But he added: 'Her description of the way the engine stopped suggests that, in fact, she might have caused the rough running by inadvertently knocking off one or both of the magneto switches.' Commenting on Jean's dramatic account of the daring way she had avoided the trees, he said that there were then none in the immediate vicinity of

the parade ground and that her emergency landing had obviously not been quite as hazardous as she claimed.

The polish and confidence Jean was developing through
1932 led her to apply for a job with Sir Alan Cobham's legendary 'flying circus' which was just starting up. Cobham, who had
been knighted for some spectacular survey flights he had made
in the 1920s to Africa and Australia demonstrating the feasibility of scheduled airline operations along the empire routes,
was to create the most celebrated of all the British prewar
barnstorming aerobatic and joy-riding operations which, in the
four years it lasted, gave nearly a million people their first experience of air travel. But the circus wasn't quite ready to take
on women pilots. After Jean had demonstrated her aerobatic
skills, Cobham's chief pilot, to her great bitterness, 'told me the
best thing I could do was go away and get married'.

But she was also beginning to meet some of the revered
personalities of the long-distance record-breaking scene. 'They
were an illustrious group,' she wrote in her memoirs, recounting
an occasion at the clubhouse when she had joined a group
comprising Amy Johnson, Jim Mollison, Charles (C.W.A.)
Scott, Tom Campbell Black and Geoffrey de Havilland,* the
eldest son of the great aircraft designer. Amy, whom she
describes as 'a very sensitive, highly strung person with strong
likes and dislikes', had by then added to her Australia flight
fame by flying across Siberia (with engineer Jack Humphreys) to
Japan and later making a return flight to South Africa in a small
Puss Moth cabin plane. Jim Mollison, with whom she had just
begun what was to be a stormy and miserably unhappy marriage, had flown from Australia to England, from England to
Capetown and most sensationally of all had, alone in a Puss
Moth in August 1932, made the first ever east-to-west solo
flight across the Atlantic – at 31 hours and 20 minutes the
longest duration flight yet made by a light aircraft. Jim, who
called himself the 'flying playboy', used to maintain his courage
by imbibing huge quantities of brandy on his long-distance

*Geoffrey de Havilland, later to become chief test pilot of his father's
company, was killed in 1946 flying an experimental tailless aircraft, the DH
108, over the Thames Estuary.

flights; he was a short little Glaswegian with bold blue eyes and a dandyish charm that proved irresistible to women; he was also notorious for the trail of debts he sometimes left behind, and for his quick temper when provoked: at a dance in Melbourne he had once punched a man insensible for what he perceived as an insult.

Charles Scott had already flown twice alone to Australia in a Gipsy Moth and once back. He was a tall, extremely handsome and arrogantly intolerant young man who, two years later, with Tom Campbell Black in the de Havilland Comet *Grosvenor House*, was to win the great MacRobertson England–Australia air race of 1934. Jean sensed the tension between Amy and Charles Scott. 'He did not get on well with her,' she wrote in her memoirs. 'Amy blamed him for her crash at Brisbane after her flight from England when he was sent to Darwin to escort her to Sydney. On arrival at Brisbane, Charles flew low over the huge crowd in salute and Amy, thinking that he was about to touch down, followed him and landed downwind with unfortunate consequences' – indeed crashing her Moth *Jason* embarrassingly in front of the huge Australian crowd.*

Tom Campbell Black, the last member of the group, a former Royal Flying Corps pilot, was a pioneer of commercial flying in East Africa who had established Wilson Airways in Kenya and flown the Prince of Wales around the colony on hunting safaris. A highly educated, kindly and modest man and a brilliant pilot (later to marry the celebrated West End comedy actress Florence Desmond who did stage impersonations of Amy Johnson) he was already, in 1932, one of the lovers of the beautiful and promiscuous Beryl Markham, the Kenyan pilot who was later to fly the Atlantic alone.

Sitting with this élite and glamorous group of aviators Jean was thrilled and flattered to be seen drinking tea at their table

---

*In fact, although Scott had done his best to demoralise Amy and undermine her confidence on the flight from Darwin, she didn't blame him for her disastrous landing in Brisbane. Attempting a steep last-minute side-slip she had overshot and careered into the far boundary fence; to a horrified gasp from the huge crowd, she had turned upside down. But to everyone's relief she climbed out uninjured.

and to find herself being treated as an equal in the lighthearted banter that surrounded a discussion, she recalled in her memoirs, on the length of a pilot's active flying career. 'Jim Mollison said very definitely, looking across at Amy who was seven years my senior and sitting next to me, "I doubt if either of you will ever reach middle age, especially you," he added, wagging his finger at me amid much laughter. "One of these days we'll be digging you out" – an allusion to a low altitude aerobatic routine I was trying to perfect.'

In the last months of 1932, when the flow of Fred Truman's money into her flying account at the club had passed its peak of generosity and funds were becoming short again, Jean met another benefactor who was suddenly to transform her long-distance flight dream into reality. She had now modified her original powerful desire to make an historic flight all the way home to New Zealand. It was obvious that she would never raise enough money to buy a plane with the huge range to make the final 1,200-mile crossing of the Tasman Sea from Australia to Auckland. For the time being she knew that she would have to settle for something less ambitious – an open cockpit biplane – and make her name instead with a flight to Australia, which she was now privately obsessed with doing faster than Amy Johnson. The man who offered to make this possible was Victor Dorée.

Victor was one of the five sons of a successful English linen merchant, Herbert Dorée, who owned a large and elegant house set in ten acres of land in what was then semi-rural Edgware on the north-western outskirts of London. The family lived in style with a chauffeur, a gardener and house servants; the gracious home, in its own large garden and orchards, breathed a warm prosperity, reflected in the Dorées' generosity to their sons and hospitality to visitors. The Dorée home was almost next door to Stag Lane aerodrome, where Victor kept his own private Gipsy Moth bought for him by his mother.

When he had left his London public school, Mill Hill, Victor had joined the family firm, going into the warehouse to learn the ropes and then on the road as a salesman. This had taken him to Australia where, in 1928, he had qualified as a pilot. Back in England, he met Jean at Stag Lane in 1932. He was then thirty and she was twenty-three.

Jean refused to name Victor Dorée in her two published books, referring to him merely as 'a pilot'. However in her memoirs, which she knew would not be published until after her death, she was a little more forthcoming and called him Victor.

I heard of his existence and the major role he played in her career, long before the manuscript came into my hands. Surprisingly I learnt about him not from any of Jean's relatives or friends, because in later years she had tried to deny his friendship but, quite fortuitously, in the slow and grinding process of day-to-day research. I happened on his name in an unlikely 1933 cutting from the Norwich *Eastern Daily Press* reporting Jean's departure on her first attempt to fly to Australia. Wondering precisely who was 'Mr Victor Dorée, a fellow member of the London Aeroplane Club' who, with her mother, had come to see her off, I appealed for information, without much hope, in letters in British aviation journals. To my surprise, there was a response from two prominent members of the de Havilland Moth Club. The first was from the enthusiastic owner of one of the world's few remaining flying Gipsy Moths, Mike Vaisey, a Hemel Hempstead quantity surveyor, who said that not only was Victor still alive, but further aroused my curiosity by adding, 'he has some tales to tell about Jean'. Almost by the same post came a note from the Moth Club's secretary, Stuart McKay, of Berkhamsted in Hertfordshire, sending Victor's address. Intriguingly his note said that Jean had once wrecked Victor's Moth. 'He is *still* very sore about it and may not want to reply to you,' he added ominously. I learnt later that Victor did indeed want to reply. But sadly, at eighty-four he was seriously ill. Before I could visit England to meet him, he died, early in 1987, at his Hampshire home at Sway, near Lymington, in the New Forest. However, before he died his wife, Mary, and his sister-in-law, Grace Dorée, sat on my behalf at his bedside and talked to him about the beautiful young New Zealand girl who had come briefly into his life fifty-five years before. Later that year I met Mary and Grace and with the help of old photographs, Victor's flying logbooks, and some remarkable and well-preserved black-and-white 16mm movie film which the Dorée family had shot in the 1930s, they reconstructed for me the hitherto unpublicised events which were to make Jean's first long-distance flight possible.

'In later years Victor rarely spoke of her – which wasn't surprising as she didn't ever bring him much happiness,' said Grace, a warm-hearted and still beautiful silver-haired woman in her seventies. Victor never spoke to Mary about Jean, but he confided in his brothers, particularly Stanley, Grace's late husband. 'I think he wanted to bury the interlude because he was so terribly disappointed by the things she did to him. He was really and truly a very splendid type of person, a genuinely kind man always thoughtful and helpful to other people. And because he was such a gentleman he could never bring himself to say anything derogatory about her, despite the hurt she brought him.

'When he first met her at the club Victor obviously found her extremely attractive and was very drawn to her, but the thing that really appealed to him, I believe, was her utter dedication to flying, her ability as a pilot and this determination to fly to Australia. I think he was also impressed that she had this great ambition without a hope of achieving it because she and her mother were so very poor. They were living in quite reduced circumstances in a very small room they had rented somewhere near the aerodrome. And they must have been going through a bad patch because Jean told Victor she couldn't afford to pay for any more flying, or even her club subscription. Victor thereupon not only paid her sub, he lent her his own plane at no cost whatsoever so she could start flying again – he even paid for the petrol.'

Victor's infatuation with Jean was subsequently confirmed for me by Bill Oliver who, with a degree of jealousy he was freely to admit, watched their swiftly developing relationship at Stag Lane. He remembered very clearly Victor's kindness. 'He was once rash enough to let me fly his aeroplane. He had a certain style. He had money. But he was a very nice chap, a bit wooden, but with a heart of gold. Yes, he was clearly very much in love with Jean – and he stole her from me. Not that I believe she ever knew my feelings towards her. He was so much older than me and I couldn't compete. No, it was a sad day for me when old Dorée hit town.'

Mary and Grace Dorée have a photograph of Jean sitting, smiling, in the cockpit of Victor's Gipsy Moth – G-AAAV. At the time he had been very proud of his association with her and not only frequently photographed her, but probably paid for an exotic and glamorous Garboesque studio study of her in expensive-looking leather flying gear which is still in Victor's album.

His generosity extended to Ellen. They both became regular guests at Oakleigh, the Dorées' home in Orchard Drive, Edgware, although Jean was probably there more often than her mother – for once again the Battens were in their perennial predicament of receiving hospitality without being able to afford to return it.

On one of her visits to Oakleigh, Jean sought the family's advice on how to get sponsorship for her flight. The family had a magnificently simple solution. Victor borrowed from his mother the money to buy Jean an aeroplane.

'She was an above ordinarily kind and generous woman,' said Grace, 'and although she'd not long before bought a plane for Victor she didn't hesitate to lend him the money for another.' Grace couldn't remember what sum was involved but as the plane was bought secondhand and had only flown about 130 hours from new, it would probably have cost something like £400 – roughly the equivalent today of the price of a used two-seater Cessna.

'It was intended to be a business deal,' Grace explained, 'but I'm very hazy about the details. I believe the idea was that if she made any money out of the trip she would pay him half, and that if she made a lot of money Victor might have gone out to Australia and joined her in some flying business they would set up.'

In *My Life*, without any acknowledgement of the virtual gift, Jean described the deal thus: 'One day at the club I met a pilot who was interested in my plan for a solo flight to Australia and agreed to help finance it. I was to have a half-share in a second-hand Moth and, in return, signed an agreement to give the other pilot fifty per cent of any proceeds from that flight and to tour Australia and New Zealand for twelve months giving passenger flights.' But in her memoirs the pilot's name is casually dropped into the narrative in one brief gesture of re-cognition: 'I was flying a Gipsy Moth belonging to my friend Victor who had managed to persuade his family to help finance a flight to Australia.' However, in a 1935 interview, she was candidly to reveal the truth: 'I was able to persuade a private family to help me.'*

In the last months of 1932 it is clear that Jean was involved simultaneously with Victor and Fred Truman and was almost certainly being helped financially by both at the same time. Whether the benefactors ever met it was impossible to discover. But Jean had become a skilful manipulator, and would probably have gone to some lengths to keep them apart. By January 1933 she had no further need of Fred; he had served his purpose in largely funding her commercial licence. The assistance she needed from here on was much more substantial – and for-tuitously the Dorée family had come on the scene at the crucial moment to provide it.

Although Mary and Grace Dorée insisted that they never believed Victor had any romantic interest in Jean – it was purely business, they said – it was not easy to accept that he didn't. It wasn't somehow credible that a man would go to his mother for a huge loan, to the worth at that time of a decent-sized house, to enable a totally unknown and patently naive young woman with a brand-new flying licence to risk his aeroplane, and her neck, in a profoundly dangerous flight through some of the most destructive weather in the world if his emotions weren't involved. Jean, in her memoirs, makes no bones about it, openly asserting that Victor wanted to marry her, and that the Dorée family would have welcomed it. They were certainly later to become much less enthusiastic at the prospect.

Whatever the precise business arrangement, the aircraft, a DH60 M Gipsy Moth (the 'M' stood for its metal-framed fuse-lage, as distinct from the wood used in some others), was purchased by Victor early in 1933 and registered jointly (its logbook shows) in the names of Jean Batten and V.H. Dorée.

---

*'The Ordinary Girl Who Became a Girl in a Million', London *Sunday Express*, 28 April 1935.

Jean was impressed to learn that it had a royal pedigree, for its previous owner had been the Prince of Wales – later King Edward VIII – who used to fly it from the nearby RAF station at Hendon where Victor had acquired it from the King's Flight, the royal flying unit, which maintained it for the prince.* Jean went to Hendon and made the five-minute flight to deliver the aircraft to its new home at Stag Lane. It was attractively painted with a blue fuselage and silver wings, but by royal decree Jean was instructed to vary this scheme and complied by repainting in pale blue a fine white line that ran the length of the fuselage. The Moth was wheeled into the hangar at the de Havilland Aircraft factory and prepared for what Jean was now telling her friends was to be an attack on Amy Johnson's women's solo record flight to Darwin. She planned to fly via the Middle East, India, Burma, Singapore and the islands of what was then the Dutch East Indies (now Indonesia). To increase the aircraft's normal range of around 250 miles (relying on its standard 19-gallon tank which sat between the two top wings) Victor had two extra tanks fitted for her. The biggest of these, holding an extra 27 gallons, was put in the front cockpit which was then covered over and ceased to be visible.

A second, 15-gallon tank was installed behind the rear pilot's seat. As the Moth's engine was gravity-fed from the standard tank up in the wing, a hand-pump was fitted in the cockpit so that Jean could top it up in flight from the two fuselage tanks. How all this equipment and engineering work, to increase her range to 800 miles, was paid for there is no surviving record, but as Fred Truman's money had been used up and Jean was wholly dependent still on a share of Ellen's maintenance, there can be no doubt that the infatuated Victor wrote the cheque, probably helped by an element of the loan from Mrs Dorée as part of the arrangement by which the family was underwriting her.

---

*Edward had first flown in 1919, but when his father, King George V, heard about it he was not amused. He ordered the heir to refrain from flying – a ban that was to remain for nine years until 1928. The following year, when the King at last relented, Jean Batten's Gipsy Moth, G-AALG, was acquired for the prince by the royal flying unit that was later to become the King's Flight.

In the weeks before her departure, in the spring of 1933, she travelled round London arranging visas, fuel supplies, and landing permissions in the fourteen countries through which she intended to fly on her 10,500-mile journey. She even compiled a list of all the marine lighthouses along the route with a note of the flashing code of each as a navigation aid. And in the evenings, back in the tiny room in which she and Ellen ate and slept, she knelt on the floor, plotting her courses on her maps. Some of them had been lent to her on a recent visit to England by her former hero, Charles Kingsford Smith who, three years earlier, in an Avro Avian biplane, had flown the route from England to Australia. He'd done it in just under ten days, breaking Hinkler's record, and had later flown it in the opposite direction. He had given her two pieces of advice which she was often later to quote: 'Don't attempt to break men's records – and don't fly at night.'

'I made a point of ignoring both of them,' she said.

More advice came from an enterprising New Zealander, Oscar Garden, who had made a remarkable, yet almost entirely unpublicised solo flight from England to Australia in 1930 a few months after Amy Johnson's epic journey, but flying it faster than she did. With a brand new licence he had walked into Selfridge's store in Oxford Street and bought a secondhand Gipsy Moth for £500 he had saved as a rabbit exterminator on a South Island sheep station. Unable to afford proper aeronautical charts he had set off from Croydon, with less than forty hours in his logbook, with some cheap school maps pinned together.

Later in New Zealand, to where he had shipped the aeroplane, Oscar Garden realised how lucky he had been to have survived. On a local trip in Dunedin the engine suddenly stopped with a loud explosion. He just managed to make it back to the aerodrome where he discovered that one of the connecting rods, linking the crankshaft to the piston, had broken. 'To think it could have happened over the Timor Sea,' he later told Jean. The incident added a further anxiety to one that had been nagging her ever since Victor Dorée had bought her the Prince's aeroplane.

It concerned the con-rods in the Gipsy engine which had

begun to replace the original Cirrus engines fitted in the earlier models of Gipsy Moths. They had been demonstrating an alarming tendency to fracture, precipitating a number of mid-air emergencies in which the engine stopped with a frightening bang. Jean had heard about Oscar Garden's flight and when she learnt that he was back in England she got in touch with him to pick his brains for route information. 'We met in London,' Oscar, now in his mid-eighties, said at his home at Papatoetoe in South Auckland. 'I remember I took her to the pictures. I can't recall the occasion very clearly now but she was a very serious, very quiet, shy girl. I think she wanted to get hold of my maps but I had to explain they weren't actually good enough. I remember taking her home on the underground and standing on the doorstep and kissing her goodnight. It was just a peck on the cheek.'*

Jean wrote of her anxiety about the Gipsy Moth's con-rods in her memoirs. 'Victor had set his heart on this particular aeroplane, although we could not find out whether a certain engine modification had been completed. Some extra work involving the fitting of new parts had been done during a top overhaul and not entered up in the logbook and, for all we knew, may have included this particular one which entailed replacing the connecting rods for it was found that, after a certain number of hours, metal fatigue developed just where the serial number was stamped. When I took delivery of the Moth at Hendon I was not really happy. Mother wisely suggested having the engine dismantled and I thought it advisable. But Victor remained convinced that all was well and kept on saying, "But it's just had an overhaul and they must have changed the con-rods." In any case the money available would barely cover expenses, so a complete overhaul was ruled out.'

The battered and coffee-stained engine logbook for Gipsy Moth G-AALG is still in the possession of the Dorée family. In a pocket inside the back cover there is an Air Ministry booklet, *Notices to Aircraft Owners and Ground Engineers 1920-1932.*

---

*Oscar Garden was to become an airline captain, a career which later led to his appointment as Chief Pilot of Tasman Empire Airways.

Jean had written her name in pencil across the front of the booklet and inside, against a lengthy notice issued in August 1932 advising on the procedure for the modification of Gipsy engine connecting rods, she had heavily side-lined several paragraphs in pencil. One read: 'Certain connecting rods on early Gipsy I, II and III engines having embossed identification letters and part number on the shank, are in commission. A small number of failures has occurred due to fatigue cracks starting from the root of the letters and spreading laterally across the rod.'

The next paragraph she had marked gave instructions for the simple but vital modification: 'During the next top overhaul, any connecting rods of the type referred to ... are to be removed. The letters and part number should then be filed off and all traces of the embossing and file marks polished out ...'

In LG's logbook for its Gipsy II engine one of the last entries by the ground engineer in January 1933, four months after this notice was issued, recorded in extensive detail all the work that had been done in the top overhaul referred to by Jean. No con-rod modification is mentioned. It is inconceivable that a modification with such life-threatening implications as that required by the Air Ministry would not have been recorded had it been done. Why hadn't it happened during the aircraft's illustrious previous ownership? Surely the engineers of the King's Flight were not going to risk by negligence the life of the heir to the throne? A check of the maintenance records for the period of the Prince's ownership during the preceding three years showed that, after the issue of the con-rod instruction in August 1932, there had not been a top overhaul required until the beginning of 1933. However, by then, it appears, the Moth was being prepared for sale.

Had Jean and Victor been seriously determined to establish whether or not the fatigue-suspect serial numbers had been removed, they had only to ask the engineer whose name appeared at the foot of the maintenance entry. Clearly they didn't. Nor, it seems, did Ellen, who took an excessive interest in her daughter's safety and welfare and who had involved herself deeply in this technical anxiety. For, without any of them taking further steps to reassure themselves that the aeroplane was safe, Jean climbed aboard and headed off for Australia. Had she not been so impatient for fame she might have avoided disaster.

CHAPTER 5

Ordeal by Sandstorm (1933)

The Dorée family turned out in force to see Jean off from Stag Lane on 8 April 1933. Ellen had gone by car to Lympne, the airport near Ashford in Kent from where departing aviators in those days cleared customs. The 16mm film of the event, kept by Mary Dorée, captures well the sense of occasion that focused on Jean that afternoon, long before she had any significance as a pilot.

The family arranged for her to be delivered to the aerodrome in style and the film shows her arriving at the clubhouse, sitting in solitary splendour in the back of the Dorées' large, chauffeur-driven Vauxhall, with Victor travelling in the front. As the car stops the door is opened for her by a close friend of the family, Ben Briers (uncle of the actor Richard Briers), and she emerges clutching her few possessions for the flight wrapped in a brown paper parcel. She is wearing a long-jacketed suit with a fur collar and a small beret on the back of her head. She looks demure, a trifle shy and a little uncertain of herself, posing self-consciously for the movie camera, chatting with the affable Major Travers, and talking to the man who designed her aeroplane, the great Geoffrey de Havilland who had honoured her by coming to say goodbye.

One is impressed by the way in which all the activity revolves around Jean. She appears as a diffident and very innocent-looking young woman of below average height – she was 5 feet 4 inches tall – holding centre stage and accepting the VIP treatment. She is composed and unexpressive, possibly overawed by the warmth of the farewell party, and in none of the scenes does she appear to radiate much joy.

The camera pans to the Moth. It is being refuelled by Jack Humphreys and we see Jean stowing away her gear in the tiny compartment on top of the fuselage behind the rear cockpit. The front cockpit has been covered over to contain the big auxiliary fuel tank, and strapped to the centre-section struts, immediately in front of the pilot, is a large bulky object wrapped in canvas – the spare wooden propeller then considered essential on long-distance flights. Jean reappears, now dressed in a long leather flying coat, wearing helmet and goggles, and poses with Victor. Then Jack Humphreys starts the engine with a casual flick of the propellor – and she is off on the one-hour flight across London to Lympne.

Shortly afterwards Victor climbed into his own Moth and took off to escort her on the short journey across Kent. The flight is recorded in his logbook with the simple remark: 'Lympne with J.B.' In neither of her two books, nor in her unpublished manuscript, did Jean describe her departure from Stag Lane that spring afternoon on what was the start of a flying career that was to realise all her aspirations for fame and success. She was not prepared to acknowledge publicly, even over forty years later, her indebtedness to Victor and his family. She appears to have viewed their patronage simply as the due entitlement of a woman of destiny.

Ellen was waiting for Jean when she and Victor landed at Lympne and they all spent the night at a hotel near the aerodrome. Next morning Jean had the thrill of seeing a glamorous picture of herself in flying helmet featured in one of the London Sunday newspapers. Victor had invited the press to Stag Lane for her departure the previous afternoon but only one reporter – from the *Sunday Dispatch* – had turned up. His story, headlined GIRL'S LONE FLIGHT – TO AUSTRALIA IN THE PRINCE'S OLD PLANE, was soon to have more journalists hurrying to Lympne to interview the unknown aviator who, the *Dispatch* said, had been planning her flight for months in total secrecy. 'Her fellow members of the London Aeroplane Club were unaware of her ambition to fly to Australia until she left Stag Lane last night. Before she climbed into the cockpit the pretty twenty-three-year-old New Zealand girl said: "I have flown about 130 hours already and I want to take up air taxi work when I get to New Zealand. By tomorrow night with luck I shall reach Rome. I am not out to break records, but hope to reach Australia in a fortnight. Flying is everything to me. I have made my preparations carefully and I am confident I can win through." '

On the tarmac at Lympne soon after dawn next morning, Ellen proudly gave the first of many interviews about her daughter. And immediately she began, boldly, to rewrite history to coincide more conveniently with the mythology she and Jean were about to create. 'Mrs Batten said her husband sent Jean over to England to learn music,' she was quoted as saying. 'Shortly after her arrival she got fond of flying and invited me over here by saying I required a holiday. She got me to Stag Lane and I have seen nothing but aeroplanes since. I shall go back when I know she has arrived safely. I was her first passenger and I am very proud of her. Her father is against her flying but she says he will be proud of her if she wins through.'

In this interview, which was widely printed throughout Britain, Ellen thus launched the fiction she and Jean were to maintain from now on to romanticise the family background. The need to distort the truth was almost certainly rooted in Ellen's deep concern to withhold from public knowledge the shame of her marriage break-up. They were always to speak of Fred as if he were part of a happy united family. And the invention of the fable that Jean had invited her mother across the world for a holiday was presumably to create the impression of a family of financial substance, a device to conceal their desperate poverty – and Jean's massive indebtedness to two individuals.

Interviewed by telephone, John Batten, who by this time had not spoken to Jean for nearly two years, entered tactfully and helpfully into the spirit of it all, as he was to do again and again, by declaring generously: 'It is rather an ordeal for all of us but Jean's a great kid and we all have every confidence in her.'

Jean's departure was a low-key affair. 'Only a few London friends were present when she took off from Lympne under ideal weather conditions at 6.25 yesterday morning,' reported the *Daily Mirror*. 'Hatless and wearing a brown tweed skirt and jumper she was accompanied by her mother and Mr Victor Dorée, a fellow member of the London Aeroplane Club. She carried her kit in a brown paper shopping bag and this was hastily put away into the machine.

'While waiting Miss Batten changed into a brown fur-lined flying suit and, combing her hair and powdering her face, she afterwards chatted with her mother and a reporter. "I am very lucky," she said. "I have a slight tail wind over to Marseilles and it is quite good to Rome."

'Suddenly she realised she had no cigarettes and hastily a whip-round was made and fifty collected. "This will be useful if I am captured by Arabs," she said [almost prophetically as it turned out]. "Somebody asked me if I was taking a gun. Isn't it perfectly ridiculous."

'She bade us goodbye, climbed into the plane and, after her mother had affectionately stroked her head, she started climbing into a north-easterly wind. The plane rose gracefully and circled the aerodrome. Once round, she waved farewell, and set out across the Channel.'

The flight began well. Unlike Amy Johnson, who had flown to the Middle East by way of Vienna and Constantinople (now Istanbul), Jean took a southern route across Europe and, with the help of her long-range tanks, made a spectacularly long hop of just under 1,000 miles nonstop to Rome. She flew at a sedate 80 miles an hour, not a lot faster than a car on a modern English motorway, and to avoid the Alps went across the south of France and the Mediterranean. She had intended refuelling at Marseilles but when she got there, six hours out from Lympne, the weather was so good and her fuel lasting so well she decided to press on to Rome. This was her first flight out of sight of land and, as she headed out across the Mediterranean, she felt for the first time the loneliness of it all and her own vulnerability setting off across the world in this 24-foot-long machine built of wood, metal tubing and fabric. 'Leaving the French coast I kept looking back time and time again until at last I could see land no more,' she wrote.

The Moth's auxiliary tanks had now come into their own. On the long flight across France she had regularly topped up her main tank above her head with long bursts on the hand-pump on the right-hand wall of the cockpit. By the time she had reached the Mediterranean she had burnt up only around three-quarters of her auxiliary petrol – in the painful pumping process that was to raise a huge blister on her right palm.

She crossed the Mediterranean in idyllic weather. 'The purr of my engine was very comforting and, to while away the time, I struggled with a leg of chicken and tried my skill at pouring a cup of coffee from the thermos flask without spilling it.' She found it impossible and finished up drinking straight out of the flask. After an hour and a half over the sea she sighted the snow-covered mountains of Corsica and 'cried Hurrah for joy', she wrote, for her navigation had been unerring – as was her landfall, right on course, on the Italian coast. She landed at the end of her ten-hour flight at Rome's Littorio airport 'to many congratulations from the Italians for being the first woman to fly nonstop solo from England'.

But to her annoyance, because it was Sunday, there was no petrol immediately available. So, as she still had enough left in her three tanks, and mindful of Amy's record, she took off again quickly and flew on down the coast to Naples. Here again, to her even greater irritation, there was no fuel. Nor, she was told, would there be any until 8.30 next morning, long after she needed it for a dawn start on her next leg to Athens. 'It was a rather disappointed little aviator who crept into bed that night,' she wrote pathetically in *Solo Flight*. But then, reflecting on her day's achievement, added: 'But England to Naples in a day is no mean feat for any man, let alone a girl without any previous long-distance experience.'

Reading the newspapers for the early months of 1933, one is soon aware that Jean was by no means alone in her venture. A small plague of long-distance solo flying activity was occurring around the world at that time. It seemed there was seldom a day without some lone aviator setting off to fly from one continent

to another. And rarely a day when the headlines weren't
expressing anxiety for the fate of one of them. Jean, in fact, was
only one of eight private pilots, simultaneously chasing records
that very day.

There was news from Karachi that a young German, Hans
Bertram, had abandoned an attempt on the Surabaya—Berlin
record, while a Spanish airman, Fernando Loring, had arrived
in Hong Kong on a record attempt from Madrid to Manila.

Much nearer home, and only twenty-four hours ahead of
Jean, was an Italian pilot, Captain Leonida Robbiano, making
his second attempt to fly to Australia. Described by the newspapers as 'a rich and handsome air ace', he had set off from
Lympne the previous morning in a Breda monoplane and by
evening had flown 1,200 miles to Bari on the Adriatic coast of
south Italy. Several newspapers invented a race between him
and Jean saying, 'she is defending Britain's air prestige against a
crack Italian airman in a record-breaking flight to Australia'.
But before the week was out Robbiano was dead, having
plunged into the Bay of Bengal.

Following Jean out of Lympne had come another tragic
figure, this one with the air of scandal around him. The much
publicised Birmingham-born Bill Lancaster, a former Royal
Flying Corps and RAF pilot, was setting off alone to South
Africa in the Avro Avian *Southern Cross Minor* in which
Kingsford Smith had earlier made one of his epic flights from
Australia to England. Lancaster had had a colourful and
anguished postwar career. In 1928 he had flown to Australia in
an Avian called *Red Rose*, making his companion – with whom
he was having a very public affair – the first woman passenger
to fly the route. She was Mrs Jessie Miller, a West Australian
known to her friends, for her rounded goodlooking features, as
'Chubby' Miller. Later, in a sensational trial in Miami,
Lancaster had been charged with the murder of another of
Chubby's lovers. But the dead man had in fact committed
suicide, framing Lancaster in the process by throwing the suspi-
cion on him. His acquittal was now being recalled in the headlines over the stories that linked his latest flight to Jean's – but
within forty-eight hours Lancaster also had disappeared. His
body, beside the remains of his biplane in the middle of the

Sahara, was not found for nearly thirty years – until 1962.

Three other long-distance flights were being made by women. A German pilot, Elly Beinhorn, who had been the second woman to fly solo from Europe to Australia, was now in Cairo on her way to Africa on an attempt from Berlin to Capetown. A French celebrity, Maryse Hiltze, already famous for her flights to the Far East, was in Hong Kong on her way, flying with a mechanic, from Paris to Tokyo. And a pioneer Australian aviator, Lores Bonney, had just set off from Brisbane to try to become the first woman to fly from Australia to England. She eventually made it in seventy-three days but not all the way by air. She had to ship her Gipsy Moth from Rangoon to Calcutta by sea after being forced down by a tropical storm on to a beach on an island off the coast of Siam (now Thailand) and wrecking her aeroplane.

Lores was a cousin by marriage of the Australian aviation hero Bert Hinkler who, in January 1933, flying a Puss Moth on a flight from England to Australia, had disappeared between London and Brindisi. Although Jean was not to know it, one of the men whose exploits she always claimed had inspired her to fly, had lain dead in the Appenine mountain snow for three months. It was several more weeks before Hinkler's body was discovered and buried on the orders of Mussolini with an elaborate state funeral in Florence.

The imaginary drama of Jean's race against Robbiano was precisely the sort of story the London popular newspapers loved. And with her spectacular first day's flight to Naples they splashed it prominently, with bold headlines and more pictures of Jean looking glamorous in her flying suit. GIRL'S GREAT FLIGHT – 10,000 MILES RACE WITH ITALIAN proclaimed the *News Chronicle*. TWO PLANES RACING TO AUSTRALIA – NEW ZEALAND WOMAN HOT ON ITALIAN'S TRAIL, declared another.

On her second day Jean flew from Naples to Athens from where, at 3 o'clock next morning, she took off by the headlights of a car for Aleppo in Syria. She had no instrument lighting or navigation lights and watched her dials with the beam of a torch. She held the torch and the throttle with her left hand and the stick with her right.

The Moth had no radio and during the long flight eastward

in the dark towards Turkey she was cold, lonely and constantly anxious about the state of her con-rods pounding away in front of her. It was physically exhausting flying a Gipsy Moth for it could not be trimmed to sit conveniently on a desired heading at a required flight level. It had to be flown manually every second of the way.

Nor was navigation easy. It demanded continuous concentration, especially in turbulence, to keep her magnetic compass needle from wandering sluggishly from one side of her required course to the other. Holding her heading with sustained precision to an accuracy of better than five degrees was not always easy – particularly, as with the passing hours, she grew more weary. However, she needed no reminding that the cumulative effect of such a seemingly small inaccuracy on a night flight, out of sight of any reassuring ground references, could build to a disastrous error of 25 miles off course over 300 miles.

She flew by dead reckoning, putting blind faith in the course she had set and the wind drift she had to assume from the far from reliable forecast supplied in Athens. For several hours, until dawn began to show her some landmarks, she didn't know with any certainty where over the Aegean Sea she was. But her navigation was superb. At daybreak, as she crossed the western coast of Turkey, she saw from her map that she had flown through the dark precisely on course.

Daylight, however, was to bring some terrifying moments. Over the Mediterranean coast, in the lee of the Taurus Mountains, she flew suddenly into such violent turbulence she thought her tiny plane was going to break up – and, unlike Amy Johnson, she was not carrying a parachute. In the space of a few moments the Moth was plucked by the downdraught flowing off the mountains in one swift movement from 5,000 feet almost into the sea. Yet her emotions were of ecstasy, she wrote. She was filled curiously with a rapturous sense of pleasure rather than fear: 'It was one of the nastiest, if not most thrilling, experiences of that flight.' Only by opening the throttle to full power and turning the plane out to sea was she able to escape the force of the downdraught and climb back to a safe height.

Two hours later, on the Turkish–Syrian border, the mountains there gave her some more bad moments. Trying to clear the cloud that hung over the 6,000-foot range she had to climb to 12,500 feet where she became numb with cold and light-headed with lack of oxygen. But above the cloud blanket she had no idea where she was and whether she had crossed the mountains and it was safe to descend to the plains on the other side. Eventually, when she judged it so, she took her courage in her hands and began her blind let-down with only the most rudimentary instruments to guide her.

All her cockpit contained, apart from her compass, was an airspeed indicator, an extremely coarsely calibrated altimeter (which responded to height changes almost imperceptibly), an engine revolution counter, oil pressure gauge, and a quaint device, a bubble in a spirit tube, to indicate when she was banking. Instrument flying through cloud was then a hazardous business with only the most basic indications – conflicting alarmingly with the body's senses – as to what the aircraft was actually doing. When she set out on this journey Jean had only a perilously superficial grasp of the technique, but this did not deter her from plunging into a huge cloud mass which could have reached all the way to the ground. The danger was further compounded by the now unreliable state of her altimeter which had been affected by atmospheric pressure changes during the eight hours she had been airborne. But it appears that she actually enjoyed the fear and the high tension it induced.

'Down, down, down I glided, my eyes glued to the instrument board until the altimeter read 1,000 feet and still no sight of the ground. Lower still to 700 feet – 500 feet, and then suddenly, to my relief, I saw green fields and half an hour later landed on the French military aerodrome at Aleppo, after a flight of nine hours from Athens.'

After lunch in the French Air Force officers' mess she took off again, anxious to cross the Syrian and Iraqi deserts and reach Baghdad, 500 miles further on, before dark. But she was now about to begin one of the most terrifying flight experiences of her life: a protracted ordeal in a series of blinding and violent sandstorms. She met the first 100 miles out of Aleppo.

'It was like a whirlwind; the whole desert seemed to rise like a
solid wall before me,' she wrote in *Solo Flight*. 'Flying entirely by
instruments, with the sand pricking my face and cutting my lips,
there was nothing for it but to fly on a compass course and land
as soon as possible. For one terrible hour I flew on, hardly
daring to draw breath.'

At last she broke out of the stinging brown wall of sand. But
within minutes she had flown into another. 'Suddenly the
machine was being tossed into what felt like an upward roll.
Then, with a shudder that made all the wires ripple, it pitched
into a spin.'

Flicking violently and giddily out of control the Moth spun
down towards the desert. She had only seconds in which to
recover – to unstall the aircraft with the stick and stop the
disorientating spin with hard rudder in the opposite direction. 'I
clung to the controls,' she wrote, 'and just succeeded in righting
it in time to pull out of the subsequent dive with only feet to
spare.'

Unnerved by the experience and trembling with shock at her
near disaster she decided, to avoid being destroyed in further
sandstorms, that she would prefer to risk the danger of a landing
on the rough desert. Miraculously she managed it on a stretch
of hard sand without damaging the aircraft.

Almost immediately another ferocious sandstorm hit her.
For an hour, with a coat over her head, she clung to the
wing, struggling to prevent the small aeroplane from being
blown over. When at last the storm passed, she calmly swung
the propeller, climbed back into the cockpit and took off again.
Back in the air her only concern, she wrote, was for the
delay on her record attempt. 'That hour on the ground was
valuable time lost,' she regretted. But she was not yet out of
trouble.

About ninety miles west of Baghdad, soon after crossing the
River Euphrates, she flew into yet another sandstorm. 'The sun
began to look like a great black sphere until at last I could see it
no more.' Presently, to her horror, she realised that the sun had
set and it was in fact night.

Flying out of the core of the storm into a fine dust haze she
was relieved to find herself in moonlight by which she could see

the texture of the desert. Another agonising decision now faced her: whether to press on to Baghdad in the hope that it would not be blotted out by sandstorms or to risk another desert landing. The latter alternative worried her for, instead of following the Euphrates to Baghdad, she had taken a short-cut across the desert where she knew no one would look for her if she wrecked the Moth putting it down.

At first she decided to fly on and chance the Baghdad weather. But a few moments later she changed her mind. In the moonlight she saw a camel track. She decided to risk landing on it. Switching off the engine to reduce the fire risk if the aircraft turned over, she glided down in the moonlight. It was another masterful performance. She flared out over the pockmarked sand, which looked alarmingly uneven in the moonlit shadows, as she drew the stick back and held her breath. She felt her tiny wheels bounce and roll through the sand. The Moth ran for a few yards, wobbling over the camel-churned ground, and bumped to a stop.

'For a few minutes,' Jean wrote, 'I remained sitting in the cockpit with my eyes closed, thanking the Almighty for my safety. Then I slowly crawled out of the machine, tired and bruised, my face chafed and lips bleeding from the sand that had been dashed onto me. My tongue was dry, my throat parched.'

She took out her screw pickets and wound them into the ground, attaching lines to secure the aeroplane. Then she covered the engine and cockpit and plugged all the exhaust pipes before sitting down on the seat cushions to eat. All she had brought for emergencies was a packet of chocolate biscuits and a tin of pineapple – but she had forgotten an opener. So she set off into the desert to look for a stone. Instead she found something else.

'I tripped over something soft and was very nearly precipitated into a large water hole. When I picked myself up a cold shiver ran up my spine. It was a dead camel in an advanced state of decomposition.' But then she gasped with fear. Something was moving beside the carcase.

For a few moments she stood in the darkness listening to her heart pounding in her ears. When at last she dared move a large creature crept away into the night. 'I learnt later that the desert was infested with land crabs and that I was extremely lucky not to have been attacked while asleep beside the plane.'

But now there was a fresh horror in the still of the desert night. 'I was just retracing my steps when I heard a cry that made my hair stand on end – an eerie, piercing howl repeated several times. Guessing it must be a jackal I fervently hoped it would stay where it was and ran very fast back to the plane.'

She had not stopped to find a rock and now smashed the pineapple tin open with her spanner. Then she spread the cockpit cushions on the ground beside the fuselage. 'Taking out a mirror and torch I was surprised to see how bruised and burnt my face looked. I had with me some very good face cream and, after dabbing some on, lay down and was soon asleep' – blissfully unaware of the frost that quickly formed on her flying suit.

The sun was high when she woke up. Looking at the desert around her, her heart nearly stood still. She was no longer alone. To her shock and surprise the aircraft was surrounded by eight robed and bearded Arabs. They sat motionless, regarding her with what seemed like sinister hostility. In the distance she could see some camels which she took to be their caravan.

She had heard stories of pilots who had force-landed in the Middle East deserts who had been tortured and mutilated by tribespeople. Men had been brutally castrated by Arab women and left to die with their testicles sewn into their mouths. As a precaution pilots often flew with what were called 'goolie chits' – reward notices in Arabic promising a large cash payment if the bearer was returned alive and unharmed. Jean carried no such chit. She found herself wondering what female mutilation might be in store.

Determined to bluff it out she scrambled to her feet and approached one of the Arabs whom, from his superior robes, she took to be the leader. 'Trembling at the knees I grasped him warmly by the hand, bidding him "Salaam" in a shaking voice. He must have seen that I was frightened for, after gazing at me in astonishment for a few moments, he called to his companions who clustered around him excitedly. I was now really very frightened.'

The Arabs began to inspect the aeroplane, walking round it, touching and probing and peering into the cockpit. 'They were obviously looking for the pilot,' Jean wrote, 'not being able to credit that a woman could have been in charge.'

Anxious to produce some form of 'goolie chit' she fished out her typewritten letter of authority to fly over Iraq. The leader stared at it uncomprehendingly. He couldn't read. So she ran to the cockpit and seized the tin of cigarettes she'd been given at Lympne. 'With shaking hand I took one myself and offered them. But they seemed reluctant and began arguing among themselves. So I lit one and, taking a few puffs, offered it to the sheik. A broad smile crossed his face as he took it. In an instant we were friends. They all now lit one and sat squatting around the machine again puffing away.'

Relieved, she now wanted to get off quickly in order to reach Bushire on the Gulf coast of Persia (now Iran) that day. But the engine was so cold it refused to start. She had no chocks and there were no stones to put in front of the wheels, which made the operation dangerous. For over half an hour she swung the propeller repeatedly without success until she was dripping with perspiration inside her fur-lined suit. She had intended changing out of it that morning, 'but in view of the company I had this was out of the question as there wasn't a tree for miles.'

The Arab leader now indicated his willingness to swing the propeller for her. Afraid that to refuse would offend him she let him try, after tying back the sleeves of his robes to keep them away from the propeller blade. But the man failed to understand the brisk technique required and his gentle pulling did not produce the smallest cough from the engine. Jean knew she would have to do it herself.

To distract the Arabs she offered them some of her biscuits and, their attention diverted, got the engine going with one vigorous swing. But again she was defeated. Before she could climb into the cockpit the tribesmen leapt to their feet and crowded around the Moth in amazement. Afraid that one of them would walk into the invisible spinning arc of the propeller she rushed to the switches and turned it off. It seemed that she would never get away from this place. However, with elaborate pantomime she demonstrated the danger, now convinced that these men had never seen an aeroplane at close quarters before. At last they got the message and withdrew a few yards. One of them now pointed into the distance. To her fresh anxiety she saw another camel caravan approaching. Desperate to get away before it brought new complications she restarted the engine, leapt into the cockpit and took off in a cloud of dust without even bothering to strap herself in.

An hour later she landed in Baghdad for a breakfast of bacon and eggs in the RAF officers' mess at Hinaidi air base. It was there that she learnt that the location where she had spent the night was notorious for its landcrab infestation and vast tracts of rolling soft sand; she had been lucky, the pilots said, to have survived her touchdown. But more to the point, had she tried to fly on to Baghdad in the dark she would not have been able to land. A violent sandstorm had been raging at the time. She would never have found the aerodrome and would probably have crashed, low on fuel, in the blinding clouds of dust.

Flying on over Mesopotamia to Basra she crossed the head of the Gulf in fading light, to land at Bushire almost in the dark. Here she caught up with her rival, the charming Captain Robbiano, who told her that he, too, had just run out of fuel and had had to force-land in the nearby desert. Someone had lent him a horse and he had ridden for two hours to get petrol. A few days later, flying between Calcutta and Rangoon, Robbiano was to crash into the sea in a tropical storm. Weeks afterwards some of the wreckage was washed up near Chittagong.

Anxious to make up lost time Jean set off again at 1 am for Jask, a lonely outpost 550 miles further down the coast at the northern entrance to the Strait of Hormuz. When dawn came she was relieved to see that she was precisely on course and entering the Strait. It was now blazingly hot. Changed into the white flying suit that was to become her most famous symbol, she put on a pith helmet, strapping it under her chin against the slipstream.

In a wall of heat she refuelled at Jask and took off to fly nonstop to Karachi. The flight was uneventful until, half an hour out of Karachi, she was once again caught in a vicious swirling sandstorm. 'I was horrified to see what looked like a wall of sand overtaking me. I put the nose down and tried to race it. Just when I thought I was outdistancing it, the sand swept upon me.'

It hit with such force that she found herself swept along the desert coast at what seemed like twice her normal cruising speed – 'dashing along like a scrap of paper in the wind'. In the brown mass of sand, being wafted up like smoke, she quickly lost sight of the ground. Descending to regain visual contact she found herself 'hurdling sand hillocks and missing obstacles by feet with visibility practically nil. Flying at this alarming rate was definitely not to my liking.' She decided yet again that she would have to force-land.

A patchwork of tiny postage-stamp looking cultivations appeared below her. She knew that they were her only chance – even if she wrecked the Moth in the attempt. Banking steeply to keep the village in sight she turned back into the wind that was racing her along. Over rows of obstructing irrigation banks she leapfrogged the Moth, heading – now scarcely moving against the wind – for a cultivation that looked marginally larger than the others. As her wheels skimmed the bank she closed the throttle and pancaked heavily into the middle of it.

'I gave three cheers as we touched terra firma. But I rejoiced too soon. Just as the plane finished her landing run the wheels sank deep into the only damp spot for yards around and the propeller tipped the mud.'

The mud was deeper and softer than it looked and the Moth tilted on to its nose. Switching off she leapt from the cockpit and scrambled underneath the fuselage. 'Standing in the mud up to my knees,' she wrote, 'I mustered all my strength to support the machine while I shouted to about two hundred natives who stood a little distant regarding me with interest.'

But the villagers, in their white turbans and long white robes, had never seen an aeroplane at close quarters. Reluctant to approach, they stood, amazed by the sight of the shouting white woman who had been delivered into their midst from out of the whirling sand like an emissary from the heavens.

CHAPTER 6

Interlude in Baluchistan (1933)

As Jean crouched in the grey Baluchistan mud, struggling to support half a ton of aeroplane on her back, the prospect of getting to Australia, let alone breaking Amy Johnson's record, seemed depressingly remote. For the second time in two days she was at the mercy of simple people whose friendliness she could not take for granted. But this time she was more desperate. Under the weight of the plane she had sunk up to her waist in the mud and her strength was fading rapidly. 'Calling upon Allah and shouting "baksheesh" I was at last rewarded by help from the Baluchi tribesmen. They surrounded the machine, and I shall never forget the relief I experienced when the weight was taken off my shoulders.'

The villagers plucked the Moth out of the mud and carried it bodily to dry ground. They were friendly people and although she could not communicate with them they treated her with reverence and touching respect. Her white flying suit and shoes, now caked with mud, her face running with rivulets of sweat, she looked a mess. But her only concern, now that the sandstorm had passed and the sun was blazing down again, was to take off for Karachi as quickly as possible. However, when she

walked round the aeroplane she was dismayed to see that the
wooden propeller had been fractured.

Most pilots would have given up at this stage and abandoned
hope of a record to Australia. But not Jean. Her immediate and
desperate concern was merely to get herself another propeller
and resume the flight. For some reason the spare propeller with
which she had left England was no longer on board – it may
have been damaged on one of her desert landings. But before
she could begin to address herself to the logistics of a replacement, she was compelled to undergo a Baluchi hospitality rite.
An elderly man in a bright red turban, who appeared to be the
village chief, arrived with a dishful of water and a white cloth.
He removed her shoes and gently washed her feet. 'It occurred
to me that these people had never seen a white girl before ...
but I soon realised they were most kindly and obviously
regarded me as a sort of goddess.'

'Now before me,' Jean wrote, 'was the difficult task of
explaining by gestures that the propeller was not as it should be
and that they must take me to white people in Karachi. A new
propeller could be either flown or motored out here, as we were
only thirty-five miles as the crow flies. So, walking up to the
propeller, I took the blade in my hand, whilst setting up a loud
wailing, punctuated by requests to Allah for aid. The Baluchis
clustered round in apparent concern. Pretending to speak
through a telephone, I said "Karachi" several times. They did
not seem to understand, but all shouted "Karachi".'

The villagers did understand. Across the language barrier
they tried to explain that there was a place called Bela from
where it was possible to communicate with Karachi. Jean
studied her map. Bela looked a long way off to the north-west
and in the opposite direction from Karachi. It didn't seem to
make sense. But she was, in fact, on the desert plains that lie to
the north and west of Karachi in what today is the Baluchistan
province of Pakistan. And although she was only thirty-five
miles from the city on the map there was no direct road. Indeed
there were very few roads at all in this remote and desolate
region and the only feasible route, she was to discover, was by a
rough, poorly defined and indirect 150-mile long desert track. It
went by way of Bela. Jean agreed to be taken there.

For the first stage, to the nearest Baluchi settlement, she was provided with a horse. After picketing the Moth down, covering up the engine and cockpit, and posting two villagers to guard it, she set off riding bareback. It was an unpleasant and scary ride. The first horse bucked and gave her a vicious bite on the leg. Its replacement went 'dashing along like the wind jumping over every obstacle we came to'. Arrived at a village she was given a meal of curried prawns and goat's milk and, now changed into her heavyweight suit, was transferred to a camel. The driver climbed up in front, sitting astride the animal's neck and, amid much shouting and waving, they set off across the desert into a sunset made crimson by the dust haze. Very soon it was dark. But presently the moon rose brilliantly, lighting up the desert with a silver glow which cast weird shadows beside the thorn and cactus bushes through which the camel picked its way.

They followed a track which was invisible in the dark and frequently lost their way. Exhausted by the events of the day she began to fall asleep, only to be constantly awakened to find herself sliding off the camel's back. After nine hours of jolting and stumbling, during which her legs were lacerated by thorn and cactus, they reached Bela at 3.30 in the morning. Here she was taken to a house where she was greeted by 'a man clad in long white robes who stood there holding a lamp and peering sleepily at us. The driver spoke briefly to him whereupon he looked at me and, to my utter astonishment, said in English: "Come inside, you must be tired"'.

She was now the guest of what she called 'the head man' of the Ruler of Baluchistan whose large white palace she had noticed on the outskirts of the town. The Ruler was away on a hunting trip but his functionary offered to send a telegram to Karachi. She demanded that a spare propeller be flown out but was told that there was nowhere suitable for a plane to land near the location of her Moth. Nor would many people in Karachi be able to find their way overland to Bela because the desert track was so poorly marked. There was, however, a lorry in Bela and a driver who knew the route. The only practical way of getting a propeller, if one existed, was to drive there and collect it.

'So it was,' wrote Jean, 'that the news of my arrival was

flashed to Karachi.' The message read: FORCED LANDED SAND-
STORM BALUCHISTAN DAMAGED PROPELLER PLEAVE HAVE NEW ONE READY
FOR ME ARRIVING ELEVEN O'CLOCK TODAY KARACHI BY MOTOR LORRY.
These were the days when the British ruled India and a white
skin was a guarantee of service and dutiful obedience. Jean was
not slow to capitalise on her privileged status, made special by
the unique circumstances of her arrival.

Now elegant in a pith helmet and back in her mysteriously
cleaned white suit, she would, with her great beauty and aura of
superiority, have commanded the unquestioning subservience
of the Baluchi people. She assumed with ease the role of their
flying goddess and rose to the occasion as if born to it. For she
viewed her flight to Australia in terms of Imperial significance,
deserving high priority in the lives of the people she encountered along the route.

Her latest transport, which arrived at dawn with a Baluchi
driver wearing a fez, was an ancient Chevrolet truck. At the
sight of it her spirits rose, but they were swiftly dashed when she
discovered there was only enough petrol in Bela to drive a
quarter of the way to Karachi. Jean quickly devised a solution.
Drive the lorry back to the aeroplane and take some of the
petrol from its tanks.

It was 4.30 am when they finally drove out of Bela to an eerie
chorus of howling dogs. However the sun had not long risen
above the horizon when, in a stretch of featureless desert
painted brilliant yellow in the early morning light, the lorry ran
out of fuel. They were still a long way from the aircraft. Everybody climbed out and a heated discussion developed in which
Jean was unable to take part. But presently she saw the Baluchis
pointing. Away in the distance, across the cactus and thorn-
bush landscape, she noticed a thin wisp of smoke. The driver
gave a brisk instruction to two of the passengers who bounded
off in the direction of what Jean hoped was a village. She settled
down again impatiently to wait.

Meanwhile, to her astonishment and delight, she was
reminded once more of her VIP status. 'A fire was lit and the
aroma of brewing tea was wafted across to me. As if by magic,
one of the Baluchis produced a small wicker table and chair for
me, while they all squatted cross-legged on the sand. They

seemed indeed to hold me in very high regard.'

Soon three camels arrived from the direction of the village, the petrol cans were roped onto their humps and Jean was helped aboard one of them. It was a shorter ride this time and within an hour and a half they had reached the Moth, now surrounded by a big crowd of people some of whom had come a great distance just to stare at it.

Fortified by breakfast of curried fish Jean, now sweating profusely, disconnected the petrol union at the carburettor and drained several canfuls of fuel out of the Moth's tanks. It took the camels three hours to get it back to the lorry. At last on the move again, she wrote, 'Fate was soon to deal me yet another blow. Looking ahead I could hardly believe my eyes. Directly in our path was a partially dried-up river, the banks of which must have been about seven feet high. Ali, the driver, pulled the lorry up with a jolt. I thought we had lost our way. But no. Picks and shovels appeared and the Baluchis set to work to excavate a ramp down to the bed of the river which flowed in a channel between the high banks. With stones and thorn bush they built a causeway through the water and then cut another ramp up the far bank.' It was the first of five such rivers to require the same expedient. In one of them the lorry got stuck in the mud. Desperate to speed up the operation Jean leapt off to help build a bridge. As she knelt, poking branches under the vehicle's threadbare tyres, she wrote, she urged the Baluchis with impatient shouts to get a move on.

Soon after crossing the last river she noticed the dust of a car approaching. Momentarily her spirits soared. 'I even dared hope it was someone from Karachi with a propeller for me. The car stopped alongside us and from it stepped a man in a white suit and a pith helmet. We shook hands and he told me he was the Wazir of Baluchistan and had motored from Karachi to meet me. I was soon sitting in comfort in his car. About an hour later we pulled up at a resthouse and there had a most excellent dinner for the Wazir had contrived somehow to bring with him an eight-course dinner on which we dined royally.'

The Wazir took Jean to Karachi airport where she met the commandant, Commander Watt. She was angry and disappointed that the propeller had not yet been delivered by the local de Havilland agent. However she was now making news. Her disappearance in Baluchistan for twenty-four hours had not gone unnoticed. Back in England the reports were being featured alongside news of Robbiano's disappearance between India and Burma and Lancaster's over the Sahara. The three stories on the same day served starkly to underline the dangers, in the early thirties, of long-distance flying in small aeroplanes.

After spending the night with Commander Watts and his wife – she fell asleep in her flying suit over dinner and didn't wake up for twelve hours – she was relieved to find her new propeller at last waiting for her at the airport next morning. How she paid for it she does not say. But she lost no time in persuading a local club pilot to fly her out with it to the disabled Moth. They took off with the propeller lashed to the side and after half an hour's flying north-west of Karachi arrived over the location of her forced landing. But, to her consternation, although they circled the area persistently, there was no sign of the little blue and silver plane. It was as if it had been spirited away in the night. Jean was flabbergasted. Despite an extensive search they could find no trace of it and, after circling the open desert for more than an hour, they returned to Karachi.

The local pilots were as perplexed as she was. One of the instructors offered to take her out again. This time they flew to Bela and worked their way southwards, combing the desert along the routes Jean had travelled on her long journeys by camel and lorry. They found the very cultivations in which she had force-landed. But of the Moth there was no trace. It was bewildering and inexplicable. Convinced that the plane must be out there somewhere, although now extremely anxious about its fate, she asked the truck driver to take her back into Baluchistan. They arrived within a few miles of the cultivation just as the sun was setting. Yet again they transferred to camels. But the six-foot long propeller proved too awkward to be accommodated on them. 'We must have presented a strange sight as we set off. Six camels each carrying two people, the boys running in front with torches and the tribesmen panting as they ran beside my camel, taking turns at carrying the propeller on their shoulders.'

Throughout this, her second night camel ride, Jean was

haunted by anxiety for the fate of the Moth. But when at last, around midnight, they reached the village the mystery was solved. 'The moon was shining brightly and by the light of the torches I was amazed to see that every part of my aeroplane – now surrounded by a great crowd of people all squatting cross-legged – had been covered with camel cloths and gunnies. Even the struts had cloths wrapped around them. I could hardly believe my eyes. I was told that a sandstorm had blown up and the kindly folk, in covering my machine to protect it, had thoroughly camouflaged it.'

Determined to get away at dawn she fitted the new propeller by torchlight, watched by Baluchis who sat on the ground smoking hubble-bubble pipes. 'The silence of the night was broken by the strange bubbling noises and the occasional howl of a jackal or hyena in the distance. One old man offered me his pipe. But I felt much more like sleeping than opium.'

By the time she had finished most of the villagers were drugged and out for the count. She was covering up the engine when she heard a shout and was surprised to see another camel train arriving out of the dark. It was the Wazir who had decided to follow her. She felt honoured that such a senior dignitary should regard her welfare so highly.

She slept on a primitive bed beside the aeroplane. 'Although it consisted only of four tree branches for posts and some hand-woven material stretched across two poles, I slept as if on swans-down.' At first light she was impatient to be off. Before leaving she discovered that the Wazir had brought a camera and persu-aded him to take a picture of her sitting on a camel alongside the plane. It is the only picture taken during her 1933 flight.

Her departure from the tiny cultivation was an emotional and dramatic event. The glamorous and demanding aviator had dominated Baluchi peasant life for miles around for over forty-eight hours. Nothing quite like it had ever happened before and people would speak of it for generations to come. Her last request was an instruction for the Moth to be pushed to the downwind side of the field. She then gave the headman who had bathed her feet some money 'to pay the camel driver and some to distribute among the Baluchis'. Then she said goodbye to the Wazir, waved to the villagers and fired up the engine, swinging the propeller herself.

The space available for take-off was perilously short and, although there was a light breeze to help her and the aircraft was now carrying little weight of fuel, she knew that it would be touch and go. The bank at the far side looked dangerously close but it was still early morning and the swamping heat of the day that would dampen her engine power had not yet arrived. She thrust the throttle wide open and held the stick hard forward to get her tail up quickly. The Moth seemed to crawl across the baked, dun-coloured ground, reluctant to accelerate. Painfully slowly the tail rose and she watched the needle of the airspeed indicator begin to creep up the dial. It was still climbing towards 40 miles an hour, and below flying speed, when the bank loomed up. With supreme confidence she did not flinch or hesitate as she eased the stick back briskly and simply vaulted the Moth over the bank, clearing it by a few feet before dropping her wheels back onto the next field. She then held the aircraft down until it had plenty of flying speed – the lifted off again and climbed away. It had been a highly risky act – a grim desperation to force the reluctant aircraft into the air at close to its stalling speed.

It was 8 o'clock in the morning of her eighth day out of England. When she had actually been flying she had been making phenomenally fast time along the route and her un-orthodox arrival in Baluchistan had brought her to what was then India in just five days. Amy Johnson had taken six days to Karachi and Bert Hinkler, whose 1928 flight was still regarded as a solo classic for the Australia journey, had taken eight. Now two days behind Amy's time Jean was anxious to reach Karachi quickly, refuel and press on across India. But this was to be the last hour of her flight. Thirty minutes after leaving the village she was within sight of Karachi and approaching Drigh Road aerodrome when disaster struck.

'There suddenly came from the engine a noise that seemed to freeze my blood. A sharp report like a clap of thunder, followed by the sound of tearing, rending, splintering metal,' she wrote in her memoirs. As dramatic proof of the fact that the engine's con-rods had not, after all, been modified and the suspect part numbers filed off, metal fatigue had developed in one of them with catastrophic consequences. The rod had snapped in half and smashed its way explosively through the crankcase. It was all over very quickly.

'I switched off the engine and looked round for somewhere to land. In less than two minutes I could have reached the aerodrome, or even glided to it had the Moth been flying higher. Unluckily I had neither power nor height, so the only alternative was a forced landing. The terrain over which I was flying was rough and sandy, so I decided to try and land on the road which ran like a dark ribbon from Karachi northwards across the featureless landscape.'

The narrow road ran through a series of large sand dunes. They had been less than 500 feet below her when the engine failed. Furthermore, there were a number of cars travelling along the road so she had to pick out a section that was temporarily free of traffic. 'I glided the Moth down towards a suitable stretch. But there was no wind to slow up the forward speed. It floated on and on until, at the last moment when about to touch down, I noticed to my horror that there were small stone marker blocks on each side.' As the road was about ten feet narrower than her 30-foot wingspan she knew that a crash was inevitable for the marker blocks were just slightly too high for her lower wings to clear.

'The aeroplane turned a complete somersault, coming to rest on its back in the sand beside the road. But for the fact that I was wearing a harness and had the presence of mind to cling to a strut on the floor of the cockpit as we turned over, my neck would have broken as surely and suddenly as the connecting rod. When I managed to undo the straps, lower myself onto my shoulders and crawl out from beneath the plane, I found it very difficult to hold back the tears.'

But she was alive and, astonishingly, apparently quite uninjured. Coolly and methodically, to reduce the risk of fire, she crawled back into the wreckage, switched the fuel cock off and retrieved her precious logbooks, her maps and her small bag of personal gear. As a car sped towards her she stood in the fierce sun beside what remained of Victor's Moth with tears on her cheeks, shocked, bruised and dejected.

'My disappointment was almost unbearable. The engine was finished and my venture had ended. In a split second all my hopes and dreams had been shattered. As I surveyed the desolate scene I noticed a tiny shadow moving across the fuselage. Looking up I saw a lone vulture circling hopefully. The sight of it made me suddenly furious. I wiped my eyes with the cuff of my flying suit and waved my arm at the scavenger bird, shaking my fist and shouting: "I know it's my unlucky day. I know, I know. But, by God, it's yours too!"

'I tried hard to smile when the car arrived and the driver offered to take me to the aerodrome. But it was very difficult while watching all my castles in the air falling about me; all my hopes for the future dashed to earth.'

CHAPTER 7

Down and Out in Stag Lane (1934)

'This was the first time in my life that I had experienced failure and tasted the bitter draught that fate had prepared for me,' wrote Jean reflecting on her Karachi disaster in her memoirs. In *Solo Flight* she said: 'I had staked everything on the venture and lost, and although now absolutely broke, I resolved to cheer up, try and be a good loser, and hope for the best. Even so, as I stepped into the car and drove to the aerodrome, it was not possible to still the dull ache of disappointment and sorrow deep down within me which was to continue, on and off, however much I smiled and laughed, throughout the greater part of the following year.'

The Moth was extensively damaged and two pictures taken immediately after the crash show that she was lucky to have survived. The aircraft is lying upside down beside the white road markers that somersaulted it. The lower wings, which hit the concrete blocks, are crumpled, buckled and bent up in the air. The propeller blade has been snapped off at both ends and the undercarriage torn away from the fuselage. The struts between the upper and lower wings have all collapsed with the result that

105

the top of the fuselage is almost touching the ground – which suggests that Jean's head, projecting out of the cockpit, must narrowly have missed being hit. In one of the pictures she is standing beside the wreckage in a white dress and pith helmet.

At Karachi aerodrome the commandant, Commander Watt, with whom she had stayed two nights before, again offered her the hospitality of his bungalow where 'in spite of my adversity I ate a hearty breakfast of bacon and eggs'. She then drove back to the Moth and watched some locally stationed RAF men load it on to a truck and deliver it to the aerodrome.

It wasn't long before the newspapers picked up the story which was soon being cabled back to London. But it made few headlines. The press was more interested in success than failure. 'The girl flyer is showing signs of physical strain, exhaustion and anxiety,' one Karachi correspondent wrote after interviewing Jean. She was indeed experiencing a sharp reaction to the trauma of the crash and later that day was visited in the commandant's home by an RAF medical officer, Dr Roach. After examining her he ordered immediate rest for three days in a darkened room for observation for signs of concussion. There were none, and she moved into a hotel to try and sort out her life.

Back in London *The Times* was delivering some trenchant criticisms of long-distance record flying. In a leader headed 'Hazards of the Air', prompted by Jean's Karachi accident, the disappearance of Robbiano and Lancaster and the continuing mystery surrounding the fate of Bert Hinkler whose body had yet to be found, it declared: 'It may be asked whether any good can come of further adventures of this kind. The routes traversed are those which have already been blazed by pioneers of the air, and the present flights can add nothing to human knowledge ... it is time to call a halt to these hazardous exploits.'

For the moment Jean's particular adventure had certainly come to a halt. As she sat on the balcony of her Karachi hotel, watching the kite hawks scavenging bread in the courtyard and an Indian laundry man industriously scrubbing her white flying suit on the stones, she contemplated the depressing reality of it all. She was in debt. She had written off an expensive aeroplane belonging to someone else. She didn't even have her boat fare home. And back in England she had no job or income to return to. She was too overwhelmed by misery to begin to think of another Australia attempt. For the moment it seemed quite beyond attainment. For several days she aimlessly walked the streets of Karachi, her mind numb with disappointment. Her entire life seemed to have come to a standstill and all ambition drained away.

Quite unexpectedly, her luck was to change. Back in the hotel one afternoon there was a message to phone the C.C. Wakefield and Company Castrol Oil representative in Karachi, Mr Chubb. She assumed he wanted to discuss the cancellation of the supplies she had arranged at points further down the route. But to her astonishment Mr Chubb had some amazingly good news. He told her that the company's founder and governing director, Lord Wakefield, reading of her plight, wanted to help her. He would pay for her, and the wreckage of the Moth, to be shipped back to London. In those few wonderful moments Jean allowed herself to think again of Australia. Four days after the crash she was enjoying a free sea voyage back to London.

The full understanding implicit in Lord Wakefield's apparently spontaneous generosity is not clear and in her memoirs, curiously, she ignores his gesture altogether. However, in *My Life*, written in 1938, she did acknowledge his help but, by then more conscious of her flawless public image, she turned her spectacular crash – which, in any case wasn't her fault – into the happier 'I made a forced landing', as if the aeroplane had survived. 'I was far too proud to ask anyone for help but it was at this stage that I first experienced the kindness and generosity of Lord Wakefield ... he had been interested in my progress during the flight to India, and with his customary generosity arranged for me to travel back to England.' One might have assumed that Wakefield's gesture was a preliminary to his company's sponsorship of a further Australia attempt. But research revealed that it wasn't. For back in England, early in May 1933, Jean was to face a period of near destitution – over five of the blackest months of her life during which she was often to sink into deep despair.

However that was all still ahead that spring day when she disembarked into Ellen's arms. At that moment she was supremely confident that she could soon acquire another aeroplane and fly off again – at somebody's expense. Her immediate hopes centred on Victor Dorée. But his financial position was about to change dramatically. Soon after Jean's return his father died. A large amount of money had to be found to pay death duties. The family estate in Edgware, and many of the contents of the large home had to be sold on a depressed market. Money was suddenly critically short and Victor was obliged to repay the large sum his mother had lent him to buy Jean the aeroplane. Since, for some reason, the Moth was not insured for the flight it represented a heavy loss; to cover it Victor was forced to sell his own aeroplane. He was about to put it on the market when Jean came to see him 'undeterred by my adventure and determined to try again'. Victor, who was patently still in love with her, was relieved and delighted to see her back unharmed – indeed, according to the memoirs, she claims he pressed her to marry him. He was acutely disappointed, therefore, when it became clear that her only interest in visiting him was to ask for another plane. When Victor explained why that sort of money wasn't available in the family any more Jean walked out of his life.

In her only published reference – in *My Life* – to that last meeting with Victor (during which she would have had some bitter things to say about what she viewed as his negligence over the con-rod modifications) she dismissed it in one brief sentence: 'On my arrival in London it was to find that the part-owner of the machine was not interested in another projected flight to Australia, so the aeroplane was sold [to the Brooklands Flying Club] and reconditioned.' But in her memoirs she elaborates: 'When I arrived back in London Victor wanted to get married and his family welcomed the idea. But I would not even consider it until I had attained my ambition, for I was determined to try again. When the family realised my inflexible determination to succeed in making a record solo flight to Australia, Victor's father transferred him to a branch of the family business in Leicester. Incidentally I was eventually able to repay Victor what he considered I owed him, and with the money he bought an aeroplane on which he qualified as a flying instructor and when the war started joined the Royal Air Force.' But it wasn't quite like that.

Grace Dorée, who read these unpublished words, insisted that Victor, shortly before his father's death, had not been transferred to get him away from Jean but entirely for family business management reasons. She also said that Jean had only partly repaid the money – she thought about half. And in an article he wrote many years later for the de Havilland Moth Club magazine (in some brief references to his financial vicissitudes in the 1930s) Victor confirmed this. Without naming Jean he referred to their ill-fated joint venture in terms which suggest that indeed the pressure to provide the money in the first place came from Jean. In 1933 'I suffered a severe financial setback as a result of being talked into a flying project by a friend far too easily. It had a disastrous result and not only did I lose all my available cash, but I was also obliged to sell my Gipsy Moth (G-AAAV) to pay off all the debts incurred.' Describing how only part of the money came back from Jean around five years later he said: 'My own personal finances having improved with the repayment of some of my earlier loss I purchased a Gipsy II Avro Avian IVM (G-ACKE) for £240.'

Victor was so hurt by the cavalier way Jean had treated him he refused to discuss it within the family for many years. He talked about it mainly to his brother Stanley, Grace Dorée's late husband, to whom he admitted, Grace told me, that 'there were sides to her character he did not admire. He said to Stanley afterwards, "Beware of women who don't get on with other women", because she didn't appear to have any friendships with other women.'

'The death of Victor's father meant that he just couldn't have helped her financially the second time,' Grace said. 'She really was very hurtful to him, yet he was such a gentleman that even at the end of his life when he was recalling all that unpleasantness he would never, despite the bitterness he must have felt, say anything derogatory about her. He had helped launch her on the path to fame but she never ever publicly gave a scrap of acknowledgment to him. All she did was wreck his aeroplane. It took him a long time to discover what she really was – a ruthless, selfish, very determined woman. But I suppose she wouldn't have been able to do the sort of things she did if she hadn't been made that way, would she?'

After several years travelling the world for the family business Victor joined the wartime RAF. When peace came he went back to the Dorées' linen company in Leicester where he started a flying club; later he moved to Beaulieu in Hampshire to launch a sailing school. He is remembered with great affection in the club sailing and flying worlds. A Scottish nurse, Isabel Stokes, now living in Auckland, was one of the few people outside the family with whom he ever discussed Jean. She met him in 1938 on a ship travelling from Sydney to London. 'He was a terrific person,' she told me, 'a real corker, full of fun, very good looking and very popular on board. I remember he played the piano beautifully and he was travelling on a sales trip with a suitcase full of ladies' underwear. He talked about Jean Batten and how she had crashed his plane and didn't want to know him after that when she discovered he couldn't help her any further. Although I met him five years after the event he was still very bitter about her.'

Meanwhile in the summer of 1933, life had become difficult and depressing for Jean and Ellen trying to survive in the depth of the Depression on Fred's slender £3-a-week maintenance payment. Even had he been inclined to, he couldn't spare any more, for his dental practice had even fewer fee-paying patients now. For five months Jean was not to fly once and her membership of the London Aeroplane Club lapsed because she couldn't afford the three guineas subscription. Nor was there a man in her life to pay it or to lend her his aeroplane – although this was to be only a temporary state of affairs. In their small room at 109 Stag Lane Jean and Ellen were now in extremely reduced circumstances and through the autumn and early winter of 1933 were frequently cold and hungry. 'I had not a penny in the world,' Jean wrote in Solo Flight, 'and had to depend on what my mother could give me out of her meagre allowance. I had not been able to scrape even ten shillings together to keep up my flying practice. There had even been times when we had to call a cup of tea dinner and, owing to lack of funds, being unable to buy coal, would go for a sharp walk and retire to bed

early to keep warm. Going to theatres or pictures was out of the
question. I had long ago pawned what few things of value I
possessed. Anyone who has been penniless in London during
winter learns to appreciate the small things of life.'

Despite her secretarial training Jean, unlike Amy Johnson,
who learnt to fly on her £5-a-week wages as a London secretary, appears never to have tried to find a job, however menial,
to help make ends meet. Although Britain was in recession
there were jobs she could have had, so the poverty was, to a
degree, self-imposed.

Furthermore, now that the Dorées were no longer part of
their lives, they had virtually no friends. And although John was
now living less than a mile and a half away at Mill Hill, neither
of them, because of the bitterness left by the quarrel eighteen
months earlier, made any attempt to keep in touch with him.
John had now married the writer Madeleine Murat,* and they
had a baby daughter Penny,† born in August 1933, who,
because of the family rift, was never to meet her aunt Jean. To
escape from the stresses of the film studios John had abandoned
his career as an actor and taken a job as a receptionist with a
plastic surgeon in Hampstead. In any case there was now little
film work to be had. Jean was never to go near him, and his
mother to do so only twice more in her lifetime. Ellen had
obviously taken Jean's side in the row, but she also disapproved,
for some reason, of Madeleine.

But Jean and Ellen at that time didn't seem to need anyone
else. They were emotionally sufficient unto themselves and the
companionship and love of one another was all they appear to
have sought – there is no record of any new men having
succumbed to Jean's charms during this period. Life in fact had
become deeply unsatisfying for her. Consumed with frustration
at the seemingly permanent loss of flying from her existence,
she was suffering very real pangs of flying withdrawal symptoms.

---

*Madeleine Murat, who also wrote under the names Martin Tree and Dorothy
Quentin, was to become a financially successful light romantic novelist,
publishing seventy-two books before her death in 1983.
†Today Mrs Penny Messer, she and her husband, Charles, live in Newton
Abbott in Devon.

Day after day through the summer and autumn of 1933 she bombarded with letters and phone calls the Fleet Street newspapers, the aircraft manufacturers, and every company she could discover that was remotely connected with aviation. She tried to see Lord Wakefield to thank him in person for rescuing her from India but the oil magnate remained inaccessible; curiously so, given his earlier concern for her welfare. The nearest she got was the office of Alonzo Limb, manager of Wakefield's Motor and Aviation Departments, who told her, she wrote, 'Lord Wakefield would need the Bank of England behind him to finance all the pilots and racing drivers who come to him.' Someone who knew Alonzo Limb well said: 'I can't help feeling that if Jean had thanked Lord Wakefield profusely for his initial help in Karachi, he would, through Limb, almost certainly have offered further financial support right away. But Wakefield *did* like to be thanked for what he had done.' There is no record of the precise terms in which Jean thanked her benefactor. However, later, when she was famous, she was always punctilious with her thank-you letters.

Sometimes, unable to keep away from the place, she would walk over to the aerodrome to watch with envy the constant stream of yellow Moths doing their circuits and landings. Even inside their tiny room at 109 Stag Lane there was the daily reminder of it all from the sharp crackle of the Gipsy engines cruising by, low and noisy, over the street. In the evenings she created for herself a fantasy world. 'I took out my maps for the England-Australia route, placed them in rows on the floor, then lay down on the carpet to browse over them. I never tired of studying them and, in imagination, flying over the fourteen countries and 10,500 miles that separated me from my goal.'

It was the old-boy network that finally rewarded her dogged persistence. One afternoon, up at the aerodrome, she bumped into Geoffrey de Havilland. The eminent and approachable aviation pioneer, who was clearly an admirer of her unusual boldness of purpose and flying prowess, offered to write her a letter of introduction to Lord Wakefield. Brimming with excitement she rushed to deliver it next day to the company's head office in Cheapside. But she got no further than the reception desk and was merely told that her letter would be acknowledged. Crestfallen she went home to Ellen. Several weeks went by without word from the company and she sank again into despair knowing that, in the middle of crippling recession, her chances as an unknown woman aviator of attracting sponsorship were in truth remote.

Just when she had nearly given up hope a letter from Wakefield's invited her to go in and explain her venture. Again she got no further than Alonzo Limb, whom she met 'with sinking heart'. He was far from encouraging. 'At the end of the interview he rose and I made an effort to smile and look the opposite to what I felt.' She sensed it was all over. But just as she was leaving, he said suddenly, according to Jean, 'Wait a minute, Miss Batten. I'll have another talk with Lord Wakefield tomorrow.'

Unknown to Jean a small file on her had been opened at Wakefield House. A note on it at this time says: 'We have had a call from a Miss Batten and have been greatly impressed by her as a young lady of strong determination as well as charm. Although she failed in her recent flight we should not be at all surprised if she did something outstanding in the aviation field.' But, unaware of the good impression she had made, Jean wrote: 'The suspense was awful. I was called to the office at Cheapside for three more interviews and had to submit a list of main items of expenditure for the flight.' But Wakefields were not in the same hurry as Jean. More weeks dragged by; and as winter came early with blizzards and heavy snow, the Battens shivered in their fireless room.

Finally the suspense of waiting became too much. She decided to try and force Wakefield's hand. Going now to the Shell company and convincing them that Wakefields were about to fund her flight, she asked if they would supply the fuel on credit. Duly impressed, Shell agreed. Triumphantly she hurried with their letter of confirmation back to Alonzo Limb. Again she was told they would think about it. The following week she was called to Wakefield House for the last time. According to her memoirs Alonzo Limb told her: 'In business, Jean, one develops a knack of assessing potential. Just in time I realised there was some inner quality about you that bore the unmistakable stamp of a winner.' And then came the good news. Although Lord Wakefield wasn't prepared to fund her fully, he would, said Mr Limb, give her £400 – 'only a fraction of what I thought would be needed'. But in that moment she knew she was on her way to Australia again. 'When I left Cheapside that day I really felt that I was walking on air, that I was the luckiest person in the world. In that moment the sky seemed blue, and all the birds were singing.'

Lord Wakefield had a shrewd intuition when it came to picking winners to publicise his oil. He took his time and did not choose them lightly. He had helped Alcock and Brown on their 1919 trans-Atlantic flight, Ross and Keith Smith the same year to Australia, Sir Alan Cobham on his 1920s airline survey flights to Australia and Africa. He'd helped Bert Hinkler, and Amy Johnson on her 1930 Australia flight. And he was well known for his support of Sir Malcolm Campbell who had then recently lifted the world land-speed record to 301 miles an hour. The correspondence between Wakefields and Jean probably still exists, but the company is today part of the Burmah-Castrol group and no one at its Swindon, Wiltshire, headquarters, was able to trace it in their vast archives. However Jean's involvement with the company was referred to in an unpublished history of Castrol Oil: 'Wakefield never sought publicity for his acts of charity. But when it came to his support for pioneer fliers or record-breaking drivers, the picture was very different! And, in 1934, a new girl star flashed across the sky. To the press of the world she was a gift from heaven. Amy Johnson, for all her brilliance as an aviator, was certainly no beauty. But Jean Batten from New Zealand was stunning.'

The reference to Amy's abilities as an aviator was perhaps generous, for her flying career was punctuated by rather more human error accidents than was Jean's. Amy frequently had difficulty with her landings. No one would have denied that Jean was the more beautiful. However, Amy more than compensated for this by the sheer natural warmth and openness of her engaging Yorkshire personality, which contrasted noticeably with the relative introvertedness of Jean's.

Emerging from Wakefield House with buoyant step, Jean hurried to the nearest bookstall to buy copies of all the aviation magazines she could find. 'That night after supper I opened *The*

Aeroplane and turned immediately to the "Aircraft for Sale" columns. My heart nearly missed a beat. "Listen to this," I said to mother. "For sale de Havilland Gipsy I Moth. Only £240."' Although suspiciously cheap for an aeroplane that was then selling new for around £700, to Jean it was irresistible.

She went to see it next day. The Moth was at Woodley aerodrome near Reading and she went out in a Green Line bus, trudging the last two miles along a country lane in melting snow. The aircraft was being sold by a company called Phillips and Powis Aircraft and in their hangar she found it. It was not quite what she had been expecting. 'In the semi-darkness I saw in a corner some wings propped up against the wall, the stripped fuselage of a Gipsy Moth with a four-cylinder engine in a wooden crate alongside. I don't know what I had expected for £240. But I felt sick with disappointment.

'Mr Powis must have sensed this because he said, "If you agree to buy it, we'll have it assembled, given a coat of paint in any colour you wish and we'll get a certificate of airworthiness for it."' The offer was tempting, but at that moment Jean, despite her burning impatience, wasn't convinced that she was looking at an aeroplane capable of making it to Australia. She wanted time to think. So, borrowing the Moth's aircraft and engine logbooks she took them home and spent the evening studying the colourful history of G-AARB.

She discovered that if she were to buy it she would become its fifth owner since it had been built in 1929. Its first had been a young RAF flight lieutenant, Richard Atcherley.* He had kept it in Amman in Jordan where he was serving but while still in the Middle East he had sold it to an Indian who wasn't a pilot but asked Atcherley to fly it to England for him. There it was later resold to a French woman pilot who had flown it all round France and North Africa before finally crashing it in Morocco. After a rebuild it had found its way to Wales where its fourth owners had used it for training and joy-riding – and then

---

*One of two celebrated RAF pilot brothers both of whom reached high rank, he was to become Air Marshal Sir Richard Atcherley and was well known in the late 1920s as a member of the seaplane racing British Schneider Trophy team.

crashed it again. 'I reasoned that it had been crashed, rebuilt, damaged and repaired so often that there must be very few of the original parts left.' She also reasoned that, if she turned it down at a price that was less than half that at which second-hand Moths changed hands in those days – and, moreover, its vulnerable con-rods had been reassuringly modified – she could forget about her Australian dream for ever. She bought it.

The November 1933 receipt from Phillips and Powis Aircraft, found among her collection of papers at the RAF Museum at Hendon, showed that in fact she paid £260 for G-AARB – £20 more than the advertised price. The receipt also shows that she bought a tankful of petrol, nineteen gallons, at one shilling and sixpence a gallon. In *Solo Flight* she described how, one afternoon in late November, she went to Woodley on the bus to collect it. 'As I swung along the country lane I drew great breaths of fresh crisp air into my lungs and felt that it was indeed good to be alive.' At the aerodrome she was overjoyed to find that the unlikely collection of dusty components had been assembled with skill and loving care into a thing of beauty. 'I felt a surge of pride and joy as I looked at it, standing outside the hangar, its silver fuselage gleaming in the weak sunshine. The registration letters, G-AARB, were painted green and the whole aeroplane looked very beautiful. My very own, I thought, at last.'

Elated to be in the air again she flew the Moth in a snowstorm from Woodley to Brooklands in Surrey where she had decided to hangar it. Why she moved from Stag Lane, where by now she was well known, to a new aerodrome where she knew no one, is not clear. But by the end of 1933 she and Ellen had also moved lodgings to a room in a house in West Byfleet to be near Brooklands. It was the home of an elderly woman 'who lived alone and seemed delighted to have two such happy people in her house. I once heard her say to mother, "Whatever do you two find so much to talk and laugh about?" to which my mother replied, "We started as soon as she was born and seem to have continued, with few interruptions, ever since."'

Jean was now walking on air. 'I don't think any feeling equals that which one experiences when actually owning something,' she wrote in *Solo Flight*. 'I used to take a great delight in asking mother to read the registration papers of my aircraft out aloud to me, and felt a great joy surge over me when she came to the part which said "Name of owner: Jean Batten."'

Brooklands was one of the cradles both of British aviation and motor racing. The aerodrome lay in the middle of the famous 2¾-mile closed-circuit banked track around which Maseratis and Bugattis then regularly roared in efforts to break the 140-miles-an-hour speed barrier. Some of the pioneers of British aviation, like A.V. Roe, Tom Sopwith and Claude Grahame-White, had flown there long before the First World War, and the factory of the Vickers Aircraft Company was soon to begin producing the celebrated Wellington bomber, created by the famous Brooklands designer Rex Pierson assisted by another designer whose name was to become a household word – Barnes Wallis. The aerodrome was also the home of the Brooklands Flying Club which vied with Heston – the head-quarters of the Brigade of Guards Flying Club – in the elegance and wealth of its members at a time when it was becoming increasingly fashionable to learn to fly. Brooklands, in some quarters, was regarded as the place to do it. Senior boys from Eton College came there to learn and busy stockbrokers would drive down from the City for lessons at lunchtime.*

One of them, who later bought his own aeroplane, was a man called Edward Fraser Walter. Early in 1934, while she was having her newly acquired Moth prepared for her next Australia attempt, he met Jean. Within a few weeks they were formally engaged to be married.

Despite the fact that she was engaged to him – and it later became public – Edward Walter was yet another of the signifi-cant men in Jean's life she refused ever to name, until she wrote her memoirs. Here she revealed him, by his first name only, thus: 'It was at Brooklands, while I was busy preparing for the flight, that I met Ted. He was quite a good pilot with his own Gipsy Moth, but only flew at weekends because he was a stock-broker and busy in the City during the week. He was rather

---

*An observer of 1930s flying club social status rankings said: 'Stag Lane was, in fact, considered to be a little "down-market" compared with both Heston and Brooklands – and, a little later, Hanworth.'

goodlooking with a nice singing voice and had been a Bengal Lancer and as our friendship developed I found that he had a decided flair for organisation. He got on very well with mother who liked him, possibly because of his military background and direct way of dealing with any problem. He did not, alas, have much sense of humour.'

Trying to trace someone who might have known Edward Walter proved a protracted business in which I had to allow for the possibility that, having been born in 1898, he might just still be alive. It took over twelve months, and more than fifty letters and scores of phone calls and newspaper appeals, to establish who he was and the fact that he had been dead for some years. For a long time all I could discover from the London Stock Exchange records was that he had ceased practising as a stockbroker in 1947. Thereafter there appeared to be no trace of him. Advertised appeals in the international aeronautical press eventually paid off. One of them brought from Winmalee, in New South Wales, Australia, a letter from Brian Whitton, who had been a stockbroker partner with Edward Walter at the firm of Nesbitt and Wilson in the early 1930s. He had also kept his own aeroplane at Brooklands and had been a not altogether happy observer of his colleague's developing friendship with the alluring young aviator from New Zealand.

'He took a shine to Jean who was a fairly attractive girl, squired her round for quite a while and gave her a considerable amount of help – for she was flat broke at the time,' Brian Whitton wrote. 'In due course they became engaged to marry. Jean was a pleasant enough girl, though she didn't seem to have much inside except a burning ambition to equal or exceed the aerial exploits of the then famous Amy Johnson. It was only later that my close friend was to discover just how ruthless she was in the pursuit of these personal ambitions.'

Later, at the Brooklands Museum, I was to be further rewarded with the discovery in the files of a photograph of Edward and Jean together – she in the cockpit of a Moth, he standing alongside. It was the only picture I ever found of her fiancé. In it he looks older than his thirty-three years and is prematurely balding which gives his genial and somewhat man-of-the-world bearing a slightly middled-aged appearance. The photograph had been given to the museum by Mrs Doreen Courtney, a retired musician from nearby Walton-on-Thames.

She told me that she used to fly with Edward in his Moth at Brooklands in the early thirties. She was a friend of the Walter family, who then lived in Bournemouth. Edward had been married and divorced and lived on his own in a flat in London. 'He was regarded by his family as something of a black sheep,' Mrs Courtney said.

Edward Walter was the great-great-grandson of John Walter I, the coal merchant who, in 1785, had founded the news sheet that had become *The Times* newspaper. Edward's ancestors (in the family tree held by the newspaper's archives) appear as generations of distinctly upper-class families whose seat was a vast Berkshire country mansion and whose sons went to significant public schools and often to Oxford, into the Army or the House of Commons. According to Edward's service records held by the Army Museum in London he spent five years immediately after the First World War in the Indian Army, serving not as Jean claimed, with the glamorous Bengal Lancers, but with a more humble foot regiment. Back in England in 1926 he had married and later divorced without children. Ellen would not have minded the fact that he was nine years older than Jean but she would have been uncomfortable about his divorce.

After I had completed the documentary programme on Jean's life I took it down to Sway in the New Forest to screen to Victor Dorée's family. Afterwards his widow, Mary, turned to me and said: 'The Edward Walter whom you showed in the film – did you know that his former secretary, Margaret Mackay, lives in the next village?' It seemed an astounding coincidence. Several days later I was able to talk to Mrs Mackay who had been Margaret Makepeace when she had worked for Edward at what was then Nesbitt and Wilson in Moorgate, in the City of London, over fifty years before.

She, too, described him as 'the black sheep – for his divorce wasn't very popular with the family whose views he always dismissed as unimportant. He was a peculiar sort of a man, definitely eccentric, but rather likeable. He was also a loner – something he and Jean would have had in common – and actually not terribly interested in women. I don't think his emotions were ever really engaged. He was much more interested in aeroplanes than in women — his bedroom was always littered with bits of Gipsy Moth. What's more he wasn't a very dedicated stockbroker. It didn't interest him and he never really took it seriously. It was just a job. Men like him with money did it in those days really only to show they had a job.'

Margaret Mackay, who was seventy-three when I spoke to her, had been secretary to both Edward and Brian Whitton. Walter used sometimes to take her out to dinner, and occasionally confided in her about his private life. He once described Ellen to her as ' "that old so-and-so — that real old bag, her mother". He didn't care much for the old lady whom I suspect would never have known how eccentric he was. Nor would she have been so keen on the prospect of her daughter's marriage to him if she'd actually known what a confirmed bachelor he really was.'

Through the winter and early spring of 1934, in the months of her shortlived relationship with Edward Walter, Jean spent many of her days at Brooklands proudly flying her new Moth on short trips around southern England, and in the hangar of Brooklands Aviation Ltd. ('I gave orders as to what I required done') supervising the installation of the long-range tanks which she had transferred from the wreckage of 'LG'. Of whether or not she paid Victor Dorée for them there is no record, but the front cockpit and luggage locker auxiliary tanks again increased her capacity to 61 gallons giving her around ten hours' endurance and a still-air range of 800 miles. For added safety she used some of Lord Wakefield's money to replace some engine parts, installing four new pistons and rings, two new cylinder heads, new valves and magnetos.

She also arranged to have installed some equipment about which she was to remain extremely reticent. It was a highly secret in-flight toilet. She was never to write about it, or reveal its existence, even in later life, to her closest women pilot friends. Indeed, whenever women journalists were bold enough to ask how she managed on long sectors, which in the Moth could take up to nine hours, she always responded with the elaborate deceit that she had prepared for her trips with a routine of strict bladder training. 'I cut down my fluid intake to camel-like levels,' she once said. 'But it made me so dehydrated over deserts. I had a silver lining to my kidneys.'

The truth was that these discomforts were nonexistent. Discreetly designed for her by Sir Geoffrey de Havilland himself, the Moth had been fitted with a discharge pipe attached to the base of her seat. Well concealed at the receiving end by the cushion on which she sat, it ended in a spring-loaded trapdoor set into the underside of the fuselage. An engineer who used to service her aircraft said: 'She had a special zipper fitted to her flying suits. With some contortions she could empty her bladder and bowels in flight. There was a small lever beside the seat which opened the trapdoor. The pipe was about seven inches in diameter and Geoffrey de Havilland had very cleverly put a kink in it to create a venturi suction effect which was really incredibly efficient when the plane was airborne. But it was a very, very taboo subject and she was extraordinarily coy and embarrassed about it. We engineers were under instructions not to discuss the contraption with anybody. It was somehow assumed in those days that women pilots didn't have those basic needs.'

Jean's route-planning for the flight was meticulous and highly professional, even by today's standards, but for the 1930s it had a rare quality of perfection. The route, which would take her through the airspace of thirteen other countries, was: Lympne - Marseilles - Rome - Brindisi - Athens - Cyprus - Damascus - Rutbah Wells (Iraq) - Baghdad - Basra - Bushire - Jask - Karachi - Jodhpur - Allahabad - Calcutta - Akyab - Rangoon - Victoria Point (Siam now Thailand) - Alor Star - Singapore - Batavia - Surubaya - Rambang - Kupang - Darwin. Twenty-five hops in all to Australia, a total distance of 10,800 miles – plus another 2,000 miles across Australia to Sydney. But the time to Darwin was all that mattered for the England-Australia women's solo record; four years later Amy Johnson's record of 19½ days still stood.

Painstakingly she set about compiling a series of journey notebooks into which she carefully typed masses of aviation route data. They contained all the information she needed 'for each proposed landing and everything connected with it. The mileage between each refuelling point, my approximate times of departure, times of sunrise and sunset in Greenwich and local times, so that I knew to the minute the amount of daylight I would have for each day's flight. The approximate number of gallons of fuel I expected to take on at the various points. A list of jobs to be done on the engine and aircraft every day so that, when leaving an aerodrome, I could consult the little book in my breast pocket to make sure that nothing had been overlooked. For the majority of the landing grounds ... I knew, before arriving, their position relative to the nearest town or village, dimensions, state of surface before and after rain, obstacles in the vicinity, whether there was a hangar, distance to the nearest hotel or resthouse, and the name and address of each oil and petrol agent.' She believed in leaving nothing to chance. 'To make doubly sure, in case the book was lost, I typed out all these particulars and glued them on to the back of my maps, together with diagrams of each aerodrome where available.'

Space in the tiny single cockpit for stowage was almost nonexistent and as the front cockpit and luggage locker were occupied by fuel tanks she had to plan on the basis of essentiality every item she intended to take. 'The cork sun helmet I carried in the cockpit together with the maps and logbooks – in leather pockets on each side – while the canvas covers for the propeller, cockpit and engine were packed alongside my seat, in front of which was a small tucker box for sandwiches and fruit.' Into the tiny headrest compartment behind her she stowed a large torch, first-aid kit, ropes and screw pickets for securing the Moth at night at aerodromes at which there were no hangars; spare inner tubes for the tyres, canvas and needles for repairs to the wing fabric, a small tin of dope to paint the patches, a toolkit, spare spark plugs, engine valves and springs. For rations and emergencies she intended to add a large thermos of water, tins of corned beef, meat and milk tablets, glucose powder, biscuits and barley sugar – 'and, to the amusement of many who saw them, a fishing line and set of hooks, a magnifying glass and a flint'.

For the small slice of space – it measured precisely 15x10x4 inches – unoccupied by the petrol tank in the rear locker she had a canvas bag made to these exact dimensions. 'I was able to pack quite a lot into it, including changes of underwear, toothbrush, soap, face cream, talcum powder, one silk frock and a white tropical flying suit. In my breast pocket I planned to carry a comb, a small bottle of eau de cologne, a powder compact and lipstick, so that I could arrive looking reasonably fresh and smart.'

With military thoroughness she practised many times until she was satisfied, loading her gear and fitting herself into the cramped cockpit. It was a tight fit which would virtually pinion her in one position unable to stretch for up to ten hours at a time. The compass (she had invested in a new one) 'was just forward of the control column so that once seated, with my feet on the rudder pedals, there was very little room to move my position but sufficient elbow space to work the hand-pump located under the instrument panel at which I would toil from time to time'.

Again she planned to take a spare propeller lashed to the centre-section struts and, when she went out to Stag Lane to say goodbye to Geoffrey de Havilland, he gave her a valuable farewell present. He went into the hangar and disconnected from his own Fox Moth a turn and bank indicator which he presented to her. It would enable her to fly with greater precision and safety through cloud than her Moth's primitive instrument panel would allow.

She went to the Royal Observatory and double-checked her list of sunrise and sunset times for the entire route. 'This list was very important for few of the aerodromes had night landing facilities so it was vital to arrive before dark, remembering that I would lose one hour of daylight for every 1,000 miles I travelled eastwards. My maps had to be revised, the magnetic variations on them verified, and the latest data obtained on the state of all the aerodromes. Finally I gave a copy of my schedule to the Air Ministry who obtained over-flying permissions from the authorities in all the thirteen countries along the route.'

It is clear from her memoirs that Edward Walter was far from enthusiastic about the flight. From his years in India he was deeply concerned for her survival in the event of a forced landing in the tropics. 'One day he arrived at the house with a mosquito net, water bottle, collapsible canvas bucket and jack-knife. On another occasion he offered me his Colt revolver and was very hurt when I burst out laughing. Nothing daunted, he presented me with a small axe and when I got the giggles he said sternly, "You wouldn't laugh if you came down in the Bay of Bengal. You'd be glad of it to hack away one of the wings for a float."' In the end she took the axe, but declined the revolver — disagreeing with Edward, and with the famous Charles Scott, who had by then flown the Timor Sea three times, and had told her he always did so with a loaded revolver in the cockpit because he preferred not to let the sharks get him.

The day before her departure in the spring of 1934, she records, Edward made one final attempt to persuade her to abandon the flight. 'He arrived with some more equipment he considered vital to my survival and when I laughed and said, "Really Ted, if I take all this stuff for an emergency why go at all," he replied, "That's the most sensible thing I have ever heard you say — why go at all? Please don't go Jean. Stay here in England with me."

'But I did go. And I took off from Brooklands without any of his Bengal Lancer equipment — but wearing his ring!'

Her second attempt to make it to Australia, however, was to end in an even more spectacular disaster than the first.

CHAPTER 8

Dicing with Death (1934)

Although she was now well known to Fleet Street as 'the New Zealand girl flier', public interest in Jean's exploits was still minimal and her departure from Brooklands and Lympne on 21 April 1934 made news in only two newspapers. The headlines now called her the 'Try Again Girl'. Ellen was there to see her go but it seems that Edward was not. In the prose of Victorian travellers, to which she was readily given, she wrote: 'Rising at 4 am in the morning, I breakfasted at the little inn at which I had stayed whilst awaiting a good weather report and drove to the aerodrome.' Clad in tweed skirt, polo-neck sweater and leather jacket underneath her heavy lined flying suit, she climbed bulkily into the cockpit, Ellen kissed her goodbye and she was off across France, this time flying into a headwind and deteriorating weather.

It was at Marseilles, where she landed in heavy rain to refuel in the early afternoon, that things began to go wrong. The grass aerodome was sodden and so badly flooded that much of it had been marked off with red flags. In the airport weather office she learnt that an intense depression with heavy rain and strong headwinds was centred over the Mediterranean near Corsica, right on her track to Rome. She was told firmly that the weather was so bad there could be no question of her continuing her flight that day. But Jean was not to be dissuaded. '"Il fait mauvais temps," they kept saying to me. But, thinking I knew more about weather conditions than the experts, and disregarding their advice, I made preparations to start.'

She now made the fatal decision not to top up all her fuel tanks. Doubting the Moth's ability to lift off the water-soaked field with a full petrol load she took only enough for seven rather than her full ten hours' endurance. She estimated that it would be sufficient, even allowing for the forecast headwinds, to get her the 400 miles to Rome with a small reserve. In her calculations she assumed the headwind would slow her down by about 10 miles to 70 miles an hour and that the flight would take no more than five and a half hours, with an hour and a half of fuel in reserve. It was to prove a ghastly error of judgement.

With the French officials loudly protesting, she strode out on to the tarmac into the torrentially driving rain and climbed into the soaking wet cockpit. But to her considerable annoyance, the airport staff had been instructed not to help her. 'On giving the order "Contact", no one came forward to swing the propeller so, thinking to facilitate matters, I alighted and swung the propeller myself.' But now an official hurried over and shouted to her in the cockpit that they were forbidding her to go unless she signed an indemnity agreeing to accept the consequences. Indignantly she switched off the engine, climbed out, and hurried back to the airport building to sign the document. 'Once again the well-intentioned French officers attempted to dissuade me, but my mind was made up. I thought if the weather became too bad it would be possible to turn back. Feeling cruel at causing these kind people so much concern, I climbed once again into my machine and set off.'

In terms of her ability to lift the heavily laden Moth off the wet grass her decision to lighten her load proved wise, for the aircraft was reluctant to unstick and climbed away only slowly, just clearing the surrounding trees. She climbed to 500 feet and looked around her. Almost immediately, as she turned to fly back over the aerodrome on her course for Rome, she knew she had been foolish. A large blanket of low cloud, now down to ground level, was beginning to engulf the airport buildings and she was suddenly gripped by anxiety and awful doubt. But she would not accept defeat and pressed on into steadily deteriorating conditions. Before long the landscape of southern France had almost disappeared under a grey pall of low-hanging stratus and she passed over Toulon without seeing the city. An hour into the flight and she decided, at last, to give up and turn back. 'But on looking round I saw to my horror that the fog had become thicker, closing in around my machine and making it extremely difficult for me to distinguish even the coastline. There was nothing for it but to fly on towards Rome and hope for the best.'

In her memoirs she referred to the decision and with hindsight rationalised it thus: 'I had to decide between a long hard flight to Rome, or wait until the weather improved and possibly being stranded on a waterlogged aerodrome. It was therefore not entirely my natural impetuosity that urged me to fly on ...' She headed out over the Mediterranean on a heading for Bastia in the far north of Corsica, flying low to maintain visual contact with the water, and was relieved presently to find herself flying into better visibility. But, as time dragged by and the coast of Corsica failed to appear, she knew that the headwind was much fiercer even than the strong one she'd been warned about. It was in fact blowing at something like 40 miles an hour, cutting her 80-miles-an-hour cruising speed in half. The brutal consequence was that her flight was going to take double the time she had estimated.

When at last the snow-covered Corsican mountains came in sight she saw that her route across the north of the island was blocked by cloud which hung low on the peaks. 'My heart sank. I was trapped and there remained only one alternative – to fly south right round the island and through the Strait of Bonifacio between Corsica and Sardinia.' So turning 90 degrees to the right she set off on a fuel-wasting dog-leg, nearly 130 miles southward, down the west coast of Corsica. It was now late afternoon and her prospect of reaching Italy before dark was slim. She thought briefly of retreating and taking advantage of the powerful tail-wind that would speed her back to Marseilles. But she knew that not only would it be dark when she arrived but that the airfield could still be under low cloud. Without radio there was no way of finding out or requesting a flare path.

Because it would now be late at night before she could reach Italy she tried to find somewhere to land in Corsica. But everywhere she looked the terrain was steep and mountainous. Whether she tried the capital, Ajaccio, she did not say in the various accounts she wrote of the ill-fated flight, but she would certainly have fared better there than she was to do many frightening hours later.

Rounding the southern tip of Corsica and turning east again she crept through the Bonifacio Strait, now fighting the wind head-on again. It took her a long time to clear the strait and the land on either side seemed to crawl past, for her progress over the sea from here on was to be barely 40 miles an hour, at which rate she knew it was going to take her another five hours to Rome – a flight for which she patently didn't have enough fuel. Furthermore the sun was already going down ahead of her.

What possessed her to keep going on this now potentially suicidal mission she never recorded but it is clear that her driving force, her deep inner compulsion to get to Australia at any price faster than the only other woman to have done it, was now overriding all considerations of her own preservation. The simple arithmetic of navigation, and the horrifying rate of consumption of her rapidly dwindling fuel must have told her it was now physically impossible to make it to Rome and that she was committed to the horrible prospect of ditching in the sea in the dark. Most pilots would have used their precious remaining fuel and daylight to search the coasts of Corsica or Sardinia for a small field in which to end the mounting anguish. But this wasn't Jean's style. She was back on the same emotional high that had brought her moments of almost sensual pleasure in the life-threatening moments of her Karachi flight. Her considerable intelligence was no longer in charge as she cruised on towards the inevitable.

She was still flying through torrential rain and presently a lowering cloud base began to force her nearer and nearer to the sea. As it got dark she took her torch out of the head-rest compartment and propped it up with maps on the cockpit floor to light up to her instruments. But she knew the batteries would go before her fuel ran out.

On the 200-mile sea crossing to Italy the Moth was soon swallowed up in the rain and darkness on its snail's-pace journey, buffeting east through the hanging tendrils of unfriendly nimbus cloud. In her memoirs she wrote that, although she was to fly this route five times in all, she never before, or later, encountered weather as terrible as this. In retrospect, in her memoirs, she identified with the famous French writer-pilot, Antoine de Saint-Exupéry, who in a P-38 Lightning fighter, disappeared on a 1941 flight from Corsica – 'and the world lost a writer without equal in ability to record a pilot's thoughts and emotions so accurately and with such lyricism'. And possibly in an attempt to emulate him she wrote in the next paragraph of her memoirs: 'The trusty little engine kept beating with unfailing regularity hour after hour, and the four spurts of flame from the exhaust pipes were my only company cheerily piercing the inky blackness outside the cockpit as I flew on.'

Long before she reached the Italian coast her fuel was nearly exhausted. She had pumped up to her gravity feed tank all the petrol in her auxiliary tanks. Now shining the torch on the crude float gauge above her head, she was dismayed to see that she had only enough left for perhaps one and a half hours' flying. 'Peering into the darkness I searched for some sign of the coast, but there was not a light to be seen anywhere. One hour passed and just when I had almost given up hope of ever reaching Italy, in the distance I saw a solitary light. It seemed to be too good to be true and I gave a great shout for joy.'

It took a long time for the Moth to creep abeam of the light and when she got there she discovered to her distress that it was an isolated offshore lighthouse. 'Now with sinking spirits I realised that I was miles and miles out to sea and there was now only about enough petrol left for a quarter of an hour's flying.' But presently, to her enormous relief she saw in the far distance some pinpoints of light shimmering through the rain. However, she knew they were almost certainly beyond reach of her remaining fuel.

'I turned on both petrol cocks and pumped hard, holding the

nose of the aeroplane up till the machine was nearly stalled, so that any petrol left would fall back towards the pump. Great was my surprise and joy when the pump gripped once or twice and I knew that there must have been a little left – yet I had pumped both tanks dry hours previously.'

Now, suddenly, she was to give herself a bad fright. Wrapped around in darkness, her world a capsule of pitch with only the torchlit flicker of her dials for reference, she had no means of knowing where the night sky ended and the sea began. Her altimeter, after more than seven hours' flying through weather zones of big pressure fluctuations, had ceased to be a reliable indicator of her height. She had forgotten to allow for the fact that in the middle of the deep depression through which she was passing it was over-reading.

As the lighthouse receded astern, 'I turned my head to look once more at the friendly beam, and casually noticing many ripples on the surface of the sea wondered what was causing them. Then suddenly horror gripped me as I realised that the slipstream from my propeller was rippling the water and that I could not be more than a few feet above it.' She climbed away in the nick of time. But for the lighthouse beam she would probably have flown into the sea.

Back at around 500 feet in teeming rain the blurred lights of the Italian coast were now visible. 'The petrol should give out any minute now and I should have to glide into the water to an almost certain death. But then why, I thought, after fighting my way through the darkness for so many hours, should I give up hope now? No – I would fly on till the petrol gave out then try to keep afloat in the hope that I might be rescued by a fishing boat. Undoing the laces of my shoes and the chin-strap of my leather helmet, I loosened all the buttons of my flying suit ... so I could slip them off and swim ... Strangely enough I did not feel frightened, but a great calm seemed to descend upon me.'

Of the events that followed Jean left several versions. The most candid and revealing reflection of her true state of mind at the time is in *Solo Flight*. It expresses the innermost depths of the shame she felt at her personal failure as a pilot. Overcome with bitter self-reproach it was not concern for her own survival that seemed to exercise her so much as regrets for the people, especially Ellen, she believed she had let down. No punishment for her reckless stupidity, it seemed to her in these moments, could be severe enough. 'My thoughts were not of sorrow for myself but of remorse and regret that I had not justified the faith that a few people had in me,' she declared. 'I had made my bed and now must lie in it. With no thought for the faith my mother had placed in me, I had set off against the advice of weather experts and now must pay the penalty ... My mother, whom I valued more than life itself, had made great sacrifices that I might do this flight ... I had dashed her faith in my ability ... A watery grave was what I deserved. If only I could reach land, never again would my impetuosity overcome my better judgement.'

She began to pray, for she was now living on borrowed time. Yet, unbelievably, as the fuel gauge float had long ago subsided to zero, the Moth kept going. 'Maybe the Almighty had taken pity on me and answered my prayers. Surely there could not be much petrol left for I had taken off from Marseilles at 3 pm and it was now 10.30.'

In a desperate and skilful bid to wring more fuel from the tanks she began to bank the aircraft from side to side to coax the last millilitres into the gravity feed lines. But the main tank was so nearly dry the engine began to splutter every time she rolled. She abandoned the tactic; the consequences were too heart-stopping.

It took her an agonising half hour to crawl from the lighthouse to the coast. But having, against all odds, been spared the watery grave she had been resigned to, and now able miraculously to be confident of personal — if not her aircraft's — survival, she made yet another incomprehensible blunder which was to seal her fate. Thanks to her superb navigation she had arrived in high winds, rain and dark, making a brilliantly accurate landfall almost on course at the mouth of the River Tiber, only fifteen miles south-west of the centre of Rome. A few minutes later she was over Ostia, looking down at a seaplane base, brightly floodlit and with a large concrete launching ramp leading into the river. To avert disaster she now had to make an instant decision. 'Should I pancake the Moth

near the slipway and walk ashore as I could easily have done —
or should I continue.'

She was still 20 miles from Littorio airport which lay on the
far northern side of the city — at least fifteen minutes' flying
time away. The city lights, sparkling through the rain, were
beginning to dazzle her. It would have needed more than a
gallon of petrol which she certainly couldn't have believed she
had. But instead of the cold logic that normally characterised
her decisions, the desperado in her took over again. With less
than a cupful of fuel remaining, she spurned the salvation of the
flying base and made the irrational and potentially suicidal
decision to head across the centre of the city.

'A forced landing between the coast and Littorio would be
difficult and I was determined not to cause injury to anyone
else. And as the aeroplane was not even insured against third
party risks I did not want to damage any property. It seemed
unreal and quite impossible that the engine should continue to
function. Yet it did and I felt that I was watching a miracle take
place. Hope surged up in my heart as I decided to take a chance
and try to reach Littorio.' What she didn't know was that the
airport staff had long given her up for lost and had closed down
the airfield lighting for the night.

She was now playing Russian roulette, but with all the
chambers loaded. 'It was almost midnight, very dark and raining
heavily. Below me stretched the huge carpet of lights marking
the city of Rome, through which I could trace, by its very blackness, the curving River Tiber.' She was approaching the city
from the south-west and the Vatican lay more or less in her
path. But trying to follow the black curves of the river she
turned in over what today is the Magliana district and was
heading straight for the huge Basilica of St Paul's when her luck
finally ran out.

'Suddenly,' she wrote, 'the engine coughed once or twice,
then cut out. Although I had been waiting minute by minute for
well over an hour for this unmistakeable sound, when it
occurred I could hardly believe my ears.' But now, when she
could have been forgiven had she panicked, she kept her cool,
reacting clinically with her brain, not with her emotions. 'I
looked desperately about for somewhere to land as the Moth

Jean, aged four, shortly before the family left Rotorua for Auckland.
(*Batten Family Collection*)

Jean, aged eight, at her first school, Melmerley College, Auckland.
(*Batten Family Collection*)

Jean the ballet dancer: an Auckland studio picture taken when she was about fourteen. (*Batten Family Collection*)

The only picture that has survived of Jean with both Ellen and Fred – taken around 1921, shortly before the marriage foundered. (*Batten Family Collection*)

Jean, aged fifteen. (*Batten Family Collection*)

Jean in the cockpit of an unidentified light aircraft while learning to fly at Stag Lane in the summer of 1930. (*Wide World Photos*)

Victor Dorée, whose family's money helped launch Jean on the road to fame. (*Mary Dorée*)

Flying Officer Fred Truman, who gave Jean his entire Royal Air Force gratuity in the belief that she would marry him.
(*Reg Truman*)

John Batten during the making of the submarine disaster film *Men Like These* on the set at Elstree Studios in 1931 – around the time of his row with Jean.
(*Batten Family Collection*)

Jean and Edward Walter, the only man to whom she was ever formally engaged. The picture was taken at Brooklands in 1934.
(*Brooklands Museum of Aviation*)

In her second aeroplane, Gipsy Moth G-AARB, Jean sets off from Brooklands in April 1934 on her second disastrous Australia attempt. Lashed to the centre-section struts is a spare propeller. (*Wide World Photos*)

Police clear a path for Jean through the crowd that greeted her at Mascot on her arrival in Sydney on 30 May 1934. (*Batten Family Collection*)

Fame at last. Jean acknowledges the Sydney crowd's roar of approval: she has broken Amy Johnson's England-Australia record. (*Batten Family Collection*)

Beverley Shepherd, probably the only man Jean ever really wanted to marry
(*Ivy Graves*)

The only surviving picture of Jean and Beverley Shepherd (right) together -
taken at Mascot aerodrome shortly before her 1935 flight back to England.
Beverley's Puss Moth is in the background. (*New Zealand Herald*)

glided silently down in the darkness. I passed over a number of buildings and a main street. Just when I thought I would have to attempt a landing in the river, I saw a small patch with no lights – what looked like an open space. After flying for so long in total darkness the lights dazzled me and accentuated the blackness of this, the only spot on which I had any hope of landing.'

Suddenly, to her consternation, she realised too late that it was not all blackness. 'It was difficult to believe my eyes when, high above the Moth, I saw a red light. It disappeared – and then another flashed on a little distance away. Leaning over the side of the cockpit with my torch trying to see the ground, I glimpsed suddenly, to my horror, a wireless mast directly ahead. How I managed to turn quickly enough to avoid it I do not know, but I had no sooner swerved to the right when I saw another mast. Turning quickly to the left, I was able to guide the aeroplane between the two. But then, when about to land on the dark patch, I saw by the light of the torch, a row of trees ahead. I had just sufficient forward speed to vault them and drop the Moth in a stalled condition from a height of about ten feet. The aeroplane pitched on to its nose and I was thrown violently against the windscreen.'

She had crashed in the middle of the Italian Navy's San Paolo wireless station in the Ostiense district, less than 300 yards from the great cathedral of St Paul's. Although the Moth was seriously damaged, apart from some bruising and one bad cut on her chin, she had again escaped with her life.

CHAPTER 9

'Jeanius' (1934)

Afraid that the Moth would burst into flames, Jean grabbed her maps, torch and logbooks and leapt to the ground. The aircraft had tipped up on its nose and the tail was high in the air. When it was clear that it wouldn't burn she jumped up and pulled the tail down. Then, standing back, she tried to assess the damage. There, in the dark, she stared at the wreckage in which, for the second time in twelve months, all her hopes of getting to Australia had perished.

In dropping the Moth from ten feet she had crumpled the bottom wings, torn off the undercarriage, buckled the struts and snapped the propeller. The spare one, lashed to the struts, had broken away from its straps and was also broken. But the upper wings, the fuselage and tail section seemed to be intact. It was still raining and too dark to see where she was but she appeared to have dropped into some undulating, marshy wasteland covered in long grass.

'On looking up my blood nearly froze. High above me, that red light was still flashing. Looking around I saw four lights altogether, one at each corner of the field. I caught my breath.' The masts were, in fact, 650 feet high and not only had she

134

flown through the middle of them, in doing so she had missed, by only a few feet beneath her wheels, several cables slung beneath them. 'Some unseen hand must have helped me guide the machine in the darkness between two of these mighty masts.'

Shocked and exhausted – she had been in the cockpit for sixteen hours since leaving England that morning – she stumbled through the marsh, weighed down by her soaking wet flying suit, shouting for help. Near the road her calls were answered in Italian and three of the wireless station staff – one she noticed was a hunchback – ran to meet her. 'One of them lit a match whereupon they all gave an exclamation of horror and pity. Wondering what was wrong I put a hand up to my face and was surprised to find it covered in blood. Suddenly I found difficulty in speaking.' In fact her lower lip had been so badly cut it was hanging on to her chin. She was taken to a nearby first-aid station and there a doctor stitched it back and inserted a metal clip. Demanding a mirror to examine the damage, she was dismayed to see that one of her eyes was blackened and almost closed.

But her greater concern was for the Moth. She instructed the doctor to phone Littorio aerodrome to report her unscheduled arrival at the wireless station and, around 2.30 am, a senior Italian Air Force officer and an airport official arrived. They promised to have the aeroplane guarded until dawn and then taken to Littorio. Changing out of her sodden clothes she climbed into a bed at the first-aid post and slept until daylight.

In the morning she went to see where she had crashed. She was amazed to discover that she had dropped on to a tiny patch of rough ground next to a high embankment beside the Tiber. She measured the distance from the river to the trees she had vaulted. It was, she judged, just thirty feet. In the dark and rain with a fading torch and dead engine she had avoided the high risk of stalling and, by some miracle – and with a good deal of skill and courage – put the aircraft on to a minuscule patch of ground that would have taxed the experience of a helicopter pilot in daylight. 'Near the field was the Church of St Paul and people said St Paul had guided me to safety and that it was indeed an amazing landing, a veritable miracle.' In gratitude she went into the cathedral and knelt to offer up a prayer for her deliverance.

The Rome correspondents of the Fleet Street newspapers, which on the morning of Sunday 22 April had reported her missing over the Mediterranean, were quickly on to the story. By the time they tracked Jean down next day she was already making light of the affair, treating the horror of it all almost as routine. Her ability to fictionalise and filter out of recent painful experience anything she wanted to forget was masterful. Still traumatised by the accident, shocked, and in pain, she was telling the London *Evening Standard* brightly next morning: 'I made a nice landing in the dark with only my torch.'

She carefully covered up her appalling mismanagement of the flight and the obsession to continue that had overruled rationality. The newspapers did not seek the comment of the Marseilles controllers who had tried to stop the crazy stubborn girl pilot. Instead she was nonchalantly telling the British public that she simply ran out of fuel. 'It was about midnight and pitch dark. I saw a field below me, but it had a tree in the centre, two wireless masts on one side and high tension wires on the other. There was no other place to land and the only thing to do was to pancake the machine with as little damage as possible.' She told Reuter: 'A local pilot told me I only managed to land and am still alive because I kept my head. I shall continue my flight.'

In *My Life*, the carefully selective account of her flying years written four years later, Jean had still further rationalised the truth, reducing the terrifying events to the dimensions of a pleasurable adventure. 'I had one of the most thrilling experiences of my career,' was how she summed it up in a brief paragraph. 'Gliding the silent machine to the outskirts of the city I managed to bring it safely down with very little damage in a small field surrounded by wireless masts.' Privately, however, as she was to admit in *Solo Flight*, she knew full well she had blown it. 'Once again I had to admit defeat and realise that I had failed for the second time. Although most of my enthusiasm for the England-Australia flight had gone, it had, nonetheless, doubled my determination to try again and benefit from the experience gained on these two failures. The first flight had failed through no fault of my own. But this failure was entirely my own and never again would I allow my better judgement to be overruled by my enthusiasm.'

Despite the careful psychological damage-control to her reputation which she was propagating, the Moth was a mess and, now dumped in a hangar at Littorio airport, it looked a write-off. Far from plummeting down safely, it had suffered extensive damage. It was not just the undercarriage and lower wings that were crushed and twisted. The aircraft, essentially a wood-and-metal framework covered by nothing more substantial than fabric, had hit the ground with such force that much of its structure, including its fuselage, was out of alignment. In G-AARB's aircraft logbook, at the RAF Museum, there are three pages in Italian devoted to the major repair work done for her at Littorio. It shows that the entire aircraft had to be dismantled and virtually rebuilt. It could have been a costly job but, full of admiration for her courage and daring, the maintenance company offered to provide the labour free of charge provided she supplied the replacement parts. The most vital of these, the lower wings, she was upset to discover were an early type which would have to be made as a special order in England and shipped out. It would take at least three weeks.

This was quite unacceptable to Jean who was now the guest of a Mr Reason, secretary to the British Air Attaché in Rome. She had scheduled her April departure from England to get to Australia before the onset of the violent flying conditions brought by the south-west monsoon to India and Burma. She wasn't prepared to wait three weeks. Desperate to find a way round the problem she went to explore the hangars at Littorio. She couldn't believe her eyes when, in a dark corner, sheathed in dust, she saw something she instantly recognised. 'It was a Moth aeroplane similar to my own. It was covered with dust, the wires were rusty and it had no engine. However, as soon as I saw it my spirits rose and I decided to have the lower wings.'

She went to see the airport director who told her that the owner of the derelict Moth was an Italian airline pilot, Signor Savelli. When Savelli returned from a flight to Berlin later the same day she was on the tarmac waiting. He agreed she could borrow the wings for one month on the understanding that she paid two-thirds of the cost of reconditioning them, and the cost of their shipment from England back to Rome. For Jean had now decided that for her record attempt she must go back to England and start again.

Meanwhile she had solved the problem of a replacement propeller by cabling Edward Walter and asking him to remove the one on his own aeroplane and air freight it urgently to Rome. Obligingly he did so and it was at Littorio within three days. Soon she was to cannibalise his Moth still further.

Ten days after her crash, with Savelli's lower wings attached to her rebuilt aeroplane, she flew back to London. A photograph of her at Littorio before departure shows her shielding with a handkerchief the wound on her chin from which the clip had just been removed. A more candid picture shows the plaster below her lip.

Back at Brooklands on 6 May, two weeks after she'd left, she was met by Ellen and Edward Walter. 'Ted was overjoyed at my return and tried very hard to dissuade me from setting off again. Mother was her usual calm, wonderful self and said: "I won't try to influence you either way. You must decide for yourself – I will support you in whatever decision you make."'

According to Jean, Ellen approved of Edward. In her memoirs she quoted her mother as saying on her return from Rome: 'I think you will be very happy with Ted. He has been wonderful these last two weeks and really has your interests at heart.' Edward did, after all, represent breeding, position and money, all things she would have regarded as important for her daughter. Nor would she have seen in the easygoing Edward any major threat to her relationship with Jean. He was not a possessive man and she probably perceived that there would always be emotional and house room for her. If, indeed, Jean ever had any serious intention of marrying him, for all the evidence suggests that the depth of her feeling for him was slight. Or, for that matter, Ellen of allowing it to happen – for there is little doubt that, behind the scenes, notwithstanding her gentle and benign appearance in public, she still jealously dominated and controlled her daughter.

Anxious to be off to Australia again, Jean refused to listen to her fiancé's entreaties to abandon the venture and marry him forthwith. '"Please don't go Jean," Ted had pleaded. "You've no idea what I've been through," to which I replied, "I'm sorry Ted but I must go otherwise I'll regret it all my life. I can sell the Moth in Australia and come straight back to you."'

But Edward had not yet exhausted his usefulness and, in a frank admission of emotional blackmail, she now claims to have said to him: 'Ted, if you love me, lend me the lower wings from your Moth.' Reluctantly, it appears, he agreed and within a few hours his own Moth had been further stripped of vital parts and the wings bolted on to Jean's aeroplane to enable her to return the set she'd borrowed in Rome. In her memoirs she said candidly of her use of yet another man: 'I had served my apprenticeship and was now a cool, ruthless, potential record-breaker.'

She took Edward's wings because the pair she had ordered by cable from Rome were still not going to be ready soon enough for her. In My Life she gave no thanks to her fiancé but earlier, in Solo Flight, she acknowledged his help anonymously: 'Once again I was obliged to borrow wings, this time from a member of the Brooklands Aero Club. I thought it very kind of him to lend me the two lower wings ... but within a few weeks was able to send the money for new wings for his machine.' In truth it was not to happen quite like that and the money was eventually to come, not spontaneously, but amid much unpleasantness.

In the frantic forty-eight hours between Jean's return to Brooklands and her departure on her third Australia attempt, she succeeded in galvanising a lot of people on her behalf. One of the aircraft engineers then at Brooklands Aviation was Ron Paine, now retired and living in Byfleet, Surrey. 'We really burnt the midnight oil getting "RB" ready for her in time,' he said. 'We knew she was racing the monsoon and we were determined to help her beat it. We all knew that she and her mother didn't have a lot of money, but Brooklands was a very classy place in those days and they were mixing with people from whom they needed support, like Edward Walter. But all the engineers were certainly backing Jean and we didn't book anything like all our time on the job that night.'

Deliberately she made her departure on 8 May 1934 – only two days after her return from Rome – a low-key affair. 'No one was at all keen for me to set off again. But one London newspaper printed a headline that raised my morale and gladdened my heart when it proclaimed: THIRD TIME LUCKY'. Only Ellen and Edward went to Brooklands to see her go at 5.30 am.

She flew to Lympne to clear customs and tank up for her flight along the now familiar route across France to Italy. 'My heavily laden Moth climbed gallantly above the boundary of the aerodrome and over the misty Channel towards the coast of France,' she wrote of the start of this, her third attempt to find fame. She was now a familiar visitor to Marseilles where the controller, M. Fournier, who offered her a cup of coffee, now regarded this wilful and formidable woman pilot with some awe. She crossed the Mediterranean, this time in good weather, reaching Rome by nightfall. On her second day, with a re-fuelling stop at Brindisi, she flew the 740 miles from Rome to Athens and on the third made a long single hop to Cyprus, then a British colony. Her arrival at the small landing ground at Nicosia created a moment of drama.

To establish the wind direction, as the windsock was inopera-tive, she threw out one of the small glass smoke bombs she carried for en-route drift estimations for her navigation (the procedure was to circle and observe the chemical-generated smoke). It had a startling result. The bomb-conscious locals waiting to greet her panicked and 'rushed', she wrote, 'into a corner like frightened ants'. But on the ground the interest in her arrival, she discovered, had less to do with her pyrotechnics than with the telegram she had sent ahead from Athens warning of her arrival: ARRIVING G-AARB ONE O'CLOCK PILOT JEAN BATTEN. 'Someone had misread it and a rumour had been circulating that a lady pilot was arriving in Cyprus in her own aeroplane with Miss Greta Garbo as passenger.'

Her fourth day's plan was to fly to Baghdad, but after re-fuelling at Damascus and setting out across the desert she ran into more of the sandstorms she had come to dread. So she diverted to Rutbah Wells, a Beau Geste-looking airline staging post 250 miles west of Baghdad, where she spent the night. In this isolated outpost in the middle of the desert, run by an Imperial Airways manager and his wife, she enjoyed a four-course meal in the company of some KLM passengers heading for the Dutch East Indies in a slow, sturdy Fokker tri-motor.

Her evening was a reminder that the pioneering days of international air travel were virtually over by 1934. Many of the world's great airlines, or their predecessors, were by now well established and companies like Imperial Airways, KLM, Lufthansa, Sabena and Air France already had extensive global networks though not yet across the world's major oceans. It had been possible to fly, if slowly, certainly in safety and with a degree of comfort, from London to Singapore since the end of 1933 and regular services to India had begun four years before that. Their establishment owed a great deal more to the route-proving surveys of the RAF and to the work of serious development pilots like Sir Alan Cobham than to any of the long-distance stunt fliers, as they were known, whose main concern was record-breaking and publicity.

Battling along in highly vulnerable little aeroplanes with permanent navigation and engine anxieties was no longer necessary on a flight to the Orient. The scheduled passengers who came through Rutbah Wells in the mid-thirties were paying £95 for the six-day night-stopping flight from London to Karachi and cruised across the desert in the comfort of the big four-engined biplane airliners, the Handley Page 42s, which carried eighteen passengers. They travelled in cabins with silk curtains, chintz-covered armchairs, carpeted floors, while being served sumptuous and leisurely meals by stewards in starched white jackets.

Jean's fifth day took her through Baghdad to a night stop at Basra where she faced her first accommodation problem. The London-bound Imperial Airways airliner had arrived with more passengers than there were beds available at the resthouse. But believing she had more need of a night's sleep than the passengers, who had paid a lot of money for their tickets, she had no compunction in displacing one of them who 'very kindly gave up his room to me and sat up all night, so I was able to enjoy my usual good night's rest'. The next night, at Jask, in the Strait of Hormuz, she did the same thing. Because of the priority she believed her flight deserved she had no hesitation in displacing from their bedroom the young Dutch couple who ran the guesthouse and allowing them to join a row of Amsterdam-bound KLM passengers from Java sleeping on iron bedsteads

under mosquito nets on the verandah. 'They were all good
sports and we had a cheery time,' she commented blithely.

On her seventh day she flew again the fateful 600-mile route
from Jask to Karachi, flying along the grim Baluchistan coast
that had spelt disaster for her the year before. She passed the
tiny village which had befriended her and shortly afterwards was
on the approach to Karachi where this time she made an
uneventful landing.

It took her two days – her eighth and ninth – to fly the
1,400-mile breadth of India from Karachi to Calcutta. The
blistering heat melted the crêpe soles of her shoes and the
rubber frames of her goggles under her topee.

Halfway between Allahabad and Calcutta she experienced
her first major problem. She began to fly into what seemed like
a dense dust haze. But, much more seriously, it turned out to be
a spray of oil from a leak in the engine. The mechanic at Allahabad had failed to tighten an oil filter union. With sinking
heart she looked for somewhere to force-land. But the terrain
was hilly and wooded – there was nowhere. She had no option
but to fly on, hypnotised now by the oil pressure needle and
trying to calculate how long it would take for the lifeblood of
her oil to bleed away and the engine to seize. It didn't. She
landed at Calcutta's Dum Dum aerodrome in a jungle clearing
with just three quarts of oil left of the eight she had set out with.

Her acute concern now was the monsoon. Then known to
light aircraft pilots as 'the wall of death', the phenomenon of
the monsoon is today much better understood as the Inter-
Tropical Convergence Zone – the ITCZ. It girdles the earth in
a continuous, irregular skirt of violently active thunderstorms,
following the sun north and south on its annual migrations
through the tropics. Today airliners use radar to steer round the
destructive mushrooms of cloud which can tower to over 50,000
feet. But the flimsy biplanes of fifty years ago had to struggle
through at low level, risking disintegration from turbulence,
icing and deluging rain.

Leaving Calcutta on the tenth day Jean now faced the most
dangerous section of her journey. On the 4,000 miles from India
to Darwin not only was the weather potentially destructive but
the jungle terrain made a successful forced landing almost

impossible. After refuelling in Akyab and night-stopping in Rangoon she hit the ITCZ next morning.

Crossing the Gulf of Martaban to Moulmein she turned south heading for the tiny British outpost of Mawthaung, then known as Victoria Point, at the southern tip of Burma. Almost immediately she met the tropical front. 'I felt a little uneasy, and looking out of the cockpit saw ahead of the machine a great black mass. It looked more like a range of mountains – too wide to go round, too high to fly over and rolling northwards towards me like a great smokescreen obscuring everything in its path.'

Faced with this daunting black wall of potential annihilation she faltered. She was still sensitised to the power of the weather from her Mediterranean experience. It tempered her customary recklessness, if not with caution, at least with a rare moment's hesitation. Beset with doubt she veered away from the endless cloud wall exploding with giant forks of lightning. It looked incapable of penetration by something as frail as a Gipsy Moth. 'I was strongly tempted to turn back,' she wrote. 'But the thought of failing a third time was too terrible. I decided to keep on.

'In a few minutes I had plunged into the thick of it, and flown from day into night. It was so dark that, although the instrument board was only a few inches in front of my eyes, I was unable to read them and had once again to rely on my trusty little torch. Very soon I was drenched to the skin and the cockpit floor was completely flooded. The machine seemed to be weighed down by the weight of the rain which was falling in torrents. At first I tried hard to keep the coastline in sight, but soon lost it altogether and was forced to fly entirely by instruments. A few minutes later, catching a glimpse of the surf, I realised how dangerously low I was.

'Giving the engine full throttle, I climbed a little higher and was horrified to hear it splutter. How unwise I had been not to turn back. It was certainly the end this time ... The spluttering continued ... I found myself shouting, "Keep on going RB. Please, please don't let me down now!" But fortune was with me for, just then, I passed out of the deluge, having flown through it for forty-five terrible minutes that seemed more like forty-five hours.'

However it had been merely the start of a series of massive storm cells through which the Moth continued to twitch and shudder. Her flying suit was soaked through, the cockpit awash with water and the engine faltered and picked up in a series of heart-stopping convulsions.

An experienced professional pilot, Gordon Thompson, today a simulator superintendent with Air New Zealand in Auckland, flew many times through the ITCZ delivering small single-engined Fletcher agricultural aircraft to the Middle East in the 1970s. Reading Jean's description of it over fifty years later he was filled with admiration for her courage. 'Once you've taken a small aeroplane through the bottom of a Cb (cumulo-nimbus) in that part of the world believe me you *are* frightened,' he told me. 'If you're not you're a fool. It's even very frightening in big aeroplanes. There are quite monumental downdraughts plucking at you around the base of those things. They take you down from 2,000 feet smack into the sea in as little as fifteen seconds.'

Another pilot told me: 'It's like flying through a waterfall. You can't hear the engine. You can't see anything. The water flows over the wings like hosepipes. And through all this you've still got to navigate. Jean Batten must have had to screw herself up to face that. The nervous tension must have been very great.'

Jean didn't lose her cool and she continued to navigate, with her customary precision, in a curtain of rain that reduced visibility to less than fifty yards, finding her way to the tiny clearing in the jungle that was Victoria Point. In her cockpit notebook, which she used as a flight progress log, she wrote that evening: '1.00 pm landed Victoria Point – teeming rain – after frightful trip from Moulmein. No hope of going on today.'

Next day, her twelfth, she took off from the waterlogged landing ground, refuelled at Alor Star in Malaya, and made it to Singapore. She was now through the worst of the ITCZ. Although she didn't know it, her flight had begun to make world news, for she was now two full days ahead of Amy's time. From now on the media interest was to become intense and, back in London, newspapers were already trying to locate Ellen for interviews.

Her thirteenth day took her uneventfully from Singapore to Batavia, then the capital of the Dutch East Indies (today Jakarta and capital of Indonesia). Here, next morning her departure was delayed by thick ground fog. But the fuel agent cleared a tunnel through it for her by driving his car frantically up and down the landing ground. She took off through the swirling hole he had briefly bored and flew across Java to Surabaya. Quickly refuelling she crossed Bali to the island of Lombok where she spent an uncomfortable night plagued by insects at a place called Rambang. Next day she went in one hop to Kupang on the island of Timor, running the gauntlet en route of erupting Mt Ende (on Flores Island) which showered hot cinders into the cockpit. She found Kupang airfield more easily than Amy who, in 1930, had put down some miles away among anthills with the result that a runway had had to be specially built to get her off.

Jean's arrival in Kupang was to thrust the story of her flight on to the front pages: she was now four days ahead of Amy's time. In London the first interviews with Ellen were beginning to appear. She had moved from the Byfleet house back into London, this time to a flat in Swiss Cottage. Besieged by reporters telephoning and knocking at her door, and by photographers demanding pictures, she had never expected anything as persistent as this. But, although inwardly fearful of the reporters, she managed to handle the Fleet Street invasion with charm and skill, talking helpfully about her daughter, extending the mythology, and successfully disguising the truth in the most sensitive areas of family history. In every interview she perpetuated the story that Jean had funded her flying training, and her three Australia attempts, from the sale of her piano and from the proceeds of the probably nonexistent New Zealand property she claimed to have sold. (As Jean, in her memoirs, went out of her way to credit Ellen with every sacrifice she made for her, it is significant that she never mentioned this source.)

Since the three individuals would inevitably be swiftly traced and interviewed, it is not surprising that Ellen avoided any acknowledgement of the extensive help her daughter had received from Fred Truman, Victor Dorée and Edward Walter — despite the fact that she was formally engaged to the latter. But it is astonishing that she gave not a shred of credit to Jean's 'patron saint', as she often called him, Lord Wakefield, whose Castrol publicity machine, she must have realised, would not be slow to tell the world of the company's fundamental involvement in her daughter's flight. The clear inference from all the interviews was that Ellen and Jean had done it all on their own by simple prudence and doggedness.

'She sold her piano and put the money towards her flying training,' Ellen told the London *Evening Standard* yet again. 'I realised some of my property and we came to England.' Sitting in her flat holding a map with Jean's route and progress marked on it, Ellen admitted: 'Secretly I thought it rather a good idea. She is doing just what I would have liked to do myself. We have much in common. We are really more like sisters.'

The stories played on the fact that Jean's last hop was the perilous long crossing of the Timor Sea. Many ran league tables comparing her day-to-day progress with Amy's, four years before. TRY AGAIN GIRL IN SIGHT OF AIR RECORD said the *Daily Mirror's* front-page headline. But the most enterprising was the *Daily Express*. It cornered the market by scooping Ellen out of reach of its rivals and whisking her, proudly clutching Jean's music certificates and samples of her teenage drawings, into its Fleet Street office – presumably for a generous fee.

On the last and fifteenth day of the flight, 23 May 1934, it was night in London and Ellen, captive in the *Express* newsroom, spent it drinking tea, darning one of Jean's socks, and talking to reporters as news of the Moth's progress flowed in. Its exclusive front-page lead story next morning was headlined: JEAN: A SILENT DRAMA THIS MORNING – HER MOTHER WAITS FOR NEWS IN DAILY EXPRESS OFFICE. 'A girl's skill and endurance are again thrilling the world. Little 24-year-old Jean Batten's last hop is across 560 miles of a sea that is peopled with sharks. The world knows that. But the story of the family split, of the three years of financial struggle, three years of hard work and no dances, that alone made the flight possible, was told to me last night. I sat with lovely white-haired Mrs Batten.

'"Her father was against her flying," said the mother of the Try-Again girl [referring to 'the family split' which was not the tightly guarded secret of Ellen's and Fred's separation]. "So Jean and I came to England on my money – which is very little. But as her heart was set on flying we determined to manage on that. We have."' Then she went on to develop the now practised fiction still further. '"She got her B certificate. It enabled her to carry passengers for money and to buy her first aeroplane which crashed last year at Karachi."' There was no mention of Fred Truman's loan of which her daughter, now two years later, had still not repaid a penny. Nor of Victor Dorée.

Asked if she was worried about the Timor Sea crossing, 'Mrs Batten grew husky. Her words came in jerks. She was evidently feeling the strain of waiting, though she would not admit it. Of course she was worried, she finally said. "But she is bent on doing it. Who am I, her mother, to stand in the way of her destiny?" And then she paused and added: "I can only help her to fulfil it ... If anything happens to her I shall at least know that she went from me doing what she wanted most to do ... if only I could have been with her ... well she's over the sharks now. But she'll be singing. Yes, she'll be singing."'

Above the notorious Timor Sea Jean was not singing. She was in an agony of anxiety. It was by far the longest flight she had ever made out of sight of land. Five hundred miles over water without a lifejacket or an inflatable dinghy. She couldn't afford the latter, she wrote, and rather than be supported by a lifejacket 'while the sharks, which I had heard so much about, enjoyed themselves at my expense' she preferred to die quickly.

It was a cloudless, brilliant blue-sky day, but the forecast headwind was stronger than estimated. She had calculated her drift when crossing the coast of Timor, estimating it at five degrees. Further out she rechecked it by dropping a small bag of aluminium shavings which broke on impact with the water, reflecting an image against which she could crudely confirm the aircraft's sideways travel with the aid of black angle drift lines painted fanwise on the trailing edge of both wings. But, when she was well over the horizon, she had suddenly remembered, to her consternation, that she had forgotten to allow also for the deviation error in her compass caused by the presence of the mass of metal of her long-range tanks. 'Much as I disliked the idea of changing course when out of sight of land I altered it by 7 degrees to compensate for the error.' On the notepad strapped to her knee she carefully logged the change and the entry shows the new magnetic heading of 112 degrees. She flew at nearly 600 feet above the sea, the better to judge from the waves any changes in her drift.

She had estimated that she would make her Australian landfall in around six hours, but when six hours was up there was no sight of land. 'Six and a half hours, then seven hours passed and still no sign ... I had long since pumped all the petrol through to the top tank and now began looking uneasily at the gauge, fearing the headwind had increased in velocity – with the danger now of running out of petrol before reaching the coast.' Her anxiety was reflected in her log entries:

'12.00 pm Having lunch – must see land soon.

12.20 pm No land in sight yet.

12.30 Should have seen land by now. Wonder if petrol will last out!

'All the self-assurance with which I had left Kupang that morning went and for once I found myself losing faith. But this would never do. I tried to reassure myself that land would soon be in sight. Every minute seemed like an hour. Seven hours and a quarter from Kupang I was straining my eyes towards the horizon, searching for some sign. Then, a tiny dark cloud.

'Surely it could not be land. I removed my goggles to get a better view. Yes, it was land. Australia in sight at last. Hurrah! My eyes were not deceiving me. I felt like shouting aloud for sheer joy.' On her knee-pad log she wrote jubilantly in large flourishing letters:

'12.45 pm Hurrah land hurrah must be about 30 miles away.'

She crossed the coast twenty miles south of Darwin and fifteen minutes later, in bush-fire haze, was triumphantly circling the aerodrome. A small reception committee was waiting for her and a Fox Movietone news cameraman filmed her climbing from the cockpit as the locals gave her three boisterous cheers and waved their pith helmets in the air. It was 1.30 pm 'on that memorable day of 23 May 1934. I was deeply conscious of the joy of achievement when I realised that my time of 14 days 22 hours 30 minutes lowered by over four days the time established by Miss Amy Johnson.'

The first thing she did was to send a cable to Ellen. There are a number of versions of this historic message, widely quoted by the newspapers of the day. But the most popular read: DARLING WE'VE DONE IT. THE AEROPLANE, YOU, ME.

Ellen was back in her Swiss Cottage flat when the cable reached her on the morning of the same day. The news had also reached Fleet Street and she was now under even greater siege from reporters and photographers. '"Fancy that little girl all alone over the Timor Sea,' she said. 'I wonder if she will wish her mother was by her side.' And then, with a tremor in her voice, she added quietly: 'I feel the happiest woman in London. I could hug you, Jean."'

That afternoon the billboards on the pavements of London were proclaiming her triumph. Perhaps the *Star* best typified the euphoria with the single word: JEANIUS. Overnight Jean Batten's dreams had come true. She was a world celebrity.

CHAPTER 10

The Empire Salutes a Heroine (1934)

In England her record flight created an explosion of newspaper euphoria. It was 6.30 in the morning there and several national dailies rolled the presses again with special breakfast editions to scoop the afternoon papers. Across Britain it was the lead story. The front pages carried glamorous pictures of Jean in flying helmet and goggles, sensationalising her flight and introducing the virtually unknown New Zealand woman to millions. Within less than twenty-four hours she had leapt from obscurity to fame. She had broken the four-year-old record of an international folk-hero whose deeds were already immortalised in verse and song. Paeans of praise poured from the leader writers. 'Miss Jean Batten's flight to Australia will make one of the most famous pages in the history of flying,' said the *Daily Telegraph*. Under the headlines MISS JEAN! SPLENDID! the *Daily Express* said: 'Miss Batten got through by skilful piloting and astonishing persistence ... Fliers all over the world will salute her triumph.' The *Evening News* declared: 'It is a splendid thing for the British race that these fine girls should be showing the world the stuff they are made of,' and the *News Chronicle* added: 'She got to

Australia by sheer grit and determination and that is why the world congratulates her.'

These were the last glorious years of Empire and some of the comments overflowed with sentimental patriotism, British pride and male chauvinism. Likening Jean to the swift-footed princess of Greek mythology, the *Morning Post*, under the heading ATLANTA OF THE AIR, said: 'She has accomplished a feat which deserves to be acclaimed throughout the Empire ... There was more eventfulness and certainly more bloodshed in the story of the Argonauts or the Odyssey – but not more heroism.'

The headlines said: JEAN BATTEN SMASHES AMY'S RECORD: TRY-AGAIN AIR GIRL THERE: MISS BATTEN'S MOTHER KNEW SHE WOULD DO IT. 'A pretty girl in an oil-stained flying suit climbed from the cockpit of her airplane here this afternoon after one of the most gruelling solo flights ever undertaken by a woman,' cabled the *Daily Express* correspondent in Darwin. 'Yet Jean Batten arrived as self-possessed as if she had been on a practice flight.' The *Mirror*'s man on the spot wrote: 'As Miss Batten got out of her machine, worn and tired after her dangerous over-sea hop, her face lit up in a triumphant smile. "Where can I get a cup of tea?" she asked. And then the plucky girl added: "I'm glad I've broken Mrs Mollison's (Amy Johnson's) record, but I'm still more pleased to have made the trip, record or no record."'

Her memoirs, however reflect the true importance to her of the record. 'My flight was hailed as a remarkable achievement and established a new record for women pilots having lowered by four-and-half days the time taken by my brilliant contemporary Amy Johnson and flying exactly the same type of aeroplane, albeit a rather older one.'

But in London later that week the aeronautical press, although saluting her achievement, were to credit the improvement she made on Amy's time to factors other than determination. Said *Flight* magazine: 'That Miss Batten found it possible to clip so much time off the "record" of another determined woman is a testimony to the improvements that have been made in the ground facilities.' And *The Times*, in one of the few leaders not to respond with fulsome praise, was again to use one of Jean's flights to strike a sour note. 'Endurance feats like those of Mrs Mollison and Miss Jean Batten will soon cease to have any good excuse,' it observed coldly. 'Solitary flights by accomplished young women will fall into the category of Channel swimming and motorcar reliability trials.'

The Times could find no merit in Jean's women's record flight, achieved 'by the simple expedient of spending less time on the ground. There was no need to prove that engine and aeroplane would stand such treatment. Mr. C.W.A. Scott* and others had driven similar aeroplanes much harder along the same route ... The flight clearly was a test mainly of stamina in the pilot ...'

In Swiss Cottage Ellen was now reaping the whirlwind. The press invasion of the privacy she and Jean had so carefully guarded was ruthless. The phone rang almost unceasingly and reporters and photographers jostled at the front door, firing questions. She was overwhelmed. 'She gazed fearfully at the callers gathered on her steps,' wrote the *Daily Express* reporter. ' "You see," she whispered, "I can't really make whoopee till she has reached Sydney." ' Inside the flat, where some of the reporters had pushed their way uninvited, 'she stripped off the great brown coat in which she had spent the night without a wink of sleep, and bent down to gather a few belongings. A wad of banknotes fell from her blouse onto the floor. "My passage money," she said briefly, replacing the notes and tightening her blouse. "I shall take the first ship out to Sydney as soon as I hear Jean has arrived." '

The stories were quick to draw attention to the close relationship between mother and daughter. 'Jean,' wrote the *Evening News* reporter, 'has a doughty champion in her mother. Even since she first thought of flying they have worked side by side, the one striving, the other encouraging ... Mrs Batten has schooled herself to be brave — but the jerky words and the strange mistiness that comes to her eyes now and then betray a woman whose whole life is centred on her daughter's happiness.' Anxious to provide background material, Ellen told

*Charles Scott in April 1932 had flown a Gipsy Moth from England to Darwin in under nine days by flying excessively long days and taking very little sleep. He had pushed the open cockpit biplane to its supreme limits.

reporters how she had pinned the picture of Blériot over Jean's cot. 'Almost the first thing her baby eyes saw was that picture of his ramshackle machine.' All the papers carried the story.

With pride Ellen again produced Jean's sketchbooks and music diplomas. 'Whenever she felt put out she would go and play Chopin. It is Chopin really who has pulled her through.' 'What about you?' one reporter asked. 'Oh I only cooked her little pieces of steak for breakfast when she went on flights and saw that she drank a quart of milk, or took a half pint of cream. Simple things I could do. Except for her flights she has never left me.' But the strain quickly proved too much for Ellen. According to the *Express* 'iron-nerved, silver-haired Mrs Batten crumpled up. She went flying off to the country away from the glamour of her daughter's achievement. She went to hide on the very day she had looked forward to for six years.'

Of where she disappeared to there is no record. But since the Battens no longer had any real friends in England it is probable that she fled to a cheap boarding-house somewhere in the home counties. For several weeks henceforth the phone and doorbell in her London flat rang constantly to no answer. And although, despite his estrangement from Jean, he had obliged the newspapers with quotes on her ill-fated 1933 flight, John kept a low profile this time. His invisibility appears to have been total. So, too, was Edward Walter's. Ellen would have regarded the engagement as no business of the newspapers. However, at Brooklands, he was identified by one enterprising reporter as the donor of a lion bone lucky charm Jean was carrying. But he was described merely as 'a friend'.

On the other side of the world, Fred Batten was reluctantly assuming the role of proud father. In Auckland, where the newspapers were calling her 'New Zealand's Amy', he was tracked down in his dental surgery, now in Vulcan Lane off Queen Street. Unlike Ellen he had not received a triumphant cable from his daughter. He hadn't even known, he said, that she was setting out on the flight until he read about it in the newspapers. He was questioned mainly about his opposition to Jean's flying. 'After all she is the only daughter we have and one is inclined to guard one's treasures,' he said. 'I was only

concerned for her safety. But of course I'm proud of her.'
However, it was obvious that Jean and Ellen did not confide
much in Fred and had certainly never told him of his daughter's
indebtedness to so many men. 'Just how she financed the flight,
he still did not know,' said the Auckland *Star*. Nonetheless,
having possibly read Francis Chichester's claim that his 1929/30
flight to Australia in the same type of aeroplane had cost him
£3,000, Fred must have been wondering where all the money
had come from. Specially as he was quite soon to learn from the
Wakefield Company that his lordship had contributed only
£400.

None of the New Zealand newspapers bothered, it seems, to
seek a reaction from Jean's elder brother, Harold, who had by
now returned from Australia with a young wife, Alma. They
had bought a farm at Waipu Caves in Northland and rarely
made the long journey south to Auckland. But there is possibly
a reason why Harold was never identified with his sister's fame.
There were lifelong tensions between him and Ellen dating
from his childhood in Auckland when he was packed off to
Wellington College, 400 miles away. His son Jim said: 'He
couldn't get on with his mother – that's all we know. Presumably it was she who had him sent away.' But the rift was
apparently to grow worse. According to Jim, during Ellen's and
Jean's 1922 holiday in Australia, Harold, then working on a
farm there, reported back by letter to Fred criticising Ellen's
conduct. What upset him Jim didn't know – he thought it
might have been Ellen's predilection for gambling on horses –
but whatever tales he had told his father about his mother, and
it is conceivable that it may have related to Jean's exposure to
the VD film *Damaged Goods*, it had led to a further deterior-
ation in their marriage. And Ellen had never really forgiven
Harold.

If Jean had ever doubted on her arrival in Darwin that she
had accomplished something for the world to applaud and
celebrate, it was swiftly confirmed by a deluge of cables from
prominent people throughout an admiring British Empire. They
came from the Australian and New Zealand Governor Generals
and Prime Ministers, from Lord Wakefield and the British
Secretary of State for Air. There was also a warm one from Amy

Johnson (now briefly Mrs Mollison).* To London reporters Amy said: 'I knew she would do it. She is made of the stuff that no sort of ill luck could thwart her purpose.' And the woman whose fame in America matched that of Amy's in England, Amelia Earhart, who, in 1932, had become the first woman to fly the Atlantic solo† was quoted as saying: 'Miss Batten's flight is an encouragement to other women fliers.'

In *Solo Flight* Jean attributed her success, as she was to do in all her public speeches, principally to Ellen. 'She made sacrifices that I might achieve my ambition, urged me on to success when I had failed, and was always at hand to cheer and help me during those dark hours when it looked very unlikely that I should ever be able to obtain finance for another attempt.'

It is difficult nowadays to comprehend the huge media interest that flights like Jean's attracted over half a century ago. The England-Australia route had by then been flown successfully in one direction or the other more than thirty times. Although often still a dangerous and high-risk adventure it had long ceased to be remarkable. Indeed the roll of honour for the journey for the early years of the 1930s lists an astonishing number of relatively unknown pilots who pitched up in Darwin at the end of totally unpublicised flights in small aeroplanes. It was certainly no longer necessary to prove that solo aviators in frail aircraft could do it. Still less were the flights contributing any helpful knowledge to the Empire's rapidly expanding commercial airline operations. By December 1933 Imperial Airways was operating passenger services from England to Malaya and a joint Imperial Airways/Qantas through service from London to Brisbane was less than a year away. The same

---

*Since her 1930 flight to Australia which had created the legend, Amy – in addition to her 1931 London-Tokyo flight with Jack Humphreys – had flown solo from England to Capetown and back in 1932 (in a Puss Moth and in record time both ways). In 1933 with her husband, Jim, in a twin-engined de Havilland Dragon, she had flown the Atlantic from Wales to Connecticut, concluding the flight – with Jim at the controls – with a spectacular crash.
†She had flown from Newfoundland to Northern Ireland in a Lockheed Vega in 15 hours, narrowly escaping death en route when her plane iced up and spun for 3,000 feet almost into the sea.

year as Jean's flight the Dutch airline, KLM, making a giant leap in speed and comfort, introduced the DC2 (the relatively sophisticated forerunner of the Dakota) on regular passenger services between Amsterdam and Java.

Nor had Jean, despite the personal triumph of the women's solo record — and there was only one previous flight to beat — made a specially fast flight. Charles Scott had done it in an identical aeroplane five days quicker in 1932; a year later Kingsford Smith, in a much faster Percival Gull cabin monoplane, had cut the time to seven days and five hours; and only a few days later, in October 1933, an absolute record of six days seventeen hours had been set by Charles Ulm and two companions in *Faith in Australia*, an Avro Ten, a smaller variant of Smithy's Fokker 3M tri-motor, the *Southern Cross*.

It really had nothing to do with speed. Jean's flight — the third by a woman alone from Europe to Australia* — created massive media interest and public adulation greater than that to surround the Apollo moon astronauts thirty-five years later, simply by reason of her gender. In the 1930s, women who weren't rich and titled didn't often do this sort of thing.

Jean had something else the media demanded: she was beautiful. Added to her deadly determination as a pilot, it made her, as an aviation heroine to the masses, a natural successor to Amy Johnson, whose public image had become increasingly tarnished by the press's remorseless examination of her unhappy private life. Amy, with her disarmingly ingenuous public speeches, her appealingly humble origins, and the provincial charm of her Yorkshire accent, presented to the world the fresh-faced image of the girl-next-door; Jean was strikingly different. Her classic dark-haired features and the strong sense she conveyed of sophistication and sexual warmth, looked out from the front pages with all the glamour of a Hollywood star. She was ready-made for fame, and proceeded to exploit herself to the full, aided by the highly receptive climate of a world deep in

*The German pilot, Elly Beinhorn, was a half-hearted second. She arrived in Darwin in her Klemm monoplane in March 1932, after a leisurely 110-day sightseeing flight with many long stopovers.

economic recession. Someone who remembered well the public mood of the day in Britain was space writer and broadcaster Reginald Turnill, for twenty years until 1976 the BBC's air and defence correspondent. 'As a young Fleet Street reporter in the thirties,' he said, 'I was involved in reporting the pioneering flights. I think much of the coverage and glorification was because their activities reflected the unfulfillable escapist dreams of the rest of us in the dreariest decade of the century. In a country of three million *really* unemployed – with half the current population – we were underpaid, underclothed and underfed, and lived in daily fear of the sack, the growth of Fascism, and the coming war.'

Jean spent only one night in Darwin before pressing on across Australia to Sydney. Much of the 2,000-mile route across the featureless heart of the Outback was extremely difficult even for professional local pilots to navigate. The list of aviators who had found their way accurately from England to Darwin, then got hopelessly lost crossing the vast tracts of desert and scrublands between there and Sydney, was a distinguished one. It even included Francis Chichester, regarded as one of the world's great navigators, and the legendary Charles Kingsford Smith, who knew the Outback better than most pilots, and was once lost there for thirteen days with his crew.

Lord Wakefield was determined that no such fate would befall his latest protégée. As he had done for Amy four years earlier, he had already cabled his Australian manager in Sydney instructing him to send the company's aircraft to Darwin to escort Jean on what she estimated was another five or six days' flying to Sydney. The plane, a four-seat Hawk Moth, cruised more than thirty miles an hour faster than Jean's Gipsy Moth. Its pilot this time was not the supercilious Charles Scott who had sped ahead of Amy in 1930 reducing her to exhaustion and tears, but a kindlier man, an Australian, Ron Adair. He flew the Hawk up to Darwin with Wakefield's Queensland manager, Captain S.W. Bird, and a Fox-Movietone cameraman, to film her flight across the country.

Wakefield was anxious to capitalise on his investment and his plans to promote Jean had no room for diffidence. 'Tell her,' an instruction to Captain Bird urged, 'that from her point of view it would pay her to be in the public eye as it will help her name in the future, and be of much more value in the aviation world than if she kept quiet like a little mouse. You know the line of stuff to put over, Birdie, so go to it as hard as you can.' Jean appears to have responded well to these new commercial pressures. She stuck a prominent Castrol logo on the side of the fuselage and back in London her features were already beginning to endorse advertisements which had her saying: IF THERE WERE A BETTER OIL THAN WAKEFIELD CASTROL I SHOULD USE IT.

Her flight across Australia in formation with the Castrol plane attracted huge interest at the small corrugated-iron Outback settlements at which she stopped. Their interest excited by constant radio bulletins on her progress, people flocked to the landing grounds to see the new flying heroine. She would climb out of the cockpit into searing heat to be greeted by swarms of flies and warm handclasps with shouts of 'Good on yer Jean' from people weirdly masked with fly nets. At the night stops they watched in admiration as she immediately set about opening up the cowling and, with great competence, attending to the ritual of her engine maintenance. Throughout the flight Captain Bird sent a stream of telegrams to his Sydney office reporting progress and the state of his charge's health. The one from Katherine in the Northern Territory said cheerfully: JEAN GOOD NIGHT'S REST. LOOKS WELL RADIANT WITH SMILES. DARWIN WOMEN STATE BEST LOOKING GIRL PILOT THEY HAVE SEEN. And from Daly Waters a few hundred miles further on: IT IS A TREAT TO SEE JEAN BATTEN HANDLE HER MACHINE. EVERY LANDING AND TAKE-OFF PERFECT. However, by the time they stopped for the first night at Newcastle Waters, Bird had noticed Jean was beginning to flag: COURAGEOUS LITTLE LADY SHOWING SIGNS OF STRAIN. IN HER WORDS 'AM GLAD WE ARE STAYING HERE I AM FEELING THE STRAIN I DID NOT THINK I WOULD'.

By the next morning she had recovered. At every stop more telegrams were waiting. There was even a handful at the vast cattle station of Brunette Downs on the Barkly Tableland south of the Gulf of Carpentaria where they landed to refuel in heat, flies and red dust in the middle of the second day. 'I could not believe my eyes when I saw that one was from King George V and Queen Mary congratulating me on my flight. This was just too wonderful. I felt that my cup of happiness was now full to overflowing.'

For commercial security, as there was fierce competition between rival oil companies to monopolise pilots they sponsored, Wakefield's acting general manager in Australia, Jock Clarke, went to the unusual length of devising eleven separate codenames for Jean, one of which was 'Brownie'. It now appeared in the message which Bird sent off from Brunette Downs: TERRIFIC HEADWINDS AVERAGING ONLY FIFTY MILES HOUR GROUNDSPEED. ENDEAVOUR MAKE CLONCURRY TONIGHT. BROWNIE DELIGHTED ACCEPT PROGRAMME YOU ARRANGE.

But they didn't make Cloncurry, spending the night instead at Camooweal in Queensland. It was in a hotel here that Jean, anxious to add romantic interest to the story of her flight, announced to the world that she was formally engaged to a London stockbroker named Edward Walter. Describing the setback of her Rome crash she told a reporter that she was now flying with the bottom wings borrowed from Walter's aeroplane. 'Miss Jean Batten's flight was literally made on the wings of love,' said the story cabled round the world that night.

But in London, at his flat in Redcliffe Gardens in Kensington, Edward was not pleased. He had newsmen banging on his door while he was still in his pyjamas. Doreen Courtney, who produced the photograph of Edward and Jean, remembers hearing about it the same day from Edward's sister Geraldine. 'He was awakened at a very early hour by a crowd of reporters demanding to know if it was true,' Mrs Courtney said. 'Teddy was furious but replied, "I never contradict a lady" and closed the door. Later, I can clearly recall him saying to Geraldine, in my hearing, "I suppose I had better send her a ring." Embarrassed by her discourtesy he wrote and asked Jean why she had done it without warning him. Her reply was: "It was good publicity."' Edward's former secretary, Margaret Mackay, confirmed: 'He was very peeved and not terribly thrilled by this publicity stunt. But because he was such a perfect gentleman he just accepted it. However it must have set him thinking a little bit harder about Jean.'

At Blackhall in the middle of Queensland, on the third day out of Darwin, the Moth was grounded for two days with a magneto problem. Here the newspapers got another story. 'The intrepid girl pilot demonstrated that, despite the hardships she had braved on her record-breaking flight, she is essentially feminine. At her hotel she changed in a twinkling to an extremely nervous young lady. The innocent cause of it all was a rat which appeared on the scene just as she was telling a small audience that she didn't feel at all frightened crossing the Timor Sea. Screaming, she jumped onto a chair and stayed there until the rodent disappeared.'

Amid the stream of messages about 'Brownie's' health and flight progress, and hour-by-hour radio reports across the country which held audiences as riveted as for a cricket test match, the two aeroplanes eventually made it to New South Wales. During the week-long journey across Australia she had collected so many hundreds of telegrams she had run out of space in the Moth to carry them; they had to be shovelled into a mail bag and stowed in the Castrol plane.

Three weeks and a day out of England she arrived in Sydney to a tumultuous welcome. A small armada of twenty aircraft, including Kingsford Smith's famous *Southern Cross*, filled with waving passengers, flew out to meet her over Sydney harbour and escorted her in to Mascot aerodrome beside Botany Bay. When she taxied into the hangar a crowd of 5,000 people was waiting to applaud her. They surged forward and surrounded the Moth, climbing on to the wings and reaching out to touch her, shake her hand, and pluck her from the cockpit. Men slapped her on the back affectionately and women fought to hug and kiss her. She hadn't quite expected anything like this.

'It was really almost overwhelming,' she wrote in her memoirs. 'It was a huge milestone in my career and quite bewildering. What a great moment it was to hear that large crowd cheering and to realise that, at last, I had truly arrived at journey's end.'

'Every rooftop,' said the *Sydney Morning Herald*, 'was crowded with businessmen and women, office girls and clerks, while sightseers craned their necks from upper storey windows. By the time she had reached the dais the crowd had become unmanageable. A dozen burly policemen went to her assistance. Rousing cheers greeted Miss Batten, whose strong captivating personality instantly appealed to all about her.'

It was 3 o'clock on the sparkling blue Sydney winter afternoon of Wednesday, 30 May, 1934. In the moments that followed, as she experienced for that first time the sensuous thrill that the crowd's roar induced in her, she recognised it was exactly this for which she'd been destined. Persistence had paid off. She was now, indisputably, a star.

Instinctively, although the noise of the engine was still roaring in her ears, she knew how to rise to the occasion with grace and charm. Clutching the bouquet thrust into her arms and surrounded by reporters and photographers, she stood before the cluster of microphones and the big, bulky cinema newsreel cameras, responding with the elegant gestures of royalty, waving and smiling as if she had been born to fame.

She was eulogised in excruciating succession by six speakers who rose to salute repetitively her achievement on behalf of the Governor General of Australia, the Lieutenant Governor of New South Wales, the Commonwealth and State governments, the New Zealand government and the New Zealand Women's Association. Their praise rose to tedious heights of extravagance in sentiments which today sound fulsome and sycophantic, but in 1934 it was what the crowd demanded. They punctuated each speech with cheers that rang across the aerodrome into the nearby suburbs where thousands more were listening to live radio commentaries of the event.

'I had no idea that I should also be asked to make a speech, having never before attempted one in public,' she wrote. 'But suddenly I found myself standing alone in front of the microphone.' The archive newsreels show her as a petite and confident figure in her white suit and helmet making her maiden speech with great poise and with excessive precision in her diction which by then had little trace of a New Zealand accent and had become just slightly affected. For a first speech it was faultlessly delivered, almost as if she had memorised it. But it was entirely lacking in warmth and spontaneity.

'I want you all to know,' she began, 'how pleased and how thrilled I am to be with you here in Sydney this afternoon, and to realise that I am so near to my native land and that I have accomplished the flight successfully. As you all know I arrived in

Australia just the day before Empire Day and I do hope that my flight will help to strengthen the great bonds between all the dominions and colonies of our great Empire.' She concluded: 'I feel that my flight from London to Sydney, which is approximately 12,500 miles, to my mind has been well worth doing if only to receive this wonderful, enthusiastic and rousing welcome. I want to thank you all once again for this magnificent welcome you have accorded me.' As the crowd erupted into prolonged cheering she smiled and waved back with the poise of an experienced actress, and great happiness showed in her face. People were already comparing her platform skills with those of Amy who would blurt out, with heartfelt innocence, things like, 'I love flying, I love Australia and I love all you people'.

From the dais she was hurried through the crowd to the clubhouse of the Aero Club of New South Wales to do a telephone interview with the BBC in London. Soon her slow, well-modulated voice and her carefully chosen, well-separated words were being heard in homes all over the world. Her dazzling but brief international fame had begun in earnest.

On the drive into central Sydney people came out of their houses to cheer as she went by and outside the Hotel Australia, where she became the management's guest, such a large crowd had gathered to glimpse her that there were major traffic jams. Describing the euphoria, one of the news reports sent that afternoon to New Zealand began: 'Nothing more inspiring has happened in Sydney in recent years than Miss Jean Batten's arrival today.'

She embarked almost immediately on a frantic round of public engagements to celebrate her achievement. On the evening of her arrival there was a huge reception in her honour at the Sydney Town Hall. The place was packed out and large numbers didn't get in. Now 'resplendent in a white lace gown and short white fur coat and silver shoes' – the first of many gifts that were to be showered upon her – she was welcomed by the Premier of New South Wales, Mr B.S. Stevens, who announced, to loud cheers, that Miss Batten had been made a guest of his State government for the length of her stay. Suddenly Australia was paying the bills; life, temporarily, was for free. She had never had a job in her life, and she would now never need one.

In her own off-the-cuff town hall speech, delivered, wrote one woman reporter, 'with complete calmness and a regard for the niceties of English diction that might easily have suggested she was reading from well-prepared notes', Jean first uttered what was to become a ritual acknowledgment of Ellen's role in her success. 'She stood by me and cheered me when downhearted and spurred me on to success,' she declared to murmurs of approval. 'Mother denied herself and made sacrifices that I might attain my ambition. Now I believe she is pleased with me. I am proud to be the daughter of a woman made of such sterling material.'

After the reception she gave a radio talk to thirty Australian stations, to New Zealand, and to England. 'A shortwave broadcast to the United States and a ball later in the evening, at which eight debutantes were presented to me, brought me to the end of a perfect day.'

She spent four weeks in Australia at government expense in a nonstop round of receptions, banquets and balls. Crowds milled around the foyer of her hotel, and wherever she went in the streets she was cheered with spontaneous warmth. She took it all in her stride as if, wrote a woman journalist, 'she had been of Royal blood and lineage'. She was showered with gifts. The Sydney *Bulletin* reported: 'It will take a lorry or two to carry her luggage down to the boat, for presents of dresses, of hats, of everything, are arriving two a minute.' Jean accepted them all graciously. She was in no way embarrassed. She told a friend she believed she was entitled to these rewards for what she insisted was her contribution to the development of the Empire air routes.

The Hotel Australia wouldn't allow her to pay for a thing. They even gave her a secretary to help answer the flood of telegrams and fan mail. She set demanding standards and throughout her neverending daily round of receptions and lunches she astonished her escorts by her stamina and vitality. A Sydney *Telegraph* reporter allowed, at her insistence, a strictly inelastic fifteen minute interview in her hotel room one morning, described the frenzy of activity: 'She had fifteen different conversations with fifteen different people while her secretary kept putting her hat on and taking it off again, the telephone kept ringing and bellhops kept hopping. Strange parcels of frocks and boxes of flowers arrived and were piled on her bed. And while all this was going on, and people tramped in and out, and the photographers were bundling up their gear, she was saying in one breathless sentence that she wanted to see the proofs, that she did not know how long she would be in Sydney and weren't the flowers lovely and did everyone like her frock.

'Trying to get into David Jones store one morning to meet the Feminist Club,' the gossip columnist continued, 'she was at once recognised by the shoppers who suspended operations and swarmed round her until she had to flee to the lift and seek safety on the top floor. When she went to the Theatre Royal one night, as guest of honour at the performance of *The White Horse Inn*, she was cheered by thousands outside and by the whole great audience as well.'

After visiting Melbourne and being fêted at a parliamentary lunch in her honour in Canberra, she climbed into her Moth and flew herself up to Brisbane where 25,000 people turned out at Archerfield aerodrome to meet her. 'I could hear them cheering even as I glided in to land,' she wrote. She arrived, to begin another hectic round of receptions, with 'Buddy', a small black kitten, presented to her by disabled soldiers at the Prince of Wales Hospital in Sydney. Buddy was to remain her mascot for nearly a year, travelling unwillingly and miserably in the Moth's luggage locker, his feeble mewing drowned by the roar of the engine. 'The poor thing became so neurotic and developed such an aversion to aeroplanes,' an Australian woman pilot of the thirties said, 'that he would run away and hide at the mere sight of one.'

It is clear that Jean came as a surprise to most Australians who met her in 1934. From the reports of her exploits they had been expecting a plain, masculine-looking woman, strong in physical appearance. But although she radiated feminine charm in public, behind the scenes she was not always the paragon her fans assumed her to be. Briefing Castrol's New Zealand manager, Bob Smillie, in a private letter in advance of her visit there, Jock Clarke wrote: 'She is chock full of grit and pluck, not only in flying but in her private life and, as a consequence, she is perhaps a trifle headstrong and, on occasions, rather rude.' Disturbed by evidence of Jean's private dissatisfaction, for she appeared not to have felt herself adequately rewarded for her success, he added: 'She has already received a substantial present from Lord Wakefield. On the morning of her arrival in Sydney, we received a cable from our Chief instructing us to pay her £1,000 (sterling) or £1,250 Australian money. Also for your private information, Lord Wakefield paid her passage from India both for herself and her plane after her first crash and, in addition, gave her £400 to pay the expenses of her second attempt. In view of this generosity she is 100% Wakefield.'

In neither of her books, nor in her secret memoirs, was Jean prepared to reveal Lord Wakefield's £1,000 bonus – enough to have cleared most of her debts, although she didn't attempt at that stage to do so. She regarded the gesture as so private she never disclosed it to anyone.

'She feels at the present that the whole flight has been, to use her own expression, "a flop",' Jock Clarke's letter continued. 'She is talking wildly about having a machine to fly the Tasman … and the Atlantic and so on and so forth … But, having known this girl for the past few weeks, I am perfectly convinced that she will make a very great name for herself.' And the author of *The Castrol Story*, in which this letter was reproduced, commented on 'the shrewd glimpse it gives of the effect of fame and glory when thrust upon a youngster not yet fully equipped to handle it'.

Others in Sydney had not been slow to notice this. One of Australia's best-known women pilots of the thirties, a diminutive, freckle-faced redhead, Nancy Bird, who had had her first flying lesson the previous year with Kingsford Smith and was later to become well known for her pioneering air ambulance work, flying nurses around the Outback of New South Wales,*

*Nancy Bird (today Mrs Bird Walton) who now lives at St Ives in Sydney, was to found the Australian Women Pilots' Association. For her first flying venture, barnstorming around New South Wales giving joyrides in small towns, she bought the famous Gipsy Moth *Miss Beefex* which had been flown to Australia in a journey which went down in the annals of long-distance light plane history for the lighthearted way it had begun: at a post-party breakfast at had met Jean at Mascot. 'When she arrived I was merely one of the adoring crowd. She was something from out of the sky, you know. It was incredible – this beautiful girl with her dark black hair and ivory skin came in, in a white flying suit, having done this quite magnificent flight. I was filled with awe and envy. Later I got to know her much better and became one of her closest Australian friends – as far, that is, as she ever got close to anybody – and I became a fascinated observer of the effect of fame on her personality. In those days she was a star. She behaved like a star. She adopted the gracious manners of royalty. Her speeches were perfect, her dresses were stunning. But in no time, just as happened to Amy Johnson, she became a bit of a prima donna.

'Poor old Jean, she allowed it to affect her life too much. She began to take herself too seriously. She actually even began to think of herself as Jean Batten the famous woman pilot. It went to her head – and she suffered for it. She began to alienate the very people on whom she depended – her colleagues in the aviation industry. They'd never met a woman who was so demanding, who expected to click her fingers and get instant service, who was so emotionally cold and personally disciplined and decisive.'

'She was a very efficient person altogether,' Peg Kelman, another well-known Australian commercial pilot, told me at her home at Buderim in Queensland. Peg, who had been a partner of Nancy Bird in her joyriding venture, was still flying in her late seventies when I met her in 1987. As Peg McKillop she had been one of the twenty pilots who had flown out to meet Jean over Sydney harbour. More than most Australian pilots, Peg Kelman understood the achievement of Jean's flight. The following year, while pregnant, she and her sheepfarmer husband, Colin, had flown from England to Australia in a light aircraft, a twin-engined Monospar. 'Not only was Jean exceedingly beautiful, she was a tremendous pilot and navigator –

Quaglinos nightclub in London in November 1931 when someone, presumably not quite sober, is alleged to have shouted: 'Let's fly to Australia.' The challenge was taken up by a civil engineer – still alive in 1989 – 'Rab' Richards, whose passenger as far as India, where she became ill, was Lady Chaytor.

altogether a very professional person,' Peg said. 'She never looked tired, never looked distraught; always totally controlled, never got into a flap. I was very fond of her and very thrilled to know her – as far as she would let me because she actually didn't want anyone very close to her.'

A much tougher assessment of Jean came from Esther Mather, another prominent Australian pilot (today living in East Melbourne) who, at the age of seventy-six, was still flying herself around Australia in 1988. A prewar commercial pilot, and married to a Quantas pilot, she first met Jean on her visit to Brisbane in 1934. She was then Esther L'Estrange.

'Australia made a huge fuss of her and she visibly blossomed with the adulation. That, I'm afraid, was life to Jean and that's what she lived for – adulation. You could never warm to her, you could never get close to her, you could never become friends with her because she wouldn't let you. She put herself up on a pedestal and could think only of herself and her exploits. She needed the adulation because she was incredibly immature. She hadn't grown up – and in many respects she never did.

'Her flying was perfectionist. It was far more brilliant than Amy's or Amelia Earhart's but her whole approach to it was uncharacteristic of a woman. I know it sounds a funny thing to say but, from watching her flying and observing her whole approach to it, it struck me very forcibly that she actually flew like a man.' When I asked Esther what she meant she said, 'Well, she just kept on going. She never ever gave up in her determination to achieve her ambition. Although those early women pilots certainly didn't lack for bravery or determination, I don't think any of them approached their flying quite so aggressively bent on winning through at all costs as Jean did. When she set herself a target nothing would deflect her from it.

'But for all her brilliance and all the heroine worship, her life was utterly empty. She had many, many acquaintances but no real friends, ever. She was cold and self-centred. Her only interest in life was Jean Batten. She was a terribly, terribly lonely person.'

But in Sydney, in June 1934, there is no evidence from any of her writing that Jean felt the loneliness Esther described. She was on the crest of the wave, intoxicated by her success. She may have had few real friends; but she certainly had acquired the first of the huge number of acquaintances who were to establish themselves on the periphery of her life.

However, the exhaustion of the long flight and the subsequent nonstop pressures of fame were now showing. According to the Sydney newspapers she had begun to falter. 'It was obvious,' said one, 'that the nervous strain was at last beginning to affect her.' Deeply frustrated that, even with its two auxiliary tanks, the Moth didn't have the range to fly the 1,200 miles of the Tasman for the triumphant return to her homeland that was her ultimate dream, she put the aeroplane on a ship, at the Union Steam Ship Company's expense, and, badly in need of a break, sailed for New Zealand.

CHAPTER 11

Shaping the Images of Fame (1934)

Her arrival in Auckland was an emotional event. Although the country was deep in recession with huge unemployment, the city fathers rose to the occasion; she was welcomed like royalty with glitter and pomp. As the ship berthed aeroplanes flew overhead, ferries hooted, flags flew and a band on the crowded dockside played 'For She's a Jolly Good Fellow' and 'There's No Place Like Home'. First on board was her father, Fred, accompanied by her elder brother, Harold, who had come down from his farm in Northland. It was clearly a proud and emotional moment for both men but, although they had seen her waving from the rail as the ship nosed in, once on board they couldn't find her. She was not waiting on deck. They located her eventually in her private stateroom tucking into her favourite breakfast of steak and eggs in solitary splendour. In none of her writings does Jean mention this family reunion. Although she was later photographed smiling, sitting distantly from Fred, she was still smouldering with deep resentment that he had opposed her flying and cut off her allowance. She was much more concerned about Ellen and the speed with which she could arrange for them to be reunited in New Zealand: 'I sent for mother to join me,' she wrote.

First to greet her on the wharf was a contingent of old girls from Ladies College who placed a garland of violets round her neck and showered her with petals. But she had risen beyond the small world of her former boarding school. One of those to greet her that morning, Zelda Percy (now Mrs McCracken) said: 'She was very gracious and very correct, a little formal perhaps and, we all thought, a trifle patronising. One of the old girls remarked unkindly, but nonetheless shrewdly, that perhaps Jean was repaying some of her former friends who had come from more well-to-do homes and might unconsciously have patronised *her* at school.' Another old girl who wrote to Jean to congratulate her, Laurel Stewart (now Lady Armstrong, living at Henley-on-Thames in Oxfordshire), was disappointed that, in reply, all she got was a formal, duplicated note of acknowledgement.

If she'd been the first woman on the moon the crowds that lined the Auckland streets could not have responded with greater fervour. They spilled off the pavements, shouting her name and cheering, bringing the trams and traffic to a standstill. 'My sudden popularity surprised me,' she wrote, 'for I really did not expect it – or all the publicity. To me the successful flight was reward in itself.' At midday she was escorted to a civic reception in the Auckland Town Hall where the mayor and six other speakers delivered eulogies. There wasn't standing room and the street outside was again blocked by a milling crowd anxious for a glimpse of the young woman whom the New Zealand newspapers were proudly calling 'Our Jean'. The Mayor, Mr Hutchison, said: 'She has brought honour to the British flag, added lustre to womanhood and enhanced the traditions of the British race.' The cheering shook the hall.

'When Miss Batten herself rose to speak it was some little time before she could make herself heard,' said the *Star*. 'She stood quietly smiling, quite collected, waiting for the tumult to cease. Then, when she did speak, each word was coolly spoken and perfectly audible. She waved her hand graciously in response to the honour shown ... A pin could have been heard drop as she spoke.' Her speech was the first of over 150 she was to make in an exhausting round of engagements throughout

New Zealand, in all of which she claimed that her flight had in some way increased the unity of the Empire. She began to speak of the great joy she felt that 'I have been able to strengthen the great bonds of friendship not only between England, our Motherland, Australia and New Zealand, but between all the dominions and colonies of the Empire.' She learnt these Churchillian phrases by heart and repeated them without a word of variation in almost every speech.

Likewise, she was unfailingly to pay her now customary tribute to Ellen, who was already heading for New Zealand to resume the direction of her daughter's life. Again and again she was to repeat the phrase: 'She has been my inspiration, spurring me on when I felt like abandoning my ambition.' With repetition also she had developed a formula in recounting her disasters, by which the nightmare of the Rome crash had lost every shred of horror and sounded like an unremarkable landing in the field she had invented. And although she would not have seen it as deceit she had become practised in explaining how a penniless young woman had funded her own flying. Although she was running the risk of being challenged – Fred Truman was back in the country – she never mentioned his name, or Victor Dorée's. Indeed she was reported in the *Herald* as saying, without a qualm, that she had owned the Moth Victor had bought for her and that, after her 1933 Karachi crash, she 'had to sell her damaged machine to repay her obligations'. The fact that the aeroplane had never been hers to sell, and that she had not yet repaid Victor a penny, apparently seemed irrelevant to her. The deadly art of investigative journalism, as practised today, did not exist in 1934 and none of the men Jean had used would have dreamed of embarrassing her with public disclosures of the truth.

Meanwhile her public relations skills were developing rapidly. Increasingly, she projected an image of perfection and infallibility. MODEST HEROINE – GALLANT LITTLE LADY – INTREPID AVIATRIX – OUR WINSOME HEROINE, the headlines proclaimed. The stories were equally generous. One reporter wrote: 'You get definitely a most tremendous thrill out of just being in the same room with her.' She took it all with deadly seriousness and the modesty the newspapers claimed for her was not always evident. 'Did you know,' she interrupted a journalist at an Auckland press conference, changing the subject, 'that in Brisbane there was the biggest crowd at the aerodrome to meet me that has ever assembled there?' The woman reporter, with insight and a candour rare for the day, was moved to comment: 'The naive enjoyment of her fame was entirely youthful and ingenuous.' Nonetheless, in the extravagant prose of the New Zealand newspapers, she was created a figure of adoration difficult to comprehend over fifty years later. 'A delightful young woman totally unspoiled by the great fame she has won ... one wonders how such a frail slip of womanhood could have braved the terrors of such a flight.'

In the crowd outside the Auckland Town Hall on the day of her arrival, a woman said: 'It's just like when the Duchess was here,' referring to the 1927 tour of the Duke and Duchess of York. And Jean was not to disappoint them. When she emerged in the long, dark brown coat with voluminous fur collar and close-fitting brown hat in which she was then most constantly seen, she stood beside the official car and waved a bouquet. When they clapped and whistled and roared back their pleasure she picked out the flowers one by one and tossed them into the crowd. 'She's just a slip of a girl,' said one man in amazement, 'but she's got grit.' In *Solo Flight*, her first book, which she had begun to write on the voyage from Sydney, she wrote: 'I did not feel in the least like a heroine and hoped I was worthy of all the homage and tribute being paid to me.'

Of how much time she spent with Fred on the day of her arrival there is no record but it is likely that she was too busy to spare him more than a few moments. From her point of view there were much more important people waiting for her in Wellington. She had been invited to stay at Government House there for as long as she wished as the guest of the Governor General and his wife, Lord and Lady Bledisloe. After only one day in Auckland, therefore, she and her kitten boarded the night train and made the 400-mile journey south to the capital. Here the adulation took on a new intensity. At a civic reception the Prime Minister, George Forbes, announced to thunderous applause that she was to be a guest of the government and awarded an immediate state grant of £500. 'We are doing,' he said, 'something we felt the people of New Zealand would want us to do.'

But in the middle of the depression not all New Zealanders were pleased. In parliament the Labour member for Waimarino, Mr Frank Langstone, gave notice to ask the Prime Minister 'whether in view of the evident buoyant state of the national finances Mr Forbes would also grant £500 to mothers of families whose breadwinners were on relief work in recognition of their sacrifices and bravery'. He was howled down with cries of 'rubbish' from the government benches. But in the newspapers the gift of so much money – then more than two years' income for most New Zealanders – raised a storm of controversy in the letters columns. One angry reader wrote: 'Miss Batten at least has a roof over her head. She has warm clothes and good food. If there is money to spare give it to the weary mothers to buy milk, clothes and blankets for their families.' But others disagreed: 'It is surely in very bad taste to make this outcry while the laurels won by her great achievement are still fresh on her brow.' The public criticism was not helped by the *New Zealand Herald* which, in the belief that it was responding to popular demand, opened a subscription for readers to contribute to a fund to replace the piano she had sold four years before. There appeared to be a feeling in some quarters that New Zealand owed her this. The subscription was a flop; it raised less than £40.

Jean was undaunted. Now installed at Government House she was above criticism and was already planning how to spend the grant. 'Many people thought I would use it to buy my trousseau,' she wrote in her memoirs, for at this point she still intended, she wrote, to sell the Moth, sail back to England and marry Edward Walter. 'But subconsciously I knew the trousseau could wait. It would go towards the purchase of a fast little monoplane.' What she had in mind was a more powerful cabin plane with the range to fly the Tasman across which she was still determined to make the first woman's solo.

During her weeks in New Zealand she was on the crest of the wave, increasingly seeing herself as a figure who would go down in world history. 'I was likened,' she wrote, 'to many famous women among whom were some of my own heroines: Joan of

Arc, Florence Nightingale and Grace Darling.'

'In truth she could well be likened to Joan of Arc – but possibly for more than the reasons she had in mind,' said Yvonne Edwards, a New Zealand psychologist to whom I turned in search of some illumination of Jean's psyche – her unusual qualities of ruthless self-centredness, her passion for fame, her obsessive need for acclaim, and her endless capacity for self-delusion. Yvonne, and her English husband also a clinical psychologist – they described their approach as 'pragmatic and behaviourist' – spent long hours at my behest seeking clues to Jean's personality from the copious material harvested from two years' research. It included extracts from her narratives, her correspondence, press cuttings, photographs, radio-tapes of her voice and extensive transcripts of filmed and sound-taped interviews with people who had known her at all stages of her life. Independently the two psychologists came to fairly decisive and almost identical conclusions.

'The Joan of Arc analogy is, ironically, very apt,' Yvonne Edwards said, 'because Joan is now known to have been emphatically androgynous: a female with a male persona, a highly female-attractive body with a male drive behind it. She was driven, she heard voices, she led armies. In her gonads – her sex hormones – she would have had a dominance of male androgens where, with most women, our estrogen gets firmly in the way and makes us nest and want to stay in one place quietly and breed. Like Joan of Arc, Jean Batten stands out immediately as a not very "biological" female because a gendering female who can take the sort of flying risks she did has a lot of male in them. From all the evidence you showed us she was quite definitely and classically androgynous. They appear in about one in twenty of the female population; but few of them, of course, come to public notice with the prominence that Jean did. She emerged not only because nature had given her the androgynous drive, but nurture came from a mother prepared to fuel it. Her mother propelled her, unlike her father who impeded her.

'Being androgynous, Jean operated in a much more aggressively male than female fashion; uncharacteristically for a woman it was perfectly easy for her to walk over other people. If it hadn't been flying she would almost certainly have found something else that was extravagant and guaranteed to gain public acclaim: like going off to find the source of the Nile. She needed adulation like fuel, like a constant essential transfusion. And, having found fame, she became intoxicated by it, driven by this powerful sense of destiny. It was that unshakeable belief that she was somehow a chosen person that took her to the heights. She saw herself as a superior being, creating her own myth and beginning to live it — and believe in it. Women like her and Joan of Arc are very rare. The chances of their androgynous make-up allowing them to develop as special people are literally one in many millions.'

Michael Edwards said: 'It was fascinating the way she actually crafted that image. The white flying suit, white helmet, they were carefully chosen. They stood for the unsullied status she didn't actually have, but insisted on projecting in everything she did, said and wrote. Even in her memoirs, written at the threshold of old age, she had to sanitise her whole life. Not only did she apparently succeed in deceiving herself but, for most of the 1930s, an amazingly uncritical public bought this image because it was exactly what they wanted.'

Accompanied by a senior government official, and escorted by another Moth, flown by an Air Force pilot, Jean flew herself in RB to civic receptions in over twenty towns up and down the country. She was fêted at lunches, tea parties, dinners and dances. She gave joyrides at £1 a time. She addressed flying clubs, women's organisations, the farming community and schools. And in every town she appeared at twice-daily performances in cinemas, holding audiences spellbound with the story of her three flights. Money was rolling in from these lectures at which she was promoted, like show business, as 'The Darling of the Skyways'. The cinemas were filled to overflowing. It cost a shilling in the stalls and two shillings in the circle. Bands beating out stirring music often accompanied her from her hotel to the cinemas where the audiences would sometimes be warmed up by a master of ceremonies to get people singing some of the many songs now being written in her praise. One five-verse ballad called 'The Song of the Flapper Ace' concluded resoundingly:

Singeing her wings at the Flames of Death
Following Jason's Quest
Daring the Fates in a Gipsy Moth
At Adventure's stern behest.
Over the globe from a Small Red Dot
To the Gates of the sun-drenched West;
Binding the twain with a firm Red Knot
Comes Grit in a feminine breast.

In her memoirs she wrote of the income her lectures were producing, saying: 'It was considered rather unbecoming for a heroine to be commercially minded.' But she considered she was worth it, adding, 'It was an endeavour to earn an honest penny.' For a small country her fan mail was prodigious. It poured in at the rate of over one hundred letters a day; with the help of a secretary she replied diligently to every one, though she usually sent the same stereotyped acknowledgement to everybody. In the schools, teachers were proclaiming the moral of her persistence, likening her flight to the story of King Robert the Bruce and the spider. In her birthplace, Rotorua, to which, because of bad weather, she travelled by train (on the day she snubbed my mother in the first-class carriage), she was given a huge Maori welcome in the steaming thermal village of Whakarewarewa where an elderly chief of the Arawa Tribe, Mita Taupopoki, placing a precious cloak of kiwi feathers around her shoulders, and in her hair one of the rare white-tipped black feathers of the extinct *huia*, described her as 'a great gem of New Zealand' and made her an honorary Rangitane, or chieftainess. The chief said they were proud to adopt her as a daughter of the Arawa people.

But while the small-town newspapers were running out of adjectives to describe her charm and modesty, behind the scenes, again, she was by no means the paragon she presented to the public. The brunt of her arrogance was taken by Wakefield's New Zealand manager, Bob Smillie, and his wife Doris, who, now in their mid-eighties, are still in Wellington where

Jean came demandingly into their lives back in 1934. They admired and respected her hugely, but neither found her easy to handle. 'By the time she got to New Zealand she'd certainly got a swollen head and was by no means backward in telling every single person she met of her achievements,' Bob said. 'We obviously had to be careful how we handled her because she kept quoting Lord Wakefield to us. For weeks I ran around New Zealand feeling like the local flunkey, carrying her handbag and becoming her cat Buddy's nurse. Every time she flew with it in the locker there was this terrible mess to be cleaned up. She would just wave her hand and give orders that someone deal with it. She could be charming if things were going well but if they weren't, then look out. She never pulled her punches. She always insisted on having her own way and she didn't use much diplomacy in getting it.' Doris Smillie said: 'After she left Government House we invited her to stay with us. But she declined. Then one day, much later, she came to a lunch party and, for the first time, saw our home overlooking the harbour in Oriental Bay. Do you know what she said to me? "Oh Doris, if I'd known you had such a nice house I'd have accepted your invitation to stay." She used to treat Bob like a servant. She wasn't a bit grateful for everything he did.'

Early in June 1934 the liner *Rangitiki* steamed into Wellington harbour, bringing Ellen to join her famous daughter. Jean was the first on board when the gangway went up. There is no record of their reunion and there appear to have been no witnesses to it. 'The personal greeting between the two took place in a stateroom,' reported the Wellington *Evening Post*. It would certainly have been a deeply emotional occasion. Afterwards Ellen and Jean held a press conference on board and were photographed standing on deck, holding hands. Ellen, a well-preserved fifty-seven, was, according to one reporter, 'very reserved and possesses the same strong personality that characterises her daughter.'

'The tall, brown-eyed woman is an older edition of her daughter with a quick eager way of talking and a certain quiet confidence in herself and in the world,' wrote another. 'It is Mrs Batten who supplies the philosophy of life for the two. "It's the setbacks in life that mould character and endurance," she said.'

With insight the story concluded: 'The explanation of Jean is Jean's mother.'

The Battens' obsession with privacy, or perhaps it was wishful thinking by Ellen, was to create even further mystery around Jean's engagement to Edward Walter. The previous week in Auckland Jean had told the *New Zealand Herald*: 'We have been engaged for three months. No date for the wedding has yet been fixed, but it will probably be in England.' Now the Wellington reporters were bewildered to hear Ellen 'state the position definitely. "They are not engaged. Before she left on her flight Jean told me he had proposed, but that she had asked to leave things as they are until she returned to England in twelve months' time as she was so busy with her flight." ' Jean did not comment on her mother's untruthful statement. She would never have dreamed of contradicting her in public. The emphatic denial of the engagement, for whatever motive, was quickly reported in London where Edward Walter read it to his irritation and astonishment. It appears that, for some reason, Ellen's early high opinion of Edward's suitability did not last.

'I had the feeling that Jean had the power,' Bob Smillie said. 'Behind the scenes, that was. But in public Jean always seemed to defer to her mother. I have to say I didn't much go for Mrs Batten. She was an older replica of Jean – a powerful, bossy person riding on her daughter's fame. And she couldn't keep her nose out of Jean's affairs. "I am Jean Batten's mother," she would keep telling people. Like Jean she demanded attention and expected to be waited upon all the time.'

Another view of Ellen at this time came from one of Jean's most devoted admirers, Joy Prime (now Mrs Burch and living in Napier). In 1934, as a young teacher of seventeen, she was learning to fly at Wellington's Rongotai aerodrome. Jean was her instant hero and she was to become a sort of one-woman fan club corresponding energetically with her for the rest of the 1930s.* 'Mrs Batten had eyes of ice,' she said. 'She was tall,

---

*Jean's letters to Miss Prime, unlike her most personal letters to members of her family, have survived. Most of them are stiltedly formal and reveal little of Jean herself. They were clearly 'duty' letters written with no personal interest in her New Zealand fan. She betrays this by her careless, alternate use of 'Dear Joyce' and 'Dear Miss Prime'.

dignified and very haughty. I think she regarded anyone with whom Jean had any relationship as a threat.'

Jean took Ellen on her South Island tour. In her memoirs she was to write: 'My mother was born in the South Island and she always seemed to me symbolic of the beautiful mountains there: strong and steadfast with a passionate love of truth and freedom.'

'I don't think Jean could ever have achieved without her,' said Yvonne Edwards. 'She would never have become famous on her own. It was the symbiotic relationship that created the great propulsion. They reinforced each other; they propped each other up. Ellen was clearly a frustrated star herself; and possibly to some degree also androgynous. A lot of successful daughters go out and achieve what their mothers have failed to do. With Jean and Ellen the symbiosis was a kind of marriage. Not a sexual marriage, but a form of tremendous bonding in which they saw in each other their own reflections. And they liked what they saw. It was a joint narcissism. The two had welded together. They were also each brimming with enormous self-will. But their unique power was that they always willed the same thing, pulled in the same direction in their drive for achievement. Which is why they got on so well together.'

'Today,' Yvonne Edwards said, 'when one can discuss these things, which in the thirties people didn't, it is tempting to ask, as some of the men who lusted unsuccessfully for her did: was Jean a lesbian? We just don't have the data on this but one can say with some certainty that she would have been far too self-centred for lesbianism; she had much too much ego. Lesbians have to give in their relationships. Jean does not appear to have been capable of that, either emotionally or materially. It was just the way she was. In any case she never allowed any other woman, apart from her mother, to enter her life other than superficially.'

Although he could only observe it all from afar through the newspapers, John Batten had his own theory about the power of Ellen's influence on her daughter. 'Jean succeeded to a large extent because of her love for Ellen,' he wrote to me. 'Mother was her bulwark, her spur, her inspiration, an incentive – no, *the* incentive – to succeed.'

A few of those who met Jean at the height of her 1934 New Zealand tour commented on her apparent lack of maturity for someone who gave the outward appearance of being such a woman of the world. Joy Prime noticed it. 'Behind it all she was really very naive and very innocent,' she said. 'There was one story that went all around the country. She had been invited to kick off at a big provincial rugby match in Auckland. It was a game between Auckland and Taranaki, and she was guest of honour at the post-match dinner. She said in her speech, in her clear and precise voice, how much she had enjoyed kicking off that afternoon. Then she added that she would be very happy to go anywhere in New Zealand at any time "to kick your balls for you". It brought howls of applause. However personally experienced she may have been with men, she didn't actually understand the *double entendre*.'

By the end of her New Zealand tour Jean had established herself as the first of the country's truly international heroes. She had also helped put a small, isolated nation on the map. And she was a great deal richer than the day she had left England over four months before. She never discussed her financial affairs, either in her writings or in her rare confidences to friends. But from the day of her triumphant arrival in Sydney, where Lord Wakefield's £1,000 cheque had been waiting, the years of penury were over. However, that windfall, and the £500 gift from the New Zealand government, were soon dwarfed by the income from her lecture tour of the New Zealand cinema circuit, where crowds had frequently been turned away at the door.

The cinema records of her 1934 tour have long been destroyed but in an interview with the London *Sunday Express* the following year she admitted: 'In New Zealand I began to make money with my successful theatre tour. I made it on a twenty-five per cent basis with the large theatres and fifty per cent with the smaller ones.' On this basis, the arithmetic suggests that she would have netted well over £2,500. Effectively she had, with the value of the aeroplane bought for her by Lord Wakefield, accumulated, in the space of a few months, an estate approaching £5,000. It did not compare with the £12,000 (worth more than a quarter of a million pounds today) paid to Amy Johnson by the London *Daily Mail* for the world exclusive rights to her Australia flight story and the promotion rights on her return to England. However it was still a considerable fortune: the equivalent in the 1990s of around £100,000. Yet, in *My Life*, she expressed disappointment that the flight 'had not been a great financial success', adding 'but I managed to clear expenses . . . and pay off most of my debts'.

Whatever debts she was referring to, they did not include the money she owed Fred Truman; nor did she offer Victor Dorée even a token amount to help him recoup what she'd lost him. It is possible that, with her enlarged egocentricity, she refused to recognise the obligation to repay money that had helped further her ambitions. 'Her morality was part of the superficiality,' said Yvonne Edwards. 'I don't think she saw needs in anybody else.'

Putting the Moth on the liner *Maunganui*, Jean and Buddy the kitten sailed out of Wellington for Sydney, where Ellen was to join her later.

Within a few weeks of arriving in Australia she had peremptorily broken off her engagement to Edward Walter. There was a new man in her life: a tall, blue-eyed, goodlooking Australian. His name was Beverley Shepherd.

CHAPTER 12

Love at First Sight (1934–1935)

In contrast to the media euphoria that had greeted Jean's first descent into Sydney, her return in late September 1934 passed almost unnoticed. The newspapers ignored her.

She took a room in Darlinghurst Road in King's Cross. 'It was the heart of the red light district,' Peg Kelman said. 'But as she wasn't familiar with Sydney she may not have known that.' Too preoccupied in any case to notice the sleazy activity around her Jean was heavily involved by now with the part she was about to play in the MacRobertson Air Race. From casual beginnings as an extra attraction in the 1934 Melbourne centenary celebrations, it had blossomed into one of the biggest aviation events of the century. Sponsored by a wealthy Melbourne sweet manufacturer, Sir Macpherson Robertson, who put up the big prize money, it had attracted, for the race from England to Melbourne, entries from some of the great gladiators of long-distance flying, including Amy Johnson, Jim Mollison, Charles Scott, Tom Campbell Black, Charles Kingsford Smith, American Wiley Post (who held the round-the-world record) and the wealthy American Jacqueline Cochran who, years later, was to become the first woman to fly herself supersonically. Although only some were to get to the starting gate, and even fewer to stay the distance, 'they were all representatives of the heroic age of aviation which was soon to die and could never be reborn. They were unique. And though some would encounter each other from time to time, they would never all meet again in such hope and heady excitement.'*

Jean had badly wanted to enter herself. But her New Zealand tour had prevented her getting back to England and seeking a backer and suitable plane in time for the 20 October start from Mildenhall in Suffolk. However, she managed to find another role in the event which was to shrink the world to half its size. She was commissioned by a radio network to go to Melbourne and broadcast commentaries on it for ten days. She knew many of the competing pilots and was familiar with the route.

When the winners of the £10,000 speed section landed at Laverton outside Melbourne in their red, streamlined twin-engined racing plane, the de Havilland Comet, *Grosvenor House*, demolishing all previous England-Australia perceptions of time and distance, in an amazing two days twenty-three hours – they had made it to Darwin in just two days four and a half hours – she was standing on the apron doing a running commentary to thirty stations. At celebration banquets she was back in the news again, photographed sitting prominently between Scott and Black. And so delighted was he with the way she had promoted his winning pilots, their sponsor, Mr A.O. Edwards, owner of the Grosvenor House Hotel in London, told her to go shopping in Melbourne and buy herself 'a little memento'. She bought a French model evening gown.

In the second plane to finish, a DC2 airliner of KLM, she flew back to Sydney. 'At this stage in my life everything seemed to be going very smoothly,' she commented in her memoirs. 'I was looking forward to returning to England for I missed Ted more than I could have believed possible. He had been so patient but in all his letters asked what on earth was keeping me in Australia. I intended on arrival in London to marry him and

The Great Air Race by Arthur Swinson, Cassell, London 1968

hoped to live happily ever after.' Within moments of her return
to Sydney, in the first week of November, these romantic
notions were suddenly, and disturbingly, destroyed. 'Fate had
other plans in store for me. It was at that precise moment in my
life, just after the DC2 landed at Mascot, that I met Beverley.'

Beverley Shepherd was a tall and very handsome young
Australian, who several people who remembered him were to
say looked uncommonly like the Duke of Edinburgh in his
twenties. He was said to be sociable, easygoing and extremely
popular with both men and women. The son of a successful
Sydney doctor, an Englishman who had become an eye
specialist, he had been dissuaded by his father from the career in
medicine he really wanted and was training to be a commercial
pilot. The family, who belonged in the upper strata of Sydney
society, lived comfortably in a large and elegant house at 3
Marathon Road in the posh eastern harbour-side suburb of
Darling Point, replete with servants and their own yacht. They
were to some extent, though possibly not as obviously
prosperous, an Australian equivalent to the Dorées before
financial problems hit the family. Indeed as Mrs Dorée had done
for Victor, Mrs Shepherd was soon to buy Beverley his own
aeroplane, a Puss Moth cabin plane, to keep at Mascot.

But on the day he and Jean met at the aerodrome he was still
learning to fly as a pupil of the Aero Club of New South Wales.
He was then twenty-three, nearly two years younger than Jean.
The 'encounter', she wrote, was to 'alter all the plans I had
made for the future'. For the first time in her life Jean claimed to
have fallen head over heels in love.

Beverley Shepherd was the fourth successive man whom she
was carefully to bury, until my researches uncovered him.
Again, she did not name him in her 1938 autobiography. Nor,
forty years later, when she had the opportunity to revise and
expand the book for its reissue as *Alone in the Sky*, was she able
to bring herself to reveal one of the closest of her many secrets.
In none of the hundreds of interviews she gave throughout her
life – when she was frequently to claim that she had had five
proposals of marriage – did she admit to his existence.

However, in her secret memoirs she disclosed his first name.
'Beverley was tall and slim, a typical Australian, very fair with

intensely blue eyes and was learning to fly, he told me, inspired by my flight from England earlier that year.' So thoroughly had she concealed all records of their relationship, it was six months before I stumbled on the first evidence of his identity and became aware of his profound impact on her life and emotions.

In search of someone who may have known her in Australia in those prewar years I advertised in newspapers across the country. At last, early in 1987 there came a response: a letter from Adelaide; from Mrs Beverley Leech. Her eighty five-year-old mother, Ivy Graves, who lived in an Adelaide nursing home, she said, had met Jean Batten in Sydney in the 1930s. In those days Miss Ivy Rudd, she had been employed as a housekeeper by Dr and Mrs Shepherd at their Darling Point home. Their son Beverley had been friendly with Jean. Later I flew to Adelaide and met Mrs Graves. Although her memory was failing and she was very frail she was able, with the help of old photo albums which her daughter brought to her bedside, to recall the handsome son of the Shepherd family and his involvement with Jean. 'She was a frequent visitor to the house and Beverley would insist that everything had to be just right whenever she came to dinner. They were very, very fond of each other. I can remember that whenever she came, or they went off on one of their picnics or flying together, Beverley would get me to make little butter aeroplanes. I made them with a pair of wooden pats and it became a sort of ritual.

'Beverley was a marvellous boy, full of fun. It was always a lively place when he was around. There was another brother, Tony, but he never seemed to be at home. The only girlfriend who ever came to the house was Jean. The servants were convinced that one day they would marry. But I was warned by Mrs Shepherd never to discuss it. Both the Shepherds and Miss Batten were very private people.'

Jean's friendship with Beverley developed into a deeper relationship than she had had with any other man. In the months of late 1934 and early 1935, by which time Ellen had joined Jean from New Zealand and they had taken an apartment at Bondi Beach, they were constantly seen together – sailing on Sydney harbour, swimming at Manly or Palm Beach, driving about in Beverley's red open sports car; or at the flying club at Mascot. They often drove far down the coast to Bulli Pass or up into the Blue Mountains to secluded places to picnic. Jean's photo albums, in the RAF Museum in London, have snaps of her, captioned in her handwriting 'Picnic with Beverley', taken in these remote places out in the bush. In all of them she looks relaxed and happy. 'Sydney can be a fascinating city with the right companion,' she wrote.

But Ellen was less happy. Despite her earlier reluctance to admit publicly to the engagement, she considered Jean committed to Edward Walter and showed her disapproval by refusing ever to visit the Shepherds' house. 'Beverley would call for me in his sports car,' Jean wrote. 'I can remember so vividly rushing to the window as soon as I heard the car, grabbing my swimsuit and flying down the stairs to meet him. But I often saw a look of disapproval on mother's face. Once she said to me: "What about Ted – you haven't answered his last letter yet," and I laughingly replied from the door: "Yes, yes, dearest, when I come home, I promise."' But the letter didn't get written and the long-suffering Edward Walter, in his Kensington flat sprinkled with bits of Gipsy Moth, became more and more exasperated as the long silences grew longer.

'I cannot remember exactly when I realised that I had fallen in love,' Jean wrote, 'but I think it may have been on one of the sailing trips with Beverley and a few friends ... a happy crowd of young people without a care in the world ... we were right out near the entrance to the harbour ... a squall hit the yacht and we were soon soaked to the skin ... Although I protested, Beverley insisted that I put on his oilskin which, as it was far too big for me, caused much laughter ... When we made our mooring and rowed ashore Beverley suggested a swim in a nearby pool which we had to ourselves ... Strangely enough I think it was there, in that pool, with the rain pouring down, that I suddenly realised I had fallen in love.' Although they were to be infinitely discreet and never to admit it, friends of both of them are convinced that they became lovers.

One of the 'happy crowd of young people' on the yacht that day was Nancy Bird Walton. 'I remember we hove to in Manly Cove,' she said. 'It sticks in my mind as the only occasion I ever saw Jean let her hair down – the only time she forgot about being the disciplined famous aviatrix.'

Jean made no mention in her memoirs of the way her feelings for Beverley Shepherd now complicated her relationship with Edward Walter. From now on she began steadily to lose interest in him; before long she was to dump him altogether. Meanwhile, her life in Sydney was idyllically happy and when, in January 1935, Beverley got his A licence and the Puss Moth from his mother, he and Jean began to fly around New South Wales in it.

In their apartment at Bondi Beach Jean and Ellen had resumed the excessively private way of life so essential to them. Although Beverley Shepherd must at times have been invited in, it was probably a spartan place. They would not have been anxious for people to see the humble circumstances in which the famous pilot was living. Nancy Bird Walton, who saw more of Jean than any other Australian woman at that time, was certainly never invited there. 'When the flying or the sailing was over, if she wasn't going to the Shepherds', she would go straight home on the tram to Bondi to mother,' Nancy said. 'I've never known such an intense mother/daughter relationship. It was quite obsessional. And so was their need for privacy and secrecy.'

Although in public Jean had a reputation in Australia for modesty and charm, in some flying club circles, in this country which made a cult of indifference to the pretensions and affectations of rank and class, she was acquiring a different reputation. Her occasionally high-handed and demanding ways were beginning to make her unpopular with a few of the men pilots. At an air pageant in Newcastle two of them decided to employ some dangerous tactics to cut her down to size. Jean was making money giving passenger-rides in RB, taking people from a permanent queue on quick trips round the circuit. But every time she tried to land the two other pilots took it in turn to sideslip from above, straight into her approach path, forcing her, to her fury, to overshoot and make another time-consuming circuit. And when one or other of them wasn't cutting in on her approach, they would taxi on to the runway and deliberately take off in the space she was about to land on. At one stage they kept her in the air with a bewildered passenger, doing circuit after circuit, unable to land for nearly half an hour. The Australians who meted out this rough and hazardous treatment were Harry Purvis and Jack Chapman. The latter, one of the few pilots Kingsford Smith would ever allow to fly his precious 'old bus', the *Southern Cross*, was later to become deputy general manager of Trans-Australia Airlines. Today he lives in retirement on the Queensland coast at Noosa Heads where he recounted this story without a shred of remorse.

'Socially she was a most objectionable woman,' he said. 'It was this brusque, bossy manner, wanting everything, uncompromisingly, done her way, always taking command, always wanting to be first. And I don't think it was altogether fame. I'm convinced it was innate. She was so different from Amy Johnson. Amy was charming, never ever rude. Jean was frequently rude. I have to say that not many of us liked her at all. And, yes, we shouldn't have interfered with her flying that day – but somebody had to take her down a peg'.

Jack Chapman confirmed another story of Jean's unpopularity which had already come from at least two other Australian club pilots of the period. It was at a time when the Aero Club of New South Wales had extended her the rare privilege, before an early morning flight, of being allowed to sleep in one of the then strictly male-only bedrooms at the Mascot clubhouse. 'The committee made this exception because of who she was,' Jack Chapman said. 'But then she made a damned nuisance of herself by going to bed at 8 o'clock and expecting members in the clubroom next door to keep quiet so she could sleep. At last there came this famous occasion when she'd gone to bed as usual and about half a dozen of us were sitting there, listening to the radio. Around 9 o'clock out she came and curtly demanded that we turn it off. When we refused she just walked across and switched it off. As soon as she'd gone, of course, we turned it on again. And back she came. But this time she walked over to the radio, plucked out all the valves and took them into her bedroom. Well that did it. I went out to the hangar where there was a similar radio, borrowed its valves and got the set going full blast again. And for good measure we pushed all the furniture up against her door for the rest of the night. I'm afraid by then it had rather turned into a thing between Jean and me. But somebody had to do something about her.' Nancy Bird Walton, who knew of the incident, said: 'She was so angry she moved right out of the club next day. I always thought it was a pity that the boys found it necessary to cut her down because she had this desire to be perfect and was normally very well-mannered.'

Jean was by now so confident of her status that she was not always aware of the way she was seen by others. Soon there was another incident at the flying club ball that concluded the annual air pageant at Cootamundra, 200 miles up country from Sydney.

'It was one of the big formal aviation social events of the year with lots of Air Force officers looking splendid in their formal rig,' said Nancy, who flew out there with Jean. 'Unfortunately, she was not the only celebrity. Into Cootamundra that day there'd flown this wealthy and attractive Australian girl, Freda Thompson, who'd just arrived from England in her own Moth. She'd hoped to break Jean's record but had crashed near Athens and been stuck there for three weeks. However, she made it in the end and had become the first Australian woman to fly herself from England. So she was a bit of a hero that evening and people were naturally making a lot of fuss of her.

'However, there was an accommodation problem. There weren't enough hotel rooms so Jean was asked if she'd mind sharing with Freda. No way would she. Nor would she agree to share with me. I don't think it was arrogance; I think it was modesty – she had this great modesty thing. She had to have her own room. So I shared with Freda and we all went to the ball. But Jean didn't seem to enjoy it. With Freda there she wasn't the star turn. So halfway through, when everyone was just beginning to enjoy themselves, she turned to the senior Air Force officer and said she wanted to go home and was her car ready. He was quite horrified but remained terribly polite and I remember he said, "Miss Batten, there isn't a car but if you like I'll walk you back to the hotel." Jean was quite put out – but she went. That little performance didn't go down very well.'

It is unlikely that Jean was ever aware of the reputation for arrogance she was acquiring away from the sycophantic adulation of the headlines. For she was now unquestionably in the big league – thrilled to be treated as an equal by her hero, Charles Kingsford Smith, who invited her into his Sydney home and was to confide some of his innermost private worries to her, as if to a close male colleague. 'She was completely accepted,' said Nancy Bird Walton, 'into the circle of the then great people in aviation. She was regarded as one of them.'

But one day she was to give 'Smithy' one of the worst frights of his life. It was in a curious looking Australian-built aeroplane called a Codock of which only one was ever built. This unique, small high-wing twin-engined airliner had been commissioned by Kingsford Smith from Wing Commander (later Sir Lawrence) Wackett for services with a New Zealand domestic airline he planned to establish. The Codock's pilot was a New Zealander, Trevor 'Tiny' White, who had served with Smithy in the Royal Flying Corps. They offered to take Jean for a trip in it and, once airborne, she asked if she could have a go at flying it – a bold request since she'd never flown a twin-engined aircraft. 'Nothing daunted,' said Nancy Bird Walton (who heard the story from Kingsford Smith's secretary, Margery McGrath, who was on board with her boss), 'she asked Tiny White to move aside and climbed into the single pilot's seat, leaving him, crouching, squeezed between the seat and the window. Well, she'd hardly got hold of the controls when she put the thing into a spin. Lawrence Wackett was on the ground watching and, believing Tiny White was in control, was shouting, "Look how beautifully she spins." Although he was prevented by the high g forces of the spin from getting back into the seat, Tiny managed somehow to reach the controls and recover with not a lot of height to spare. Marge told me later, "She damned nearly killed the lot of us."'

Jean was never to mention the incident. It joined her training crash at Stag Lane in the list of events she was too ashamed to recall. But she and one of the world's greatest pilots had come close to perishing in one spectacular crash that day.

She threw herself into the launch of her book, now published in Sydney, going from shop to shop signing copies and being photographed by the newspapers. *Solo Flight* does not appear to have made much impact or to have been widely reviewed, but where it was noticed in the Sydney papers it was praised highly, not for its literary merit, but for the quality of the flying adventures it described. 'It is not a brilliant book,' said the critic of the *Sydney Mail*, 'but the flight of her narrative is much more heroic than any flight of imagination for it had to be lived before it was written.' The *Sydney Morning Herald* also liked it, saying 'One finished the book with a very genuine admiration and liking for the charming and intrepid young New Zealander.' Despite the kind reviews, the book sold badly. She would have done better, as some of her famous pilot colleagues had done, to have had it professionally ghosted. Four years later she was to repeat the mistake with equally disappointing results.

There are several versions of how Jean, now in love with Beverley Shepherd, broke off her engagement to Edward Walter. It appears to have happened in March 1935 soon after she had announced her intention to fly RB back to England and was about to make a brief farewell visit to New Zealand.

On her way to the ship in Sydney she was incensed to see her name on the billboards of the sensation-seeking Sydney newspaper *Smith's Weekly*. 'Quite dazed', she stopped and bought a copy. Her picture was on the front page beside the headlines: JEAN BATTEN'S LOVE AFFAIR – FAMOUS FLYING GIRL'S BRIDEGROOM IS PUZZLED – WILL SHE MARRY ENGLISH STOCKBROKER?

'There were all the details of my recent engagement laid out bare in black and white,' she wrote indignantly in *My Life*. 'It appeared that a rumour had been circulating that I was flying back to England to be married. Before leaving I had become engaged, but on arrival in Australia realised that I should have to choose between matrimony and my career. What made the situation rather difficult ... was that my fiancé had been interviewed in London about my forthcoming flight a few days before receiving the letter suggesting that we should break off our engagement. I really felt that if I married at this stage I could not devote myself so wholeheartedly to the programme I planned for the next few years.'

'Jean Batten, famous flying girl, has left a gentleman up in

the air,' *Smith's Weekly* said. 'Rumour had it that she was soon
to marry a well-known London stockbroker. He himself thought
so, too. But Jean seems to have cast a doubt on the matter.' The
newspaper had sent its London correspondent to interview
Edward Walter. 'I am not sure whether I'm engaged to Jean or
not,' he had said. 'Just a short while ago her mother published a
statement in New Zealand denying the engagement .... I don't
know whether there will be a wedding at all.'

As Jean boarded the *Monowai* to sail to Auckland, the *New
Zealand Herald's* Sydney correspondent asked for her comments
on the *Smith's Weekly* story. 'Of course my engagement is
broken off – I thought everybody knew that,' she snapped as
she went up the gangway. She was now getting herself into a
mess. According to Edward Walter's partner, Brian Whitton,
newspaper reports now appeared in London quoting Jean saying
'My engagement to Mr E.F. Walter has been broken off at my
request and I am leaving for New Zealand immediately.' Mr
Whitton said, 'That was the last my unfortunate (or perhaps
fortunate) friend ever heard of Jean Batten. No goodbye call or
letter of explanation. Nothing.' Edward's friend, Doreen
Courtney, said, 'I know that he and his family were very
annoyed and it led Teddy to say that, after that, he had no
intention of ever remarrying.' And Edward's former secretary,
Margaret Mackay, recalled: 'It was rather appalling that he
should have to learn from the newspapers that his own engagement was broken off.'

Nancy Bird Walton's version of the story confirmed the
significant part Beverley Shepherd played in it. 'Her friendship
with Bee, as he was always known, was no secret at the Aero
Club. I think there's no doubt that she was very much in love
with him. But of course she would never have revealed it to
anybody – she was so intensely emotionally reserved that I
sometimes wondered if she had any emotions at all. I remember
the *Smith's Weekly* story well. When he saw the "Will Jean
Batten Marry?" headline Bee is supposed to have said, "She'll
marry all right – but not the person they think she'll marry." By
then there's no doubt she wanted to marry him. He actually
helped her compose the letter sending the ring back to her
fiancé. I can even remember the day they went together in his

car up to Mascot post office to send it. From then on it was a foregone conclusion that they would marry, but of course only a few of us knew.'

By the time Edward Walter got the letter the damage had been done. His response was brisk and, as Jean was to write in her memoirs, angry. 'He wrote a very bitter letter, accusing me of telling the press before letting him know. This was quite untrue. Although in those days letters to England took very much longer, I had nevertheless allowed for this when I wrote and returned his ring. I knew that Ted had a violent temper when aroused so was not surprised to learn that he had actually thrown a reporter out of his office in the City.'

Edward's letter contained more than his personal bitterness. He attached a bill for all the money he claimed Jean owed him for the various parts she had cannibalised from his aeroplane. 'It was a carefully prepared statement in his beautiful handwriting, asking me to pay as soon as possible. I agreed. It was fair enough that I should pay everything down to the last penny.' But she didn't do it immediately, merely noting: 'I made up my mind to do so as soon as I could.' Reflecting the sense of relief she felt at what she now saw as a narrow escape from a man who could behave so ungallantly, she wrote: 'There were the two lower main planes – "the wings of love", I thought ruefully – the propeller sent to Rome, and dozens of small items of expenditure, which he must have jotted down in a book at the time. I now realised that everything had happened for the best. Although I would never cease to be grateful for the help Ted had given, I knew in my heart that I could not have been really happy with someone possessing such an analytical mind.'

There is evidence that, despite Jean's claims for her mother's acceptance of Edward, Ellen was not wholly uninvolved in the termination of the engagement. Not only had she earlier denied to reporters that he had become her daughter's fiancé, she was later to say emphatically of the relationship to Nancy Bird Walton: 'I put a stop to that.'

Jean didn't allow the unpleasantness to bother her for long. 'I decided that if I were to make a success of the flight back to England I would have to put it all out of my mind,' she wrote coolly.

'There was only one thing in her life: her own fulfilment; everything else was secondary,' Yvonne Edwards said. 'Her engagement to Edward Walter had been secondary. She didn't want it publicised because that would have created a deviation from her main drive. And that was an all-consuming passion, not in the emotional sense, but in the cold sense. She seems to have been able to pick people up and discard them with ease. I think she, and her mother, saw men as providers of money. Her drive was ruthless. I don't think she saw needs in anyone else.'

Of whether or not Jean ever repaid Edward Walter there is no record. According to Brian Whitton, she didn't. 'As far as I am aware the loaned wings were neither returned nor paid for,' he said. But, in *My Life*, Jean claims that she did so on her return to Sydney from her brief visit to New Zealand. 'I was able to repay him a few days after my arrival ... when I cabled the amount I had borrowed.' But in her memoirs, in which she went to great pains to shape the image she wanted to leave the world, it is significant that she made no reference to repayment at that point in her life story.*

Her elation at escaping from his clutches, as she prepared to fly the Moth back to England in April 1935, is made evident in *My Life*: 'Now that I had tasted the fruits of success and felt the urge to rise to even greater heights, any responsibility, however light, that would in any way hinder or deter my progress was not to be considered. In short, I suppose ambition claimed me and I thought no sacrifice too great to achieve the task I had set myself.'

With the long-range tanks reinstalled in the Moth, Jean set

*According to Brian Whitton, Edward Walter subsequently made a startling career change. Leaving the Stock Exchange after the war, he joined London's Windmill Theatre as assistant stage manager where he became friendly with the well-known racing driver, Sheila van Damm, whose father owned the theatre, famous for its chorus girls. Edward Walter is now dead. 'The last I heard of my old friend,' said Mr Whitton, 'was that he was fed up with England and told me he was going off to live in Portugal with some Portuguese girlfriend and drink red wine and lotus-eat on the beach – that would have been sometime around 1960.'

off from Sydney on 8 April in an attempt to fly back to England faster than she'd flown out nearly a year before. The strength of her feelings for Beverley had tempted her to abandon the dangers of long-distance flying, and her return to England. She made a disguised reference to her uncertainty in *My Life*: 'I was very reluctant to leave Sydney, however, and right up to the moment when I climbed into the cockpit ... I thought seriously of cancelling the flight and remaining in Australia.' But as always her heart yielded to ambition. She was careful, however, to avoid a public declaration of her new record hopes, declaring she was returning for the Jubilee of George V and Queen Mary, saying, as if making an airline booking, 'I have decided to fly to London to witness the wonderful pageant.'

Her departure from Mascot attracted very little publicity for she had kept the date a secret until the last minute. She preferred the adulation when she'd earned it, at the end of successful trips. But Beverley (who had agreed to keep Buddy the kitten) was there to see her go and, in a fascinating roll of archive newsreel film, he can be seen holding her wing as she taxied out and waved goodbye to him from the cockpit – one of the few pictures I ever found of them together, for, years later, she carefully removed from her albums any shot that showed her with any of the men in her private life. That was not quite the last she and Beverley were to see of each other in 1935. In his newly acquired Puss Moth he escorted her all the way to her first night-stop, 400 miles away at Bourke in northern New South Wales.

A second escort, another Puss Moth, was provided by the rising long-distance Australian star, Jimmy Broadbent. Jimmy, later to challenge Jean's records on the England-Australia route, was accompanied by his mechanic, Arch Steinbeck, whom I was to meet in Peg Kelman's home at Buderim. Arch had become friendly with Jean when she worked on her Moth in the de Havilland hangar at Mascot every Sunday afternoon. 'I watched her friendship with Bee Shepherd developing,' he said, 'but I never knew until much later how serious it was – she was so undemonstrative she never gave us an inkling of her true feelings; never betrayed the smallest sign of affection for him. She certainly covered it up all right.'

Jean successfully navigated her own way across Australia back to Darwin in four days. From there, on 12 April, she set off across the Timor Sea – and very nearly disappeared for ever.

CHAPTER 13

The Black Hole (1935)

Although she had had the Moth's engine overhauled in Sydney, Jean could not escape a nagging sense of unease that April morning as she climbed away from Darwin into a thick red haze and headed out north-west to cross the 500 miles of sea most feared by all the pilots who ever flew the Australia route.

The haze, which extended for hundreds of miles offshore and rose for thousands of feet into the air, was created by massive dust storms sweeping Northern Australia and blown out over the Timor Sea by a strong south-east wind. To get abcve it she climbed to 6,000 feet for the six-hour ocean flight to Kupang in Timor. As usual she carried no life raft, lifejacket, or radio. She just hoped the engine would keep going. This time it didn't.

The trouble began about three hours out of Darwin, almost exactly halfway to Timor. The nightmarish events that followed, which some people who knew her believe affected her for the rest of her life, she described in closely similar terms in My *Life* and in her memoirs.

'Below me floated a cloud carpet tinted orange by the dust; occasionally through a gap in it I would glimpse the sea. About 250 miles from land the engine suddenly gave a cough. Were my ears deceiving me? I listened intently. There it was again. A sudden falter which shook the entire structure. A few moments later the engine gave a final cough – and then there was just dead silence. A terrible feeling of helplessness swept over me as the plane began a slow, silent, glide towards the cloud carpet.'

Quickly she tried to diagnose the problem. She had just pumped up some fuel into the main gravity tank so there was no shortage. She jerked the throttle vigorously backwards and forwards hoping the engine would clear itself. But there was no response, 'no sound to relieve the terrible silence except the whirring, sighing noise as the lifeless plane glided down'. It must, in those appalling moments, have seemed like the end. From the day she had learnt to fly she had pushed her luck so often the law of probability dictated that sooner or later, in aeroplanes a great deal less reliable than they are today, her number must come up. The mechanics of her predicament were simple, and the remedies limited entirely and helplessly to pumping the throttle handle beside her knee. She had no starter motor with which to turn the engine over and no radio for an SOS to give her a small chance of being located and rescued from the sea.

So she left the throttle wide open in the hope that whatever was blocking the fuel jets in her carburettor might become dislodged. The only factor in her favour was her altitude. From her usual cruising level she would have been in the sea in little over a minute. But from 6,000 feet, at the Moth's rate of descent (with the heavy weight of fuel still remaining) of around 350 feet a minute, the anguish could be drawn out for over a quarter of an hour.

'Fascinated, I watched the altimeter unwind to 5,000 feet, 4,500, 4,000 – I was in the cloud layer now, but it wasn't very thick and at 3,000 feet I emerged to see the blue expanse of sea stretching into infinity. It was agonising.' But, as always, when death stared her in the face she claimed in her memoirs to have felt no panic. 'I experienced a feeling of complete detachment – as if I were an onlooker, not the central figure in the drama. In fact I didn't even think of mother or Beverley. Instead I found myself thinking first of Charles Scott and the loaded revolver he always carried over the Timor Sea to defeat the sharks – then of

Ted and the little hatchet he'd given me to cut away one wing
for a float, at which suggestion I had laughed so heartlessly at
the time.' (Her cynicism was, in fact, justified; the suggestion
that a small axe could sever the wing timbers was ludicrous.
Even had the axe done its job, which was unlikely, the wing
would have been prevented from floating free by inter-plane
bracing wires.)

With five minutes of gliding time left she began to pray 'as I
have never prayed before with every nerve and cell of my being,
while I watched the altimeter, hypnotised by the needle which
seemed almost eager to reach zero. I forced my gaze away from
the instrument and looked over the side at the approaching sea
which, fortunately, was fairly calm for I was now determined to
try and land the machine on the water as best I could. I undid
the buttons of my flying suit, loosened my shoe laces, then
reached into the leather cockpit door pocket for the despised
hatchet. The propeller was still just ticking over. Those last few
minutes were torture. In a final desperate effort, just before
attempting to land, I opened and closed the throttle lever once
more – but nothing immediately happened.

'I had just convinced myself that there was no alternative to
the sea, when a sudden roar broke the silence like a clap of
thunder and sent the blood surging through my veins. Like a
great sob the engine burst into life again.'

For several minutes the Moth skimmed the surface of the sea.
Then, holding her breath, she coaxed it gradually up to a safe
height where, euphoric with relief, she began to sing. But the
anxiety was by no means over. Within a few minutes the engine
was faltering again and she wondered if the whole terrible
procedure would be repeated. 'For the next three hours, until I
was flying once more over land, my mind was tortured with
doubt.'

Despite its nerve-shattering unreliability and more coughing,
faltering, shuddering spasms, the engine got her to Timor. 'On
landing at Kupang I offered up a prayer for my deliverance and
the kind Dutch people listened with ashen faces as I told of my
experience.' A Dutch mechanic concluded that some of the
Australian dust had caused a temporary blockage in the fuel
system. So she thoroughly cleaned the fuel filter and the car-

burettor jets. But this was not to rectify the fault. The experience had subjected her, whether she would admit it or not, to a more prolonged and punishing episode of intense fear than she had ever before known. 'It had shaken me more than I cared to admit at the time, or fully realised, and I did not feel my ususal confidence return until I neared England toward the end of the flight.'

'The nervous tension must have been very great,' said Sir Peter Masefield. 'She never showed it at the time. But I think it was there in the background for the rest of her life. I'm quite sure it's what came to the surface years later when she just couldn't stop talking about it all.' One of Britain's most eminent aviation patriachs, Sir Peter knows what it's like to feel vulnerable in a small aeroplane over the ocean: with his son, Charles, he flew from England to Australia in the 1960s in a light executive twin-engined aircraft. He knew Jean on the London flying club circuit in the 1930s and was to meet her again in the 1970s. Her personality fascinated him.*

'I've always had a belief', he said, 'that she nursed a latent yearning for quiet domestic security. And security was at the end of the flight in contrast to the tremendous anxiety on the way. Talking to her later I was convinced that was the reason she always pushed herself so hard. It's rather like hitting your head against a wall – it's so nice when you stop. It was nice when she got to the other end of a long flight. And with it she

*Sir Peter Masefield's distinguished career has ranged from air and war correspondent of the London *Sunday Times*, Secretary of the War Cabinet Committee on British Air Transport in Sir Winston Churchill's Government, and first British Air Attache at the British Embassy in Washington D.C., followed by Director General of Long-Term Planning and Projects at the British Ministry of Civil Aviation. He was subsequently Chief Executive of British European Airways, Managing Director of the Bristol Aircraft Company, President of the Royal Aeronautical Society, Managing Director of the Beagle Aircraft Company, Chairman of the British Airports Authority, Chairman of the Royal Aero Club, Chairman and Chief Executive of London Transport, Chairman of the Royal Society of Arts, and Vice Chairman of British Caledonian Airways. His son, Charles, is Managing Director of the British Aerospace Commercial Aircraft Company at Hatfield, Manchester, Chester and Prestwick.

got applause and acclaim. And however much she pretended this didn't count it did count a lot. It replaced the security that otherwise she'd never had and wasn't getting.'

'The Timor Sea incident must have been quite terrifying,' said Esther Mather. 'But it was only one of a whole series in her career. Yet, you know, she never gave up. It always used to amaze me that, having frightened the hell out of herself, she would simply turn around and do it again. You had to admire her determination – and her bravery.'

Although Jean carefully cleaned her fuel filter and carburettor jets in Kupang and at every subsequent landing, she never eliminated the problem. All the way back to England, flying, with minor variations, the same route she had followed on her outbound flight,.the engine continued to cut out at critical moments, plaguing her journey with one stressful crisis after another. She managed this time to get through the Inter-Tropical Convergence Zone by dodging the worst of the storm cells. However, once in the northern hemisphere, the strong prevailing westerly headwinds that persisted as she crossed India and the Middle East slowed her down so badly all prospects of a record began to fade. Then, on top of her fuel problem, over the Mediterranean she developed magneto trouble and her engine began to splutter and misfire worse than ever.

Over the Appenines the Moth refused to climb and she had to turn back, with the engine firing only intermittently, to make a semi-gliding descent into Foggia in southern Italy. When she got to Marseilles there was just time, with luck, to make it to London in one hop and break her own record by a few minutes. But her bad luck persisted. She now got a puncture and further magneto problems developed. She was so dispirited she locked herself in a room at the aerodrome. 'She is terribly disappointed,' a French official told reporters. He quoted Jean as saying, 'It is a dismal shame to be held up like this. I cannot go on now unless I have some rest. I can talk to no one until I reach home.'

Her troubles were still not over. Next day, over central France, flying low through mist and rain, the engine cut out completely. It only picked up seconds before she was well down her final approach for a forced landing in a waterlogged field.

When, with hands blistered from pumping petrol, she finally made it to Croydon in seventeen days and sixteen hours from Darwin, having failed by two and a half days to break her own England-Australia record, she was exhausted and depressed. Even for a Gipsy Moth it was not a particularly fast time. Jim Mollison had flown back from Australia in one four years earlier in less than nine days – half her time. If she was going to soar to greater heights in the record-breaking firmament she knew she wouldn't do it in a fifth-hand, 100-horsepower biplane. She needed a much faster aircraft.

She told reporters that her failure had lost her film and newspaper rights worth £500. There was only a handful of people to meet her at Croydon and she was greeted by an official of Imperial Airways merely as a courtesy. However although she hadn't drawn a crowd this time the London newspapers applauded her as the first woman to fly solo to Australia and back. Choosing to ignore Lord Wakefield's sponsorship that had made it possible, she told one of them: 'I accomplished it all without help, influence and money. All I had to help me was God's gift of persistency.' The *Daily Telegraph* saluted her achievement in a leader: 'Miss Jean Batten has firmly established herself among the record-breakers of the air,' and the *Sunday Express* splashed her life story, with new glamorous pictures, under the headline THE ORDINARY GIRL WHO BECAME A GIRL IN A MILLION. Her face began to appear, too, in the glossy society magazines; from now on she was regularly to grace the pages of *Tatler*, *Vogue* and *Sphere*.

There were no personal friends to meet her at Croydon because, despite her now significant fame among the ranks of the great aviation heroes, she actually had none. She and John were still not speaking, Edward Walter was still smarting from her cavalier treatment, and Ellen was in Sydney preparing to sail to join her.

Instead of an obscure room in an unfashionable part of London, her public image now demanded that she be seen in accommodation fitting to her status. She was driven by a *Daily Express* reporter to the prestigious and expensive Grosvenor House in Park Lane where she would never have dreamed of paying for a suite herself and was almost certainly the guest

either of the owner, Mr Edwards, who had bought her the costly
dress in Melbourne, or of the *Express* who wanted the ritzy
ambience for their photographs. Unlike Amy Johnson who had
stayed there on her triumphant return from Australia in 1930,
she was not a centre of crowd hysteria. The *Daily Mail* had
estimated that a million people had turned out to welcome Amy
at Croydon, to line the route to London and to lay siege to her
outside the hotel. And when Amy had stood on the balcony
outside her room overlooking Park Lane that night and waved,
the fans, who had brought traffic to a standstill, roared like a
Wembley cup-final crowd. There was no crowd for Jean. She sat
quietly in her room, drinking tea and being photographed with
her flying helmet, goggles and pith helmet composed around
her. 'I have come back to work for my living,' she told the
Express man.

She certainly had no intention of doing so conventionally.
She had convinced herself that she had Joan of Arc qualities;
she had a lot more destiny to fulfil and she saw her livelihood
coming from the fruits of fame, not from a demeaning and
boring office job. Almost immediately she set out to capitalise
on the publicity her return flight was generating.

'The morning after my arrival I rose at 6.30 to give an Empire
broadcast from the BBC,' she wrote. On her way to the studio
she was delighted to see the early morning billboards declaring:
HOME, JEAN. It was the start of a nonstop round of engagements
at many of which she was guest of honour. She was invited to
lunch at the Royal Aero Club, to the Royal Aeronautical
Society's garden party at Hanworth, to join Jim and Amy
Mollison as guests of honour at a League of Airwomen's ball at
Grosvenor House, to lunch with the directors of the de Havilland Aircraft Company, to New Zealand House to be entertained by the High Commissioner, Sir James Parr, back to the
London Aeroplane Club to be made a life member. Everywhere
she was lionised. And everywhere she stood up she told the
same story: a detailed account of her three attempts to fly to
Australia and her trouble-plagued journey back. The audiences
were riveted.

The Gaumont British film company signed her up to appear
for two weeks at a West End cinema to introduce an RAF

recruiting film they had made and which was preceded by a
newsreel item of her arrival in Australia the previous year.
Introducing Jean, who appeared twice daily in a spotless white
flying suit, the Air Minister, Sir Philip Cunliffe-Lister, said that
her Australia flights 'would live as one of the greatest voyages in
history'. The poet John Betjeman who was there described her
'as attractive as the bestlooking film star, entertaining and
modest'. 'I felt very proud,' Jean wrote. 'The cream of British
aviation was there.'

From the *Sunday Express*'s 'Girl in a Million' story and from
Gaumont British she was topping up her bank account 'and
earned more than enough to repay Ted', she wrote in her
memoirs. I puzzled over this, because, in the highly sensitive
matter of her debts to Edward Walter, she had earlier written, in
My Life, that she had already cabled him the amount from
Sydney. Was he ever fully repaid? Or was Walter's close friend,
Brian Whitton, right when he insisted that he didn't get any of
his money back. Whether he did or not (there is no firm evidence either way) there emerged from her friendship with the
stockbroker, unlike any of her relationships with her other male
benefactors, a deep concern to be seen in the public record to
have been scrupulous. The most compelling reason, probably,
was that Edward Walter was the only man in her life ever to be
fully named and publicly linked with her. With the others,
whom she carefully concealed from the outside world, it didn't
matter.

Surrounded by bowls of tulips and roses in her Grosvenor
House suite she was in constant demand for magazine interviews. Her abruptness and inflexibility in dealing with some of
the requests to promote her image in print was described in the
New Zealand Freelance by its London correspondent, Iain
Aitken: 'The person at the other end of the telephone was
being persistent. "No, I cannot give another interview until I
return from Scotland," said Jean the Celebrity. "I am sorry but I
am absolutely booked up. No, no it's quite impossible. Well –
wait a minute. Fifteen minutes at the most, the day after
tomorrow – Saturday at a quarter to eleven. What? But surely a
quarter of an hour is a long time for an interview? I'll try and
make it twenty minutes then – I've never given a longer inter-

view than that in my life. What is it you want? No I can't do that. I'm tied up to write my life story – I don't want to spoil my own story."'

Jean turned to Jain Aitken and said, 'I am enjoying the rewards of a successful flight. I wouldn't be done out of them for anything.'

One of the tangible rewards, the first of many showered upon her, was the Challenge Trophy from the Women's International Association of Aeronautics in America. It was given for 'the best woman's flight' for 1934. She was to win it three years running.

Now moving in the upper levels of British society she was being entertained by the rich, the famous and the noble. 'The Jubilee celebrations exceeded my greatest expectations,' she wrote in *My Life*. 'At the invitation of the Countess of Drogheda I watched the brilliant procession from the balcony of a lovely house in the Mall. Shortly afterwards I visited Scotland as the guest of Viscount and Viscountess Elibank and spent several happy days at their home in Peebles ... Among the guests was the Marquis of Londonderry at whose lovely home I had been entertained several times and experienced the lavish hospitality for which the Marchioness is famous ... At this dinner I had the unique experience of having my toast proposed by Lord Sempill.'

'She loved gracious living and important people,' said Nancy Bird Walton. 'She was flattered by their attention.'

Although her book is liberally sprinkled with the names of prominent figures, Jean made close friends with none of them for she was a loner who survived independently of normal social needs. Her acquaintance with these noble people was always cordial, immaculate and superficial. She presented herself to them from her pedestal. They paid her homage because she had achieved. They found no warmth in her; she was never loved, only considered a transient, glamorous star of the moment whom it was briefly fashionable to entertain, but who scarcely left an imprint in their lives.

By the end of the summer of 1935, the English social round was no longer providing the satisfactions Jean needed. Only another spectacular flight could recharge her cup of happiness.

New routes to conquer were running out by the mid-thirties; but she managed to find one worthy of her reputation: the South Atlantic.

It had been possible to cross it as a passenger in great luxury since 1932 in a Graf Zeppelin airship which flew between Germany and Brazil; and Air France's predecessor, Aeropostale, had been running mail services across it since 1928. But it was not a popular route with record breakers. Bert Hinkler, Charles Lindbergh (with his wife) and Jim Mollison were among the few who had flown it and, by 1935, the record (from West Africa to Brazil) was held by a Spanish pilot. No woman had yet flown it solo. To tackle it Jean sold the Moth and bought a comfortable, brand new and very expensive cabin monoplane.*

The model she chose was a Percival Gull, a startling improvement on the gentle, flimsy Gipsy Moth. It was twice as fast and, fitted with a huge auxiliary tank, had twice the range. Designed by an Australian pilot, Edgar Percival, who had flown with the Royal Flying Corps during the First World War, it was considered radically sleek and efficient for its day. He set up a small factory at Gravesend in Kent to build them; only a relatively small number of this pedigree, and today exceedingly rare aeroplane, was ever made.†

Compared with the mass-produced, draughty, and very basic open-cockpit Moth the Gull was luxurious. It was a low-wing cabin monoplane complete with starter motor, electric fuel pumps, metal propeller, brakes and flaps. The model Jean chose

---

*She sold G-AARB to Michael Sassoon, a member of the prominent merchant and banking family. His younger brother, Siegfried Sassoon, was the well-known author, distinguished for his *Memoirs of a Fox-Hunting Man*. In a letter to her fan, Joyce Prime, in New Zealand, Jean wrote: 'So she is in good hands and is very well cared for as the new owner is very proud of her and rightly so. I can always fly RB if I want to.' By early 1939 the Moth had been resold to the National Women's Air Reserve who based it at their headquarters at Maylands airfield in Brentwood in Essex. Sadly, during the war, a major hangar fire destroyed it there.
†Excluding the high-speed single-seat Mew Gull, of which there is no Percival Company record of the number made, a total of 138 Gull 4s, Gull 6s and Vega Gulls were built. The Gull 6, which Jean bought, was the rarest; only nineteen ever existed.

was a Gull 6 three-seater, powered by a 200-horsepower de Havilland Gipsy Six 6-cylinder engine. Instead of struggling along at 80 she now had the means to cross the world at 150 miles an hour. In a slightly different model Kingsford Smith had already flown from England to Australia in just over seven days, almost breaking the 'one-week barrier'.

'All this luxury cost money of course,' she wrote in her memoirs. 'By the time the auxiliary tank was fitted, and I had bought a few extras, it was the best part of £2,000 – practically every penny I possessed.' There is evidence that, from the income from her Australia flight, from the sale of the Moth, and whatever fee the *Express* and Gaumont British paid her, it was far from being her last penny. It is probable that she had begun to invest the surplus of her lecture tour revenue for, in later years, when people were to ask how she managed, her response was always that she had 'invested wisely' in the 1930s.

In the section of her memoirs dealing with the extravagance of buying a luxury aeroplane at a time when she owed several people a lot of money, she discoursed about her deep-rooted dread of debt: 'Even had it been possible at the time, I would never have considered buying the Gull on time payment, for I have always had a horror of making myself a slave of the hire purchase system,' she declared. 'If I could not save up enough to buy something I wanted, I would go without rather than pay more in the end, and endure the worry and anxiety so bad for the health ...'

On her twenty-sixth birthday, 15 September 1935, she went down to Edgar Percival's factory at Gravesend and took delivery of her shining new aeroplane. It was an exciting event for, with this powerful new machine which could fly 2,000 miles in one hop, she had plans to make her mark on aviation even more indelibly. She flew her proud new possession, painted in gleaming silver with the green registration letters G-ADPR, to Hatfield aerodrome in Hertfordshire to where both the de Havilland Aircraft Company and the London Aeroplane Club had now moved from Stag Lane. Because of the Gull's huge endurance, she arranged with Sir Geoffrey de Havilland to have another secret on-board toilet tube fitted – identical in operation to the one he had designed for G-AARB.

Ellen had now returned to England. To be near Jean's new flying base, they rented a small terraced house, their biggest accommodation luxury to date, in Endymion Road, Hatfield.

Jean was actively planning her South Atlantic attempt for November. She intended to fly to Dakar in West Africa and make the 1900-mile crossing from there to Natal in Brazil, and then to tour South America. She spent her days in London collecting maps, aerodrome information, flying permits and visas. At Shell's headquarters at Shell-Mex House in the Strand, where she went to the aviation department to confirm her fuel supplies, she was met, she wrote, by 'a most engaging young man with a slight limp, with very blue eyes and dark curly hair'.

Intrigued by her proposed flight the man went to a shelf and produced a page from a magazine. '"Here's a present for you," he said, "a picture of Cap San Roque – so you can recognise your South American landfall." It was a tiny picture, about one-and-a-half inches square, of a sea-girt point with a few palm trees. I said, "Thanks, this will be a great aid to navigation. All I have to do is count the palm trees." We laughed and the young man said, "Gosh I wish I was going with you." He wrote on the back of the picture "Good luck from Douglas." I said, "Douglas who?" and he replied, "Bader".'

On the day of departure Jean took the bus to Hatfield aerodrome, where disturbing news awaited her. She was handed a letter from the French aviation authorities forbidding her to fly over the Sahara to Dakar without a radio on board. 'Why had they waited until the last moment to deal this blow which meant cancellation of the flight? I sat down quietly and tried to think what to do ... It must be a very new regulation indeed ... Perhaps the authorities in Casablanca and West Africa might not yet have been notified ... Here, I decided, was a situation that called for the "Nelson touch" ... I re-read the letter, committed the contents to memory, then went into the ladies room where I tore it into tiny pieces and flushed it down the toilet. "Getting rid of a love letter before leaving, Jean?" one of the girls laughingly asked. "You'd be surprised if you knew," I replied mysteriously and walked out to the aeroplane with the thrill of anticipation and exhilaration that glowed in my heart before every big flight.'

Jean flew to Lympne where she spent the night at the Swan Hotel and arranged for a 3.30 am weather forecast for the first leg, nonstop to Casablanca in Morocco. Undecided when she got it in the foggy cold dark of the small hours, she went back to her room to think it over. 'With a start I realised it was Armistice Day (11 November 1935). That anniversary, synonymous with courage and quick decisions, decided me. Yes, I would go.'

Despite her misgivings about the en-route weather she changed into her brand new white flying suit, knotted her New Zealand flag round her neck, pulled on a heavy woollen 'Teddy Bear' overcoat and went across to the hangar. In *My Life* she described, with childlike excitement, the sight of the Gull that dark November morning. 'The big hangar doors swung back, revealing a low-wing monoplane. Its silver surface, glistening and gleaming under the powerful electric lights, made it look like some lovely thoroughbred, groomed and polished in readiness for a great race and straining to be away.'

As the aircraft was wheeled out two disturbing things were on her mind. The morning newspapers carried the story of the disappearance of her friend Kingsford Smith and his co-pilot Tommy Pethybridge off the coast of Burma. Smithy, ill and in financial trouble, had been trying to raise money with an attack on Scott and Black's England-Australia two day and four and a half hour record. A major air search had been mounted to look for the big missing single-engined Lockheed Altair. But Smithy and his companion were never to be seen again.*

To add to her concern, the previous afternoon at Lympne the young pilot of a small ultra-light Flying Flea had crashed, injuring himself before her eyes on the aerodrome. A few

---

*In her memoirs Jean described how she met Smithy in England shortly before he set out on his last flight. 'I thought he looked tired and rather frail,' she wrote. 'Although I would not have dreamt of trying to dissuade him from his latest England-Australia record attempt, I did ask him why he needed to do it when he had already achieved so much. He was happily married and owned a lovely home at Darling Point in Sydney where I had been a welcome visitor. "I've got to do it, Jean," he told me, "I desperately need some money." But I sensed that he was not really at all happy about it.'

minutes earlier he had presented her with a tartan scarf as a good luck memento for her flight. She refused to look at the wreckage as it was removed to a hangar and confided in a woman reporter that she was now afraid the scarf would spell bad luck for her flight. 'Why don't you discreetly stow it in your luggage locker?' the journalist suggested. Jean took her advice.

Soon after dawn she was off on the 1,500-mile nonstop first leg to Casablanca. She had never been able to make hops as big as this before, crossing France at 150 miles an hour, high above the cloud at the hitherto unattainable altitude of 14,000 feet to clear bad weather over the Pyrenees. THE TRY-AGAIN GIRL IS TRYING AGAIN said the headlines; JEAN BATTEN OFF ON ATLANTIC BID. But not everybody was cheering. The flying magazine *Aeropilot* declared negatively: 'Not cheerfully could we entertain the thought of the great risks to her involved in a long ocean crossing for no very useful purpose.'

After a night in Casablanca she flew on south round the bulge of Africa, landing briefly to refuel at Villa Cisneros in Spanish Sahara. By the end of the second day she was at the badly overgrown military aerodrome in a jungle clearing at Thies, forty-five miles inland from Dakar in French Senegal. She had been instructed to make her South Atlantic departure from Thies because the airfield at Dakar was under repair. In the event, when she got there, Dakar was serviceable again but it was too late in the day to fly on and she unhappily accepted the penalty of the extra miles now unnecessarily added to her critically long ocean crossing to Port Natal in north-eastern Brazil. She calculated that the total distance on this, the longest single sector she'd ever flown, was 1,907 miles and that it would take her around thirteen hours.

Her original plan had been to rest in West Africa and wait for ideal weather. But she had made such fast time from England she decided that, though tired, she would push on and go not only for the South Atlantic record but also for the one from England to Brazil, then held by Jim Mollison who had done it in just under three and a half days. But, to her dismay, she now learnt that all her petrol was waiting for her in Dakar, four hours' drive away. She exploded in fury. '"I haven't flown three thousand miles to be held up by a wretched fuel agent," I cried.

It was difficult to control my anger for I was tired and hungry.'
The French airfield commandant reassured her that the fuel
would be in Thies by morning. '"That's no good," I cried.
"They must start immediately. And I don't care if they do have
to drive all the way in the dark. It will teach them a lesson."'
The fuel was there by midnight.

She supervised the filling of her five tanks, four in the wings
and a large cylindrical 85-gallon one which occupied the whole
of the rear half of the cabin. Her total 147-gallon capacity, she
knew from the 10-gallon-per-hour consumption tests she had
carefully established on flights at Hatfield, would keep her
in the air for a theoretical $14\frac{1}{2}$ hours. She also filled her
auxiliary 10-gallon oil tank which had been installed in the
cabin on the right-hand side of her seat and with which – using
a hand-pump in flight – she could periodically top up her
engine levels.

But having loaded the Gull with maximum fuel she was now
worried that the small military field would be inadequate for the
long take-off run she was going to need. So she decided to
lighten the aircraft. She removed the heavy signal pistol, her
revolver, rockets and cartridges, torch, toolkit, spare engine
parts and emergency water drums. She put them in a pile on the
floor of the hangar, ready to jettison the lot. But then she had a
second thought. 'Smiling at my own optimism I surveyed the
assorted collection and selected two evening dresses, which
weighed practically nothing – one of them my Patou gown from
Melbourne – and to the surprise of all present, put them back
into the locker. After all, if I crossed the Atlantic successfully
they would be more useful than the toolkit ... And if I didn't –
well ...'

Again she was not carrying a life raft. It wasn't cost this time
but the weight penalty she couldn't afford. And again she didn't
have a lifejacket, still believing it provided only temporary
survival in an emergency.

It was midnight when she got to bed, sleeping in the
commandant's bungalow. He wakened her at 3.30 with the
Atlantic forecast. 'It was bad and my heart sank as I read it.
There was a depression right on my track immediately north of
the equator – the region French pilots called the "Black Hole"

– an area of black storm clouds and heavy rain. Without radio it would be impossible to make a detour round the centre of this permanent depression ... attempting to regain the original course would be unthinkable ... to deviate a fraction of a degree from the heading I intended steering could spell disaster.' But, as always, she threw caution to the wind and went.

Conditions for her overladen take-off from Thies were highly dangerous. The moon was obscured by low cloud, it was drizzling, and there was no wind. Nor was there a flarepath. She took off at 4.45 am by the headlights of the commandant's car. Like so many of her take-offs in the previous two years, it was a very unsafe operation.

'Holding the control column fully forward I gave the engine full throttle and the Gull roared through the darkness towards the lights. Would the tail never lift, I wondered, as we plunged across the dark aerodrome. At last, as I felt it rise, I tried to lift the aeroplane off, but it just sank heavily back to the ground. I had to think quickly now. Forward with the control column again and give it the full length of the aerodrome. I was now rapidly nearing the lights. The commandant's words rang in my ears: 'If you're not off by the time you're level with the lights – stop as best you can." But just as the headlights flooded the cabin, dazzling me, the wheels lifted as, with one final effort, I heaved the machine off the ground. I kept the nose down for a few seconds to gain flying speed, then eased up into a gentle climb, rising above the dark shadow of the jungle. Skimming the tree tops I flew for miles before gaining enough height to turn back towards the coast.'

Twenty minutes later she was out in the blackness of the Atlantic, setting course for Brazil. As she settled down to await the dawn the light of her torch fell on a note she had carefully written and underlined on a pad beside her: *1 degree of deviation to north or south of magnetic track = error of approximately 34 miles at destination*. It was, she wrote, 'a sobering thought'. For although she now had a much faster and more comfortable aeroplane its navigation and flight instruments were no more sophisticated than the Moth's. Her only steering aid – apart from a simple protractor to measure courses on her map – was still a primitive, imprecise magnetic compass. As in the Gipsy Moth, it needed great skill and concentration to hold a sustained course to an accuracy of five degrees, let alone one tiny degree. It was the biggest navigational challenge of her career and anxiety as to where precisely she was, hour by hour, over the vastness of the South Atlantic must have been intense. With such crude navigation facilities, on such an absurdly narrow fuel margin, and with no radio, nobody in their right mind would attempt such a flight today.

She flew low, cruising at only 600 feet above the sea to help monitor her drift, which she judged by aligning the aircraft's nose against the waves. Since she never used a sextant and astro-navigation techniques to check her position by the sun, the total success of her flight rested on the skill with which she was able to detect her right or left drift – and it was rarely consistent for long. If she didn't get it almost exactly right she would miss her landfall at the north-east corner of South America at Cap San Roque. Quite a small error either way and she would finish up with perilously little petrol left, heading towards the Amazon, or far out at sea flying southward parallel with the east coast of Brazil until her tanks ran dry. But Jean had supreme confidence in her abilities; the risk did not worry her — for she had an absolute belief in her own indestructibility.

When at last a grey overcast dawn began to filter into the cosy warm night-world of her cabin it was a lonely scene she began to register outside. 'In every direction stretched the vast blue expanse of the Atlantic, not a ship in sight, my only company the roar of the engine as I winged low over the ocean like a solitary bird ... I might have been the only person in the world.'

The flight went smoothly until she estimated she was around 200 miles north of the equator. Here she flew into the South Atlantic convergence zone, the familiar black wall of rain that rose threateningly from sea level to much higher than she could fly. She plunged into it determinedly but it was so torrential she had to drop to within 50 feet of the water to maintain visual contact with the sea. Afraid she would accidentally dive into the waves she opened the throttle and climbed to 1,000 feet where, for what seemed an eternity, she flew on her few simple instruments, grateful now for some blind-flying instruction she had taken at Hatfield before setting out. Most desperately of all she clung to her compass heading of 242 degrees.

But now came another of the moments of sheer terror that, throughout her flying years, were never far away. 'Suddenly to my horror I saw the compass needle slowly swing around the dial. It must be imagination, I thought. Drawing my hand across my eyes I felt the tiny beads of perspiration on my forehead as the needle continued its ghastly movement. Slowly it swung through 180 degrees. I was lost ... If I followed the compass now I should go round in a circle.' In the blackness of the rain that hammered on her windscreen she looked for some point of reference, however small, with which to orientate herself. But there was not a glimpse of sea, sky or sun. She struggled to resist the rising panic.

'I must not lose faith now, I told myself, my eyes fixed on the turn indicator, trying to hold my course on it independently of the compass. But I knew that I couldn't accurately steer another thousand miles to Natal on that alone ... Perspiration was now trickling down into my eyes ... every muscle in my body was tensed.'

She didn't record how long the local magnetic disturbance lasted. Air France pilots who flew mail planes down this route were later to tell her they were familiar with the phenomenon, having experienced it regularly while flying through severe electrical storms. But Jean didn't know this. Her brain semi-paralysed with fear, she sat there bathed in the sweat of her deep anxiety, convinced that she was hopelessly lost with no means of steering her way accurately to South America or even back to the coast of Africa. But, after what seemed like an eternity of terror and despair, but was probably only a matter of minutes, she was amazed and relieved to see the compass needle apparently swing back, agonisingly slowly, to magnetic north. And almost immediately the Gull burst out of the darkness of the rain into brilliant sunlight.

'The relief was tremendous. All my taut muscles relaxed and I sank back in the seat breathing a prayer of thanks. I took out my handkerchief and mopped my wet forehead, then slid back the window and let some air into the stifling cabin. I couldn't take my eyes off that compass needle. But it remained steady and once more I thanked God for my preservation.'

During the magnetic crisis she had crossed the equator and now estimated her position as 1,100 miles from Africa with 800 miles to run to Brazil. She had been in the air for over seven hours. 'A strong south-easterly wind was now increasing and blowing me to the north; I could see I was being carried well off my course. I spent the next few minutes trying to ascertain accurately the amount of drift and calculated it at 8 degrees to starboard. I altered course 8 degrees to port to compensate for it. This should take me to Cap San Roque. I began to feel very lonely. The empty blue sea everywhere made me long for the sight of other human beings – a ship to relieve the monotony of the vast blue waste.' Exhausted by the storms and the frightening compass incident she opened the lunch parcel the French commandant's cook had produced for her, and began to devour sandwiches and a whole chicken. 'After a drink of black coffee I felt quite refreshed.'

Nine hours out from Africa, 600 miles from the Brazilian coast, Jean was cheered to see a ship approaching over the horizon. 'It was a cargo vessel evidently bound for Dakar and my course lay right along the ship from tip to stern. I was almost breathless with joy, for she must have come from Natal in which case I was absolutely on the right course.' But then a sudden, nagging doubt entered her mind. Glancing at her map she saw that the ship – which she could now read as the *Belgique* – could just as easily have come from Pernambuco (now Recife), 160 miles south of Natal. Perhaps she had over estimated her drift and her 8-degree correction had been too much. But refusing to believe she'd got it wrong, she opened the window, trailed her scarf in the slipstream and dipped in salute over the ship. She resisted the temptation to circle the waving crew and held her course for what she prayed was Natal.

She was now searching the horizon for the small volcanic island of Fernando de Noronha, 250 miles offshore. But she didn't see it. Instead 12½ hours out from Africa, on her last tank of petrol with fuel for only one more hour's flying, she saw a large land mass ahead. As always when she made a landfall, 'I shouted aloud for sheer joy. Land, land, I shouted ... Surely Columbus himself could not have been more pleased when he sighted the New World.'

It was a lonely coast of sand dunes and palm trees and, as she crossed it with singing heart, she searched about for landmarks to establish where she'd hit Brazil. And then, almost to her disbelief, about half a mile to the north she saw a slight promontory covered with palms. Almost afraid to look at it she fished in her pocket for the tiny picture Douglas Bader had given her. One glance was enough. ' "Cap San Roque," I cried, hardly able to believe my tired eyes. It seemed too good to be true that, after steering for thirteen hours over almost 2,000 miles of ocean, I had made landfall within half a mile of the point I had been aiming for. Such luck seemed unbelievable.' Then, suddenly, she was assailed by doubt. Her map and the photograph showed a lighthouse. Her heart sank as she realised she couldn't see one. Just a sandy headland covered in palm trees. She could have arrived anywhere on the vast coast of Brazil. She turned and flew north to inspect the promontory more closely. As she flew over it she saw to her relief that, sitting among the trees, was a red-painted structure, 'a strange, lonely-looking edifice, but nevertheless a lighthouse. And an exact likeness of the little photograph.' Her navigation, which was much more than luck, was again almost supernaturally brilliant. The achievement owed much to her awesome powers of self-discipline which directly generated the concentration and ruthless attention to detail that the thirteen-hour flight, out of sight of a single landmark, had demanded. She had crossed the South Atlantic, with the aid of a sloppy compass, with the same precision 747s were to achieve fifty years later with sophisticated radio direction-finding aids and space-age inertial navigation systems.

She turned again and flew south along the coast. Within a few minutes she came upon a harbour and a town. 'It was like a dream come true to see real houses and civilisation. Passing over the town I gave another shout for joy: "Port Natal".'

She found the aerodrome in a jungle clearing on the southern outskirts and glided down to a perfect landing. Her only thought at that moment was for the record. 'Immediately the wheels touched the ground I checked the stopwatch. It registered 13 hours 15 minutes – my time from Thies. It was exactly 7.45 pm GMT on 13 November, which made my total elapsed time from England to Brazil 2 days 13 hours 15 minutes for the 5,000-mile journey. I experienced a wave of pleasure on realising that I had lowered the record from England by almost a whole day and I had crossed the Atlantic in the fastest time in history.'*

Her elation, however, was mixed with relief that the ordeal and the high stress was over. She was to tell reporters back in England that she had not believed such intense loneliness could exist and that she would not want to do it again.

The handful of people who greeted her were astonished to hear that the diminutive senhorita had come in such a small plane all the way from England. They were even more surprised when she climbed out and declared: 'I'm not particularly tired – I'm going on to Rio in the morning.'

She spent the night with an English family in Natal and listened with pride to a BBC news report of her record flight. 'Until I heard that broadcast,' she wrote, 'it had all seemed unreal, like a dream. But now the realisation that the flight was accomplished came to me and I experienced once again the greatest and most lasting of joys: the joy of achievement.'

Once more she was on the front pages of the London newspapers. The fact that this time she had beaten the time of Britain's aviator idol Jim Mollison had made her even more emphatically one of the great fliers of the day. The leader writers struggled to find adequate words for their hymns of praise. Her picture was now as familiar throughout the land as Amy Johnson's. And not only in Britain. In Paris *Le Figaro* said of the flight: 'We must realise the cool deliberation, the

---

*The previous fastest times outside of airline operations were 16½ hours flown by a Spanish pilot, Señor Pombo, and 17½ hours by Jim Mollison whose time from England to Brazil had been 3 days and 10 hours. However, Jean's greatest triumph lay in the 22 minutes she cut off the recently claimed record of an Air France crew flying a four-engined mail plane.

unusual courage, and the skill and authority which went into
its achievement. These are qualities one is scarcely accustomed
to find among women and which a lot of men will certainly
envy.'

But the boldest headlines came a day later. On the morning
after her epic trans-Atlantic flight she took off from Natal to fly,
in one ten-hour hop, the 1,400 miles south to Rio de Janiero.
By nightfall she had not arrived.

CHAPTER 14

Mother says No (1935-1936)

JEAN BATTEN MISSING – OVERDUE AT RIO – AIRCRAFT SCOUR JUNGLE FOR HER. The London headlines shouted the news and every BBC bulletin carried the story throughout Friday 15 November 1935. She had left Natal at 7.30 in the morning without refilling all her tanks but with adequate fuel for the ten-hour flight to Rio where she had been due to arrive at 5.30 pm. She was last sighted late morning over the town of Bahia less than halfway. When she hadn't reached Rio by dark the British Embassy arranged for an air search to begin at dawn.

For several hours a squadron of Waco biplanes of the Brazilian Air Force searched the line of her route north of Rio without success. But around mid-morning one of the pilots spotted the Gull, apparently intact, on a beach. It was near a village called Araruama, 175 miles north-east of Rio, but of Jean there was no sign. The pilot landed on the beach to investigate. He found that the Gull was bogged down in deep sand and its metal propeller had been damaged. A few minutes' walk away he found Jean in a fishing village. She had spent the night there, sleeping on the floor of the hut of one of the families. She explained that she had developed a major fuel leak; when, about seventy minutes out of Rio, she had switched to her last tank, she had been shocked to find that it had almost drained dry through a loose connection. Without enough petrol to continue she had put down on the beach. The landing had been perfect but, in taxiing clear of the incoming tide, she had sunk into loose sand and bent the tip of the propeller. She had regarded it, she said, as a minor price to pay for her salvation: had the petrol connection come adrift the day before in mid-Atlantic she would not have made it to Brazil.

The Air Force repaired the propeller and a formation of Wacos escorted her to their base at Campo dos Alfonsos to a warm welcome. In *My Life* she played down the Araruama beach incident, dismissing it in a few lines. Like the Rome accident it was not good for her image and she carefully avoided any reference to the damaged propeller because it implied carelessness and minor pilot error.

To the Brazilians, the beach adventure merely added spice to her reputation as a dashing and fearless young aviator. For a week they fêted her in new heights of heroine worship. The President, Dr Vargas, decorated her on the spot with the gold cross of the coveted Brazilian Order of the Southern Cross. 'The first British woman other than Royalty to receive this decoration – no wonder I felt pleased,' she wrote. The Brazilian Army and Naval Air Forces each made her an honorary officer. She was again showered with gifts, jewellery and money, including £500 in cash from the British Chamber of Commerce. She went from one reception and banquet in her honour to another, deeply impressing her hosts with what was described as quiet-spoken modesty.

She flew south to the Argentine and Uruguay. On landing at Buenos Aires the Gull was swamped by a huge crowd which a squad of mounted police, wielding whips, failed to contain. The passion of the Latin welcome was frightening. People threw their hats in the air, snapped their arms in salute, cheered and shouted and fought to touch her. She was snatched from the cockpit and carried shoulder-high into a hangar which was besieged by thousands of people who smashed windows and tore doors off the hinges in their determination to get near her.

In the newspapers she was featured as LA FAMOSA AVIADORA and CLAVEL DEL AIRE – the (carnation) flower of the sky. She was fêted from morning till night. She flew the Gull across the River Plate to Uruguay. In Montevideo the demanding ritual was repeated.

Back in Buenos Aires, in the first week of December 1935, she was showered with offers from the local British business community to stay in the Argentine and capitalise on her fame in sales promotional jobs. But much more attractive to her was an offer to fly the Gull up to do a coast-to-coast lecture tour of the United States. It came from the celebrated Charles Lindbergh, the first of America's great pilot heroes whose 1927 nonstop flight from New York to Paris had made him rich. 'It was a very tempting offer,' she wrote in her memoirs. 'While I tried to make up my mind a positive avalanche of telegrams arrived from the States urging me to accept.'

It was an opportunity that could have altered the entire course of Jean's life. It would have put her on show before a vast new prosperous public who, until then, had scarcely heard of her. She would have realised her ultimate dream of a ticker-tape welcome and been promoted and packaged more professionally than ever before. She would, more importantly, have earned money on a previously unimagined scale. But she turned the offer down.

Almost simultaneously the Royal Mail line had offered to take her and the Gull back to England for free 'to spend Christmas in London with mother'. It was the least lucrative of all her options at this critical point in what she knew, as a stunt flier, would be a short career.

How her decision was finally made she recounted in the 1970s, to Peg Kelman in Australia. 'Not many people ever knew how very badly she wanted to go to the States,' Peg said. 'Lindbergh's was an offer she knew she just couldn't refuse. And it was just the right moment in history. She'd made the magnificent return flight to Australia and now done the South Atlantic. She'd made some far more brilliant flights than

America's own Amelia Earhart, and with far less money. In the States she would have gone on a fabulous lecture tour and made a mint of money – not to mention the colossal adulation that she needed like a drug.

'Well, for some extraordinary reason, she felt it necessary to cable her mother for permission. And guess what her mother said? She cabled back that, on no account was she to go to the States – she was to put the Gull on the ship and come straight back to England. Fancy a girl of twenty-six, with all her ability and having done all the things she had, actually having to do what mum said. Jean never told me why. Perhaps her mother thought she'd be seduced or corrupted in America. It wasn't until all these years later when Jean told me about it that I came to realise what a diabolic woman Mrs Batten really must have been; a sort of Svengali with a peculiar hold over her daughter. I'm sure she stopped all Jean's relationships with people – men as well as women.'

'It was incredible,' said Esther Mather. 'She was never actually allowed to grow up and think for herself. She was ruled by her mother.' Ramai Haywood commented: 'Few people realised how emotionally dependent on her mother Jean became. It kept her in a state of unbelievable immaturity for the whole of her life.'

At Ellen's bidding Jean had the Gull loaded onto the liner *Asturias* and sailed out of Buenos Aires for England on 6 December. She was back in England two days before Christmas rejoining Ellen in the small terraced house in Hatfield. All their Christmas cards were forwarded by Thomas Cook, for no one, not even Fred, was allowed to have the address of their retreat. Here, content in each other's company, and cut off from all risk of social intercourse through the festive season, Jean would have listened to Ellen's explanation for insisting she turn down the biggest financial and publicity opportunity of her life. Presumably she saw her mother's will as wisdom. But it was to be a long time before America called again.

After Christmas Jean went back to Southampton to collect the Gull to fly it to Gravesend for an engine overhaul at the Percival Aircraft factory. On the way, trying to cross the South Downs in West Sussex, she crashed.

She never ever discussed the incident or wrote about it, and went to some lengths to keep the story out of the newspapers. I stumbled on it when, among her private papers at the RAF Museum in London, I found a small snapshot of the Gull, wrecked in a field and surrounded by onlookers. The date was 28 December 1935. But the extent of the damage was only revealed much later when an Australian engineer, Bruce Shaxson, wrote from Adelaide sending pictures of the unhappy looking G-ADPR. Then a boy, he had photographed it with his box camera the day it came down on his family's farm near Treyford at the foot of the Downs near Midhurst.

Mr Shaxson's pictures showed how disastrously the flight had ended. The undercarriage had been torn off, both port and starboard wings had been twisted from their roots, the engine cowling had been ripped open and the propeller was bent underneath the engine.

I eventually found the story in the files of the *Daily Express*. Its reporter tracked Jean down to a nearby hotel where she had gone after being treated by a doctor, to recover from concussion and a bad cut on her forehead which required stitching. She at first refused to speak to the *Express* man but he was persistent and finally got his story. 'I was on my way back to Gravesend,' she said, 'and over the Downs had to drop low to get beneath cloud. Suddenly the engine cut out. It came to life again for a second or two and then packed up for good. I picked what looked like the best clover field and glided down. I tried to clear a small willow hedge, but the undercarriage hit it and one of the wheels was carried away. I pancaked and slid on crazily for a short distance. I felt quite cool about the whole matter. But as I crashed I went forward and my head hit the windscreen. Blood was streaming down my face as I pulled myself out.'

I was never to discover the cause of the engine failure. The Chief Inspector of Accidents at the Royal Aircraft Establishment, at Farnborough in Hampshire, had a search made for me of the accident files for 1935. Curiously, since there was major aircraft damage and personal injury, there was no record of Jean's mishap. It was no longer possible, therefore, to discover the cause of the engine failure she claimed. In a letter she wrote a few weeks after the accident to a Montevideo newspaper, she speculated that it was a fuel blockage 'caused by water or grit in the system'.

A 1930s pilot who was familiar with the bad weather problems of crossing the South Downs, and knew of her propensity for fiercely guarding her reputation as a pilot, was sceptical of Jean's explanation. 'I strongly suspect that there was, in fact, no engine failure,' he said. 'It is much more likely that, flying when out of practice, in very low cloud, and possibly with winter dusk coming on, she tried to squeeze through a non-existent gap between the low cloud base and the rising tops of the Downs. She could well have hit a hedge with her under-carriage – and the rest would have followed.' In one picture at the crash scene Edgar Percival is visible beside the Gull, clearly anxious to establish what went wrong. He had the wreckage moved by road to Gravesend where, in the early months of 1936, the repairs must have cost many hundreds of pounds – whatever the true cause of her abrupt and violent arrival in the field.

Whatever the financial setback of the accident, Jean had, by early 1936, quickly resumed her public buoyancy. The *Daily Express* bolstered her morale when it named her, along with the Queen, one of the five 'Women of 1935'. International awards and honours were now beginning to arrive in pro-fusion. For the most meritorious flight of the year by a British subject in 1935 she was awarded the Royal Aero Club's pres-tigious Britannia Trophy. Jointly with Amelia Earhart (who had made the first-ever solo flight from Hawaii to California) she was given the Harmon Trophy for the most outstanding flight by a woman in 1935. She later told friends that Colonel Clifford Harmon, the wealthy American businessman who personally presented it, and who was over thirty-five years her senior, had wanted to marry her, but that she had turned him down.

She was awarded the gold medal of the French Academy of Sports and, for the second year running, the Challenge Trophy of the American-based Women's International Association of Aeronautics. The French government announced that it wished to confer on her the honour of the Croix de la Légion d'Honneur; Charles Lindbergh and Amelia Earhart were among the few previous aviator recipients.

The trophies joined the spectacular bronze-winged figure 'The Spirit of Aviation' presented to her by the Brazilian Air Force and she had herself professionally photographed holding each one. Unlike Amelia Earhart, who had been showered with honours ever since her first woman's North Atlantic solo in 1932 and was reputed to keep them modestly hidden away, Jean luxuriated in the insignia that acknowledged her brilliance.

Her fame had spread far beyond the Empire and she was now much in demand in Europe. The French treated her like one of their own heroes and invited her to Paris where she was entertained by the nobility and established a firm friendship with the famous, still vigorous, Blériot whose picture Ellen had once hung above her cot.

In the spring of 1936, the Gull at last repaired, Jean and Ellen set off on a leisurely flying holiday to Spain and Tangier. From Valencia they made a side-trip by sea to Majorca, falling in love with this appealing Spanish Mediterranean island. They stayed two weeks, swimming on its remote beaches, exploring its mountain villages, in days long before the world's airlines poured the tourists in. They spent hours wandering through the monastery at Valldemosa where Jean's favourite composer, Chopin, had written the 'Raindrop Prelude' she had once played when she was depressed. They were so enchanted with the island they nearly decided to take a villa there and stay for the rest of the summer. The rumbles of the Spanish Civil War changed their minds, and it was to be forty-six years before Jean would return to Majorca.

Back in London an argument was developing in Whitehall about the award Jean should receive in the forthcoming King's Birthday honours. The New Zealand Prime Minister, Michael Savage, was pressing the British government to have her created a full Dame of the British Empire. But in 1936 the dominion governments did not enjoy their present-day autonomy in these matters and the decision lay firmly in London. Had Jean ever known about the controversy that raged privately for several months between Whitehall and

Wellington over the doubtful perceived worth of her flights, she would have been mortified. The exchanges read like a script from the television comedy *Yes Minister* and were fascinatingly revealed to me, fifty-one years later, in Air Ministry minutes retrieved from the Public Record Office at Kew in Surrey.

The saga began with a secret and personal telegram to the Secretary for the Dominions, Malcolm MacDonald, from New Zealand's Governor General, Lord Galway. 'My Prime Minister has it in mind,' he cabled, 'to recommend award of DBE to Miss Jean Batten in recognition of outstanding achievement. Glad to learn as early as possible whether such recommendation would be appropriate ...' Knowing it had strong views about the activities of the long-distance fliers, the Dominions Office sought a reaction from the Air Ministry. The latter was strenuously opposed to the whole institution of private record flying and was less than sympathetic to the award of high public honours to the pilots who competed with one another for their own satisfaction. New Zealand had requested an unprecedently significant honour for a woman pilot — the equivalent of a knighthood. It was not surprising, therefore, that the conservative, male establishment of the Air Ministry bridled at the sheer audacity of it.

The Air Minister, Lord Swinton, was briefed on the implications by the Director General of Civil Aviation, Sir Francis Shelmerdine, who, to his slight embarrassment, had become privately friendly with Jean. 'We have done what we could for some years past to discourage such flights as this, which involve a wholly unjustifiable risk for no good purpose,' Sir Francis wrote to his Secretary of State in March 1936. He went on to list some of the recent honours bestowed on private pilots — the Air Force Cross to Charles Scott, a knighthood to Charles Kingsford Smith and an OBE to Lores Bonney, the first Australian woman to fly solo from Australia to England (who in fact had made part of the journey by sea). He reminded the minister that no award had ever been made to the celebrated Jim Mollison or to the winners of the 1934 Melbourne air race. On balance, he thought that Jean's flights merited at the most an OBE.

In New Zealand the suggestion was badly received. If the national heroine couldn't become 'Dame Jean' then the cabinet insisted she be rated at least as highly as Amy Johnson who got a CBE. Less than a Dame, but infinitely better than the much more frequently awarded OBE.

The matter was now becoming so diplomatically delicate that Lord Swinton decided to confer with his colleague at the Dominions Office. Malcolm MacDonald persuaded him, as the Air Minister was later to minute, 'that in all the circumstances it would be very difficult to contend with the New Zealand government that Miss Batten should have a lower honour than Mrs Mollison. On the other hand we ought to stand out very definitely against a DBE as that would certainly land us in all sorts of claims here.'

And so, in the 1936 Birthday honours, it was announced that Jean had been awarded a CBE – Commander of the Order of the British Empire. She was over the moon and a few weeks later went to Buckingham Palace to receive it from Edward VIII. 'It was indeed gratifying,' she wrote. 'I placed it proudly alongside my French and Brazilian orders.'

Among the letters and telegrams of congratulation that poured in through Thomas Cook, there was none from her brother John. But he was no longer in the country. Unable to get work as an actor he had given up his job with the plastic surgeon in Hampstead and he and Madeleine, with their three-year-old daughter Penny, had gone to live in Tahiti where Madeleine continued to write. It is highly probable that neither Jean nor Ellen knew they had gone.

Although her public persona was that of an elegant and glamorous filmstar, taking it all in her stride, the truth was that Jean was finding fame highly stressful. For each public performance she had to hype herself up days beforehand, carefully rehearsing her speech, choosing her clothes with Ellen's guidance, calculating the timing of her arrival to guarantee she was never upstaged. Then, to escape from the glamour and pressure of it all, she would hurry back to Hatfield. The wall that mother and daughter had erected around their private lives was now so impenetrable that, in two years continuous research, during which I traced scores of people who knew Jean in the 1930s, I did not find a single one who had ever been invited into their home.

'The curious thing about her,' said Sir Peter Masefield, 'was that she never socialised in the way that in the thirties was so common in flying circles. She never came, like most of the women pilots, and propped the bar up. She didn't seem able to talk informally about things other than flying. She would come to the aerodrome, do whatever she had to do, and go. It was like a ghost materialising then disappearing. I remember one big dinner we gave for her at the Royal Aero Club in London. This highly attractive, hugely respected woman arrived apparently from nowhere, alone. She spoke well and the acclaim was enormous. But as soon as the formalities were over she didn't hang around as guests usually did. Out she went, into the taxi and was gone. And none of us knew where she went, or where she lived.'

Peg Kelman, also temporarily living in Hertfordshire – at nearby Harpenden, and flying at the London Aeroplane Club at Hatfield – made several attempts that summer of 1936 to socialise with Jean, not always with much success. 'I'll never forget one occasion,' she said, 'when I went around to their house in the village to try and get her to make up a four for tennis. Well, I knocked on the door and waited. Nobody came. Then, at last, I heard someone come down the stairs. But, very strangely, the door wasn't opened. However, at a nearby window, I suddenly caught a glimpse of a hand. It moved the curtain slightly aside and an eye looked out at me before the curtain swung back. There was a pause, and then I heard the footsteps retreating upstairs. After which there was complete silence. I thought, how very odd. Next day I met Jean and asked her what on earth had been going on and she said, "Oh, that was mother. She didn't want me disturbed – I was resting."

'Well,' said Peg, 'I never got into that house and I never met her mother. I just knew she was there. It was quite weird the lengths to which they would go to prevent people encroaching on their privacy.'

The secretiveness of Jean's private life was beginning to attract wider comment. The *Sunday Express* came out with a story claiming that she was going through a bad patch and was depressed. Its air correspondent, Victor Burnett, wrote: 'She had become uncertain of herself. The outside personality she had come to adopt when facing cameras, newsreel microphones, reporters, guests at dinners, kept stealing over her when she was with friends. They were becoming afraid of her – were thinking about the airwoman and not the girl. She decided to take a country house and keep her address secret. Nobody knew where she lived ... She was never seen at restaurants, parties, clubs or airfields. All that was known was that she had gone to live in the country with her mother ... But it didn't have the result she wished. People began to say that she had gone away and hidden to get greater publicity.'

'I had the impression,' said Sir Peter Masefield, 'that she was really two people. She was the person that drove herself on to attainment to prove she could do things, and to get the acclaim she needed. But curiously this never actually made her happy, because the other side of her would have liked dearly to have escaped from the headlines, find the right man and lead a comfortable, secure married life. Perversely, she seemed driven to do the very things that, having brought the acclaim, she had then immediately to run away from. It was almost a form of schizophrenia.'

One of the explanations of Jean's disappearance that summer was that she had gone to earth to plan the fulfilment of her greatest ambition of all – the first-ever through flight by anyone from England to New Zealand. For several weeks she wasn't even at her country retreat. She and Ellen had gone off on an eighty-mile walking holiday along the length of the South Downs. It was intended as a fitness training exercise instead of the daily stints of walking and skipping she had done for previous flights. Spending the nights in hotels they went from Amberley in Sussex to Hythe in Kent. 'As you walk all the petty little worries and doubts that sometimes crowd the mind disappear, and in Nature's soothing presence new thoughts and inspirations come as if by magic,' she wrote.

Back at Hatfield at the end of July she set about her flight preparations in earnest. She had the huge long-range tank

reinstalled in the Gull's cabin and spent her days in London
arranging her over-flying permissions, buying the latest route
maps and checking on aerodrome facilities; they were a great
deal less primitive than when she had set out in the Moth in
1934, and for over a year it had been possible to fly on the
connecting airline services of Imperial Airways and Qantas all
the way from London to Brisbane. The pioneering days were
well and truly over, but this in no way diminished Jean's belief
that she was about to write a significant new page of aviation
history.

What she didn't know was that someone else was also hoping
to write it. And he was also a New Zealander. Ernle Clark, a
twenty-nine-year-old sheep farmer from North Canterbury and
an Oxford University graduate, had come over that summer on
holiday with his mother. While in England he had learnt to fly
and bought himself a Percival Gull. It was a Gull 4, a lower-
powered and slower version than Jean's but, in late September
while she was quietly making her final preparations, Ernle
unknown to Fleet Street, was also having a huge, long-range
fuel tank fitted in his rear cabin.

Apart from his mother, very few people appear to have
known of his secret plans. He had only 100 hours of flying
experience and a mere five hours on the Gull, but his bold
intention was identical to Jean's: to make the first direct flight
between the two countries. Neither appears to have known of
the other's plans. Ernle was a taciturn, extremely laid-back man
who, unsure of his flying and navigation skill, was cautiously
keeping it a low-key venture and telling the few people in whom
he confided that he 'was going home for the shearing' which
was also true.

It would not have been until the first week of October that he
would have read the first newspaper reports of Jean's proposed
flight. Her plans were further advanced than his and the deliberately short notice she was in the habit of giving the world of
her flights meant that her invisible rival didn't have time to
expedite his own. But not only was he to leave from Lympne
only three weeks behind her, he was, to Jean's astonishment, to
make it successfully, if with very little publicity, all the way to
New Zealand.

At Hatfield to see Jean off on her customary short positioning hop to Lympne was Peg McKillop; she was accompanied by her sheepfarmer fiancé, Colin Kelman, whom she was to marry shortly before their own private flight back to Australia two months later. 'We were the only people there to say goodbye,' Peg recalled. 'No one from the flying club bothered to turn up. There was just one other person, a young man in a navy blue suit, whom I didn't recognise. When she saw him Jean went quite funny. She turned slightly pink with embarrassment and said to him, with a rather strained voice, "Oh I didn't expect to see *you* here." She quickly left us to go and talk very briefly to him but was obviously too taken back even to introduce us.'

There were two men who could have reappeared in Jean's life at that time, either still in love with her, or hoping to discuss the repayment of debts. Edward Walter's reaction to the treatment he had received had been so violent it is unlikely he would have wanted to witness her flying off in an expensive new aeroplane. Victor Dorée is the more likely candidate. Although she still owed him for his wrecked Moth it is evident from letters he continued to write her, some of which have survived, that his admiration and affection had not been wholly blunted by the unhappy events of two years earlier.

Whoever it was he could not have failed to have noticed the new prosperity that surrounded Jean, who was now in a position to fund this flight herself. Compared with their early London days of hunger and penury she and Ellen were now mildly affluent. Aware of this, Fred Truman, now engaged to Rose, and working as a paint salesman in Auckland, had a few weeks earlier made another cabled plea for his money. The text of her reply was to go down in his family's history. It read: SORRY UNABLE TO OBLIGE STOP WILL HAVE TO WAIT YOUR TURN – JEAN. Fred's brother, Reg, who quoted the cable to me fifty-two years later, said: 'He really was desperate for the money by that time. He'd been waiting four years; he was right down to the bottom of the barrel.'

Another observer of Jean's last lonely moments at Hatfield before flying to Lympne that day was Terence Dancy, who now lives at Elkins, New Hampshire, in America. He was eleven at the time. His mother, who was friendly with Ellen, had taken him to the aerodrome for a bit of plane-spotting. 'We went into the refreshment room,' he recalled fifty-five years later, 'and there, sitting all by herself at another table, was Jean Batten! This was a thrill for me since she was so well known to young boys interested in flying records. But, despite my mother's urging, I was too shy to go and speak to her. I just remember being amazed that such a famous person was all alone at such a time.'

At Lympne, in the bright autumn moonlight before dawn on 5 October 1936, as Jean walked out to her aeroplane bathed in the newsreel camera arc lights, and prepared to set out on the most spectacular flight of her career, her former boyfriend who had made it all possible was nowhere in her mind. But Fred Truman's fuse burned slowly. He had by no means exhausted his patience; nor had he fired his last shot.

CHAPTER 15

The Cup of Happiness is Full (1936)

The media turnout for her at Lympne that morning was the biggest ever. In the arc lights she recorded a brief message: 'I want to cut my 1934 flying time to Australia by at least a week,' she said. She did not add that her real objective, apart from getting to New Zealand, was to break the standing England-Australia solo men's record of six days twenty-one hours, flown in a Gull by Jimmy Broadbent.

Ellen was not there to see her go, but back in the sitting room of the Hatfield house she had hung a large map on the wall and was ready with a collection of flags to plot the Gull's progress down the route.

The London newspapers spoke of the secrecy of the flight, saying that not even her own mechanics at Hatfield had known Jean's full intentions.

With her ability to cruise for fourteen hours at a stretch, and with her six-cylinder engine driving her along at 150 miles an hour, she sped across Europe and the Middle East to India faster than Kingsford Smith had ever done it on his own. She drove herself as she had never done before, flying with singleminded intensity, obsessed with the need to keep her time on the

233

ground to a minimum, ignoring her body's craving for sleep, flying by day and night. She flew at altitudes up to 14,000 feet, avoiding the worst of the turbulence and storms that had rendered her so vulnerable in the Moth. Sitting in comfort with a cabin heater to warm her at high level, her seventy-two feet of strip maps joined in one long concertina, and her logs arranged around her without risk of being whipped overboard by the slipstream, she nourished herself contentedly on the high-energy food Ellen had prescribed and packed for her: barley sugar, chocolate, raisins, malted milk tablets and flasks of coffee.

Stopping to refuel at Marseilles, Brindisi, Cyprus, the H3 landing ground in the Syrian desert and Basra, she reached Karachi in only two-and-a-half days. After just a few hours' sleep she took off again at 3.30 am and, with a refuelling stop at Allahabad, flew the 1,900 miles from Karachi to Akyab in Burma in one very long day.

Now setting her alarm for 1 am she tried to make the 1,300 miles south over Burma and Siam (Thailand) to Alor Star in Malaya in another big hop. But she hit the inter-tropical front and, although in the Gull the furious rainstorms gave her fewer bad moments than in the open cockpit, the ferocious rain still drove inside the cabin and soaked her to the skin. Forced to fly low to maintain contact with the ground she almost killed herself in southern Burma near the coastal town of Ye, not far offshore from which, beside the island of Aye, Kingsford Smith and Tom Pethybridge had plunged into the sea eleven months before.

Believing she was following the coast she didn't notice in the driving rain that she was actually flying up the dead-end of an inlet. 'Trying to keep the dark blur of the coastline in sight, I suddenly saw, straight ahead, a high, dark mass that looked too solid for cloud. In a split second I realised that it was a mountain top.'

It was a narrow estuary with jungle hills on both sides. There was no room to turn and the mountain ahead rose steeply up into the cloud which merged with the grey wall of rain. She couldn't risk trying to climb over it for she had no idea of its height. There was no time to waver. Instinctively she did the only thing possible. She made a stall turn – a fairly dramatic and risky aerobatic manoeuvre. Heaving back the control column and closing the throttle she pulled the nose up high until the Gull sagged into a stall. As it did so she kicked hard on the rudder and the aircraft fell slowly back through 180 degrees to face the way it had come. Opening the throttle she headed back up the inlet away from the lethal high country. 'I felt badly shaken,' she wrote. 'After that I decided to climb to a safer height, fly out to sea and trust to the instruments and my faithful compass.'

A moment later, clear of the coast, she was horrified to see that the leading edges of the wings were slowly turning pink. The silver paint had been beaten off by the rain and she was looking at the red undercoat on the fabric covering. 'If the canvas split it would rip off in seconds. But there was no time to contemplate such a catastrophe. All my thoughts were for survival, for the Gull was being tossed about like a feather and whirled along at terrific speed.'

It was several hours before she flew clear of the Convergence Zone. So dangerous were the landing conditions at Alor Star, with thick nimbus cloud blanketing the surrounding hills, she had to fly on south to Penang to refuel. Here she hurriedly patched the worn wing fabric with adhesive tape from her first-aid kit and went on, in the few remaining hours of daylight, to Singapore where the RAF made more substantial repairs for her. She had flown to Singapore in four days and seventeen hours; Jimmy Broadbent's record was now within reach. But it wouldn't allow her time for much sleep.

After a shower, a meal, and a brief rest at the station commander's bungalow, she was back in the air before midnight and heading south over Sumatra at 14,000 feet in moonlight on a lengthy night sector on which she flew above the weather for nearly 1,000 miles to Rambang on the island of Lombok. She was now having difficulty keeping her eyes open. After only fifty minutes on the ground she flew on to Kupang in Timor for the night. Only the Timor Sea now separated her from Australia, a certain new record and heightened fame.

But now she had her first major setback. The Gull's tail-wheel got a puncture. By the time the fuel agent had driven into Kupang and returned with an armful of sponges to stuff inside the tyre it was too late to get to Darwin before dark. However, she was still well ahead of Broadbent's time and knew that, if she took off at dawn, the record could still be hers. In any case she was almost dropping from exhaustion and couldn't see straight. 'I was landing with one eye closed because I couldn't any longer focus with two,' she later said. Since leaving England she had slept for only seven hours in five days. The delay gave her a badly needed rest.

With memories of her last traumatic experience crossing the Timor Sea she set off from Kupang at dawn on 11 October, inevitably with some anxiety. But the Gull's engine never hesitated.

She reached Darwin in just under four hours, half the time the Moth had taken and, according to the *Sydney Morning Herald*, her attempts to land were unexpectedly spectacular. 'The large crowd assembled at Darwin aerodrome to cheer her had an experience they will never forget. On her first attempt, her throttle jammed open and she came in at great speed. Her wheels did not touch ground and she opened the engine out again, clearing the hangar by only a few feet. On her next attempt she shut off the engine, but still came in fast. When she put on the brakes, the right one locked and the plane swung round in a full circle before coming to a standstill.' The hydraulic fluid in one brake had leaked away; only one wheel had braked and she had spun into a vicious ground-loop. But the Gull wasn't damaged and she climbed out to a tumultuous welcome. She had flown to Australia in five days twenty-one hours, knocking exactly twenty-four hours off Jimmy Broadbent's record. It was not a woman's record this time; it was an absolute solo record and within hours the story was on front pages round the world. Her time was to stand for forty-four years.

It had taken her a week to struggle across Australia in the Moth; the Gull did it in two days with only three stops — at Brunette Downs, Longreach and Charleville. She flew the 2,200 miles this time without an escort and her navigation without radio was unfailingly accurate.

Her one night stop was at Longreach in central Queensland. Hundreds of people drove great distances into town in the hope of seeing her. But she spurned them retreating to her hotel room and refusing to come out even for a few minutes. Said the *Longreach Leader*: 'Miss Batten's reticence and the manner in which she retired from the public eye was a disappointing feature of her stay on Monday night ... After remaining at the Qantas hangar until her machine had been refuelled she retired to her room at the Imperial Hotel. Though she answered one Sydney telephone call from a close friend, she refused to be disturbed for the numerous other calls and retired early.' The manager of the Longreach radio station 4LG was bitterly disappointed when his request for an interview was flatly turned down. The editor of the *Longreach Leader* got a similar response.

The one phone call she did take from 'the close friend' was undoubtedly from Beverley Shepherd. It is clear from Jean's memoirs that they had been in frequent correspondence during the eighteen months since they had last met. Disappointingly, none of their letters have survived.

Among the large number of telegrams that arrived while she was in Longreach was an affectionate one from Fred. 'We are very proud of you,' it said.

Her arrival in Sydney next afternoon, 13 October, in only eight days' flying from London, produced new frenzies of praise and adulation. Again an armada of aeroplanes flew out over the harbour to escort her in to Mascot while many schools gave pupils half a day's holiday to go to the aerodrome. Despite her exhaustion, she arrived looking immaculate. 'There was not a spot on her white overalls,' a reporter wrote, 'and the green silk handkerchief around her neck looked as if it had just come out of the box.'

When the speeches were over the huge crowd surged forward to the truck, on which she was standing in front of a battery of radio and newsreel microphones, to get a closer view of this legendary woman. But as she was only five foot four inches tall the deputy mayor of Mascot, Alderman Galloway, trying to be helpful, whispered to her, 'Put your arm round my neck and stand up on the side of the lorry.' Jean, according to reporters present, went rigid. Drawing herself quickly away from the stunned alderman she hissed testily, 'They can see me all right.'

'It was an unforgettable welcome,' Jean wrote, 'surpassing the one I'd had two years earlier. All the way into the city there were groups of cheering people.' Inside the hotel, where 1,700 telegrams were waiting for her, she couldn't get to the lifts for the jam-packed crowd. The famous Scottish music-hall singer Harry Lauder, who was touring Australia, happened to be there. He leapt onto a chair among the seething mass and in Jean's honour sang in his rich Scottish voice 'I Love a Lassie' to roars to applause.

When she finally got into the lift and it began to rise there was such a groan of disappointment from the crowd that she instructed the operator to take it down again. The doors were opened and, like the star she was, she stood waving a bunch of lilacs and smiling for several minutes. 'Sydney has witnessed similar demonstrations of enthusiasm, but never one that was more spontaneous. The name of the New Zealand girl was on everyone's lips throughout the day,' wrote one reporter.

Meanwhile the London newspapers were again singing her praises. 'Miss Batten must be the most extraordinary young woman in existence. Is she human or superhuman?' asked the *Daily Mirror*. Under the heading 'Bravo Bonny Jean', the *Daily Mail* said: 'There must be heroic stuff in Jean Batten.' And the *Daily Telegraph* declared boldly: 'No man can expect to surpass Miss Batten's courage and perseverance.' In Australia the press were equally generous. The Sydney *Sun*, under the headline JEAN, EMPRESS OF THE AIR, said: 'There is something about Miss Batten's flight which staggers the lay imagination.'

During the two days she spent in Sydney waiting for bad weather on the Tasman to improve, Jean was the centre of two storms of her own. One was the battle for the now valuable media rights to her story; the other an attempt by the Australian Civil Aviation Department to ban her from making the flight at all. 'I had no idea until I got to Sydney of the great controversy raging as to whether I should be allowed to fly the Tasman,' she wrote in her memoirs. 'I was even more staggered to find hundreds of letters and telegrams urging me not to attempt it.'

The Department's ban centred on the simple technicality that, to fly the 1,200-mile width of the Tasman, the Gull would have to carry so much fuel that its take-off weight would exceed that permitted in its certificate of airworthiness. But it quickly became an emotional issue as well. The Tasman had been flown sixteen times since Kingsford Smith and his crew had first done it in the *Southern Cross* in 1928. But thirteen of the seventeen flights in both directions had been made by multi-engined aircraft, most of them by Smithy in his Fokker tri-motor and by Charles Ulm in his *Faith in Australia*, an almost identical aeroplane, an Avro Ten. From Australia to New Zealand it had been flown only three times by single-engined aircraft.* No woman had yet flown it. The Tasman was notorious for its stormy weather and, although the length of New Zealand represented a target of nearly 900 miles of land to head for, the prevailing strong south-westerly winds had nearly drifted one of the light aircraft disastrously past the top of the country and out into the Pacific. But Jean suspected that most of the public concern was to do with her sex. 'I was a woman flying alone and in those days Australia, like New Zealand, was very much a man's country,' she wrote.

The Australian navigator Harold Gatty who, in 1931, had with American Wiley Post made the first flight round the world – he was once alleged to have said, 'women of charm don't take up aviation as a career' – was quoted as saying, 'She should be stopped.' Beau Sheil, who had been Kingsford Smith's business manager, said: 'To attempt the Tasman in a single-engined machine is crazy. If the engine stops all the skill in the world will not prevent disaster. She is already the world's greatest aviatrix. She cannot add to her honours by a Tasman flight.' The mayor of Auckland, Ernest Davis, deeply anxious, cabled her, 'There is a pronounced feeling in the community that you should not fly the Tasman.' Even Lady Gowrie, the wife of the Australian Governor General, tried to intervene; her plea was reported under the headline GOVERNOR'S LADY APPEALS TO JEAN AS 'WOMAN

---

*Guy Menzies in an open cockpit Avro Avian did it in 1931 in 12 hours; Ray Whitehead and Rex Nichol, sitting in turns on each other's laps on one seat in a Puss Moth, took 14 ½ hours in 1934; and Pat O'Hara in a Klemm Eagle nearly 13 hours in 1935. The only other solo crossing had been in the reverse direction, with two stops, in 1931: Francis Chichester had flown a Gipsy Moth floatplane across via Norfolk and Lord Howe Islands. But despite these successes, still fresh in people's memories was the first single-engined attempt in 1928 by two New Zealanders, George Hood and John Moncrieff. They set out from Sydney in a radio-equipped Ryan monoplane, heading for Wellington. But, although they carried a rubber dinghy and signals were heard from them for over 12 hours, they were never seen again.

TO WOMAN' NOT TO GO ON. And in Auckland Fred told reporters, 'I would feel a great deal easier in my mind if she would come home by steamer.'

But nothing was going to deflect Jean from the crowning glory of her flying career; indeed the whole point, in her view, of six years of hardship and struggle. So she bypassed the Civil Aviation Department and demanded to see the Federal Minister of Defence, Sir Archdale Parkhill. She showed him the British civil aviation special permit authorising her to take off with an overload of 1,000 pounds. It was good enough for the Australians. The opposition to her flight was withdrawn, although the Controller of Civil Aviation said he still hoped she could be persuaded not to do it. Her answer was to announce to the newspapers that she intended to take off the moment she got a favourable forecast.

Meanwhile she faced another dilemma. It concerned the media rights. She was now a vastly more valuable property than in 1934; for the first time since she became famous, media interests were competing for exclusivity. It was all happening in her large suite at the Hotel Australia where she had organised a formidable secretariat, complete with bodyguards and secretaries who waited on her hand and foot, even laying out her clothes each morning.

Within an hour of arrival, there was an offer of £600 from a radio network to do one fifteen-minute broadcast. It was more than two years' salary for most people. She quickly found time to fight her way out of the hotel, through the crowds who held permanent siege in the foyer, and drove to the studio to make it. Back in her suite she was flattered to receive a request for a meeting from the famous Australian newspaper baron, Frank Packer. She was flabbergasted when he rapidly came to the point and offered her £5,000 not to fly the Tasman but to stay in Australia and do a lecture tour. 'The girl who has beaten the men's solo record – it's really terrific – everyone wants to see you Jean,' she quoted him in her memoirs as saying. It was a staggering sum of money in 1936. Invested in its own right, it would, she knew, be sufficient to keep her and Ellen comfortably for the rest of their lives. But she could not bring herself to sacrifice the Tasman flight.

'I'll fly on to New Zealand, then come straight back and do your tour,' she offered. 'No,' she claims Packer replied, 'you must do the tour right away while the publicity value is white hot.'

In her memoirs she described how she dealt with this huge temptation. 'Now at practically the last minute, just when my morale was beginning to be affected by all the controversy, came this substantial offer. Should I take it, I wondered. After all £5,000 was a fortune for me at just twenty-seven. The temptation was almost irresistible. I needed the money. There was so much I could do with it, I thought: a new aeroplane, a lovely fast car, some beautiful clothes. The possibilities were endless. And I did not even dare to allow myself to think that it could mean staying in Australia and not having to leave Beverley.

'It would have been so easy to say yes. To be able, apart from anything else, just to sleep for a whole day. But I also knew it would mean foregoing my greatest ambition: giving up before I had reached the ultimate goal. In my heart I knew that all my life I would regret it if I did not go. After all money was not everything.

'And so there was a gasp of surprise from Frank Packer and his colleagues when I rejected the offer. "It's all very well for you to talk of linking England and New Zealand and risking your life, but what on earth do you gain from it?" Frank Packer asked in amazement. "The honour," I replied quietly. And they all looked at me pityingly.'

Just at that critical moment, Jean claimed, a secretary came in with another sheaf of telegrams. 'My spirits rose when I opened one and found that it was from mother, wishing me luck on the Tasman crossing. "My thoughts and prayers go with you and I am confident you will succeed," it read. My spirits soared. In that moment I had regained all my former confidence.'

But the process of commercialising her flight was not over. 'I had financed the venture alone. It was imperative that it should pay for itself,' she wrote. That it might, she now entered into several deals. One was with a consortium of newspapers which included the *Sydney Morning Herald* and the *New Zealand Herald* for exclusive worldwide rights to the story of her forthcoming flight for three days during which she undertook not to be interviewed or photographed by any newspaper not party to the contract. Another was with a New Zealand cinema chain, Amalgamated Theatres, to lecture throughout the country for two weeks, as well as providing the group with exclusive cinema newsreel rights. A third concerned the sale of all radio rights.

In her own writing Jean was remarkably reticent about the arrangements and there is no longer any record of the sums involved. There was, however, much wild speculation by newspapers on both sides of the Tasman who had been excluded from the deals. One of them was the aggressive *Smith's Weekly* which, under the headline BIG SCRAMBLE TO BATTEN ON JEAN BATTEN, claimed, without substantiation, that 'Jean will reap £20,000 at least'. The story said, 'The Batten hotel suite has become a cockpit of the money battle,' adding: 'It is astute management that scoops the gold dust from the heavens.' But the paper's extravagant guess appears to have been crudely based on nothing more than the fact that Kingsford Smith and Ulm, and their two companions, had received £25,000 in recognition of their historic first flight across the Pacific. But those were not media sales: £5,000 had come from a grateful Australian government and £20,000 from a nationwide public subscription. Furthermore the money was shared by four people.

Between making the deals, in which she was closely advised by Lord Wakefield's Australian management and their lawyers, and her fight to be allowed to fly the Tasman at all, Jean spent her few spare moments with Beverley Shepherd. He was now a fully qualified airline captain flying with a company called Airlines of Australia on the Sydney-Brisbane route. However the time she devoted to him during the two-and-a-half days she spent in Sydney was a great deal less than he had expected.

On her first night in town she eventually went to bed dizzy with exhaustion. On the second, Beverley invited her out to dinner. She declined in favour of an offer of £150 to make a personal appearance at the city's Luna Park funfair. Beverley was exceedingly put out when he heard that he had failed to compete with what he saw as her need for more adulation. However Jean viewed it as a commercial necessity.

'He was pretty peeved,' Nancy Bird Walton said. 'After eighteen months apart he'd made himself available for the whole of her stopover. And then he had to wait until the third and last night to take her out and see her properly. He told me that she gave him no priority at all. You see, he really was in love with her. She with him? Yes, well, I think so.'

Jean flew the Tasman on 16 October 1936. To provide her with a long runway and a flarepath for her overweight take-off in the early morning dark she was invited by the Royal Australian Air Force to use its base at Richmond to the west of Sydney. She flew the Gull over from Mascot the evening before. Despite her customary outward calm she was now very much on edge. Nancy Bird Walton recalled an incident shortly before her departure from Mascot: 'She was walking out to the Gull with the Shell representative,' Nancy said, 'when she discovered that he had failed to do something she'd asked. It was something quite minor, but she just flew into a rage. She stormed aboard her aeroplane and, as she closed the door, she shouted threateningly: "The world will hear about this."'

At the airbase Jean was made a guest in the officers' mess where they made a huge fuss of her. But she didn't sleep. The public controversy about the flight had begun to undermine her confidence and her wakefulness wasn't helped by a sentry placed on guard outside her room who marched up and down in heavy boots throughout the night. At midnight, still awake, she put on her coat and crept out to ask him if he could guard her from a stationary position. But before she could speak to him she caught sight of a large contingent of reporters and photographers talking and smoking at the end of the corridor, waiting for her departure. To escape them she hurried back to her room and lay on the bed knowing there was no hope of sleep now.

At 2.30 she couldn't wait any longer. She got dressed and went over to the station met. office where she saw the commanding officer, Group Captain Cole. Together they studied the forecast for the Tasman. It was not good. A deep depression lay in the middle of the ocean right on her track. If she waited a few hours for it to move she knew she wouldn't reach New Zealand until after dark and this she wanted to avoid because the grass at Mangere in Auckland was under repair and the landing area temporarily restricted. She had considered an offer from a rival aero club at New Plymouth, 150 miles south of Auckland, to make the historic landing there instead. But

Auckland was a more prestigious destination and would produce a much bigger welcoming crowd and higher ranking dignitaries – things that were immeasurably important to her. In the end she decided to risk the weather and go, aiming to make her landfall at New Plymouth to provide the shortest distance – 1,330 miles – over water; then to head north for Auckland.

Group Captain Cole escorted Jean out to the Gull. In the media contingent waiting there was the nephew of the famous Charles Kingsford Smith who had been killed the year before. John Kingsford-Smith, now in his eighties, was then a young cameraman with the Cinesound newsreel company. He will never forget that moment. 'Jean turned to the group captain and said, rather imperiously: "Has my aircraft been fuelled?" He confirmed that it had. "Did you check it?" Jean then asked. "No, Miss Batten," he said. "It was fuelled and checked by the sergeant," and he named the man. To my amazement Jean then snapped at him: "I'm not prepared to accept the word of a sergeant. I want you to check it." There was a moment's embarrassed silence, and then I can still hear Cole saying, very slowly: "I have no intention of checking it, Miss Batten. Neither I nor any of my officers will do so. If my sergeant says it was fuelled, it was fuelled." It was a tense moment. In a peeved voice she said: "Then I'll have to do it myself. Get me a torch." But the group captain had had enough by now. He replied very politely: "Miss Batten, I have no intention of doing so." Whereupon she leapt into the cabin, found her own torch, and checked the tanks herself. Her rudeness was quite unforgiveable.'

Yet again she was carrying no survival equipment. A Sydney company had offered to provide a radio, but in those days the equipment was bulky and heavy, with only a Morse code facility, and she declined. However for the first time she compromised. An Air Force Officer came out to the Gull with an inflatable lifejacket and insisted she take it. Reluctantly she put it on.

'The scene,' she wrote, 'was quite memorable. There were rows of press men, photographers and newsreel cameramen silhouetted against the flames and smoke from the burning oil curling up into the night sky from the long lines of drums marking the flarepath.' Photographs confirm the sense of drama: an eerie scene, like a gathering of the Ku Klux Klan, made slightly sinister by the brilliant white-smoking magnesium flares of the newsreel cameramen.

As she climbed into the cabin and started the engine a radio reporter ran forward with a microphone asking for a farewell message. Determined to end the opposition to the flight once and for all she decided it was the moment for a dramatic gesture. 'I want to speak to the group captain again,' she shouted above the roar of the engine. The station commander hurried over, and she declared: 'If I go down in the sea no one must fly out to look for me. I have chosen to make this flight and I am confident I can make it. But I have no wish to imperil the lives of others or cause trouble or expense.' A woman reporter who heard this wrote: 'She is something fine and brave and rare, something more than an ordinary girl.'

Jean waved goodbye and taxied out to the runway. It was 4.30 am and still dark as she took off and climbed out over the lights of Sydney, heading for New Zealand. For the next ten hours thousands of people on both sides of the Tasman kept their radios tuned to the stream of news bulletins that speculated on her progress.

Her memoirs quote an English newspaper headline that day: THE WORLD HELD ITS BREATH AND WAITED. And certainly in Australia and New Zealand it was true. Jean's nephew, Jim Batten, was then growing up on his father Harold's farm at Ruakaka in Northland. 'I must have been about eleven,' he said. 'In 1936 we didn't have a radio. Mum, Dad and we three kids, I remember, walked three miles across country to an old bachelor's house to listen to the commentary. It was a very emotional occasion.'

The flight was another triumph. She flew the Tasman in nine-and-a-half hours, like a homing pigeon. It was a record for the crossing. Flying through many heavy rainstorms she cruised below 1,000 feet much of the way to observe her drift. Her observations were, as always, almost supernaturally accurate. But in mid-Tasman she had no means of knowing this, and with the world watching her as never before, some of her unshakeable confidence had this time deserted her. 'The strain was terrific,' she wrote. 'And my spirits sank when, nine hours out from Sydney, there was still no land to be seen.' By all her calculations she should have reached the New Zealand coast in nine hours – but outside the cockpit there was just sea and torrential rain. The 8,000-foot high welcoming landmark of Mt Egmont, which trans-Tasman pilots can sometimes see from over a hundred miles out, was buried in sombre grey cloud. According to Nancy Bird Walton, who heard it from Ellen, Jean later confided to her mother that, for the first time, she nearly lost her nerve on the Tasman that day.

'Mrs Batten told me that those last couple of hours had been very, very traumatic. She actually thought she might have missed New Zealand altogether. It must have been hideous. I know. I've been lost at sea in a small aeroplane. I can tell you 'it takes a lot of courage to fly out of sight of land at all, let alone fly 1,300 miles.'

As the miles went by with no landfall, twitching through squall after squall, her arms growing tired of struggling with the control column, she began to think again of some whales she had seen earlier – and a persistent new worry began to grow. She knew, so she thought, that at this time of the year whales migrated through Cook Strait between New Zealand's North and South Islands. Her increasing belief was that she was off course and flying in zero visibility on instruments through the two halves of the country; heading out into the Pacific. She tried hard to reason that she could not have drifted, undetected, so far to the south of her intended track. But the worry remained and, with every minute, it grew.

Then suddenly through the curtains of black hanging nimbus cloud she saw it at last. 'A dark blur loomed ahead through the rain and the Gull flashed past a small rocky island. "Land!" I shouted with joy, recognising the island . . . Within a few seconds I swept over New Plymouth, absolutely on course, 9 hours 29 minutes after leaving Richmond and 10 days 23 hours 45 minutes out from England.'

She was within a hundred yards of her course. Her confidence flooded back and she dipped the Gull in salute over the disappointed crowds standing in the rain, hoping she would land at New Plymouth aerodrome. As she reset her course for Auckland and headed north on the last leg she was filled with elation.

CHAPTER 16

Breakdown (1936)

Jean's arrival in Auckland shortly after 5 o'clock on the afternoon of 16 October 1936 will remain for ever one of the greatest events in New Zealand history. Many people who are still alive, who rushed out to the small grass aerodrome at Mangere, beside Manukau harbour, that day still talk of it. Nothing quite like it had ever greeted even a royal visitor.

It was the first direct flight ever made from England to New Zealand. Her time was eleven days forty-five minutes. Remarkably it was to stand for forty-four years.*

Throughout the day as radio commentators built up the suspense, 6,000 people poured out of Auckland in cars, taxis, buses, motorbikes, by bicycle and on foot. By 4.30 there were 2,000 cars lined up on the aerodrome and still pouring in; a special squad of mounted and foot police had to be sent to control the crowd. Many shops and offices had let their staff off early to go to Mangere and the city was strangely quiet. Fred

---

*Her Sydney-Auckland Tasman record (for all types of aircraft) of 10½ hours didn't last long. It was cut by 1 hour and 20 minutes in 1937 by an Imperial Airways Short Empire flying boat.

had closed down his surgery in Vulcan Lane and left pinned to the door a note which said proudly: GONE TO AERODROME TO MEET JEAN.

In a crumpled suit, with a partly-buttoned old fawn cardigan, he had been standing at Mangere in the official enclosure, pacing up and down, scanning the southern sky anxiously through his binoculars, for over three hours. People said he looked a lonely figure. He had never fully come to terms with Jean's flying and he often told friends that he preferred not to hear about her flights until she was on the way. He believed that her Tasman risk was unnecessary and, until news came from New Plymouth that she had made her landfall, he had been restless and edgy with worry.

Now the sun shone for the first time on a grey and wet day. The tiny speck his glasses had spotted had materialised into the Gull, it had landed and taxied in, its fuselage and windows glazed with the grey stains of salt spray, so close to the sea had she flown. He felt intense relief and much pride as he walked towards it. The cabin door opened and, in her white helmet and flying suit under a belted camelhair overcoat, his daughter, visibly fatigued but smiling happily, climbed briskly out of the cockpit.

Despite warning shouts from the mounted police the crowd broke through the rope barriers and swarmed round the plane, cheering and shouting her name. It was a highly emotional event that somehow excited the most phlegmatic hearts. The newsreels show that even the press photographers, then dressed like business executives in suits and waistcoats, were moved to pause in their picture-taking, lowering their cameras, standing respectfully to attention, and solemnly raising their hats high above their heads.

Jean stood momentarily on the wing, holding the flowers that had been thrust into her arms, waving as the crowd's roar rose to a new crescendo. As she stepped down Fred greeted her with a hug. But she didn't respond very affectionately, people said. She said, 'It's good to be home,' but turned her head away as he tried to kiss her, smiling instead at the cameras. Alice Carrick-Robertson, with whom Jean had stayed after she had been ill as a child, said: 'I wasn't at the aerodrome but I saw the newsreel.

When I watched the cold way she greeted her father it actually made me cry.'

The newsreels show Fred proudly trying to escort her by the arm. But she pulls free and strides away, aware only of the presence and force of the crowd – responding with practised waves and a fixed smile, distancing herself from her father. As she climbed the dais her smile was only for the cameras and the reception committee led by Auckland's mayor, Ernest Davis. Reflecting the universal relief at her safe arrival, he immediately led the crowd in a prayer of thanks for her deliverance. People stood in respectful silence with bowed heads for several seconds. Then with unconscious chauvinism characteristic of his generation of New Zealand men, Mayor Davis startled the crowd by saying: 'Jean, you are a very naughty girl and really I think you want a good spanking for giving us such a terribly anxious time here.' Paternalistically he added: 'But we glory in what you have done and we glory in your wonderful and magnificent pluck dear.'

Jean's speech was preoccupied with her pride in her achievement. 'I was able to fly from England to New Zealand in the fastest time in the history of the world,' she said. 'I think I can say that this is the very greatest moment of my life.'

'Her Serene Highness' the *New Zealand Herald* called her next morning and it spoke of the tears of thankfulness in the crowd at her safe arrival. 'The brave little beauty,' it quoted one man as shouting; 'and he wondered why his eyes became wet.'

On the dais at Mangere Jean first became aware of the implications of the media contracts she had entered into. There, behind the microphones, she was introduced to two smartly-dressed middle-aged executives, two of the country's most experienced journalists: Mr H. McD. Vincent and Mr K.H. Usmar. They had been appointed as a bodyguard to keep rival newspapermen at bay. One or other of them was rarely to be out of her sight for the next two weeks and they were to do their job with ruthless efficiency for an era when chequebook journalism was in its infancy.

But Jean had already begun to make money – £225 had been collected for her at half-a-crown a time from parking fees. And within a short time of her arrival the Gull, with the New

Zealand flag and the emblems of three South American air forces on its rudder, had been locked away in a hangar out of sight of prying eyes. It was to be another source of revenue: a store in downtown Auckland had arranged to put it on display.

With the siren of an escorting police car wailing, Jean made a triumphant entry into the city. Along the fourteen-mile route cars pulled off the road and the occupants stood and cheered as she sped past led by a police motorcycle.

At the Grand Hotel the now familiar cables were pouring in. In London *The Times* called her Tasman flight 'an act of deliberate courage'. The story even made the front pages in American newspapers for the first time. In France it was splashed exuberantly. In Sydney a well-known member of the late Charles Kingsford Smith's crew, John Stannage, declared that her Tasman journey ranked with Smithy's great 1928 trans-Pacific flight. 'She has set a mark that will take men a great deal to equal,' he added. In newspapers everywhere she was being hailed as one of the outstanding aviators of the world, her name now linked with the two greats, Amy Johnson and Amelia Earhart in a revered triumvirate of airwomen.

Although exhausted from nearly two weeks of flight stress and lack of sleep, Jean found the strength to go that evening to a big Auckland cinema to deliver the first of the talks demanded by her theatrical contract.

She was now obsessed by money and the need to seize every opportunity to make it, including a large number of lucrative advertising deals to promote products from Shell petrol and domestic radios to tea and breakfast foods. No source of revenue was too small. For the first time she even began to charge for her autograph. It was announced that the books should be left in town halls for signing at a shilling a time. They were to pour in in their hundreds.

However, the tour began to affect her health. People started to notice how strained and pale she looked behind the outward radiance. On the journey to and from the Auckland cinema, to minimise the public's view of her, she was hustled by her minder, Mr Vincent, into a car. The crowds lining the streets hoping for a glimpse didn't know that she was approaching the end of her tether. Yet because of her desperate need for money she drove herself on. 'As I was entirely dependent on myself,' she wrote, 'it was of the utmost importance that I should more than clear expenses to enable me to continue my flying activities.'

But her phenomenal reserves of stamina were nearly exhausted. Although she spent her first weekend sleeping and resting, by Monday morning, when the grinding lecture tour began in earnest, she was not her normal resilient self. She had never before known commercial pressures like these which demanded that her bodyguards intercept every phone call to her room – and later those made by rival journalists to Fred as well. Even when out shopping she had to be accompanied.

On the Monday the pressures began to mount. Four secretaries had to be installed in the hotel to handle the mountain of letters and telegrams. To help her reply to every message the government offered her a free postal facility. There was the inevitable huge civic reception at which she was presented with a testimonial scroll which said: 'You have rendered to the Empire a service which upholds the highest traditions of pioneering endeavour.' Fred, who was there in the packed town hall, was invited to speak. 'Although she is a very famous pilot,' he said, 'to me she is just my little girl.'

As the latest round of adulation continued there is evidence, however, that Jean was at last beginning to tire of the endless platitudes and the sound of her own voice repeating to seas of faces, in cinema after cinema, the identical phrases that described the details of her latest flight 'linking the Motherland with its farthest-flung dominion'. For the first time she actually wanted to run away from it all. But she knew she was trapped. She expressed something of the isolation she now felt in her memoirs: 'I have experienced the cool, rarefied atmosphere of the Olympic heights where the famous dwell in lonely solitude.'

For the first time she began to say she was tired of flying, tired of the constant engine noise and the back-strain from long hours at the controls. She refused an offer by the government to be flown on her lecture tour round the country, saying she would prefer to go by train.

Meanwhile a nationwide public subscription, to which individuals and local bodies were encouraged to contribute, again brought some bitter opposition. Nonetheless it produced £2,000 for her. It more than paid for the Gull. And from an insurance policy in which she had prudently invested before leaving London, she now collected a further £350. In her memoirs she conceded: 'I was earning quite a lot of money at last.'

But it was not bringing much happiness. Indeed the evidence of her prosperity was now about to precipitate a showdown at long last with Fred Truman over the money she had owed him for four years. His pleas had been renewed soon after her arrival and were growing more persistent. He had begun to write pressing letters and to telephone her hotel. She ignored him, screwing up his letters and refusing to take his calls.

His patience finally exhausted, Fred decided the time had come for more drastic measures. He went to see her father and poured out the whole story. Horrified, Fred Batten called Jean to see him and asked her if the debt was real. She confirmed that it was.

What happened next was described to me by Fred Truman's brother Reg. 'Mr Batten told Jean that, as he saw it, the family honour was involved. He was apparently pretty blunt. He said she was not going to leave the country until she repaid the debt. And to make sure she did something about it he set up a meeting at the Grand Hotel between Jean, Fred and himself. Well, when my brother got there Mr Batten was waiting in the foyer but there was no sign of Jean. Eventually she came down the stairs. She had a cheque in her hand. But she virtually ignored my Fred – she just walked up to him and, without a word, thrust the cheque into his hand and walked out of the hotel. He looked at the cheque. After all that it was only for about half the amount: something like £250.

'He never pursued the rest. I think he knew when he was beaten. He was just relieved to have got anything at all, and I believe it helped him and Rose get married – by which time he'd joined the New Zealand Air Force.'

Jean was never to mention the incident. In truth she had probably never accepted Fred Truman's life-savings as a debt; it is likely that she saw him, as she did all men, as a provider and the money her due entitlement to fund her central ambitions and her contribution, as she genuinely saw it, to Empire and aviation.

Whether or not she was upset by her father's intervention there were now some developments that tellingly began to strike at her self-confidence. The New Zealand public was not this time queuing up so enthusiastically for her lectures. Where, in 1934, people had often been turned away, the cinemas now were rarely full. This was first painfully evident in Auckland. But as Jean travelled south, the poor attendances were, to her distress, repeated in Hamilton. From there she was escorted on the night express to her next engagement in Wellington by Mr Vincent. Her lecture contract required her to keep public appearances, including civic receptions and walkabouts, to a minimum, so she didn't go all the way on the train. To avoid an encounter with reporters and a large crowd of hero-worshipping fans at Wellington's Thorndon station she was taken off the express at the small township of Paekakariki, thirty miles up the line, and driven secretly into the city, 'half hidden behind a large hat box'. The crowd and the press were not amused. According to the *New Zealand Observer* 'only eight people including a reporter and a photographer saw her arrive at the Hotel St George and saw the smile she bestowed on those favoured few. If Auckland people saw little of Miss Batten ... Wellington saw even less. And at the hotel she was kept in comparative seclusion.'

She managed, however, to call on the Minister of Defence, Mr Fred Jones, who had been at Mangere to welcome her on behalf of the government. The junior secretary in the minister's office at the time was Mary Dennehy, who is still working in New Zealand's Parliament House. 'I'll never forget her arriving in the office in her white flying suit,' she recalled. 'Looking completely sophisticated and glamorous, she sat herself down on a couch and demanded a gin and tonic. She then told us she was "a perfect size 12" and would like to be outfitted at government expense in some new clothes. We were rather taken aback. I'm afraid she didn't get them.'

The strategy to keep Jean out of public view proved badly

counterproductive; the less that was seen of her the less was reported to maintain public interest and attendances at her lectures. By the time she began her South Island tour in Christchurch in late October she was visibly depressed. She was also beginning to detect a falling off of the veneration to which she had become accustomed.

Wakefield's man in New Zealand, Bob Smillie, was a close observer. 'She didn't get on with the hotel staff,' he said. 'She behaved as if she was Lord God Almighty and felt they didn't pay her enough respect. On top of that she was depressed by the poor attendances. She began to think the tour was a flop. It was that – the sense that things were no longer going her way – which, I'm convinced, precipitated her final breakdown.'

My Life contains, for Jean, frank admission of the impending disaster: 'I had to gather my remaining strength ... When I set off I knew that I was overdrawing on reserve energy, but insisted on continuing.' In Christchurch she finally ground to a halt. Alarmed at the state she was in – increasingly depressed and rapidly slowing down – Bob Smillie, who was on tour with her, consulted the senior government official seconded to the party and they decided that a doctor should see her urgently. Reluctantly Jean at last admitted that she wasn't well. The doctor saw immediately that she was both physically exhausted and in a highly nervous state; she had lost a stone in weight since leaving England. He advised cancellation of the lecture tour and complete rest.

Her collapse was reported in the newspapers in one brief sentence which said that 'to avoid any further strain' she had been ordered to rest by her medical advisers and would be leaving at once for a long holiday. At the prompting of Bob Smillie, who quickly got word to the Prime Minister, Michael Savage, the holiday was provided at government expense. She went off to the west coast of the South Island and spent much of November resting at the Franz Josef Glacier and trout fishing on Lake Wakatipu. Bob Smillie persuaded his wife, Doris, to come down from their home in Wellington to be with Jean during her convalescence. Doris told us: 'She was extremely quiet and withdrawn during those weeks, I remember. Always very courteous, but I didn't get much out of her. She never spoke of how she felt or confided anything personal at all.'

Jean's breakdown quickly had Ellen aboard a ship steaming to the southern hemisphere. It was agreed that, when she was better, Jean would sail to Sydney to meet her and they would return to New Zealand for Christmas. Jean wanted to see Beverley again. Although the copious correspondence they exchanged, according to her memoirs, during this period was destroyed, it is clear that she believed herself deeply in love with him and that her long-term plans, about which she was consistently evasive to the press, were to give up long-distance flying, marry him and settle down in Australia.

Before leaving New Zealand her morale was given a boost by the news that her latest flight had brought her three further international honours. For the second year running the Royal Aero Club had awarded her the Britannia Trophy 'for the most meritorious flight of the year by a British subject'. Then came word that she had been given the Segrave Trophy 'for the most outstanding demonstration during the year of the possibilities of transport on land, water or air'. And a few days later she was excited to hear that for the second year running she had been awarded the American Harmon Trophy for the 'greatest flight of 1936 by an airwoman'. She had shared it with Amelia Earhart the previous year; this time it was hers outright.

The awards received little publicity in New Zealand, where her illness had abruptly removed her from public view. Her face had disappeared from the newspapers and her voice from radio. She had gone to earth again, distressed at the failure of her remarkable stamina and at the serious financial loss from the abandonment of the tour. It is significant that in her exceedingly detailed memoirs she chose to ignore this tour completely, though it was, in effect, the celebration of her greatest achievement.

She did, however, record her reunion with Beverley in Sydney in late November while waiting for Ellen's ship to arrive. Her memoirs confirm that it was a deeply happy occasion. 'They were golden days, those few we spent together, each one shining in my memory like a highly polished jewel. Time seemed to stand still. We made wonderful plans for the future;

with the supreme confidence of youth we were quite sure they would materialise.

'I had just turned twenty-seven and had everything anyone could desire: youth, perfect health, good looks – and fame. I had realised my greatest ambition and Dame Fortune was smiling on me. And now, although few people knew it, I was deeply in love with someone who shared my enthusiasm for flying and with whom I knew I would be happy to go through life. It seemed almost too good to be true that a mere mortal should be so lucky. And so it was,' she added sombrely, 'as events were to prove.'

Her memoirs are the only source of information on those carefree weeks. They spent the days, during some of which Beverley took leave from the airline, sailing, picnicking in the Blue Mountains, flying up country in his Puss Moth and discussing the married life they planned during long evenings in restaurants and nightclubs. 'How handsome he looked in his navy blue captain's uniform. I felt very proud that I had inspired him to take up flying as a career.' But there were, she confesses, some major psychological difficulties for Beverley coping in public with someone so constantly recognised as she was.

'I remember how annoyed he was on one occasion when, as we entered a nightclub and were being shown to our table, the band struck up "See the Conquering Hero Comes", at which many people rose to their feet and applauded. Beverley's blushes were mercifully hidden in the soft lights. But I promptly got the giggles – which was interpreted by the band leader as pleasure, for he promptly played the tune again.

'I leant across to Beverley and whispered, "How do you know it's for me? Maybe they're playing it for you – it would be quite appropriate!"

'He was not amused and I spent the rest of the evening trying to humour him while shaking hands with well-wishers and signing menu cards.

'"I supposed I'll have to get used to sharing you," he murmured, adding rather bitterly, "to being known as Jean Batten's husband."

'I had to laugh and replied, "Is that such a terrible fate to reflect upon? You know, there are lots of men – some of them here tonight – who would consider it quite a pleasant prospect."

'To which he replied, "That's the trouble, you don't understand how much I would hate to lose you now."

' "Don't be so morbid," I said. "You won't lose me for at least fifty years" – at which he laughed and I added, "Besides, all this adulation will soon die down when another heroine comes along."

' "That's just where you're wrong, Jeannie," he said. "There's only one girl like you – for you're one in a million and all those people know it as well as I do. There never will be another you." '

When I first read this preposterous dialogue I thought Jean had been writing tongue-in-cheek. But as my knowledge of her grew, and the scale of her ego became more apparent, I came to understand that, in matters affecting her self-opinion, she never joked. Once in a Sydney shop, Nancy Bird Walton recalled, she was with Jean when she wrote a cheque. 'She turned to me and said, with total seriousness, "When they see the signature they won't cash it, you know, they'll frame it." '

Nancy added, 'I would be surprised if a man ever got very close to Jean.' But Jean does appear to have believed that she was in love with Beverley. Indeed her memoirs hardly mention Ellen's eventual arrival from England. She tells us instead that, when they later set sail together for New Zealand, Beverley flew his Stinson airliner over the ship in salute as he flew off north on a scheduled service to Brisbane. 'And so it was,' she wrote, 'that although I returned to New Zealand, I left my heart in Australia.'

In New Zealand they went to ground for three months and there is today little trace of their movements during this period, when Jean was clearly at a major crossroads. In her memoirs she wrote vaguely: 'The weeks passed pleasantly enough and my time was fully occupied', but how she did not record. Curiously, in view of her parents' estrangement, she and Ellen and Fred were to spend Christmas together. They went back to Rotorua, where Jean was honoured with another traditional Maori reception at which she was given the name *Hinerangi*, Daughter of the Skies. Later she and her parents went to stay at a beach cottage at Maketu in the nearby Bay of Plenty. Since Ellen and

Fred's separation was still not public knowledge, the sight of them all together must have helped maintain the impression, important at least to the women, of an outwardly happy marriage. Indeed they went to the extraordinary length, to help foster the lie, of arranging an adjoining flat, its front door directly opposite Fred's, in Courtville Mansions in central Auckland.

This must have cramped Fred's style for he was by no means lacking in feminine company and, at the age of fifty-seven, was conducting a number of affairs. One of them was remarkable for the regularity of its consummation: every Friday evening soon after the last patient had left, on the floor of his dental surgery.

Fred had a much deeper, long-term relationship with an Auckland woman, Gertrude Perry. More than twenty years younger than him, she remained single and devoted over thirty years of her life to him as he passed from middle to old age. At one time she had been his dental nurse. She used to visit him at Courtville Mansions but, because Fred was still technically married to Ellen, they never lived together. Someone who knew Fred well said: 'There were certain nights when you just didn't go to Courtville – if you didn't want short shrift!'

Jean spent the whole summer out of the public eye. 'Lazing away the hours, sunbathing on the golden sands of wide beaches and swimming in the clear blue waters, I let the world roll by for a little and felt utter contentment,' she wrote in *My Life*. She was now under some pressure 'from many of my friends' to keep things that way by giving up flying while she was still alive. '"Why not rest on your laurels and settle down?" they suggested. "Why go on until your luck deserts you?"' On which she comments: 'I wanted very much to settle down in my own country and lead a calm peaceful life, but in my heart I knew only too well that I was destined to be a wanderer. I seemed born to travel and, in flying, I found the combination of the two things which meant everything to me: the intoxicating drug of speed and freedom to roam the earth. In my innermost thoughts I knew the fire of adventure that burned within me was not yet quenched, and that urge was drawing me on – to what?'

Her memoirs tell a different story: that all she wanted was

marriage to Beverley. It is clear she was missing him badly. 'Had there been an air service, we could have met and the blow that fate struck might have been averted.'

In every letter he wrote Beverley demanded to know what was keeping her in New Zealand. By the middle of February 1937 she could wait no longer: she booked a passage for herself, Ellen and the Gull on the liner *Awatea*. Shortly before sailing she got a letter from Beverley to whom she had written with the ship's arrival time. 'Isn't that just my luck,' she quotes him as replying. 'On that day I have to take the Stinson to Brisbane. But I'll be back in Sydney the day after.'

But in mid-Tasman she was delighted to get a long telegram saying he had managed to rearrange his roster. Instead of staying overnight in Brisbane he had been given permission by the airline to return on a southbound service the same day, flying as co-pilot. The telegram ended: SEE YOU AT MASCOT.

The *Awatea* arrived in Sydney on 19 February. At the dockside reporters questioned her about new rumours – they never ceased through her years of fame – that she was secretly engaged to be married. It was, of course, true this time but the press didn't know of her friendship with Beverley. So she denied it, saying, 'There is no truth whatever in the rumours. I am going to devote my life to aviation.'

She took Ellen to the Hotel Australia then hurried out to Mascot to receive the Gull when it arrived from the ship and to await Beverley's plane which was scheduled to land at 5.30 pm. He had booked a restaurant table for that evening. 'Just before it was due I walked over to the tarmac to watch it land,' she wrote. 'Talking with a group of friends I didn't notice the minutes slipping by until someone came out of the office and said, "The Stinson's late. Go and have a cup of tea while you're waiting, Jean. I'll let you know when it's sighted."'

She went across to the clubhouse she knew so well. The Stinson, she assumed, had been delayed by a headwind. But 'the minutes stretched into hours until eventually darkness engulfed the aerodrome. And although a flarepath was lit everyone knew without saying a word that by now the Stinson was down somewhere.'

Throughout that long night she paced between the clubhouse and the office of Airlines of Australia. She had such confidence in Beverley that it didn't at first occur to her that the problem was other than a forced landing in some remote place and that, before long, his cheerful Australian voice would come reassuringly through on the phone. But it didn't. By 3 o'clock in the morning the last of the oil flares on the runway had flickered out. With it seemed to go much of the earlier hope. By dawn the Stinson had still not been found anywhere along the 450-mile route.

It was not to be located for nine days when, against all the odds, some survivors were found beside its burnt-out wreckage. The days of anguish and uncertainty were to be among the most heart-rending of Jean's life. But she was never to speak of it to anyone, sharing the torment only with Ellen.

CHAPTER 17

'A Dagger in my Heart' (1937)

The loss of the Stinson airliner in February 1937 remains one of the most emotional events in Australian aviation history. Fifty years later it was still being remembered with reunions of the rescuers and a television drama which movingly recreated the tragedy.

By today's standards the three-engined eight-seater aircraft was small. But when Airlines of Australia, a forerunner of Ansett, proudly introduced them on the intercity routes in the mid-thirties, they represented a phenomenal advance in comfort and speed. Cruising at 170 miles an hour the squat, slightly sinister-looking monoplanes with their smart blue logo had become a familiar sight on their twice-daily schedules up and down the coast between Sydney and Brisbane. They were so punctual farmers were said to check the time by the unmistakeable snarling whine of their engines.

But, on Friday 19 February, the 1 pm Brisbane-Sydney service failed to arrive at its scheduled intermediate stop at Lismore in northern New South Wales. It hadn't caused much concern at the time because a fierce storm had been raging in the area; it had been assumed that the pilot had decided to avoid the 4,000-foot MacPherson Mountains on the aircraft's direct track to Lismore, and flown down the coast to the east of the ranges. However, despite nearly seventy reported sightings, the City of Brisbane with its five passengers, flown by Captain Rex Boyden, had mysteriously disappeared.

The aircraft was normally operated by one pilot, but on this day Beverley Shepherd was being allowed to return to Sydney as supernumerary pilot – virtually as a passenger – to enable him to make his dinner date with Jean. He was occupying the right-hand seat on the small flight deck, but playing little part in the operation of the aircraft which, unlike most other Stinsons in the fleet, had not yet been equipped with radio.

A huge air search began at both ends of the route. Soon, over forty civilian and Air Force planes were scouring the Stinson's flight path across southern Queensland and down the eastern side of New South Wales. One of the first search pilots into the air at daybreak from Mascot was Jean Batten. For the whole nine days she flew the Gull up and down the coast like someone possessed, driving herself to the limits of her endurance.

'She was the first out every morning and the last back every evening,' said Nancy Bird Walton. 'She pushed herself like never before. I had a Leopard Moth by then and she came up to me at Mascot and said, accusingly, "Why aren't you taking part in the search, Nancy?" and I had to tell her bluntly that I just couldn't afford it. I didn't have the money to fly back and forth day after day along 500 miles of coast. In any case almost every spare plane in New South Wales was already out looking. All I could do was lend her my maps. But I don't think she understood. She just seemed deeply resentful that more people weren't out looking for her boyfriend.'

Nancy was struck by how little emotion Jean displayed. 'Her self-control was quite astonishing. She was calm and quite coldly analytical about the whole thing, conducting the search grimly and methodically. No one would have known that she was in love with the co-pilot.'

'Although the newspapers reported that Jean had joined the search they did not know her reason. Why, when in a few days they were due to announce their engagement to the world, she had to conceal her love for one of the crew, seems hard to understand. But to Jean and Ellen it was simply none of the public's business. And because it wasn't she wove into the Stinson narrative of My Life the sad understatement: 'One of the pilots was a great friend of mine.' And then, cautiously: 'He was a very skilful airman and I thought highly of him.' It was the nearest she ever got to a public disclosure of the most important man ever to enter her life.

In her memoirs much later, where she occasionally dropped her guard, she poured out the tragic truth. 'During the fruitless search I seemed to be living in a vacuum, shut off from the outside world ... in a dream with only one object: to find the Stinson and Beverley.'

Misled by numerous sightings of other aircraft on the fateful day, the search organisers had directed the heaviest concentration of aeroplanes to scour the Broken Bay and Hawkesbury River Valley area in what would have been the last few minutes of the Stinson's flight into Sydney. But increasingly the belief was growing that it had plunged into the sea, and an oil slick found on the day of its disappearance added credence to the theory. After five days the search was abandoned. Jean, angry at the decision, refused to give up. One of the few pilots now left in the search, she pressed on determinedly, pouring petrol into the Gull day after day, flying out of Sydney, Newcastle and Brisbane. 'Although I was feeling tired and disheartened it never occurred to me to give up.' And occasionally, as she flew low over the tangled hills, densely cloaked in eucalypt forest, circling through pink smoke and dust haze, her heart would lift momentarily. 'I would see what looked like a smoke signal and fly hopefully towards it – only to find it was an isolated bush fire ... it seemed quite incredible that an airliner with five passengers and a crew of two could have vanished so completely.'

In Newcastle she stayed for a few nights with one of the town's most prominent families, the Rankins. Their daughter Sue (now Sue Duval), whom I went to see, told me they had no idea that Jean was searching for the Stinson because her boyfriend was on it. 'She never mentioned it,' said Sue. 'Yet day after day she would go out at five in the morning and come back to the house after dark exhausted. Yet she behaved as if she was just helping out on a search for some anonymous aircraft. Wasn't it extraordinary?'

On the ninth day, Sunday 28 February, she flew dispiritedly back to Sydney intending to resume the search from Mascot at first light next morning. She spent the night being consoled by Ellen in the room they shared at the Hotel Australia. Driving out to Mascot next day she was stunned to see a billboard: WRECKAGE OF STINSON FOUND: TWO SURVIVORS.

'I felt my heart turn over,' she wrote. 'An icy hand seemed to clutch at my throat as hope and despair struggled for supremacy in my mind.' In a daze she stopped the car and bought a newspaper. But she couldn't bear to read it immediately, wanting to postpone the moment, prolong the hope. She threw the paper on to the back seat, she wrote, 'for I could not bear to look at it just then'.

For nearly twenty minutes she drove on, her mind racing wildly, tense with the now self-imposed suspense, afraid of what she might read. But as the aerodrome came in sight she knew she could delay the moment no longer. She parked the car and reached for the paper. 'As I forced myself to read it,' she wrote, 'it seemed almost as if I deliberately drove a dagger into my heart.'

The Stinson had been found in deep tropical rainforest 3,000 feet up on a steep ridge of the MacPherson Ranges on the Queensland-New South Wales border. It had been discovered by a young bushman, Bernard O'Reilly, who ran a remote guesthouse in the mountains. Hearing reports from farmers in the foothills that they had seen the airliner go over, flying dangerously low in and out of the cloud base, he had set out on his own to search the jungle ridges and ravines. He had found the wreckage and, beside it, gaunt and hollow-eyed, two survivors – both passengers, who had kept themselves alive on water and berries. One of them had a badly fractured maggot-infested leg.

The Stinson had caught fire within seconds of the crash and only its twisted metal framework remained. The two other passengers and the two pilots had been unable to get out in time: they had died in the fire which burned for several hours and their blackened bodies lay in the wreckage. Not far away O'Reilly found the body of the fifth passenger; he had survived the crash but died of injuries and exposure after falling down a waterfall trying to get help.

The last minutes of Beverley's life were described by the surviving passengers (who two days later were carried out of the mountains on stretchers by a small army of volunteers). They had been able to see into the cockpit from the Stinson's cabin through a window in the flight-deck door. As the aircraft had approached the mountains, they had looked out and been concerned at the startling proximity of the treetops flashing by below. 'I was about to press the button to call the attention of the pilot,' one of the passengers said, 'when I looked through the glass panel in the cockpit door. Boyden was conversing unconcernedly with Shepherd so I didn't think there could be anything to be alarmed about.'

His reassurance was shortlived. 'Within seconds,' the subsequent accident report said, 'the trees were only a foot below the aircraft and the view through the windows was suddenly filled by a heavily timbered mountain slope, just off the starboard wing. Another glance toward the cockpit showed that the co-pilot's expression had changed to one of urgency and he was reaching across to manipulate something with his left hand. The Stinson lurched to starboard, then there was a splintering crash as it rode over the top of a large tree and ... fell through the timber to the ground ...'*

The Stinson had been caught in a powerful downdraught, in the northern lee of the mountains, created by a 70-miles-an-hour wind on the edge of the cyclone. The aircraft's three engines at full power had been unable to climb against it.

In a suburban street beside Mascot aerodrome that morning of Monday 1 March, Jean sat alone in the car staring at Beverley's name among the list of the dead. Her horror was profound and for a long time she was immobilised with shock, scarcely aware of the crackle of the engines of the light aircraft

---

*'The Stinson Story', *Aviation Safety Digest*, Air Safety Investigation Branch, Australian Department of Transport (1976).

doing early morning circuits overhead as rare tears streamed down her cheeks. With the cruel news in her lap she sat there, Beverley's presence still unbearably close with reminders of him all around her in the car in which they had shared some of her life's happiest moments.

In a moving passage in her memoirs she described how she eventually started the car again and turned round to drive back to Ellen: 'I felt numb with grief and have no recollection of driving back to the city; only of rushing up the stairs and flinging open the door, knowing that mother would be there waiting for me to return, as she always was when I needed help.

'This time she did not speak, just held out her arms to me and in a flash I was in them sobbing my heart out. I remember her stroking my hair and murmuring softly, "Never mind little one, some day you'll find someone else," but at that moment I thought I never would.'

Beverley was buried where he died, high up in the subtropical mountain rainforest on the Queensland border. He and his fellow captain, Rex Boyden, and the two dead passengers, were laid in a communal grave beside the contorted metal skeleton of the Stinson. A small cairn of stones, with a simple cross of metal rods crudely fixed together, was placed on top. It is a lonely and inaccessible place, lying half forgotten, with still visible fragments of the wreckage, at the head of Christmas Creek, half-an-hour's drive from the southern Queensland town of Beaudesert. It takes all day to struggle up there and back from the road-end and the crude track climbs steeply in places on a gradient of one-in-one – as difficult of access as the day Bernard O'Reilly stumbled on it more than half a century ago.

In *My Life*, Jean was to lay a smokescreen over the tragedy, dismissing it matter-of-factly: 'a young bushman made the discovery and heroically rescued two passengers who were the only survivors.' However Beverley's death, people said, was one of the most traumatic events in her life. Nancy Bird Walton said: 'Mrs Batten told me later that Jean would never be the same again. Of course it was kept such a secret that very few of us knew of the depth of the relationship. And because it wasn't supposed to be public knowledge none of us went to the hotel to try and comfort her: I think we thought it would have been an intrusion; with her mother there she wouldn't have needed anybody else.

'It was a foregone conclusion that they would marry', Nancy added. 'Years later Jean told me: "I nearly became an Australian."'

Esther Mather agreed: 'I think that Bev Shepherd would have been the ideal person for Jean. I think his death was the original tragedy of her life.'

'It was, in truth, a double tragedy,' said Sir Peter Masefield. 'For it led to her enforced return to the smothering influence of the Machiavellian Ellen.'

If we are to believe what Jean wrote forty years later, she cared very deeply for Beverley. And, from all the evidence, it seems likely that, had he survived, they would have married in Sydney sometime during 1937. Indeed Jean was many years later to tell a friend in New Zealand that wedding presents had begun to arrive – but had later been stolen by a burglar.

Whether the marriage would have worked is another matter. There would have been the immediate and formidable impediment of Ellen – and she was to live for nearly thirty more years – who would have been a powerful and threatening force in the inevitable triangle. It is doubtful whether the generous, easygoing nature of Beverley, himself reputed to have been a highly indulged 'mother's boy', would have been a match for the dominion of his wife and mother-in-law who were, in a sense, already married to each other. All the evidence suggests that he would have come off a poor third. To have done better would have required a radical change in Jean's abnormal relationship with her mother, which Ellen would undoubtedly have resisted with every emotional weapon at her command.

The marriage might well have been at risk for another reason also; there would immediately have been a power-sharing problem between Jean and Beverley. With her boundless egocentricity, her tendency to exploit the opposite sex, her desperate need to be the centre of the universe, and to be treated as someone exceptional, Jean could never have been easy to live with, and one wonders whether Beverley could have handled it. How long, as an attractive and popular personality in his own right, would he have tolerated the public role of 'Mr

Batten'? From Jean's accounts of the adulation in the shadows of which he moved, it is apparent that he hated it. Yet public applause would always have been necessary to Jean's psyche.

Would she really have settled down, abandoned flying and reared Beverley's children? Might she have used the marriage as an escape from Ellen's tyranny, as many saw it? Would she have repeated the family pattern, ignoring her sons to develop a new symbiosis with a daughter of her own? The subsequent events of her life suggest that, whatever the consequences to her marriage, she would always have needed both Ellen and hero-worship.

In Sydney, in the late summer of 1937, as she tried to bury her grief, her love focused again on Ellen. They moved out of the Hotel Australia and took a flat at one of the beach suburbs; nobody who knew her at that time could recall where. As they always did when something was too painful to bear, the Battens retreated from the mainstream of life; Jean even stopped going out to the flying club at Mascot. Astonishingly, according to her memoirs, 'We did not discuss the disaster or any of the subsequent reports.' Perhaps trying to pretend that it hadn't happened made it more tolerable. As an antidote to sorrow they drugged themselves with sun, lying for hours on the beach and going for lonely picnics up into the Blue Mountains, never speaking of the Stinson and rarely mentioning Beverley's name. But the pain did not go away. 'There seemed an unreality about everything,' she wrote. 'I spent each day trying to convince myself that it was all true – not a horrible nightmare from which I could hope to awaken.'

Despite the acuteness of her depression, she made the effort to visit the Shepherd family at Darling Point. Ivy Graves, who waited at table during these visits, remembered her coming and recalled that she made the effort to put on a smile for the benefit of Mrs Shepherd who had been deeply affected by the tragedy. 'She was never the same again,' Ivy said. 'Beverley had been her whole world. She idolised him. I never saw her cry. But she just seemed slowly to waste away and a couple of years later she died – I'm sure of a broken heart.'

Describing one of her visits, Jean wrote: 'I held my breath when I was shown a tree in the garden on which Beverely had carved his name when a boy ... I marvelled at the courage and composure of his mother. My intention had been to console her – but the reverse happened: we just sat together on a bench in their lovely garden holding hands and looking out over the wide blue sweep of the harbour.'

In her memoirs Jean describes how her persistent grief and lassitude began to worry Ellen. 'One day mother looked up when I entered the room and said, "You must try and take a grip on yourself: you don't want the press to get hold of this do you?"' The thought that her love for Beverley, and the way she had been demolished by his death, could be splashed across the newspapers, was too shocking to contemplate. 'So I now tried very hard to master my grief,' she wrote.

As a challenge to her diminished self-confidence she decided, probably with Ellen's persuasion, to accept an invitation to give an Anzac Day address at St Mark's Church in Sydney. She took as her subject 'Faith and the Elimination of Fear', commenting, 'All my life I had believed in faith as indispensable if one were to achieve success in any undertaking.' There is no record of the address but it would almost certainly have been illustrated with some of her own narrow escapes from death in the air – in all of which she was convinced she owed her salvation in large measure to the fervour of her prayers at the time.

On all her long-distance flights Jean wore round her neck a gold and enamel medallion given to her by Ellen. On the back were inscribed two verses from the 139th Psalm. But Ellen must have quoted them from memory for she got the psalm wrong, calling it the 138th, and misquoted the words: *If I take my wings early in the morning and dwell in the uttermost parts of the sea, Even there also shall thy hand lead me and thy right hand shall hold me.* For some inexplicable reason she had rewritten the most famous line of all: *If I take the wings of the morning* ...

Newspaper reports of her great flights frequently referred to the importance Jean attached to the medallion. But she was not, in truth, a deeply religious person. However, in the 1930s, it was helpful to her public persona to be seen as a woman for whom faith was important. Hers was a faith in God the Father rather than God the Son – a belief in cosmic forces rather than in committed Christianity. 'Faith in God and confidence in oneself. That's my philosophy,' she once said in an interview. In none of her writing or correspondence are there clues to suggest that she was in any way devout. She appears to have drawn on the comfort that religion offered in some of her worst physical and emotional crises. Her belief in an afterlife focused principally on the hope it raised of permanent reunion with Ellen. She went to church intermittently, usually Anglican, but with pragmatic facility was equally prepared to accept Catholic communion. Before one such occasion, to a friend who said she would not, as a Protestant, be welcome, she replied: 'The priest will not dare to refuse Jean Batten.'

Someone who knew her well said: 'It would be fair to say, I think, that she went to church in situations where she felt it was expected of someone of her significance – that she should set an example. It was never something she sustained; she could drop it instantly for long periods of her life. Her religious face was really part of her chameleon character. Certainly she was much too selfish and self-centred ever to have qualified as a genuine Christian. But she did believe most emphatically that, as one of the world's chosen people, the Almighty was watching over her. And one has to agree that for much of her life, in terms of her own preservation, He certainly was.'

While Jean was still in the grip of despair in that Australian autumn of 1937, John and Madeleine Batten and their daughter Penny, now four, passed through Sydney. They had grown dissatisfied with lotus-eating in Tahiti and were on their way to live in New Zealand. John went to see Ellen – the last time they were ever to meet – but it was arranged in such a way that he would be spared the embarrassment of an encounter with Jean; their rift was to continue unhealed. In any case, Jean would not have wanted John and Madeleine to see her acute depression.

During most of the eight months she stayed on in Australia, now unsure what to do with her life, she took to driving off to lonely places around Sydney where she would sit in the car for long periods, brooding. One of these spots was the high rocky point on the southern head of the harbour entrance where she would park near the lighthouse. Sitting there one evening, looking across at the lights of the Sydney Harbour bridge, she claims to have tried desperately to put some meaning back into her life.

'There was nothing to keep me in Australia now and it seemed that the only hope I had of recovering from the dreadful blow ... was to go away from the city in which I had been so happy and where, now, everything reminded me of Beverley.' She thought of going back to New Zealand but somehow her homeland had become too small and provincial for her. It was England that called again: 'I realised how very homesick I felt for the country where I had learnt to fly and been given the chance to prove myself.'

The turning point, she wrote, came one day in September 1937 when Ellen drew her attention to a newspaper report that Jimmy Broadbent was planning an imminent attack on her England-Australia record. In her memoirs she describes how it was Ellen who persuaded her to go out to Mascot for the first time in six months and confirm the truth of the report. Ellen's pressure on her to divert her thoughts from Beverley, confirms her role, which many people suspected, as an active partner driving Jean on to new hazardous flying ventures.

Out at the flying club Jean learnt that Broadbent was indeed planning to lower her record. 'It was such a lovely day,' she wrote, 'that I took the Gull up for a flight over the Blue Mountains.' It was the first time she had flown since her search for Beverley. With the control column back in her hands ambition was rekindled, the limelight called again. Next day, in a bold gesture, she announced to the Sydney newspapers that her response to Broadbent's plan would be a counterattack on his Australia-England record of six days and nine hours. To prepare for the flight she went immediately into training with daily skipping exercises, jogging, swimming and walking. She had the Gull overhauled and, to see her daughter arrive for the first time, Ellen booked her sea-passage to England.

To try and make money out of the flight Jean went to see newspaper chief Frank Packer, whose £5,000 offer she had turned down the year before. She was taken aback to be told that she was no longer big news. 'There's an air service to England now,' he reminded her. 'Soon there'll be a worldwide network. The pioneering days are over, Jean. And the game's no longer worth the candle, is it?' He was referring to the recent disappearance of Amelia Earhart, who was never to be seen again.*

But there was one story Frank Packer was prepared to buy. '"What people want nowadays, Jean," he said, leaning across the desk, "is love interest. Now a really good love story is worth something." He paused, looking at me intently.

'I wondered how much he knew. I couldn't trust myself to speak so remained silent, for my own love story was not for sale, not for any amount of money. It was far too soon for the fragile, beautiful flower that had bloomed in my heart to be pressed and preserved for all the world to gaze at.'

In the end they compromised. Jean refused to talk about Beverley but Packer agreed to pay her 'several hundred pounds', she said, for the exclusive rights to the story of her new record attempt, provided she cabled a 200-word report every night en route. The *Daily Express* in London was to share in the rights. It was more than enough to cover the expenses of the trip and Ellen's boat fare.

Ellen sailed in September and Jean, a pad strapped to her thigh on which to write her reports, left Sydney for Darwin in the Gull on 14 October. After some weather and minor technical problems she began the record attempt from Darwin on the 19th. Despite Frank Packer's pessimism, she was still making news and the Australian papers were enthusiastically calling the flight a BATTEN-BROADBENT DUEL. Jimmy Broadbent was preparing to leave Lympne to fly in the opposite direction and Jean was

*Earhart, by then married to the wealthy American publisher George Putnam, was on a round-the-world flight in a sophisticated twin-engined Lockheed Electra accompanied by Fred Noonan, a former Pan American Airways navigator with an alcohol problem. On 2 July 1937, heading for Howland Island in mid-Pacific, they took off from Lae in New Guinea. Although Amelia's voice was heard loudly and clearly on radio at Howland Island near the end of her long flight, the Electra never arrived. Despite their radio navigation equipment, Amelia and Noonan failed to locate the tiny island and went down in the sea. Stories which have persisted ever since that they had put down on a remote atoll and were later executed by the Japanese for spying, have never been substantiated and are highly improbable.

carrying a small bunch of roses which, she told reporters, she would present to him when they met en route.

By sacrificing sleep and flying much of the way at night, and often in cloud on instruments for hours at a time, she set a cracking pace, battling her way through the rain and turbulence of the inter-tropical convergence zone over Sumatra in the dark and reaching Rangoon in only a day and a half from Darwin. In the sun's fierce heat, crossing India at 500 feet to minimise the effect of the headwind, the crepe soles of her shoes again began to melt and stick to the rudder pedals as she grew drowsy with exhaustion.

On the ground in Karachi in 'a semi-coma', she said, 'I ate a meal and fell asleep with the last mouthful. 'After only four hours in bed she flew on to Basra, Damascus and Athens. Her next intended stop was Rome but when she arrived there the weather was so bad and the cloud base so low she couldn't let down without risk of hitting the masts of the San Paolo wireless station – for which, understandably, she had a particular aversion. So she turned back to Naples. When she landed there she was in such a state of nervous and physical exhaustion she had to be lifted from the cockpit. Too ill to speak to reporters she gave her story to KLM's airport manager, a young Dutchman, Frederik Meuser, who phoned it through to Fleet Street for her. 'She is completely deaf,' he told the Sunday Express. 'We had to give her stimulants when we took her from the plane but she is a little better now. She should go to sleep but it is difficult to make her do so. She worries all the time about what the weather ahead will be like. If she could she would return to her plane and fly away this evening. Of course that is impossible. However, she says she intends to take off tomorrow whatever happens. She is not going to let the weather cheat her of her record now.'

Jean's ability to land in Naples, where all airline operations had been suspended by the weather, astonished the airport officials. But the price she paid shows starkly in her face in pictures of her slumped in the cockpit before she was lifted out. Normally, however exhausted, she could always muster a smile for the cameras and turn to face them (avoiding her profile which showed her slightly prominent chin). But the Naples pictures caught her offguard. They show her, almost unrecognisably, with sunken eyes and drawn features, looking ill and profoundly unhappy.

But overnight, she bounced back. And at dawn she was cheered to be handed a pile of cables of encouragement from England – one of them, to her utter astonishment, from Edward Walter wishing her luck. 'It touched me deeply,' she commented, obviously surprised by his generosity of spirit. There was also news of Jimmy Broadbent. She learnt that they had passed the previous day without seeing each other, between Greece and Italy – so he didn't get his roses. (Later he was to run out of fuel and force-land in the desert near Baghdad.)

On Sunday 24 October she made it across Europe, threading her way through storms, to land at Lympne in the middle of the afternoon, five days nineteen hours fifteen minutes from Australia. She had not only broken Broadbent's Australia-England solo record by fourteen hours, she had improved, against the prevailing headwinds, on her own outbound record of the previous year, and had become the first person to hold both out and back solo records at the same time.*

Sunday afternoon crowds, excited by newspaper reports of her latest triumph, lined the south coast cliffs to watch her arrive from France. At Lympne, where crowds didn't normally gather, there was a hugely enthusiastic welcome: but because she was seized with cramp and could not walk, she was carried shoulder high to the customs house where she said, 'It was a filthy flight. I never want to do it again.'

And although she didn't know it, in the crowd, but unable to get near her, were Victor Dorée and his mother. It was a touching indication of his pride in her achievement, and of his continuing fondness for her, that had led him and Mrs Dorée to drive across southern England in the hope of being able to congratulate her personally. But, as on the day at Mangere

---

*Remarkably, she was within only 4 hours of improving on the fastest time in which any type of plane had ever flown from Australia to England – the five days 15 hours record of Owen Cathcart Jones and Ken Waller on their 1934 return flight from the Melbourne Air Race in the DH 88 Comet racer (not to be confused with the equally famous post-war DH 106 Comet jet airliner).

when she had seemed hardly to notice her father, she was back on her pedestal, high on adulation. But this time she was more shatteringly exhausted, and her cramp was so painful she had to be carried back from the customs house to the Gull. Deciding that this wasn't the moment to reveal a shade from her past, Victor reluctantly hung back in the crowd. Wistfully, and one suspects still in love with her, he watched her climb slowly back into the cockpit and close the cabin door – refraining from sharing the moment of glory his generosity had helped make possible.

'For a moment,' one reporter wrote, 'her smile vanished and the lines round her mouth told of the ordeal she had been through.'

Within a few minutes she was back in the air, escorted by newspaper aeroplanes with photographers, heading for Croydon. And she still had the will and the strength to put on lipstick, rouge and eyebrow pencil for the cameras she hoped would be waiting. She was not disappointed. At Croydon she got the most feverish welcome of her life. It was on an epic scale, the sort of homecoming she had often dreamed of. It was the crowning public salute of her flying career.

'All day the cars had been streaming out of London down the Brighton Road to what, in those days, was London's international airport. North and south of the aerodrome there were major traffic jams and extra police had to be called in to control the ten thousand people who had swarmed into the airport to meet her.

Not even Jean, with Packer's discouraging words ringing in her head, had expected her flight to create such huge interest. Writing about it in *My Life* she said: 'My mother, who had always been the inspiration and the guiding light of my whole life, would be there to meet me and probably a few friends, I thought. Not for one moment did I expect the tremendous welcome which awaited me. The boundaries of the aerodrome were black with people.' As she climbed out of the cockpit on to the wing in her camelhair coat and white helmet, ten thousand voices on the tarmac, and from the roofs of the airport buildings, roared their approval. But Jean had eyes for only one person. For the first time Ellen was there to share the delicious moment. In her memoirs she was moved to write: 'Mother was one of the first to greet me and a newspaper had a photograph of her looking up at the sky, smiling, and the caption, Milton's beautiful words, "They also serve who only stand and wait".'

Holding armfuls of bouquets she said into the newsreel microphone, 'I didn't expect to break the record by such a large margin — I am glad the flight is over but am annoyed with myself for losing so much time.' And then, as she was hoisted, waving like a popstar, on to people's shoulders, she was mobbed.

'There followed the most amazing scenes ever seen at Croydon,' said one newspaper report. 'The crowd went wild, pushing and fighting to get near the aeroplane. It is estimated that 8,000 people joined the rush. The police charged the crowd, scattering the people fanwise, then formed an invincible blue wall around the official party which they escorted to the safety of the hangar.'

But the crowd felt cheated. 'A rumour was quickly circulated that Miss Batten would make a secret exit from Croydon whereupon pandemonium broke out ... People were running in every direction colliding and shouting: "Where is Jean leaving?" Women were knocked down and walked upon as a kind of frenzy seized the spectators. But they were tricked after all, only people standing six deep on the roadway seeing the official car whisk past en route to a London hotel.'

The hotel was again the exclusive Grosvenor House and, again, the suite was provided by the owner, Mr Edwards. Among the waiting flowers was a box of orchids and a generous note from Jimmy Broadbent still stranded in Iraq.*

That evening Jean and Ellen gave a brief press conference. The reporters were more interested in Jean's immediate prospects of marriage than her latest flight. Afraid that news of

---

*Broadbent's next attempt the following year also failed. Only 500 miles from Darwin he was forced down on the island of Flores in what today is Indonesia. However, later in 1938, in his Vega Gull, he broke Jean's Australia-England record, doing it in 5 days and 4 hours. He was killed in 1958 when an aircraft he was flying for a Portuguese airline disappeared over the Atlantic between Lisbon and Madeira.

her friendship with Beverley might have leaked out she didn't dare trust herself on her most sensitive and distressing subject. Not even lightheartedly would she be drawn. 'I refuse absolutely to make any statement about that,' she said firmly, returning immediately to a description of her passage through the monsoon. Adding, 'She's always too busy for romance,' Ellen cheerfully set about resurrecting the old myth of how she had funded her daughter's training. 'It was as much as I could do to manage it,' she said yet again, adding that Jean's success had ultimately been due to her Christian faith.

The story of her record flight dominated many of the front pages next day. The *Daily Express* banner headline somehow summed it all up: THE GIRL WHO HAS BEATEN ALL THE MEN. But it was to be the last time the presses would roll with her glamorous figure waving from the front pages. The era of the long-distance record-breaker was virtually over.

CHAPTER 18

The End of an Era (1937–1939)

The exploits of the stunt pilots were to recede into history faster than any of them would have believed possible.

Amy Johnson, who had resumed her maiden name and was in the process of divorcing Jim Mollison for numerous infidelities, declared publicly the week of Jean's return: 'Our job is done. Record-breakers are wanted no more. It is no longer a life's work.' Amy, whose years of enormous fame had brought her much ill health and unhappiness, was broke and looking for a job. With war threatening in Europe, and the violent images of the Spanish Civil War daily on the front pages, the aeroplane was now unhappily viewed as a vehicle of destruction. Furthermore, the world's airlines had moved out of the biplane, fabric and wicker seat era and were entering a new age of reliability with sophisticated metal monoplanes. Anyone with £195 could now buy an Imperial Airways ticket from London to Brisbane and the airline was about to introduce the luxuriously comfortable Empire Class flying boats on the Australia route; they would take longer to get there than Jean did, but would do so in considerably greater safety.

Yet she had survived where many of her famous colleagues

had lost their lives. Hinkler, Kingsford Smith, Ulm, Earhart — all were dead. Tom Campbell Black had been killed in his cockpit on the ground when, at Liverpool, a military aircraft had taxied into his little Mew Gull and its propeller had sliced into his canopy.

'It was an heroic era in its way, an almost Arthurian period in aviation,' Sir Peter Masefield recalled. 'The people who did it became legends not only in their sometimes very short lifetimes but in aviation history. There's never been anything quite like it since — space flight perhaps, but that's rather too remote. With the pilots of those little aeroplanes, battling their way through the monsoons, landing at aerodromes where anybody could go and see them and touch them, the public could identify as never before.

'Of course they didn't contribute much technically, despite their claims, to the development of the air routes. But what they did do was capture public imagination in an unbelievably successful way. They put aviation on the map and their achievements shouldn't be underrated because the public feeling that helped foster confidence in aviation was developed from that.

'Jean Batten was undoubtedly one of the best of them,' Sir Peter said. 'In those days the fact that she was a woman made it doubly meritorious. And she survived because she planned all her flights so meticulously — they had the thoroughness and professionalism of a modern airline operation; that was rare among the amateur pilots of the thirties. Given that, obviously, there can be no comparison with a modern professional pilot, I think history will rank her as a competent, determined — and, eventually, experienced and skilful — amateur.'

Her success to a high degree, Sir Peter claimed, resulted from what he called her 'all-consuming obsession' to fly from England to New Zealand. 'Between 1930 and 1936 it dominated her life to the exclusion of everything else — except the influence of her mother. And determination to succeed in that one objective enabled her to overcome the obvious fact that she was not a natural pilot. Indeed, she learnt the hard way — through two disastrous Australia attempts — to become reasonably adept at long-distance light aeroplane flying and, eventually, to modify her earlier obsessive "press on regardless" approach. I would rate her also as one of the great women navigators of the world.'

Jean was to fly again but only on short trips around Europe. She was never to embark on another record attempt. Her name dropped out of the headlines as swiftly as it had arrived there. Her period of fame had lasted only four crowded years, from 1933 to 1937. And she had achieved it all with only five successful long-distance flights involving less than sixty-five days of flying. But these years were to sustain her emotionally for the rest of her life. She had just turned twenty-eight.

In the two precarious years before Europe was plunged into war, she made the most of the public's rapidly fading memories of her fame. She went live on one of the BBC's early current affairs television programmes and broadcast to eight million people on radio. Her effigy was cast in wax at Madame Tussaud's. The Gull went on exhibition at Selfridge's store. For a few days she was followed about by photographers. She embarked again, but now for the last time, on a nonstop round of banquets, balls, lunches and receptions in London's high society. At none of them was Ellen ever seen.

The Lord Mayor of London invited her to tea at the Mansion House with Lord Wakefield. She went to the House of Commons to address the Conservative Air Committee, impressing the seventy MPs with 'her disarming modesty and charm', as she described at great length her flight to New Zealand. Later she was the only woman at a banquet in her honour at the Royal Aero Club where she was thrilled to be presented with the club's Britannia Trophy and its gold medal. The *Evening Standard* said: 'The hardened pioneers of the air, accustomed to listening to long-distance fliers' stories, broke into round after round of applause.'

Her fame and her ability to hold audiences with accounts of her flights had her, for a few heady months, in such demand as a speaker she had to hire an agent. As a result she was soon guest of honour at scores of major functions from the Brighton veteran road race dinner to the Variety Club's annual ball where she proposed the toast to the famous singer Gracie Fields. Her face had moved from the front pages to the society columns but she was firmly back among the rich and famous, frequently photographed with distinguished peers of the realm, air marshals and other eminent achievers like Sir Alan Cobham and Sir Malcolm Campbell. She began to travel round the country opening new department stores and lecturing to clubs and societies.

Her proudest moment was to be summoned to Buckingham Palace. King Leopold of Belgium was a guest there and he asked to meet her. While there she had a private chat with Queen Elizabeth and met King George VI. JEAN TALKS WITH TWO KINGS the headlines said, and she was quoted as saying of King Leopold: 'I was very flattered by his familiarity with the times I had put up on my various flights.' Meanwhile more international honours were descending on her, including the most coveted of them all: the medal of the Fédération Aéronautique Internationale. She was the first woman to receive it, voted by the representatives of twenty-two countries.

Jean and Ellen had moved into a flat in Kensington but, as usual, nobody knew where it was. Their address, even for Fred in New Zealand, stubbornly remained Thomas Cook and Son. And it was by this circuitous mail route that, in November 1937, the faithful Victor Dorée wrote in the hope that she would meet him. He had earlier phoned her at Grosvenor House but she had declined to see him. Victor's letter hasn't survived but Jean's reply has. 'It was very nice of you and your mother to go all the way to Lympne to see me land. I was so sorry I could not see you the morning you telephoned but felt you would understand. Let me know a few days before you are next in London and we can arrange to have lunch or tea together ... In two weeks' time I shall not be so frightfully busy as at present.' Coldly and formally she concluded: 'Yours sincerely, Jean Batten.' For whatever reason they did not meet. One suspects that, despite the offer to do so in her letter, Jean actually had no wish to see him for she could not have handled the awkwardness she must have felt whenever Victor reappeared in her life – as he was to do yet again.

From Kensington the Battens moved out of London to St Albans in Hertfordshire. They took a flat at Wickwood Court, a large old country house with a tennis court. It was here that Jean must have finished writing her second book, *My Life*, which was published by George Harrap in May 1938. Again people found it a difficult book to read and enjoy. It flowed awkwardly as a clumsily written travel narrative, spiced with the names of every important person she had ever met. It was extraordinarily egotistical, bursting with the names of kings, presidents and peers who had saluted her achievements; even the detailed descriptions of her great flights were somehow flattened and made unsatisfying by her pedestrian prose. Her own clippings archive did not contain any reviews of the book whose title she was, many years later, to describe to friends as mildly preposterous for an author of twenty-eight. However, she did send a complimentary copy to the King – probably in the belief that it was expected of her. The Palace sent her a formal letter of thanks, but whether His Majesty ever read the book will never be known.

It is possible that the absence of reviews among her own papers is due to their highly critical tone, if the single one that has survived was typical. It was written by the outspoken editor of *The Aeroplane*, C.G. Grey. 'Miss Jean Batten, at the age of something less than thirty, has chosen to write her "life". Considering all the extraordinarily unwise things she has done in the course of a good many hundreds of hours flying she is very lucky to have a life to write,' he said scathingly. 'There seems no more reason for reading it than for taking the needless risks which Miss Batten took … All her flights had been done before, most of them in better and in safer conditions, so she added nothing to human knowledge.'

One suspects that Jean, having read Grey's attack both on her book and her motives, would have been entirely nonplussed. Her belief in herself was still too unshakeable – fuelled by the adulatory newspaper prose of the day – for her to have seen in it a grain of relevance or truth.

Unrelated to the publication of the book, there were beginning to appear in London some less than sycophantic opinions of Jean herself. A writer, Charles Graves, in the *Bystander* magazine, set out to examine why, with so many flying triumphs to her credit, she had attracted wide public admiration but little affection. 'When you meet her you understand why,' he wrote. 'Jean Batten is a sweet but rather grim

girl. She speaks evenly and steadily. She is very sure of herself
... But where she fascinates is in her absolute acceptance of
everything at its face value. Amy Mollinson, and also my old
friend Jim, are perfectly aware that they are leading stunt lives
and that the ballyhoo is crude, but inevitable; laughable, but
ultimately cruel ... Miss Batten, however, is as literal as the
alphabet and takes everything equally literally.' Referring to the
actress Florence Desmond's then hugely popular stage impersonations of famous people (Amy Johnson had once been
mortified to be in the audience and hear her Yorkshire accent
taken off mercilessly), Graves concluded: 'Miss Batten will have
to be very careful if she ever meets Miss Florence Desmond. For
between you and me, Miss Desmond is almost bound to find her
a most intriguing subject for study, flying helmet, profile and
all.'

Equally unkind were the comments of a woman writer, Betty
Ridell, in the *Aeropilot* magazine: 'Try as they may, the newspapers will be unable to turn her into a sideshow because she is
too practical, too unobtrusive, works too hard and says too
little. It is characteristic of Jean Batten that articles on her
flights, her success, her life, have to be padded to such an extent
that even casual readers can see the wadding sticking through
the story. This is because she has actually nothing to say to the
press, unless it is information on how much petrol the tank will
hold and where she expects to break her flights ... So the
reporters have to do a good deal of fine writing about her
"determined little chin" and tell again and again how she sold
her piano to help finance her first record-breaking flight.'

Early in 1938 Jean began a lucrative lecture tour of Britain
and Europe. In France, where she arrived glamorously in the
Gull, the aviation community lavished hospitality on her and
she stayed with Blériot's widow. In Belgium, amid some speculation that she was having an affair with him, she was entertained
again by King Leopold and swam in his exotic pool set in a
hothouse in Laeken Palace among tropical plants imported from
the Congo. But it was in Sweden, still in the grip of late winter,
that she found the greatest enchantment. Here she was received
like a national heroine and the entertainment flowed from the
highest quarters. Immediately claimed by the nobility, she was

fêted by the Swedish royal family and photographed at banquets dining and dancing with the King's son, Prince Bertil. The Crown Prince, Gustaf Adolf, presented her with the gold medal of the Royal Swedish Aero Club and a Swedish Air Force Officer, Count Mac Hamilton (his name curiously deriving from a distant wave of Scottish immigration) took her ice-yachting on a lake near Stockholm. There are photographs of her looking like a large beaver, swathed in furs, being carried across the frozen lake laughing in the Count's arms.

That summer she flew the Gull to Milan to accept an invitation to stay with the KLM man, Frederik Meuser, who had befriended her when she'd arrived exhausted in Naples the previous year. She spent the holiday at his villa on Lake Como. Meuser's Serbian widow, Mila, who now lives in St Moritz, in Switzerland, I succeeded in tracing through a letter she had written to Jean in 1982 and which was found in one of the latter's suitcases after her death. She remembered Jean's 1938 visit very well. 'She was a very shy person and obsessed with the need for privacy,' she said. 'I remember she never wanted to be photographed and was always hiding when important persons wanted to speak with her. At the time we knew her there were no men in her life. Men could not have been interested in her, she was too cold. Later, during the war when my husband was serving with RAF Transport Command, he bumped into her in the street in England. He tried to give her a kiss, as one does with friends. She was shocked and escaped and that was that.'

From Meuser's villa Jean sent Fred a brief postcard. Like all the cards she ever sent him it is remarkable for its lack of warmth. It is concerned only with the weather and the Lake Como scenery and one is struck by how formally she signs it: 'Best wishes, Yours affectionately, Jean.' Not even a conventional word of love.

The postcards to Fred compare remarkably with the one surviving card which Jean wrote to Ellen, in which she sent her mother a million kisses. She sent it from Holland, only a few weeks before the one from Italy to Fred. 'Dearest,' it began and concluded: 'Take care of yourself dearest. All my love Jean (1,000,000 XXXX).'

According to the aircraft's journey logbook Jean did a lot of flying in the Gull during 1938 and 1939. She appears to have been using it like a taxi, hopping in and out of Europe to deliver lectures or receive awards. The aircraft was now based at Hatfield. One of the de Havilland company's ground engineers who used to service the Gull there was Alan Carlisle, who now lives in Auckland. Sometimes after maintenance work on the aircraft Jean would invite him to fly with her. On one occasion, he recalled, 'We were no sooner airborne, one misty November morning, than the windscreen fogged up. So I reached into the door map pocket for a rag and quickly wiped it clear for her. When I'd finished I looked at the cloth and saw that in fact it was a pair of apple-green satin French cami-knickers. I remember noticing that they were a rather daring style for the time.

'Both of us turned a delicate shade of pink and as we approached to land we studiously avoided catching each other's eyes, carefully studying the sky out of opposite sides of the cabin. Glancing at her I saw that she had gone almost scarlet. I thought it wise not to look again.'

Alan Carlisle added: 'We regarded it as a great honour to work on her famous Gull and all of us loved Jean as "our girl". She was, of course, much more reserved than Amy Johnson who would go out and knock a football round with the lads. With Jean it was all maps and technical stuff. Curiously, looking back now, although she was physically very beautiful she actually had no sex appeal. Amy used to flirt outrageously with the blokes in the hangar. But not Jean. She gave out no warmth; one certainly never fantasised about a romp in the hay with her. It was noticeable, too, that someone so unusually attractive never arrived at Hatfield with a man friend. We were all mystified. We used to ask: why is such a beautiful girl always on her own?'

The same question was often in the minds of the Willey family, who had earlier been the Battens' Hatfield neighbours. Squadron Leader Malcolm Willey, who was a boy at the time, and whom Ellen once took to see Jean's waxwork at Madame Tussaud's, wrote to say: 'I don't recall ever seeing Jean with a male friend. When she came home it seemed that it was always to relax and unwind only with her mother. I don't remember ever seeing anyone else there. My mother once said that Jean had told her that she had sacrificed many a friendship for her flying – whenever they threatened to become too intrusive or demanding.'

For her most publicised lecture tour of all, arranged by the British Council in early 1939, Jean decided to avoid weather delays flying and go by boat and train. The tour was to Scandinavia and the Baltic States. First she went to Norway. Before boarding the ferry at Newcastle she was asked by a reporter: 'Are you lecturing on flying?'

'Oh dear, no,' she replied. 'I'm going to lecture on the British Empire – on its potential influence as a power for world peace. I want to try and create better relations between other peoples and the Empire.' Reports which came back to the British Council in London were effusive in their praise. 'I do not think you could find a better representative for your country,' wrote the man in Oslo. And one of his Baltic colleagues said, 'Miss Batten is the best propaganda item that has appeared in Lithuania under the Council's auspices.' The British Council report concluded: 'We *must* find someone of this type and calibre for next season.'

Now fairly flush with funds – she claimed to have been, for a time, the highest-paid lecturer on the prewar European circuit – Jean decided to take Ellen for a holiday. In the spring of 1939 they went on a lengthy Caribbean cruise. During the trip they landed in Jamaica where they hired a car and spent several days exploring the island. So taken were they with this tropical paradise they decided that, one day, they would return to live there.

Back in England in the late summer of 1939 Jean set off on another holiday, this time alone; back to Sweden. She went in the Gull. It was 9 August when she left from Lympne and the days of peace in Europe were numbered. In Stockholm she was met by her host, Axel Wenner Gren, a Swedish millionaire industrialist and his wife Marguerite. They lived in grand style in Haringe Castle outside the city. Impressed when she heard this, Ellen, who now sent lengthy and extraordinarily detailed progress reports of Jean's triumphant tours to Fred for his regular information, wrote: 'She stayed with very rich people

who arranged for her to have 1½ hours' rest every evening
before dinner.' Indeed the last occupant of the 'huge carved
four-poster bed with Beauvais red canopy and hanging,' Jean
wrote, had been Greta Garbo who had made an offer to buy the
castle from the Wenner Grens.

From this visit persistent and enduring rumours sprang that
Jean had had an affair with a member of the Swedish aristocracy
– indeed, some stories claimed, with a member of the royal
family no less. Nancy Bird Walton understood the affair had
been with a Swedish count. She said: 'If Jean ever did succumb,
then it would have to have been at least with a count.' Fuel was
added to this speculation by a letter which came in 1987 from
Sven Hugosson, Secretary General of the Royal Swedish Aero
Club, whose members down the years have remained among
Jean's staunchest admirers in the international aviation frat-
ernity. I had written to the club to enquire if anyone survived
from the late 1930s who might remember any particular attach-
ments Jean formed on that celebrated visit. Mr Hugosson wrote:
'The member of "Swedish society" with whom Miss Batten was
very friendly would have been (Count) Mac Hamilton. He is
now dead. Other people are alive, including Mr Carl Jacobson*
who disappeared for three days in 1939 with her in a car
"borrowed" from Baron von Eckerman. The local police at that
time did *not* investigate this escapade as they very well knew
what the couple were doing ... As you will see Miss Batten is
rather well remembered in Sweden.'

I tried, without success, to get Carl Jacobson's address. Now
in his eighties and long since happily married (I was told) he
proved elusive. However another member of the Royal Swedish
Aero Club, who knew him well, undertook to speak to him on
my behalf. Later he telephoned to say that Carl Jacobson
claimed he had never met Jean Batten. And there the matter
rests. As Jean, contrary to the opinion of some of the women
who knew her best, did not preserve her maidenhood, the
Swedish police may indeed have arrived at a valid conclusion.

Later, when I had discovered Jean's memoirs and read her

*Because he is still alive his name here has been changed.

lengthy account of that Swedish holiday without a single reference to Count Mac Hamilton or Carl Jacobson, I wrote to tell Sven Hugosson (who had by then viewed my documentary on Swedish Television). He replied: 'The witnesses to Jean Batten's fling with Carl Jacobson are still sure of their opinion: they were away for three days. That does not, of course, guarantee any physical affair. What happened between her and Count Mac Hamilton cannot be further clarified; the people involved are dead. I would dare to say, though, that the omissions of "sensitive" pictures and of names in her memoirs, could quite as well be a cover-up for, and suppression of, acts that she would have regarded as very taboo. Memoirs sometimes tell more by what is omitted, than by what is committed.

'As seen from the film, she was certainly very beautiful. But her body language and speech did not seem immediately seducing ... The lasting impression is one of a lonely and emotionally suppressed girl, compensating for this by performing with men "up to the brink".'

Not only, in all probability, was Jean enjoying a transient affair with an aristocrat on that Scandinavian holiday, she was also being seduced by the warmth of the Swedish hospitality. Seemingly unconcerned by the approach of the Second World War, then little more than a week away, she dallied rather too long in Stockholm. From a letter she wrote to Fred on 18 August it would appear that she was so wrapped up in her role as a visiting celebrity she was almost naively oblivious of the imminence of hostilities and their inevitable repercussions on her Swedish idyll. Far from any expression of concern the letter, which describes her hosts as 'among the nicest friends I have', discourses on the medieval history of the castle and tells Fred that she will, in fact, be extending her flying holiday to other countries.

'I am greatly enjoying my holiday for I love Sweden and have many good friends here. Before flying home I shall visit Finland (Helsingfors* is only 265 miles from here) then Oslo. The

*Helsinki

lecture season commences again in October so I shall be very busy again.'

But Jean had been deceived by the charm and hospitality of the Wenner Grens. They were not quite what they appeared to be. The immensely wealthy Axel, who had founded the international electronics company, Electrolux, and whose armaments business made the famous Bofors gun, was in fact the subject of a major British Intelligence dossier at that time and was also being closely watched by the FBI. Not only was he a pro-Nazi sympathiser, he was a close personal friend of Goering and, earlier that year, had gone to London to try and see Prime Minister Neville Chamberlain to act as a go-between to negotiate an agreement for Hitler that would avoid war between Britain and Germany. His mission having failed, he was later to cultivate the friendship of the exiled – and pro-Nazi – Duke of Windsor, by then Governor of the Bahamas, as a result of which the latter was to receive a blunt warning from Winston Churchill that Wenner Grenn was 'suspected of being in communication with the enemy.'*

In short Jean, although she was probably never to know it, was the unwitting guest in neutral Sweden of a man suspected by the Anglo-American security services of being an active German spy. But, oblivious of the sinister undertones surrounding the activities of her suave and cultivated host, and apparently unaware that the Swedish newspapers were dominated by reports of the inevitability of war, she was picking mushrooms on the vast lawns of Haringe Castle, enjoying midnight swims with the Wenner Grens and playing Chopin to them on their grand piano in a large tapestry-hung room. But suddenly in the last week of August as, innocently, she was about to fly the Gull across the Baltic to Finland, a telegram arrived from London to shatter her peace of mind. It was from the Foreign Office warning her, on no account, to attempt to fly home across Germany.

At last reality struck. She rushed with the telegram to

King of Fools by John Parker (Macdonald, 1988)

Wenner Gren for his advice on how to get the Gull immediately
back to England without a long flight across the North Sea. To
her utter surprise he promptly picked up the telephone and
called Berlin. It is highly likely that he spoke to Goering himself,
since he was head of the Luftwaffe. Within a short time Gren
had obtained a special clearance for Jean to use German
airspace. It required her to fly via Copenhagen and to proceed
below 500 feet to Hamburg for a further clearance. Now in a
state of some anxiety she packed her suitcase and set off
immediately. 'When I got to Hamburg I found around 150
Messerschmitts lined up ready to go into action and, as I
stepped out, many of the pilots whistled and blew kisses to me.

'Waiting for my clearance from Berlin, I sat alone drinking a
coffee in the huge airport restaurant, deserted except for a solitary waiter. I felt inexpressibly sad as I flew on towards Holland
that sunny afternoon, disregarding the frequent smoke signals
warning me to land, for I knew that things would never be the
same again for me or any of my generation.'

After a night in Amsterdam she crossed the Channel, cleared
customs at Lympne, and flew back to Hatfield where she arrived
in the middle of the afternoon. It was 27 August 1939, seven
days before the outbreak of war. She climbed out of the Gull,
not knowing that she had flown herself for the last time. In nine
years' flying she had accumulated around 2,600 hours. Her
golden years, quite suddenly, were over.

She hurried home to St Albans, to Wickwood Court and
Ellen. They spent an anxious week never far from the radio,
listening to the news of a world moving into war. And the day it
was declared she announced to Ellen that she would offer
herself and the Gull for immediate communications flying duties
with the RAF.

On 4 September she wrote a personal letter to her friend
Captain Harold Balfour,* Parliamentary Under-secretary of
State for Air. I tried to trace the letter in the labyrinths of the
Public Record Office at Kew. But the Air Ministry's files for the
period were not fully indexed and the task would have taken

---

*Later Lord Balfour of Inchrye.

literally years. However, in Jean's archive at the RAF Museum, I found Captain Balfour's prompt reply of 5 September.

'Dear Miss Batten,' he wrote. 'Many thanks for your letter of the 4th September offering your services and your Percival Gull G-ADPR for despatch-carrying or communication work. I am at once communicating with Sir Francis Shelmerdine with a view to your name being included in a pool of civilian pilots for employment on Royal Air Force organisation and delivery work or general communication flying, and I am asking him to communicate with you direct in the matter. Yours sincerely, Harold Balfour.'

Sir Francis Shelmerdine, the former Director General of Civil Aviation, who had moved to Bristol to head National Air Communications, a new organisation responsible for the civil aviation war effort, was also quick to write to Jean. He knew her as a friend and had been deeply involved in the Whitehall controversy over her CBE. On 8 September he wrote acknowledging her offer and said: 'I am looking into the question of enrolling a certain number of women pilots for ferrying or communication work and will communicate further with you as soon as possible. It may take a little time to make any arrangements so I would ask you to possess your soul in patience.'

The organisation Jean hoped to join was the Air Transport Auxiliary which had been formed at the outbreak of war to employ a pool of experienced pilots ineligible, by age or fitness, for RAF service. The pilots – whose job was to ferry anything from Moths to four-engined bombers from factories to RAF bases – were at first only men, but early in 1940, under pressure from one of Jean's former flying club colleagues, Pauline Gower, the Air Ministry created a small women's section at Hatfield and Gower was appointed to command it. One of the pilots she was later to recruit was Amy Johnson.

Jean, a considerably more competent pilot than Amy, was not accepted. She claimed that she failed the medical. She was (she wrote in her memoirs) dumbfounded. And, to add to her distress, her wings were further clipped when, in July 1940, the Gull was peremptorily commandeered by the RAF and taken off to be flown for the first time by pilots other than herself. Her disappointment must have been bitter, her emotional trauma very great indeed. From now on, without the mystique of flying to sustain her, a lot of the joy was to go out of Jean's life for ever.

CHAPTER 19

War without Wings (1939–1946)

It was her eyesight, Jean claimed, that had her rejected by the Air Transport Auxiliary. In her memoirs she dealt with it only briefly, calling it 'this terrible disappointment'. She said: 'I failed my medical because of poor near-ocular vision, which apparently could have been caused by excessive eyestrain during my record flights through peering at maps in dim light when suffering from exhaustion.'

Near-ocular vision is shortsightedness but it would not have been caused in the way she suggested; an opthalmologist commented. The eyestrain theory was one of the popular misconceptions surrounding the condition of myopia, he said. It was normally an hereditary problem simply rectified by wearing glasses.

In later years, it emerged, Jean had also admitted privately to another vision problem. The eye that had been bruised in her 1934 Rome crash gave her double vision for some time afterwards because the muscles had suffered temporary local contusions. It had not healed by the time she came to make her successful flight to Australia throughout which, although she didn't admit it at the time, the double vision had caused her much stress, particularly during the moments of fine judgement needed on landing.

But not everyone I spoke to about her failure to get into the ATA was convinced that she needed to accept the apparent rejection so easily. Sir Peter Masefield, who knew many of the women ferry pilots, said: 'I think it shows that she had actually, by then, lost the determined urge which was such a characteristic of her earlier career. The fact is that, early in the war, the ATA was eager to recruit all, and any, of the small band of experienced women fliers. Initially they found only nine – though they kept a tenth place open for Amy Johnson. All of them had a fair amount of flying experience – but few with as much as Jean Batten. What's more a number of them had poor eyesight.' Sir Peter added: 'Experienced women pilots were accepted on their record of achievement without bothering too much about eyesight tests. Later – and after a number of accidents – they tightened up on their requirements. I myself flew for a time with the ATA – with glasses, or rather with goggles with appropriately corrected lenses in them.'

On 16 December 1939 the newly appointed commander of the ATA women's section, Pauline Gower, invited twelve well-known and experienced women pilots to the airfield at Whitchurch near Bristol for flight tests. Pauline Gower (who made up the total of nine founder women pilots) was authorised at that stage to recruit a maximum of eight. They were to be Winifred Crossley, Margaret Cunnison, Margaret Fairweather, Mona Friedlander, Gabriel Patterson, Joan Hughes, Rosemary Rees and Marion Wilberforce. Amy Johnson was committed to another flying job for the time being. However, despite her track record and her 2,600 flying hours, Jean was not (according to Joan Hughes) among those invited to Whitchurch. In the light of her earlier enthusiastic attempt to serve this was curious.

Not only did some of the ATA's pilots have vision problems but, according to a New Zealand woman pilot who flew with the ATA, Trevor Hunter (today Mrs Trevor Colway, who lives in Wanganui), at least one of her women colleagues flew with glasses. Indeed one of the men in the ferry group, Stewart Keith-Jopp, who had been a First World War fighter pilot, delivered a continuous stream of Hurricanes and Spitfires –

with only one eye and one hand. Why then did Jean Batten, one of aviation's greatest megastars of the thirties, not join Amy Johnson in the sisterly comradeship of the Air Transport Auxiliary when her short-sightedness was probably not an impediment? Had she, as Sir Peter Masefield suggested, lost her once all-powerful flying drive? Or was there another explanation? That she still saw herself, in the fantasy world she inhabited, as the super-being the media had created. When she had offered herself and her Gull for military service within hours of the outbreak of war it is not improbable that she had assumed that the Air Ministry would have been honoured to accept her and her plane as a glamorous package. But the service didn't operate that way. It quickly seized the Gull and, almost certainly, would, quite separately, have found a flying job for its owner in the uniformed and commissioned ranks of the ATA — whether or not she had to fly with glasses.

So why did she not persist in her attempts to join? Perhaps the prospect of losing her star status, of becoming just an anonymous member of a team, did not appeal to her ego. As a loner she would not have taken happily to the military discipline, and would, too, have been deeply bothered by the inevitably competitive spirit among the women pilots. (She was known always studiously to avoid exposing herself to risk of defeat in club flying competitions.) Nor would she have been happy at the thought that she might have to share a room with another woman. Or relished the certain routine of having her rarely scrutinised abilities exposed to the ATA's flying tests and assessments — to the critical appraisal of service instructors. Did her deep-rooted insecurity prompt her to run away from this whole intimidating and, for her, emotionally vulnerable scene in which she would not have been number one? And how far did Ellen, who was still a powerful force in her life, influence the decision? Somewhere in the wartime files at Kew, clues to the truth may possibly lie.

The records might also just possibly throw some light on yet another theory, believed by some of the women ferry pilots: that her eleventh-hour dash back to England across Germany had somehow made her a security risk. I could get no confirmation of this. However, if her loyalty was suspect it would much more

probably have resulted from her friendship with the notorious
Axel Wenner Gren. There is evidence that Pauline Gower
knew the truth. According to Joan Hughes, several of the first
women pilots to join the ATA asked why Jean had not been
recruited. Significantly she replied that the flying heroine
'would not be doing so'.

Jean was compensated by the RAF for the Gull with a sum
her memoirs do not disclose. What she called 'our happy and
successful partnership' ended in the summer of 1940 when the
aircraft went off – under military registration AX866 – to begin
six years of undistinguished service with a succession of RAF
units around Britain; it was used, among other things, as a
station 'hack' and as a target for anti-aircraft and searchlight
training.

She was so mortified by her inability to get into the ATA on
her own terms that, for years afterwards, she rationalised the
reason for her 'rejection'. She told people that the British
Government had valued her services much more highly in other
areas of the war effort. But for the first three years of the war her
jobs do not appear to have benefited much from her former
considerable accomplishments.

She first became a driver with the Anglo-French Ambulance
Corps. It operated in France, but before she could be sent there
the German armies reached the Channel coast; she was chilled
to learn later that some of the women drivers had been captured
and sent to Ravensbruck concentration camp. She spent only a
few months in the job, most of it around England on campaigns
to raise funds for more vehicles. She looked exceedingly glamorous in her uniform and in June 1940 was attractively featured at
the wheel of an ambulance on the cover of the huge circulation
Picture Post.

When the corps was disbanded after the fall of France she
went to work on the production line at the Royal Ordinance
factory at Poole in Dorset, inspecting the Hispano Suiza 20 mm
guns used in the Spitfire. There she worked a six-day week and
twelve-hour day which began on the assembly line at 7.30 am
when, with blueprints, micrometers and calipers, she would set
about checking the fine measurements of the gun parts. She
rented a small apartment nearby and wrote in her memoirs that

she spent many of the nights with plugs in her ears sheltering under the bed to avoid being hit by falling plaster dislodged by German bombs which fell on Poole night after night. Whenever she got leave, which wasn't often, she would hurry up to Hertfordshire, to St Albans (and later to new lodgings her mother was to acquire in Dorchester much nearer to Poole), to spend the brief time with Ellen.

The Battens' wartime years in Britain are virtually undocumented and are the beginning of a period of nearly thirty years during which they appear to have communicated only rarely with Fred and to have cut themselves off from almost every single friend Jean had made during her years of fame. There is no explanation other than that, as they grew older, their love for each other deepened and the psychological fusion between them – spiced for Jean, highly probably, by occasional casual affairs – increasingly found less and less need for the fellowship of others. But, that is, for one notable exception soon to enter her life.

Not even the long rift with her brother was healed by the wartime spirit of camaraderie. John and Madeleine had been divorced in New Zealand in 1940 and he had later joined the Royal New Zealand Navy as a dental mechanic seeing action at sea in the cruisers *Achilles* and *Gambia*. For six months in 1943 he was given special leave to play a role in a British film about the air-sea rescue service, *For Those in Peril*. It took him back to London where, for six months, he lived in Chelsea and worked at Ealing studios. But he didn't meet his mother or his sister and in an interview at the time said he didn't even know where they were.

Jean's memoirs ignore John's visit to work on this major wartime feature film, which she and Ellen may well have gone to see. Nor, surprisingly, does she refer to the tragic circumstances of the death (in early January 1941) of her former record-breaking colleague, Amy Johnson. Amy, whose standards of airmanship were less meticulous than Jean's, was delivering a twin-engined Oxford trainer from Scotland to an airfield in Oxfordshire. On the last leg south she took off in bad weather from Blackpool against the advice of the duty officer. She got lost and finished up to the east of London where she ran out of fuel and baled out. Her parachute opened but, with appallingly bad luck, she was over the Thames Estuary. She landed in the sea and perished in the bitterly cold water before she could be rescued. The death of the most legendary woman pilot of all time left Jean one of the very few survivors of the tiny élite band for whom the war spelt oblivion.*

There is no record of how long Jean worked at the gun factory but, according to her memoirs, which for the duration of the war are devoid of dates, an attempt was made at some stage by an organisation called the National Savings Committee to have her released from her munitions job and engaged as a lecturer in support of major wartime fundraising campaigns to collect public donations for guns and aeroplanes. The Air Inspection Directorate, for whom she worked at Poole, resisted fiercely. But at some point – it would appear to have been during 1943 – the Savings Committee's argument that, as a celebrity, she was more valuable in the propaganda industry, finally won the day. Jean moved back to London and she and Ellen took a flat in Baker Street.

She began an exhausting schedule of visits to factories, dockyards, textile mills and town halls throughout Britain, exhorting her audiences to put their hands in their pockets and support campaigns with names like 'Salute the Soldier' and 'Wings for Victory'. She addressed fourteen thousand dock workers at Chatham naval base from the back of a truck and gave a pep talk to Welsh miners at the coal face deep underground.

'It was hard work travelling about the country in wartime,' she wrote, 'especially during the winter months, enduring long journeys in unheated trains and trying to appear happy and confident speaking in icy, blacked-out halls, often during air-raids.' On three occasions she spoke to huge crowds in the centre of London in Trafalgar Square, once standing on a

---

*'Towards the end of her life,' wrote Constance Babington Smith, her biographer, 'Amy had no doubt as to how she would die: long-distance record-breaking fliers always "copped it" in the end. "I know where I shall finish up – in the drink," she told one of her friends.'

platform beside a complete Lancaster bomber and with air-raid sirens wailing throughout her speech.

Even in Trafalgar Square the skeletons from her past continued to haunt her. Victor Dorée's brother, Stanley, was proud and delighted to see her there during one of her rallies. His widow Grace said, 'He went up to speak to her afterwards – but her face just froze. She just said, "Hello", turned on her heels, and walked away.'

But it seemed she was never to escape from unwanted encounters with her early benefactors. Victor Dorée had joined the RAF as a flying instructor, serving at Elmdon near Birmingham until invalided out with duodenal ulcers. However, he was later to take a job as an RAF ground instructor at Sidmouth in Devon. Quite by coincidence, Jean was to visit the station on a fundraising drive. Grace Dorée said: 'The CO said to her in the mess, "By the way we happen to have a friend of yours here." She turned round and there was Victor standing there. Although she was polite the encounter clearly made her very uncomfortable. Victor said later that when she first saw him her face just dropped.'

A handful of photographs and newspaper cuttings are all that survive as reminders of Jean's fundraising tours. She is seen with workers in factory canteens, lecturing on public platforms surrounded by phalanxes of local dignitaries, and on daises outside town halls in industrial Midlands towns taking the salute as soldiers and RAF men, led by bands, march past. She was clearly in her element again, a celebrity come to town, and the centre of much respect and attention – GRIMSBY WOMEN INSPIRED BY MISS BATTEN was typical of the provincial headlines she attracted.

Her speeches pleaded for personal contributions from her civilian audiences, reminding them of the sacrifices the fighting men were making to keep them safe at home. 'If we could recapture that wonderful 1940 spirit that pervaded the country after Dunkirk we would very soon win the war,' she would exhort. According to her memoirs her appearances were extraordinarily successful in helping the money to roll in. 'At the Savings Committee's headquarters in London one day,' she wrote proudly, 'I was shown a telegram from one of the towns which read "Doubt if we can reach target by end of week stop can you send Jean Batten".'

Towards the end of the war in Europe Jean was to meet the last of the men with whom she claims to have fallen in love. She revealed his existence for the first time in her memoirs but gives his name only as Richard, an RAF bomber pilot. 'Mother had said that I would meet someone else one day,' she wrote, 'and so I did – a young pilot who combined the boyish enthusiasm of Victor, the calm wisdom of Ted and the debonair charm of Beverley. Once again I made wonderful plans for the future with Richard, quite sure that when the war ended everything would come right.'

Sadly it didn't. 'Alas fate had set a precedent: instead of the forest-covered mountains of Australia the scene this time was a war-torn night sky over Europe.

'I recall so well that particular morning when I switched on the radio to hear the news. It ended with a brief report of a raid over Germany: "Last night targets in enemy territory were attacked ... fourteen of our bombers failed to return."

'Unlike the previous occasion when I had been able to fly off in the Gull and search, this time all I could do was wait for the telephone call that never came. I felt numb with grief.'

That is virtually all she tells us about the tantalisingly mysterious Richard who, it appears, had found a place in her heart comparable with that of Beverley Shepherd. But where a number of people were to learn of her secret love for Bee, in very few was she ever to confide her feelings for the young RAF pilot and to none did she disclose his surname.

To try and trace members of his family who might have known of his friendship with Jean was a challenge I could not resist. But it was immediately a formidable task: in effect, over forty years after the event, to attempt to put a surname to the one of the thousands – probably tens of thousands – of Richards who had been killed in action on a bombing raid over Germany sometime during the war. There wasn't even the approximation of a date.

In England, in the summer of 1988, I decided to invest a strictly limited amount of time to the search by dedicating one week exclusively to it. I began by re-reading the sparse and guarded references to Richard in Jean's memoirs, searching for the smallest clues to the date of his death. Her reference to him followed immediately upon a description of a journey from Hull to London in a train packed with troops on their way to Normandy, immediately after the D-Day (6 June 1944) invasion of Europe had begun.

From a 'Salute the Soldier' campaign programme found in her archive at the RAF Museum I discovered that she had been lecturing in Hull on 9 June. Assuming that her narrative was here following roughly the true chronology of her wartime years – which, by and large, her writing usually did – I decided to concentrate the search from D-Day to the end of the war in Europe, on 8 May 1945: a period of eleven months. But the crucial clue on which all my hopes rested was her reference to the fateful BBC radio news bulletin that had reported fourteen bombers missing from the previous night's operations. On how many nights in the last eleven months of the war had precisely fourteen bombers failed to return? I reasoned that the odds were that there would probably not have been that many. I was right.

At the RAF Museum the normally enthusiastic Keeper of Aviation Records, Peter Murton, was dumbfounded when I explained the task. 'My advice, quite frankly, is forget it,' he said discouragingly. 'You'll spend literally hundreds of hours on a search that will almost certainly prove fruitless – beyond finding perhaps a Flight Sergeant R. Smith or a Flight Lieutenant R. Jones.' I knew he was probably right. Nonetheless, I was determined to try: to give it just the one week I had promised myself.

Searching records at the RAF Museum and the Air Historical Branch in London I established the very small number of dates during the eleven-month period when fourteen aircraft were recorded as failing to return from night operations over Europe. It was only then that it occurred to me that the dates were, in fact, quite irrelevant. What I really needed first were the nights for which the BBC – however right or wrong the true figures – *reported* fourteen aircraft missing. I went straight down to the BBC's Written Archive Centre at Caversham Park, a small, military-looking establishment in a Berkshire woodland, near Reading. Here, on microfilm, were all the memorable wartime news bulletins of the Home Service.

It took me five days to work through them – a process I often found deeply moving as I read, in one endless kaleidoscope, the simple hand-corrected scripts of the bulletins that the voices of Richard Dimbleby, Alvar Lidell, Frank Phillips and Chester Wilmot had spoken to the world in days when the fate of mankind had often seemed to hang on their words. There were over two thousand bulletins from D-Day to the end of the war. I read them all. Astonishingly there were only two nights when they had reported fourteen bombers missing, and neither were dates targeted by my preliminary research. They were both in July 1944: the nights of 4/5th and 15/16th. I had not believed I would get so close so quickly. Surely there could not have been a large number of Richards among the notional twenty-eight pilots killed on those two nights?

To try and answer this I went, now with some excitement, to the vast Public Records Office. Through a computer terminal I requested a copy of the Bomber Command Headquarters Operational Record Books for the two nights in question. When I opened the pages my heart sank. Suddenly I was looking at the huge haystack in which I had not wanted to believe the tiny needle lay. Nearly six hundred aircraft from scores of squadrons had gone out on both nights to attack targets in Europe. To identify the missing pilots it would require endless weeks of searching the operational records of fifty-six separate squadrons. This I could not justify.

However, just as I was on the point of abandoning the search for Richard, I had a rare stroke of luck. I stumbled by accident, in an RAF records index, on a volume with the promising title *Missing Aircraft Register 1943–1945*. No one had ever mentioned the existence of such an obviously relevant document. Five minutes later the books were in my hands. And suddenly my search was focused only on the aircraft that hadn't come back on those crucial nights. Here, yet again, were totals which bore no relationship to the figures in the BBC's bulletins: on 4/5th July twenty-eight aircraft were shown as not returning and on the 15/16th only five. Thirty-three bomber crews in all which, at that stage of the war, meant only thirty-three pilots in the seven-man crews. Their names were all listed by role, rank, number and surname. There were no initials or first names. But if Jean was being literal when she quoted fourteen aircraft – and she tended to be exceedingly precise when she *was* prepared to reveal information about herself – then, in theory, one of these thirty-three bomber captains was the man she might have married.

Only one stage of research remained: to track down the missing first names. They lay for some reason in old-fashioned filing cabinets at the RAF's Historical Branch in Lacon House in Holborn. There, next day, it took only minutes to search the Bomber Command 'aircraft loss record' cards. Frustratingly they supplied only the aircrews' initials, but on each of the two nights in question, amazingly, there was only one captain with an R among his first names. To turn the initials into names required one final act of detection – perusal, in yet another filing system, of the RAF's 'casualty cards', helpfully arranged alphabetically.

With mounting excitement I flicked through them. Unbelievably, at the end of the long search there appeared at last to be the elusive name. Only one of the two pilots on my short list had the name Richard, but somewhat disappointingly it was his middle, not his first name.

Pilot Officer Ronald Richard Smith, a twenty-one-year-old Australian from Sydney, flying a Lancaster of 57 Squadron, had flown from East Kirby in Yorkshire on the night of 4 July 1944 to attack a flying bomb storage site at St Leu D'Esserent in France. The aircraft had been shot down and all the crew had died.

Pilot Officer Smith seemed somehow extraordinarily young to have been involved with Jean, who was then approaching thirty-five. Somehow I had been expecting a squadron leader or wing commander, still in his twenties, but a little nearer her age. However, she did have a strong romantic attachment to Australia and perhaps Pilot Officer Smith was mature beyond his years. Although the fact that his first name was Ronald didn't sound promising, having come so far I felt compelled to learn more about him.

Through the wartime RAF community in Australia I managed to trace not only a 57 Squadron colleague who had actually seen Ron Richard Smith shot down that night, but Smith's mother who was still alive in Sydney. They both confirmed that he had never spoken of a friendship – of which he would most certainly have been proud – with the famous Jean Batten. What's more he already had a close girlfriend back in Sydney.

In one last attempt to locate the real Richard who, I still felt somehow, did exist, I published appeals in all the magazines read by the now aging Second World War RAF aircrew community. Nobody who could help ever replied.

One can only speculate about the true place in Jean's affections of the young bomber pilot who had the 'debonair charm' of Beverley and whom – had he, against heavy odds, survived the war – she claims she would have married; if, indeed, that is, Ellen had not put a spoke in the wheel. The only person I was to meet in whom Jean had, in the 1970s, confided her love, was not to learn much about him. Indeed Jean didn't reveal what his peacetime profession was, where he lived, or how she met him: probably during the 'Wings for Victory' campaign when RAF pilots joined her on the speaking platforms. Or why in fact, when custom favoured wartime marriages, they had decided to wait. And much more to the point, was he, in truth, in love with her? Would he, had he survived the war, really have married the famous woman so much older than himself? Undoubtedly she had a brief wartime affair with an RAF pilot living on borrowed time. But was there a degree of fantasy about the brief encounter? Did her morale at that time require the image of a brave and romantic new figure in her life?

It was yet another enigma. Richard must remain an insubstantial shadow in her memoirs, in which she wrote wistfully, 'If only I had met Dick years earlier. Or if only the war had ended sooner – if, if, if . . .'

In the last months of war the Baker Street flat was damaged by bomb blast. The windows were blown out and thereafter the roof leaked so badly, despite a tarpaulin cover, they had to collect the water in buckets and dishes. Ellen, now approaching seventy, had suffered more or less continuous colds and flu during every winter of the war and had pleaded with Jean, according to her memoirs, to take her to live in a warmer climate when peace came. With memories of the island from their 1939 cruise they already had their eyes on Jamaica which had appealed to them as an idyllic permanent home. Jean says she, too, now wanted to leave England to escape from the memories of Richard. 'Only a complete change could dispel my obstinate grief.'

And so mother and daughter, as they did so often during their closeknit existence, sold all their furniture, all their books and the Steinway grand piano they had bought in their prosperous years immediately before the war and, in November 1946, flew in a British South American Airways converted Lancaster bomber to Jamaica. They were to stay for six years, during most of which few of their former friends actually knew they were there. For their address, at their insistence, was to remain Thomas Cook and Son in London.

They were not to find their Utopia on this lush Caribbean island. Instead, for Jean, it was to bring only deep personal tumult and dissatisfaction. Many people made the sad observation that life had apparently ceased to have much meaning for her.

CHAPTER 20

Islands in the Sun (1946–1966)

On arrival in Kingston, the hot and humid Jamaican capital, the Battens made immediately, in the new car they had bought, for the cooler habitat of the island's north coast, sixty miles away over the mountains. Blessed by a benign tropical climate, the coast was not the crowded tourist scene of smart hotels and souvenir shops it is today, but a world of unspoiled silver sandy bays. One could drive for hours without finding habitation larger than a fishing village.

In this tranquil paradise, among a population whose pigmentation ranged across a spectrum from ebony to pale white, Jean and Ellen, late in 1946, rented a house in St Ann's Bay, seven miles west of what today is the busy tourist town of Ocho Rios. The house had an exotic view through coconut palms on to the Caribbean and was set in a garden bright with tropical flowers and alive with tiny, darting humming birds. For the first time in their lives they enjoyed the luxury of servants – a cook and a gardener. But, as so often in their nomadic existence, they were not to remain long. 'Hidden in these idyllic surroundings there was an unsuspected serpent,' Jean wrote dramatically in her memoirs. 'But for mother's uncanny intuition, either one or both of us would have met a violent and terrible end.'

Ellen, she claimed, told her one day: 'I sense a sinister under-current and have a feeling of foreboding.' Despite Jean's protestations Ellen insisted they leave within forty-eight hours. So they drove back across the island and rented a cottage in a British Army camp at Newcastle in the cool air 2,000 feet up in the Blue Mountains. Here they learnt that Ellen's prescience had been no eccentric whim. Two days after they had left the St Ann's Bay house, the eighteen-year-old gardener – 'a well-mannered young boy' – high on *ganja*, the local marijuana, had gone berserk and in a drug-crazed frenzy destroyed the entire contents of the house with an axe.

Despite this chilling news the seductive quality of life on the north coast was soon to lure them back. They gave up the mountain cottage, bought a plot of land by the sea and, in 1948, built their own home. The site was a barren tract of almost bare rock sprinkled with coconut palms, in the then virtually undeveloped stretch of coast immediately to the east of Ocho Rios. The place was called Tower Isle and, close by, one of the north coast's first tourist hotels was being built by Mr T.A.D. Smith, a local construction engineer. Jean persuaded him to build her house.

'Tad' Smith, as he was known, who still lives in Jamaica, remembers the job well. Inspecting the site (he told me in a letter) he asked her what sort of house she wanted and how much she was prepared to spend. 'Jean gazed skyward for some time, as if she were in a dream; then with a gleam in her eyes, said very precisely: "The sky is the limit."' Accordingly he set to work to design what he called 'something skyward and uniquely beautiful – with a cost to match'. He presented her with the plans and the budget. Jean couldn't afford it. For a quarter of the price he built her a simple, conventional house.

'During construction her mother would sit and watch. One day she climbed the ladder to inspect the roof tiles. Jean was so proud of her agility in her seventies she kept saying to me: "Isn't she marvellous?" There was, I observed, a very close relationship between them. Jean was always standing and gazing skyward, as if in some wonderland. To me she was just not all here. One day I did ask her why she was always gazing upward.

She said that ever since she was a child she had done it – imagining herself up there in a plane. She was obviously missing it very badly.'

Jean called the house Blue Horizon and around it built a wall. Within a few months, with imported soil, she had transformed the rock wilderness into a fertile garden, splashed bright with bougainvillea, frangipani, hibiscus and poinsettia. And in front of the house, on the edge of the beach, she had a swimming pool built which she filled with sea water.

The shrubs soon enveloped the barren site, melding with the tall coconut palms to conceal the house from the gaze of strangers. Within the walls of Blue Horizon Jean and Ellen settled down, in the late 1940s, quickly succumbing to a new pulse of life made gentle and serene by the welcoming warmth of the Jamaican people and the soothing climate – a lifestyle of enviable ease and comfort in which, waited upon, they did little more than read and swim, tend the garden and go for long walks. Jean had, in effect, retired and, on the income from the money she had made in just five profitable years, they were now happily self-sufficient.

But, in the small expatriate community of the north coast, it proved more difficult than they had imagined to cut themselves off from society. For Jamaica was beginning to be discovered by the rich and the famous. Only a few miles to the east, near the township of Oracabessa, in a large but spartanly furnished house called Goldeneye, perched on a cliff-top above the Caribbean, the writer Ian Fleming, who came to the island every winter, was shortly to give birth to one of modern fiction's most lucrative characters – James Bond. And a few miles further east again, on a hillside overlooking the market town of Port Maria, the playwright and actor Noel Coward, who spent several months of the year in a large two-storied house called Blue Harbour, was still in the full flower of his genius. Jean was to meet them both, and Coward was often to speak of his great admiration for her courage and determination as a pilot. But more often than not the Battens remained behind their closed wrought-iron gate; their social life was muted in a society dominated by wealthy, cultivated and often titled expatriates and prosperous plantation families. It was for some a lotus-eating paradise, devoted to the pursuit of pleasure and characterised by rounds of parties, late nights and late rising, long siestas, hard drinking – and a high incidence of casual affairs. Even had the Battens wished to they could not often have afforded to participate in this costly social scene.

One of the island's best-known figures, a former plantation owner, writer, and friend of Noel Coward, Morris Cargill, said: 'We had some fairly legendary playboys here in those days. They were kept extraordinarily busy squiring frustrated American Mid-West schoolteachers who rapidly lost their inhibitions when they got here. I remember the owner of one hotel, where they used to stay, would actually provide these local studs with free drinks and meals provided they gave satisfaction to his guests.'

In the midst of this hedonistic society, one suspects that Ellen must have felt some concern for her daughter's moral welfare. But although an apparently withdrawn and unsociable figure, Jean was not inexperienced. Although she probably never confided in her mother, it is highly likely that she indulged in some sporadic affairs out of range of Ellen's surveillance.

However, her memoirs carefully avoid naming any men during her six Jamaican years and, forty years later, trying to establish even the few open friendships she enjoyed proved exceedingly difficult. Indeed, although her memoirs devote several long chapters to the period, they are more descriptive of the island than of people. And they make not even guarded reference to the psychological traumas with which, I was to discover, she was beset in Jamaica.

When I first visited the island in 1987 it took three days to find anyone who had ever heard of Blue Horizon – its name long since changed to New Horizon. A modest Spanish-style house, it lay still concealed beside the busy main road between Ocho Rios and Port Maria, on a narrow coastal belt of spectacular beauty, with palms, banana plantations and jungle framing the brilliant blue of the sea. It was now flanked by other houses and modern apartments and the insistent rhythm of reggae wafted across its garden. The owners were away but their Jamaican caretaker obligingly took me on a tour of the small three-bedroomed home where Jean and Ellen had once so effectively cut themselves off from the world.

Next door, buried under its own canopy of palms and bougainvillea, was a more elegant house called Tradewinds. It had been built while the Battens were at Blue Horizon and its owner in those days, Mrs Anne Keighly, I managed to trace in Ocho Rios. 'They were both recluses,' she said immediately. 'Although we lived next door for over a year we never actually met them. People rarely saw them coming or going. Nor were they really involved socially with the rest of the community, Jamaican or expatriate. One day, I remember, they just weren't there any longer. I don't think they even said goodbye to anyone.'

This was a disappointing start. However, I was later to meet someone who, in the late 1940s, had become a deeply concerned observer of Jean and her now mounting personal problems. Beth Jacobs was the widow of the Battens' north coast doctor, a distinguished Jamaican, Dr Lenworth Jacobs, celebrated for his fight for the acceptance of family planning on the island.

Beth, when I met her in 1987, was still elegant and attractive in her early seventies. Her entry in Jamaica's *Who's Who* was as impressive as her late husband's — she had been a member of the island's Legislative Council and the first woman director of Barclays Bank anywhere in the world. She met Jean soon after the latter's arrival on the north coast; she was going through another bad patch and had come to Dr Jacobs to seek help for psychological problems which were causing her deep distress. The complex roots of it all will probably never be known for, even forty years later, Beth Jacobs felt it professionally unethical to reveal all she knew. But it was evident that she had been much involved in her husband's efforts to help with the crisis Jean was facing as she tried to handle life out of the headlines.

Treating famous people was something Dr Jacobs' practice took in its stride at that time. Among his patients had been Sir Winston Churchill, Sir Anthony Eden, Noel Coward, Ian Fleming, the Duchess of Gloucester, Princess Alice and a host of dukes. As patients, Beth said, they were all gracious, easy and informal. 'But not so Jean Batten who, I have to say, disturbed me. She was a real enigma. I had rarely had anyone quite like her in my home before. She remained stiff and formal and simply refused to unbend.' Because there was no psychiatrist locally and he didn't have the time for protracted counselling, Dr Jacobs asked his wife, who had much experience as a social worker, to help by trying to establish a rapport with Jean.

'I remember he said to me one day, "I want you to do something about Jean Batten." We used to try and make our home a healing home. Patients would come and I would listen to their problems, get to know them and, in the process, we were sometimes able to help. At the end of these visits I would usually feel that perhaps we had healed a little – but, sadly, never with Jean Batten.

'I found her so locked up within herself I just could not reach her. I felt she was arrogant and a little bit condescending. I had the feeling that here was somebody who was curiously unfulfilled. Emotionally something was missing. Yet she was famous, had been blown up by the media, had drunk life's champagne and enjoyed everything the world had to offer. Yet within her I couldn't find a real person. I found someone who was looking for something that would never be there. She came across as an international celebrity who was still standing there waiting for the applause. But I'm afraid I didn't applaud and perhaps because of that it was to a degree my fault we couldn't communicate.'

Beth and her husband had, on an earlier occasion, been invited to dinner by Jean and Ellen. She had only faded memories of that evening but was later to wonder if Mrs Batten was not a significant cause of her daughter's problems. 'I was left with a strong impression of a very overbearing mother dominating her life. I am convinced that something must have happened to Jean in her formative years that made her afraid of being hurt, made her afraid of the normal life. Her problem seemed to be a total inability to readjust to life after fame, to accept that the champagne had stopped flowing. I have to use the word awesome when I describe her, for she was undoubtedly a great woman. But perhaps a sad human being.'

Dr Jacobs saw Jean on a number of occasions and Beth spent many hours walking with her along the beach and sitting talking over cups of tea trying to break through her defences. When the visits came to an end Beth and her husband had to accept that they had failed. But some years later they were surprised to receive a letter from Jean thanking them for the helpful things they had done during those apparently futile weeks.

On the nearby beach at Roaring River another family was often to observe Jean's lonely figure striding along the sand. Fiona and John Edwards, now in their seventies, live in a multi-turreted old wooden plantation house which sprawls across the top of a hill at Walkers Wood in the mountains between Kingston and Ocho Rios. Fiona, who before her marriage was a Pringle, one of Jamaica's most prominent landowning families in the island's nineteenth-century plantocracy, is an incisive woman with colourful memories of those days.

'I can still see her walking that beach, this rather ascetic lady, looking so much alone, and wondering what she was thinking about. She came to the house on a number of occasions but she didn't talk a lot to me. We would sometimes meet her at cocktail parties with Noel Coward and others in that set and she would always be looking elegant and beautiful and misty up-in-the-skies so to speak. She was actually not a very sophisticated person and exceedingly remote with an aura that was all her own – a sort of Jane Austen figure, rather unattainable. Somehow you knew she was someone just passing in the night.'

Occasionally, visitors to the island who had heard that the famous pilot was living there, would seek her out. One was an Australian journalist, Jim McDougal, who, in Sydney, recalled how he had managed to find Blue Horizon in 1951. As an intruding stranger he was indeed lucky to have been invited in. 'But,' he said, 'it was a very, very brief meeting. The gate was locked, I remember. She was polite and aloof and clearly didn't welcome my presence. I didn't meet her mother. I came away thinking what an eerie place. With its wall and locked gate it felt cloistered – like a retreat.'

Some of the most elegant formal parties to which Jean was invited were given by Sir Harold and Lady Mitchell. Sir Harold was an immensely wealthy baronet with business interests across the world in coal, oil, coffee and farming. A former vice-chairman of the British Conservative Party, he owned a large estate near Ocho Rios called Prospect and the parties were held in its eighteenth-century mansion house. Sir Harold is now dead. Lady Mitchell befriended the Battens on their arrival in Jamaica. She was to become exceedingly fond of Jean and was able to throw some further light on her character for me.

The Mitchells were often hosts to important visitors, and always Lady Mitchell made a point of inviting Jean to meet them. Although now in her seventies Mary Mitchell is still an inveterate world traveller, commuting throughout the year between her principal home in Bermuda and others in Jamaica, Boston, Switzerland and Rio. For this reason we never managed to meet but we did have several phone conversations and she wrote me many helpful letters about her friendship with Jean whom, interestingly, she did not find remote.

'She was a very attractive and intelligent friend,' Mary Mitchell wrote. 'She devoted her entire life to her mother whom I met on several occasions, a tall and very goodlooking woman who I think was most fortunate in having such a self-sacrificing and devoted daughter. But despite her great achievements I fear that she never found happiness. I always felt that she was a little envious of me with a nice husband, a lovely home and an attractive daughter; she loved children and was devoted to my Mary-Jean for whom she often danced ballet in the Great House at Prospect.'

It was at a party at the Great House in January 1953, towards the end of the Battens' stay in Jamaica, that Jean and Ellen were to meet Sir Winston and Lady Churchill who had come to spend a holiday there. It appears to have been one of the rare occasions on which anyone remembers seeing Mrs Batten in public. Jean wrote in her memoirs about the evening with the British Prime Minister. 'It was one of the happiest memories I have of mother in Jamaica. She was wearing a black velvet sheath frock with long full silk-net sleeves and looked very lovely sitting with Lady Churchill and Captain Molyneux who may even have recognised one of his pre-war model gowns.* During the evening Sir Winston, who was in a happy mood,

---

*Edward Molyneux (1891–1974) was one of the most prominent British fashion designers of the years between the wars.

glanced round the room and said, "I am the oldest person here tonight", then looking across to where mother was standing, added with an impish smile, "– by two years". Mother inclined her head in acknowledgement, raised her glass, and gave such a charming smile that Noel Coward rushed forward and said "Mrs Batten you look so romantic tonight, may I kiss you?" and did so whilst mother pretended to swoon in his arms.'

Although Jean's memoirs don't mention it, she and Ellen occasionally invited Noel Coward to dinner at Blue Horizon. On one occasion he was accompanied by his lifelong companion, Graham Payn, who told me from his home in Switzerland that his principal memory of it was that 'it was a very quiet evening'. He recalled that Ellen hardly spoke at all; she left all the talking to Jean. 'Noel,' he added, 'always thought Jean was marvellous.'

During her six years in Jamaica one wonders whether any men entered her affections, other than in fleeting and furtive affairs. Her memoirs reveal none. But during my research and filming on three visits to the island the names of two men cropped up. One was an Italian banana planter, long since dead, John Paraccini. His name was suggested by an Ocho Rios land surveyor, Ertis Morrison, who had done some work on the Blue Horizon property for Jean and who was later to run a wine bar in the town.

'I used to meet her at parties,' he said. 'She seemed to move in the same clique as John Paraccini who worked the Llan-rumney estate near Port Maria which had once belonged to the island's famous pirate governor, Sir Henry Morgan. I sometimes saw them dancing together. She was a very withdrawn sort of woman, but a very good dancer.' I could find no confirmation of any sort of relationship apart from an apparently innocent social one between Jean and John Paraccini. However, it transpired that Mr Paraccini had a quite formidable reputation in the early 1950s as a man who enjoyed a constant succession of girlfriends from the increasingly plentiful flow of tourists to the north coast. Someone who knew him well said, 'He certainly did his duty by Jamaica in those days.' Although he would probably not have fitted Ellen's specifications for male companionship for her daughter, it is highly likely that, since she saw a great deal of him, she would, at some stage, have yielded to his charms.

The other alleged lover proved more of a mystery. He was (according to one of the island's best-known real estate agents, 'Bobby' Alexander) the local manager for an American airline. 'Jean was actually living with him in a house at Montego Bay,' he said. 'She had taken up playing a guitar, classics only, and was very intense about it. I thought they were married.' However, when after twelve months' search I managed to trace the now elderly former Pan American Airways man to his home in Massachusetts, he said he hadn't been in Jamaica during any of the years of Jean's residence there. Bobby Alexander remained insistent that she had been 'shacked up with someone'. Who it was will probably remain a mystery.

'In my opinion she had very few friends,' wrote her house-builder Tad Smith in his 1989 letter. 'Once, I remember, Abe Issa (owner of Tower Isle hotel) asked me to introduce him to her. But when I told her of Abe's request she said most abruptly, "What for?" and it never happened. She was defin-itely an isolationist. I never ever saw any men fooling around with her. I have to say I came to the conclusion she was a recluse.'

What persuaded Jean to leave this island paradise early in 1953? In her memoirs she describes the apparently impetuous decision with disarming simplicity: 'We have been so very happy in Jamaica and yet, after six years, we both began to get wanderlust unknown to each other. Quite by accident one day I learnt that mother wanted to return to Europe as much as I did. Sitting on the patio and reading from the airmail *Daily Telegraph* a report of a forthcoming art treasures auction at Christie's, she said, "I wouldn't mind being in London for it."

'"What's to stop you?" I said. "Let's go."

'"But that's not possible," came the reply.

'"Oh yes it is," I said laughingly. "Just think of it: London, Paris, Rome, Venice and Madrid for a start. What fun we could have," I cried.'

She claimed that Ellen remonstrated, urging deeper consider-ation before such an upheaval, but that she brushed aside saying:'"There's nothing to think out. You want to go, so do I, and that's all that matters."'

Almost immediately, it appears, they put Blue Horizon on the market. It was to be sold later for £10,000 to the Countess of Onslow, who within a few months, in a state of severe depression, was to drown in Jean's pool. But the Battens didn't wait for the sale. As a final shrewd gesture they bought as an investment − and as a possible place to which to return one day − three plots of land at nearby Discovery Bay, sold their furniture and car yet again, and boarded a ship for Liverpool.

Few people on the island knew they had gone. 'One evening,' wrote Tad Smith, 'I called at the house only to be told that they had removed. This was certainly a great shock to me.'

'It was really most curious the way they just faded away,' said Beth Jacobs. 'But that was really Jean Batten, wasn't it − something a little ethereal about her.'

There is a theory that the Battens who, insofar as they held any strong political views, were mildly reactionary and emphatically right-wing, may have left Jamaica to avoid living under black rule. Although the island didn't get its independence until 1962, at the time they left the anti-colonial ripples had already begun. In the event they would have noticed little difference in their security and lifestyle. On balance it is more likely that their deep-seated rootlessness was the reason for turning their backs on one of the most attractive places in the world.

They went back to England in an Elder and Fyffe banana boat, the *Manistee*, on which, a few days out from Port Antonio, seven stowaways emerged from among the bananas. Jean and Ellen dined each night in the places of honour at the captain's table. Recalling the twelve-day voyage nearly forty years later, Captain J. Kinsley, of Stoke Poges in England, wrote: 'Mrs Batten sat on my right and Jean on my left. Among other passengers were three Jamaican ladies taking their teenage daughters to a finishing school in Switzerland. One of them, a widow, eventually became my wife. She often joked to friends that the only reason she started to take an interest in me was to take me away from Jean − with whom I was becoming too friendly!'

It was the spring of 1953 when they arrived back in England

and took delivery of a new Vauxhall which Jean had arranged to be waiting on the Liverpool dockside. The Battens were on the run again, determined not to put down roots anywhere in the foreseeable future. They embarked on a sightseeing tour of Europe which, incredibly was to last seven years. During the whole of this period they lived like nomads. It is the least documented period of their many years of isolation; all that survives of it, apart from some imprecise narrative in the memoirs, are a few impersonal postcards to Fred in New Zealand.

When the protracted tour began in 1953 Jean was in her forty-fourth year, Ellen in her seventy-seventh. They appear to have been permanently on the move, like gypsies, driving through France, Holland, Belgium, Switzerland, Italy and Spain; once they put the car on a ship and visited Malta. The tour appears to have had a strongly cultural bias for they went sedulously from one famous art gallery to another. 'In Paris mother would say, "Let's go and pay our respects to Monet." To tour the great art collections of Europe with her was a revelation. She was also such good company – someone to laugh with.'

From the memoirs it seems that they were constantly 'helpless with laughter', a phrase Jean repeats again and again. They were undoubtedly always at ease in the close sisterhood they jealously guarded. They were 'shaking with laughter', she wrote, as they drove through France 'devouring three kilos of cherries and leaving a trail of stones behind us'. They laughed in the evenings as they sat cosily in small restaurants growing expansive and giggly on champagne. Twenty years later Jean was to describe the seven-year holiday as the happiest time of her life. She told a friend in Sydney, Layne Glanville Williams, that her mother's greatest attribute was that: 'she made me laugh. We knew each other so well that we could be sitting in a restaurant knowing we were the only English-speaking people present. Something would be going on in a foreign language which we didn't understand. Mother only had to turn to me, raise an eyebrow, wink, blink, or drop a single word in English that would be a perfect commentary on the scene – and we would both be in instant paroxysms of laughter.' Jean and Ellen appear to have been in protracted orbit during those years. A collection of snapshots among her papers at the RAF Museum shows them beside the car in many of the cities of Western Europe or picnicking graciously on the roadside with hampers of food, bottle of wine, and tablecloth laid out elegantly on the grass. Their progress through Europe is also mapped in Jean's sketchbooks in which she recorded with competence some of the landscapes that caught her eye.

At the end of 1954 they mysteriously returned to Jamaica, but only for the winter. The visit was confirmed by a photograph of her sitting with the celebrated British MP Sir Robert (later Lord) Boothby at the Shaw Park Hotel in Ocho Rios. She went back to the island, she said, to supervise the development of her Discovery Bay plots which, by 1957, had all been sold at a handsome profit bringing the total value of the sale of her Jamaican properties, including Blue Horizon, to over £16,000. In its own right, the revenue from these deals then represented an investment on which they could live comfortably. They would certainly have needed the money, for their 'flitting about Europe like two little birds just escaped from a cage' would not have been cheap since they stayed in hotels – admittedly low-budget ones – and ate in restaurants.

During their cultural pilgrimage, owning no permanent home, living out of a motor car, suitcases, and seedy rooms, Jean moved from her mid-forties to her early fifties, dedicating her life to Ellen and virtually denying herself whatever prospect of marriage remained. But from the commitment and bondage of her relationship with her mother it is clear that she found a deeply satisfying substitution for the real marriage she was never to experience.

Deliberately excluding all other people from their lives they remained almost entirely out of touch with friends. The three women pilots who had welcomed Jean to Australia in her epic years – Nancy Bird Walton, Peg Kelman and Esther Mather – hadn't heard from Jean now for twenty years.

But in the late autumn of 1955, having returned briefly to England to change their Vauxhall as an economy for a small Austin A30, they had taken temporary roost in the south of France where an invitation reached them from Sir Winston Churchill, who had recently retired as prime minister, to a small cocktail party at Lord Beaverbrook's villa at Cap d'Ail, near Monte Carlo. It was not to be Jean's last meeting with Churchill, who remained one of her many staunch admirers. His daughter, actress Sarah Churchill, was present later that year when Jean came on her own for dinner at the villa. In a subsequent letter (later published in her autobiography*) to her mother, Lady Churchill, she described the unhappiness and disillusionment they detected in Jean that evening.

'Jean Batten, the flier, came to dinner; she is exactly Diana's age.† It was obvious she is a deeply unhappy and frustrated woman. Her nice character and self-discipline keep her going, but cannot hide the fact that she feels life is over. The war stopped her flying at the peak of her career – and there is really no more personal pioneering in this field at the moment. She must wait for spaceships I suppose.

'She talked with gentle resignation. It did some good to Diana for none of us is alone; but equally that is never an answer. Papa was intrigued with Jean Batten and said she must search for new horizons – search, *not* demand – that the next part of her life might be something, *must* be something, different but not *necessarily* less great.

'She laughed and went home, promising to come again and saying it had been a wonderful and inspiring evening – but we all felt sad despite Papa's words and he looked contemplative himself as he watched her drive herself away up the narrow winding drive in her small Austin, after the glories of the open sky.'

She and Ellen didn't stay long on the Riviera. As they had extended from one year to another their seemingly endless travels through Europe they had been drawn more and more to the climate of the south of Spain and had begun to spend all their winters there to spare Ellen, now in her eighties, from the cold she was increasingly unable to deal with. Indeed from

---

Keep on Dancing (Weidenfeld & Nicolson, London, 1981)
†Diana Churchill, Sarah's sister, was later to commit suicide. She and Jean were forty-six at the time of the visit to Cap d'Ail and Diana was going through bouts of acute despair.

Ellen's British passport, in Jean's archive, it is clear that, from around 1956, they must have been living more or less permanently in southern Spain, for it shows frequent crossings of the frontier into Gibraltar where they had opened an account with Barclays Bank.

It would probably have been in Spain that Jean learnt of the death in 1959 of Jim Mollison, one of the last of the 'greats' among the prewar record-breakers. He died, as he had lived much of his life, an alcoholic. Since (according to her memoirs) Charles Scott had shot himself with a revolver in Germany shortly after the end of the war, Jean, and the much less widely publicised Beryl Markham, were now almost the only surviving members of the era's big league.

Eventually Jean and Ellen found the Costa del Sol so agreeable they decided, for a while, to sink roots. They chose the small fishing village of Los Boliches where, in 1960, they bought a villa by the sea, calling it La Paloma in memory of Jean's birth music. Again their stay was to last six years.

Information on their life in southern Spain, as Ellen grew into her late eighties, is almost nonexistent. However, among her snapshots in the Batten family's collection of her photographs and cuttings, I found some tiny faded prints. One showed Jean in a pinafore standing outside a Spanish villa. Another had her in a bikini on a beach with a dog; on the back she had written: 'Fuengirola'. On a map I located it: a town on the Mediterranean coast about twenty miles south-west of Malaga. I went there.

It proved, in 1987, to be in the midst of the continuous tourist colony of apartment blocks, hotels, villas and hoardings that now extend in one long fusion all the way from Malaga to Gibraltar. The fishing village of Los Boliches at the eastern end of Fuengirola had long since disappeared under high-rise developments. However, with the help of the 1961 snapshot, I was able to locate the approximate spot where Jean had been photographed by Ellen. Close by I found La Paloma. It had been converted into an Arab restaurant, the Sheherezade, which was now derelict.

At the back of the former villa I stood among the detritus of abandoned restaurant chairs, tables and broken glass on the terrace where Jean and Ellen so many years before must have sat and laughed together, comfortable in the knowledge that almost certainly no one knew of this sanctuary they had created in the obscurity of southern Spain long before the tourist invasion brought any risk of the intrusions they so dreaded.

I tried to find people who might have known them during their six years at La Paloma – a period Jean inexplicably dismissed in one sentence in her memoirs. But despite appeals on local radio and in the English language press on the Costa del Sol, no one ever came forward. It seemed as if, in their Spanish retreat, they had now grown so close that any other relationships would have been superfluous. As confirmation of their deepening isolation, Jean's address book, which I was later to acquire, contained not a single name that could be traced to those years on the Costa del Sol.

In a 1970's interview in New Zealand Jean was to talk about Ellen's remarkable state of preservation as she grew very old, describing how she would insist at Los Boliches on walking a mile every day. 'Even nearing ninety mother was tall, elegant and with a beautiful head of hair. When she was eighty-nine she had me drive her to Gibraltar for her first reading glasses. She used to read *The Times* every day.'

I also drove the two hours down the coast to Gibraltar and visited the Bristol Hotel in Cathedral Square at the foot of the Rock. She and Ellen used to stay there on their regular visits from Spain to go shopping, see their bank manager, visit the dentist and license their car, which they felt happier having registered under the British flag. But there was no one at the hotel old enough to remember them.

Somehow towards the end of her La Paloma days an un-expected echo from her glorious past came from New Zealand. It was a letter which eventually reached her by the slow and devious means she had devised via Barclays in London and their branch in Gibraltar. It came from the Auckland Regional Authority whose chairman, Mr Hugh Lambie, was inviting her to be a guest at the official opening in January 1966 of the city's new international airport. It had been built on the site of the small grass aerodrome on which she had landed at the end of her triumphant 1936 flight from England.

A copy of her reply, written from the Portuguese North Atlantic island of Madeira, on 29 December 1965, is on display to this day in the airport terminal building. 'I am sorry that I can't accept your invitation,' she wrote, 'for to do so would involve me in considerable inconvenience and expense. I am travelling with my car and have already booked to ship it to Tenerife and Las Palmas then to Casablanca from where I intend driving it to Rabat and Marrakesh for several weeks and back to Tangier at the end of the winter.'

They were on the move again. Jean had already taken all the large shabby suitcases containing the memorabilia of her years of fame – a small mountain of photographs, press cuttings and correspondence – across the frontier to Gibraltar where she left them, probably with Barclays Bank, happy in the knowledge that they were in British hands. Shortly afterwards, in the late autumn of 1965, they had sold La Paloma and, incredibly as it may seem, as Ellen was now in her ninetieth year, had once more divested themselves of most of their possessions and set out on the extended winter holiday, which Jean had described in her letter, to Madeira, the Canary Islands and North Africa. It seems a possibly unwise venture with someone as old as Ellen, but there is not a clue in the memoirs to explain what appears to have been yet another of the reckless impulses that seized them at regular intervals. It is possible that the rising tide of tourism had helped to drive them out of southern Spain; but where did they intend living the following spring?

In one of the last pictures ever taken of her, Ellen is seen in the centre of Seville feeding the pigeons and, although still tall and erect, her features under her white hair have begun to shrink and she looks for the first time frail and vulnerable.

We will never know what their long-term plans were because they were to become irrelevant. After leaving the Costa del Sol, Ellen's passport shows that they drove across the border into Portugal to Lisbon from where they shipped the car to Madeira, arriving late in November and staying until 7 January 1966. The car was now driven on to another ship and they went south to the Spanish Atlantic islands of the Canaries which were next on their itinerary. They first visited Tenerife, arriving at the port of Santa Cruz on 8 January.

For some weeks they drove about this beautiful and rugged island, its landscape dominated by a central 12,000-foot high dormant volcano. They were looking for somewhere remote, well away from the reach of tourists (who then anyway came only by sea and in tiny exclusive numbers) to settle for a few months before sailing on to Las Palmas and then to North Africa.

At last, to their delight, they found what they were looking for – a successor to Los Boliches as they had first discovered it: the tiny unspoiled fishing village of San Marcos. Here, in a small rented second-floor apartment, perched on a cliff high above a spectacular rocky cove, looking out across the Atlantic, on 19 July that year, just three months short of her ninetieth birthday, Ellen Batten died in Jean's arms.

CHAPTER 21

Grief (1966–1969)

'I can hardly see for the tears to write this letter for my heart is breaking. She passed away quite suddenly the day before yesterday. The last thing she said as I held her in my arms was, "Now none of that or you will make me feel unhappy."

'We took her yesterday to the tiny Anglican cemetery at Puerto de la Cruz in a lovely white car. I had prepared her myself, bathed her and arranged her hair and put a pale blue silk scarf over her head – she always liked to be well-groomed – a lace handkerchief in her pocket with a sachet of *Jolie Madame*, her favourite perfume. The casket was the best I could find – solid mahogany padded with mauve satin and lined with glass.

'She lay there looking like a sleeping princess – peaceful, fragile and beautiful – I was so proud of her. The Vice-Consul, Mr Reid, was able to obtain at short notice a lovely bouquet of ninety red roses, my last gift to her – one for every year of her life.

'The casket is placed in a niche in the wall so I can move it again if I want to take her with me to Europe. I think I will stay here until her birthday. I am trying so hard to be brave but it is

Gipsy Moth RB. Jean had the names of her thirty-five refuelling stops between Lympne and Sydney painted on the fuselage. (*Batten Family Collection*)

In the early morning dark of 5 October 1936, Jean climbs aboard the Gull at Lympne for her flight to New Zealand. The rear cabin is filled by her huge long-range fuel tank. (*Fox Photos*)

The 1935 crash that Jean never spoke of:
the badly damaged Gull after her emergency landing
in a field near Midhurst in Sussex. (*Bruce Shaxson*)

The aircraft logbook in which Jean triumphantly recorded her 1936
England-New Zealand records.

(1) JOURNEY FROM Richmond-Sydney		(2) TO Auckland New Zealand		
OPERATING CREW.			**VISA.**	
(3) Names.	(4) Duties.	(5) Incidents and Observations.	(10) By the Aeronautical Authorities.	(11) By the Customs Authorities.
Jean Batten Pilot		Left RAAF Station Richmont N.S.W. at 04.35 hours local time for New Zealand		(a) Passenger Lists :— No............ (b) Manifests :— No............ (c) Visa :—
(6) Date.	(7) Places of Departure, of intermediate landings and of arrival.	(8) Arrival. (9) Departure.	16.10.36	Group Captain Commanding R.A.A.F. Station Richmond N.S.W.	(a) Passenger Lists :— No............
15.10.36 Sydney		18.30	Lympne-Auckland 11 days 45 mins First Direct Flight England-New Zealand	No............ (b) Manifests :— No............
16.10.36 Auckland.		5.05	Sydney-New Plymouth Record Flight ever Tasman Sea 9 hrs 29 mins	(c) Visa :— (a) Passenger Lists :— No............
			16 OCT 1936 McIntosh	(b) Manifests :— No............ (c) Visa :—
(12) SIGNATURE OF OFFICER IN CHARGE Jean Batten				

16 October 1936: the crowd of 6,000 that turned out at Mangere to greet Jean at the end of the first ever flight from England to New Zealand. (*New Zealand Herald*)

Jean and her mother on the ship that brought Ellen hurrying to Sydney late in 1936. (*Sydney Morning Herald*)

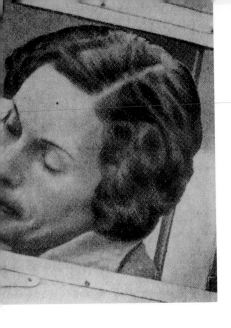

Headlines like these
made Jean famous
for four years.
(*Daily Express*)

Ill with exhaustion,
Jean had to be lifted
out of the Gull
cockpit on arrival in
Naples from Australia
on her last epic flight
in October 1937.
(*Daily Mail*)

Jean features at the
top of a group of
record breaking
celebrities in a 1937
London newspaper.
(*Batten Family Collection*)

Legs numb with
cramp, Jean
is carried through
the crowd at
Croydon in 1937,
having just broken
the Australia-
England solo record.
(*Daily Mail*)

Daily Express

RADIO PROGRAMMES: PAGE 23.

No. 11,681 MONDAY, OCTOBER 25, 1937 ONE PENNY

from springtime into autumn . . . Last week I was sun-bathing, and now . . .

HE GIRL WHO HAS BEATEN ALL THE MEN

. AT CROYDON
DAY :: TRIUMPH

Lucky Comb Was Lucky Again!

Dictated in the Daily Express office last night by

Jean Batten

(World Copyright)

PLEASE let me sit here pretty close to you so that I can hear you ask me questions. And put me on a hard chair. My ears are still singing, and if I sit in that armchair I shall just go off to sleep. You see, I've had only eighteen hours' sleep since I left Darwin.

MARRIAGE? NOT YET, says Jean

[illegible]

'The Good Companions', Jean captioned this picture of her and eighty-nine-year-old Ellen in Seville, Spain. I[t] was taken on Jean's fifty-sixth birthday in September 1965, ten months before Ellen's death.
(*Batten Family Collection*)

Looking like a woman in h[er] thirties, sixty-year-old Je[an] goes back to see her Gull [at] the Shuttleworth Museum [at] Old Warden in Bedfordshi[re].
(*Batten Family Collectio[n]*)

Hair dyed blonde, Jean, at sixty-seven, flew to Auckland in 1977 to open an aviation pioneers' pavilion at the Museum of Transport and Technology. (*MOTAT*)

In the intake of an Air New Zealand airliner at Auckland, Jean, approaching sixty-eight, poses youthfully with the model of her Gull made for her by Captain Bob Miles. (*New Zealand Herald*)

No.	Name	Age	
138	Ophelia Martinez 61	83	C
139	Francisco Jimenez Correa 62	62	C
140	Günter ...		V.
141	Catalina Ripoll Garau	91	V.
142	Andrea Rigo Char	79	S
143	Gabriel Brunet Sancho	79	C
144	Antonia Cardona Trasanc	30	C
145	T. del flor Pompar/Tesquiry	46	C
146	Jean Gardlner Batten		Judicial
147	Florfluno Martinez Comino	57	C
148	Barblome Mateu Vicens		
149	Antonio Riera Riley	60	C
150	Nadal Cladera Perello	68	C
151	Geronimo Cheva Conard	80	C
152	Miguel Puigserver Puig	88	C
153	Jose Valent Segura	62	C

Jean Gardner Batten's name, and her burial number, 146, in the Spanish cemetery register. Her middle name was misspelt. (*Author*)

The final loneliness of the long-distance aviator. (*Author*)

taking me all my strength.'

Jean drafted and redrafted this text using the heavily amended final version as a master-letter to copy, with small variations, to the people she notified of Ellen's death. She sat alone in the small apartment above the little fishing harbour, numbed and shocked by grief. Although there is no record of it she probably sent a cable to Fred.

But she could not bring herself to tell John that their mother was dead. She wrote instead to Harold who later showed his brother the letter. 'It was a very touching note,' said John. 'She and mother were so close, it must have been like husband and wife. She must have been desolate.'

Although she had ignored him John now wrote to Jean – his first letter since their 1931 row – trying to persuade her to come back to New Zealand and even offering to give her a home in his house in Auckland; but she did not reply.

Jean told the Anglican vicar in Tenerife, Canon Phillip Miller, that she would never leave the island without her mother's bones. But the truth was that she had nowhere to go, no real long-term friends with whom she had kept in touch. Emotionally devastated, and now approaching fifty-seven, she clung to the only prop she had – the memory of Ellen. To be close to her she decided to stay on the island. She was to do so for sixteen years.

In the geography of Jean's life Tenerife occupies the most psychologically traumatic position of all. I flew there early in 1987 to try and find people who might have known her during those years of grief. From the files at the British Consulate in the island's capital, Santa Cruz, it was possible to identify the tiny village of San Marcos where Ellen had died. Still largely unspoilt, it was set in steep black volcanic sea cliffs on the island's west coast. The registration card, showing that Jean and Ellen had applied for a *residencia* (a short-term foreigner's residence permit), had given their address as the Apartamentos Baez. Since renamed the Miramar, its owner, Señor Baez, actually remembered Jean and Ellen taking No. 7 early in 1966. The old woman, he said, was *muy tranquila* – so quiet he suspected that she was unwell. He saw very little of them in the following months because they rarely left the apartment. He wasn't surprised when, after a few months, he heard that the mother had died.

I found Ellen's grave in the small British Protestant cemetery, protected by a high rectangular wall, next to the police station in the tourist town of Puerto de la Cruz. The grave was high up among scores of concrete niches and the headstone Jean had put there said simply: ELLEN BATTEN BELOVED MOTHER OF JEAN BATTEN 21.10.1876 – 19.7.1966.

Two things were remarkable about the inscription. Although Ellen's husband, Fred, was then still alive and so were her two sons, Jean chose to ignore them on the plaque as if they did not exist. And presumably because of her sense of self-importance, she had instructed the stonemasons to carve her own name in letters prominently larger than Ellen's. It looked incongruous, and at first glance gave the impression that she, not her mother, was buried there.

Who had Jean turned to in the years of the abnormal grief that was to paralyse her emotionally and from which she never was quite to recover? In her memoirs she appears to have shared it with no one. It is clear that she was so totally demolished that she rapidly slipped into deep depression, struggling through each day 'in a sea of numbing misery and despair ... drifting away', she wrote, 'beyond recall and hope of recovery'.

In one of her few frank and desperate admissions, she described how she felt herself lacking 'the courage and strength of character to rise above it. I appeared incapable of doing so, alone as I was, in a foreign land with no one to turn to, stunned with grief and really frightened for the first time in my life.' She wrote that she lost two stone (nearly thirteen kilos) in weight. But she made no attempt to seek medical help.

Her first instinct was to run. But to where? She had spurned the overture from her brother. And she had long since cut herself off from her friends in New Zealand and Australia where she had once been revered and would still have been warmly and sympathetically received. Most of her English friendships had been transitory, on the crest of fame. In Spain she and Ellen had, apparently deliberately, established no new friendships at all. But in Jamaica, to where she had already once been drawn back, there was somebody.

His name was Oswald Girling, an English businessman and planter, well known as a racehorse owner, and a former neighbour at Blue Horizon. His wife had died and, according to Lady Mitchell, 'he was a great admirer of Jean'. Little information exists about their relationship, but it was clearly sufficiently warm for Oswald Girling, early in 1967, on hearing of Ellen's death, to invite Jean to his Ocho Rios home, Blue Shadows, for a holiday.

But before accepting this lifeline she came, for the first time in her life, under some emotional pressure from Fred to visit him for what he knew would be the last time. Now in his late eighties he was living out his days in a retirement village in the Auckland suburb of Mt Roskill where he was visited daily by John who now lived on his own in the city where earlier he had worked as an announcer for one of the local radio stations, 1ZB.

According to Ramai Hayward, in the months following Ellen's death Fred had begun to plead for Jean to come back to see him for one last time before it was too late. She said his requests became more and more persistent and that, for some reason, early in 1967, he had, to his great excitement, come to believe that she was about to make the journey. But Jean, swamped by grief and misery, was torn between the pressure on her to visit her dying father and her greater desire to escape to the soothing environment of the Caribbean to restore her emotional equilibrium.

In the event she succumbed to Oswald Girling's invitation. Jean and Fred (according to John) had rarely corresponded, but she now wrote to her father saying, in a phrase she frequently used in letters she found difficult to write, that she hoped he would understand. It is apparent that Fred didn't understand and that he was bitterly disappointed. Shortly afterwards he suffered a minor stroke and his letter of reply, the only one of his to Jean that has survived, is in someone else's handwriting – highly probably that of his longstanding friend, Gertrude Perry. It was undated.

Masonic Village
Mt Roskill
Auckland

Dear Jean

You will doubtless get a surprise at receiving a letter from me but the truth is letter writing is too much for me – I fizzle out after a few lines. May the Lord help me, a friend of mine is writing this letter. She is thoroughly trustworthy and I have known her for years. You must miss your Mother – my letter of condolence fell short I know. However it comes to all of us sooner or later. What actually happens to us we can't know. Well take care of yourself and enjoy your winter holiday.

Love from

Dad.

The letter betrays the sadness Fred felt that he would never see Jean again. He had been hanging on to life, friends said, in the hope that she would make it. Although he had bitterly opposed her flying activities out of a genuine concern for her safety, it is clear that he was deeply fond of her and much distressed at her unwillingness to make the effort to visit him.

As Fred, his jaw paralysed by his stroke, moved into the last months of his life, Jean flew to London and boarded a ship for Jamaica to stay with Oswald Girling. 'I forced myself against my better judgement to go in the hope of easing the terrible grief that held me in a vice-like grip,' she wrote, making no reference to Fred's pleas.

She does not mention Girling anywhere in her memoirs. Yet he was in fact (I discovered very late in my research) one of the two men she claimed in her narrative to have 'nearly married' on the rebound from grief. It was from Lady Mitchell that the truth came. After viewing my documentary in Jamaica early in

1990, she wrote expressing surprise that Girling had not been mentioned in the film as one of the men in Jean's life. The reason for her surprise, she explained, was that during Jean's 1967 holiday when she and Girling had been alone together at Blue Shadows for many weeks, 'he had asked her to marry him – but she refused'.

Jean's memoirs would appear to confirm this – although naming neither of the two men. 'On both occasions,' she wrote 'I changed my mind until I could think more clearly, for I still found it almost impossible to free myself from the constricting web that grief had woven round my spirit.'

On her Jamaican holiday she made contact with few of her former neighbours and acquaintances and insisted that Oswald Girling not advertise her presence on the island. Ertis Morrison said that he thought he was seeing a ghost when, one day, she passed him as a passenger in a car near Ocho Rios. 'It was still a small community of residents,' he said. 'None of us knew she was there.'

Back in Tenerife Jean also went to some lengths to avoid the British expatriate community and moved 'into the old house of a friendly Spanish lady named Carmen who used to address me as Juanita'. While she was lodging there news reached her of Fred's death. He had died peacefully on 20 July 1967, three months before his eighty-eighth birthday.

Unlike the lengthy account her memoirs give of the bitter grief Ellen's death caused her, Fred's passing is dismissed in a few lines: 'It came as a terrible shock. I loved both my parents so deeply and any success I may have achieved I owe to their guidance and help in my formative years and to the wonderful bond of understanding, based on mutual trust, that developed between us as I grew up.' She could not, even now they were both dead, bring herself to reveal that she had been the product of a divided and unhappy home.

In fact for the last thirty years of his life, Fred had mattered very little to her. John Batten commented: 'Dad idolised Jean – the converse was not the case. Mother disliked my father. Jean worshipped mother: the two only lived for each other and nobody else – but *nobody* – counted.' But Jean's indifference to Fred did not diminish his great affection for her – as she was to discover when the provisions of his will were communicated to her.*

In an effort to find people among the Tenerife expatriate community who knew her during this desperate period, I went to the British Club on the slopes above the town of Puerto de la Cruz. But she had never set foot there. Nearby at the English Library, where elderly expatriates retired from Ealing and Chelmsford sat reading the Daily Telegraph and Time magazine, one of the librarians, Irene Davis, who told me she was over ninety, paused from date-stamping books to say, 'Yes, I knew her by sight. When you spoke to her in the street she barely acknowledged you. She would pass by shielding her face with a big straw hat. Have you tried Annette Reid?'

Annette Reid was the Rhodesian-born sister-in-law of the honorary British Vice-Consul who had handled Jean's and Ellen's Spanish residencia applications in 1966. A handsome woman of great courtesy and charm, I took her to be in her sixties when I met her at her large villa on the hillside above Puerto de la Cruz in 1987. She had met Jean through the Vice-Consul soon after Ellen's death and had been an affectionately sympathetic witness of her grief.

'I remember being very struck by this woman who appeared to have everything: fame, beauty, and a striking personality. But she was enveloped in tremendous sadness ... one could see that she had received a really knock-out blow to her whole psyche. Whenever I met her in the street in those months after her mother's death she would just dissolve into tears and her

---

*Among Fred's effects was a trunk full of memorabilia of Jean's years of fame. It included one of her most sacred medals. John had earlier taken it to Auckland airport to present to the English pilot, Sheila Scott, during her celebrated 1966 round-the-world solo flight of her Piper Comanche Myth Too. When she got back to England, Sheila wrote to Jean: 'When I went to take off from Auckland there was a very shy, but sweet, man standing by the aircraft, who turned out to be your brother. Naturally I was thrilled to meet him and, during our conversation, he handed me your 1937 Harmon Trophy medal to carry back to England and maybe to give back to you one day. He said that it would keep me safe and get me home all right.' Subsequently Sheila (who died in 1988) was herself awarded the Harmon Trophy for her global flight.

terrible grief just poured out. She told me she owed absolutely everything to her mother who had been her life's greatest support and companion, had sacrificed all for her – and was the only person who had ever understood her.'

Annette Reid tried hard to befriend Jean, but found her tearfully reluctant to communicate. 'She put up this huge barrier. She was very aloof. I'm afraid she didn't open many windows to let you peep inside. But I began to realise that she didn't have a single intimate friend in the world – not one genuine friend – and I don't think at that time that she actually had such a tremendous desire to live. I always thought of her as a wonderful star that had shot across the firmament and burnt itself out. There was nothing left.'

'There were lots of people who would have liked to have befriended Jean,' Esther Mather said. 'But she didn't know how to unbend and mix with ordinary mortals. She had become so possessed by her mother that when she died she became a lost soul.'

Despite her now desperate need for friendship Jean rebuffed most of the overtures made to her on Tenerife and increasingly people were beginning to find her distinctly eccentric. She would go to services at the Anglican church in Puerto de la Cruz, always arriving a few minutes late to avoid having to speak to anyone. She would sit at the back and, just before the service ended, hurry off before she was obliged to socialise.

Jean, who spoke fluent Spanish, walked about the streets of Puerto de la Cruz carefully avoiding the English community and at times behaving curiously. 'I'll never forget the day I met her in town and tried to introduce her to a friend who was with me,' Annette Reid said. 'I was about to explain who Jean was when she turned abruptly on her heels and, without so much as a word, just walked off. I was absolutely flabbergasted.'

Sometime during 1968, when Tenerife's first international airport was starting to pour the tourists in, Jean moved out of Carmen's home, sold her car, and bought a tiny flat on the sixth floor of the Apartamentos Residencia Avenida. The block was in the Avenida del Generalissimo Franco, one of the main streets in the now rapidly developing holiday town of Puerto de la Cruz. The apartment, characteristic of her spartan style, was austere and cramped. It comprised just one very small room with a minute separate kitchen and a shower cubicle. Here she withdrew more and more into herself. The few people to whom she ever spoke found her total absorption with her dead mother distinctly morbid; one of them said: 'She seemed actually to resent her mother's action in dying — as if the old lady had deliberately deserted her.'

One day Annette Reid went to the apartment with a woman visitor to the island who had a letter of introduction to Jean and was keen to meet her. 'I rang her bell and she opened the door. I heard a man's voice inside. I was about to open my mouth — but I didn't get that far. Jean just took one look at the woman and slammed the door shut in our faces. Next day, alone in the street, I bumped into Jean. She apologised. She said she had had a friend and his wife from England visiting and we had arrived at an inconvenient moment. I didn't take umbrage but my friend will never forget the rudeness. Jean was not a particularly compassionate woman. She was only interested in people she viewed as being as significant as herself. Ordinary human beings and their problems, I'm afraid, didn't much appeal to her.'

One of the few other people on Tenerife who remembered Jean was an elderly widow, Mary Ireland. She must once have been a lively and extrovert woman but, sadly, when I met her in her flat in Puerto de la Cruz she had recently suffered a major stroke and lay ill in bed, looked after by a Spanish maid. But she had insisted on meeting me and, although her speech had become badly slurred, was anxious to talk about Jean whom she candidly described as 'a very odd fish'. 'She used to go for long lonely walks round the town and up into the hills and would sometimes just knock on the door and walk in here — usually at the oddest times extraordinarily early in the morning.'

'But', said Mary Ireland, 'what problems that woman had. She was totally bound up in a mother complex which I found quite morbid — she talked endlessly about her and the bones she was going to take wherever she went in the world. Her loneliness was quite desperate.'

For the three remaining years of the 1960s, Jean sat in apartment 606 fighting her grief. She began to seek comfort from the writings of the great Spanish and French ancient mystics, searching for guidance from their personal spiritual experiences of God as the ultimate reality. 'One day,' she wrote, 'I found a passage in a translation of the autobiography of St Thérèse of Lisieux which seemed like a lifeline to cling to. I might have written it myself so perfectly did it express my feelings for mother -- the words of another woman whose grief must have nearly matched my own; I read it again and again: "Dear mother, it was you who taught me to sing from childhood upwards, it was your voice that thrilled me, and it is quite splendid nowadays to hear people say that I remind them of you. Not that I'm in the least like you really; but I do hope, with all my disabilities, to join my song with yours in eternity."

Out on her balcony she would sit, looking up at the deep blue sky at the streaming silver contrails of the big jets passing over the island on the high-level airways to and from South America to where she had flown so long ago. And every morning she put out scraps for the birds whose companionship she preferred to the members of the English retired community. She avoided her neighbours in the Avenida apartments, hurrying in and out of the building always with a large hat covering her face. She began a routine of daily exercise often striding off on long walks soon after dawn to avoid bumping into other expatriates who might intrude into her life. Avoiding the lift she would run down the six flights of stairs from her apartment. 'It's good for the ankles,' she told the amazed people who asked why she did it. She went regularly to the cemetery to gaze moist-eyed at Ellen's grave high up on the wall and to change the vases of flowers. Equipped with a snorkel, she began to go swimming every day in a small harbour a few minutes' walk from her apartment, after which she indulged in the ritual of a quarter bottle of Spanish champagne.

On her daily swims she was sometimes joined by the elderly vicar, Canon Miller. He was to tell friends how one day he had taken her elbow to guide her across the street but had been startled when she recoiled and hissed at him, 'Don't ever touch me.' Aghast and embarrassed he never extended old-fashioned courtesies to her again.

After nearly three years of persistent depression Jean decided at last to seek help. She went, in the summer of 1969, to see a doctor. Although it is not clear from her memoirs it seems probable that, to avoid gossip on the island, she flew to London to the anonymity of Harley Street. The doctor tried to help her, she wrote, by reassuring her that she was suffering from no more that acute grief and telling her she should be grateful that Ellen had lived to such a ripe old age and had gone without suffering. How she was treated, in view of her total aversion to drugs of any description, is not known. All she records of the consultation is the doctor's apparent amazement at her physical state of preservation for a woman now just turned sixty. 'He tested my lungs, heart, blood-pressure and announced that I was in the twenty-seven-year age group.'

Her self-esteem moderately restored, Jean flew back to Tenerife. She hadn't been home very long when she received a telegram which was to propel her, in one swift leap, out of depression, and to change the whole course of the rest of her life.

CHAPTER 22

The Comeback (1969–1977)

The telegram was an invitation to the start of a major air race from England to Australia planned for December 1969. It was to commemorate the fiftieth anniversary of Ross and Keith Smith's first flight in 1919. Sponsored by British Petroleum and organised by the Royal Aero Club, it was due to be started from Gatwick by the pioneer aviator and round-the-world yachtsman, Sir Francis Chichester.

Although Jean claims in her memoirs that the invitation came 'literally out of the blue', the truth was that she had engineered it. She had written to the race director at the club offering to be involved. Although her name was by now only a memory in aviation circles the race officials were not slow to capitalise on her publicity value. Not only did they promptly send her an invitation, they arranged for her to be flown from Tenerife and put up at the Waldorf Hotel in London as their guest.

Although this came as a tonic to her depression Jean was assailed by momentary doubt. 'When the war ended, and my career with it, I had wanted to be remembered, if at all, as a happy, smiling young girl in a white flying suit,' she wrote. 'Was it wise to make a come-back at sixty years of age?' But she managed to reassure herself: 'After all I did look only half my age and felt no more than twenty-five. Mother, who had always seemed ageless, once said to me, "I doubt if you will ever grow old for you've never really grown up."' But although young in spirit, looking in the mirror she could see the first disconcerting evidence of her advancing years. She decided to deal with it by flying to London again and having a face-lift. Few of her friends were ever to know of the operation which was done privately at the expensive London Clinic. It was paid for by money Fred had left her. He had provided for John, Harold and his long-term companion Gertrude Perry, but had left the lion's share to Jean.

Back in Tenerife she went into hiding until the scars had healed. But although the surgery had removed the worst of her facial lines she was disappointed (she later admitted to a friend) that it hadn't rejuvenated her more obviously. She went on a shopping spree in Puerto de la Cruz. As painstakingly as she had done in the golden years she set about crafting a suitable image for her renaissance. She dyed her short brunette hair a startling jet black. And, to heighten the illusion of youthfulness and embrace the fashion of the swinging sixties, she bought some mini-skirts. They did not look amiss for her legs were still appealingly shapely. With the help of the surgery, and with not a strand of grey hair in sight, she looked in her new attire not a day older than forty.

She arrived in London in mid-December in a white leather coat, white hat and white boots looking, as the *Sunday Express* said 'like a snow queen'. It was just like old times.

At that moment in the greyness of the English winter of 1969 Jean's animus was reborn. Presenting a façade of great happiness, she re-entered the English aviation scene with grace and gusto.

She was photographed with Sir Francis Chichester as he flagged away the air race competitors, none of which, to her open delight, managed to lower her five days twenty-one hours solo time to Darwin – which had now stood for thirty-three years, far into the age of jet-powered flight.

But her outward gaiety didn't deceive everyone. She caught

up again with Sir Peter Masefield, now chairman of the British Airports Authority, who organised a dinner party in her honour and invited her to his home in Reigate. He hadn't met her for over thirty years and was struck by the change in her personality. Behind the buoyant exterior Sir Peter sensed that she was deeply insecure and that her life had lost direction. 'Her flying had been a way in which she'd found expression: she appeared still to be searching for something to replace it. She came to spend the day with us. We found her emotional and talkative. From the moment she walked into the house about ten o'clock in the morning until she left around seven in the evening she never drew breath. And she talked entirely about herself – all about the past which was where she was still living. She'd become a sad and lonely figure. However good her navigation had once been, she had now clearly lost her way and was concerned about her future. We felt very sorry for her.'

Few of the people Jean was now meeting had known her in her heyday, however, and most lacked Sir Peter's perception. Not many were aware of the private struggle she faced searching for something to fill the great vacuum Ellen's death had left. Her public wit and sparkle deceived most of her new admirers.

She was interviewed on BBC radio and television; was guest of honour at the Press Club; became an enthusiastic member of the British Women Pilots' Association, honoured to have one of the great names of aviation unexpectedly in their midst; and she went up to the little grass airfield at Old Warden in Bedfordshire where, at the Shuttleworth Collection of historic aeroplanes, she had an emotional re-union with the Gull. After its RAF wartime service it had been bought by its manufacturers, the Percival Aircraft Company, and put back on the civil register. The Shuttleworth museum had acquired it in 1961 and had flown it regularly at air shows. Although she no longer held a flying licence the museum had hoped to take her for a short flight for old times' sake. But the Gull was growing tired. Parts of its wooden frame needed re-glueing and the bottom of the fuselage had become soaked in oil. By the time she got to Old Warden it had been grounded.

Instead she was taken to Fairford in Gloucestershire and

shown the prototype of the British Concorde airliner. Photographed with its chief test pilot, Brian Trubshaw, on the flight deck she declared a new ambition: to fly to New Zealand in it in half a day. It was a dream that was later to become an obsession.

In her interviews, and at the many functions at which she was, once again, the guest of honour, she demonstrated precise recall of the details of her flights and records now forgotten by most people; for few of those who met her had been old enough to remember the bold headlines she had once made and the excitement and public admiration she had created. Her journeys, and her place in aviation history, had, over three decades later, assumed a new perspective. Their significance did not always lie within the comprehension of her 1960s audiences who had seen men walk on the moon. Where once she had been the heroine of the hour she was now viewed as a quaintly anachronistic figure from the past. Her legend had not endured like Amy Johnson's, whose name was permanently etched in British history. She was uncomfortably aware that people were having to be reminded exactly who she was. Yet, once she began to relive those flights, taking her listeners back to the brave days of Empire and her wood-and-fabric aeroplanes, she never failed to have people spellbound.

But not everyone knew quite how to take her. One of her air race hosts, who preferred not to be named, took her to dinner at the famous Rules restaurant in London. Towards the end of the meal, when both were mellowed by wine, he was startled to feel her knee exploring his under the table. 'I could not have been mistaken: she was clearly playing kneesy,' he said, confessing that he had discreetly withdrawn his leg. Before long other men were also to be startled by Jean's unexpected explicit overtures — some in much more intimate circumstances.

Occasionally the beautiful celebrity of the thirties was recognised. One of the air race's public relations men, Gavin Cochrane, took her to dinner at the Savoy. From a distant table she was spotted by Noel Coward who was dining with the actress Merle Oberon. The playwright's unmistakeable mellifluous voice hailed her affectionately across the restaurant: 'Jean, Jean — is it *really* you?' as he waved, then hurried over to greet her.

The air race committee had booked her into the Waldorf for a week for the period of the race. They were surprised when she was still there, at their expense, two weeks later. In fact she stayed on for Christmas and New Year. 'In the end she was there for a month,' one of her hosts told us. 'We had the devil's own job actually prising her out.' But the success of her comeback had made her restless and reluctant to return to her solitary existence. 'The excitement of it all had unsettled me,' she wrote. Her depression had magically begun to slide away and she was actively seeking a new stimulus to replace the psychological tonic of the air race.

She found it, she said, in Regent Street – at the reservations office of BOAC.* Lonely and suddenly seized again with wanderlust she went inside to get a timetable, out of curiosity to see how the routes had grown since the days of Imperial Airways. Half an hour later she emerged: in her handbag was a round-the-world air ticket – and a seat booked to leave Heathrow two days later.

Feeling, for the first time in thirty-four years, an urge to view again the green and folded landscape of her homeland, she flew to New Zealand. On the journey she spent much of the time on the 707's flight deck with headphones clamped on, listening with fascination to the torrent of radio voices that she had never known in the loneliness of the Moth and Gull cockpits. She astonished the pilots (she claimed in her memoirs) with her knowledge of the route.

Descending into the now vast and sprawling city of Sydney, she was briefly overcome with a spasm of emotion, she wrote, as vivid, painful recollections of Beverley Shepherd flooded back and 'the bittersweet memories filled my mind'.

During a six-day stopover there, in mid-January 1970, however, she made no attempt to trace any of her former women pilot friends. Nor did she attempt to publicise her presence in Australia.

At the now modern airport in Auckland where, thirty-three years before, she had made history, the young immigration

*British Overseas Airways Corporation, now British Airways.

officer glanced at the name in her passport without a flicker of recognition. There was no cheering crowd to meet her this time – merely, she later disclosed to a newspaper with customary mysteriousness, 'one person, an Auckland friend, forewarned'. In fact, although forewarned, the person waiting to greet her had never met her before. He was Lionel Murray, chauffeur for British Petroleum, sent by the company's Auckland area manager, David Kelly, who had been asked by London headquarters to look after her. The national heroine had so lost touch with relatives and friends in her own country she no longer knew anyone well enough to suggest they meet her.

No one gave her a second glance as she walked into the terminal building in her white mini-dress and was driven off in the company's large Chevrolet Impala by Lionel Murray. He told me that Jean had been so anxious to remain incognito that, after a few days in an international hotel, she borrowed his name and booked into a small motel as 'Miss Murray'.

She appeared to have no plans and Lionel Murray spent several days driving her around Auckland on nostalgic sightseeing trips looking at the streets and houses where she had lived as a child. 'I found her a bit stand-offish and very demanding,' he said. 'On the last day she made a curious remark. She said she was surprised that a man and a woman could spend a week in each other's company and still remain friends at the end of it.'

However her anonymous visit was not to remain so for long. The *New Zealand Herald* discovered and interviewed her. 'It was the first we knew she was in the country – we were astonished,' said her nephew, Jim Batten, who was farming at Ruatangata in the Far North. 'She may have come home to see the family but she certainly didn't tell any of us. I immediately phoned my brother Rick who was also farming not far away and he rang her at her Auckland hotel. She seemed thrilled to hear him and he invited her up.'

To avoid the two-and-a-half-hour bus journey Jean asked BP to deliver her to Rick's farm at Ruakaka in the company Impala. A large assembly of Battens gathered to meet her: her nephews, Jim and Rick, and their wives, Rhoda and Margaret, her niece Isobel Gunson and her farmer husband, Jim, and their various children. It was a red-letter day and the family were impressed when their famous aunt Jean swept up to the door of the farmhouse and emerged graciously in mini-skirt like a trendy fairy godmother. They invited her inside for a cup of tea and, with informal Kiwi hospitality, suggested that the chauffeur join them. 'But Jean wasn't having any of that,' Rick told us. '"The driver will have his outside," she said very firmly.'

Absent from the family reunion were Jean's two brothers. John had left New Zealand for good in 1968 after Fred's death, having tidied up his father's estate. Harold, whose wife Alma had died in 1966, was the father of Jim, Rick, Isobel and a third son, Colin, who had gone to live in Australia. Now sixty-seven, Harold had been suffering for some years from epilepsy and his mental instability, which had necessitated psychiatric treatment, had long been a source of concern to his children – particularly his occasional outbursts of violence. Jean was later to visit him on his farm nearby. 'It was a terrible shock to her to see what had happened to my father,' Isobel told us. 'She had so completely lost touch with us all she hadn't known anything was wrong.'

The reunion was a happy occasion. The family made a great fuss of the distinguished aunt. They were flattered to be entertaining her, but a little on edge for it was a bit like having royalty in the house. At the end of the day Jean was driven back to Auckland but soon returned to stay for some weeks in turn with Isobel, Jim and Rick. Having her in their homes they got to know her much better; they became fond of her but found her exhausting and demanding. 'She didn't seem to comprehend that we were all busy working farming families – and not making a lot of money any of us. It was as if she could not accept that other people had lives outside of her own,' said Isobel. She and her husband were farming at Whatitiri west of Whangarei and Jean, as she was so often to do to her hosts in the years ahead, went for a couple of weeks and stayed for two months. 'She was desperately lonely and craving family companionship,' said Isobel. 'But she got on our nerves after a while. She expected the farm to revolve around her. And she was quite helpless domestically. I suppose her mother must have looked after her all those years. She couldn't cook: it took her an hour one day to make a tiny, wizened little omelette – and she didn't even seem to know how to iron: the one time she offered she burnt the clothes.

'She was also very cautious with her money – plain mean in fact. She wrote a lot of letters and never paid for a single stamp. Almost every day she'd hand me a pile and say, "Could you just post these for me, dear." Nor did she ever offer to pay for a long-distance phone call. The only thing she ever bought us was a new toaster because ours didn't work properly and annoyed her.'

Towards the end of her stay at the farm Jean began to express a wish to come back to live in New Zealand. She got Isobel to drive her around Northland visiting real estate agents and looking at beach cottages for sale. One on Whangarei Harbour she very nearly bought. The families sensed that what she really hoped for was an offer to move in with one of them, but none could quite face the domestic stress it would have created.

'There was something artificial about her – she was not a natural person,' said Rhoda Batten, who had Jean to stay for a week. 'She made such a drama out of everything. I remember she insisted we plant a special fern garden to commemorate her visit; she didn't do it, of course, but took charge and directed the operation. She liked bossing people up.' They also found her very right-wing. Jim Batten said: 'She was a great admirer of Ian Smith, the Rhodesian Prime Minister, and the stand he had taken to block black rule.' (As a product of the old British Empire – throughout which she regarded the lower orders of all non-white races as 'natives' – there is evidence that Jean had difficulty coming to terms with postwar change. Throughout her life she never wavered from the belief that mankind was best served by pure white government.)

The Batten family found some of Jean's fastidiousness about her food frankly eccentric. 'Her tea had to be made in a strange and special way,' said Rhoda, 'and her poached eggs became a nightmare. The eye – the embryo – always had to be located and picked out. But we did it to humour her.'

Back in Auckland Jean's unexpected reappearance had her briefly in demand. She went on television. She opened a school near the airport that had been named after her and was appointed patron of the New Zealand Airwomen's Association. At the Auckland town hall she was invited to address a group of women. David Kelly, who drove her there, said: 'She was asked to sign the mayor's visitors' book. So was I. I put my name underneath hers. You've no idea the fuss she made. She turned to me indignantly and said, "I'm not accustomed to having people sign on the same page as me." She really meant it. I remember noticing then, although she was very beautiful still, what a hard face she had in repose.'

In her hometown, Rotorua, Jean climbed aboard a Cessna floatplane to be flown out to be the guest of a prominent businessman and his wife, Sir Noel and Lady Cole, at their lodge on the shore of Lake Rotoiti. The pilot was another aviation folk-hero, Fred Ladd, whose zany style of flying, singing ballads of his own composition and playing practical jokes on his passengers, had made him a national legend.* He had been fascinated by the Batten mystique since, as a young man in Hamilton in 1936, he had driven into town to hear her address a large crowd from a hotel verandah. Now he was meeting her for the first time. 'She was really two people, I quickly discovered,' he said at his home in Taupo shortly before he died in 1989. 'She was actually a very introverted person, but with the ability to switch on a highly extrovert performance whenever she was the centre of attraction. When she wasn't centre-stage I found her cold and unsociable as if the fuss being made of her was all a bit of a nuisance. When we landed on the lake at Moose Lodge that day it was all rather shattering. There was no one waiting on the beach to meet her. So I waded ashore carrying her in my arms and eventually a caretaker turned up. He said Sir Noel and his wife had just driven off to Auckland. There'd been some communication foul-up. She wasn't expected. I must say it was a chilling moment. The caretaker invited her into the house. But she absolutely refused. There was no way she was going near it. So I carried her out to the

---

*Captain Ladd was renowned for his vast flying experience and skill as well as his antics. When he died, aged eighty, the former bomber pilot and airline captain had logged 21,000 hours.

plane again and flew her back to Rotorua. It definitely wasn't her day.'

Jean's appearance in New Zealand made few headlines; mostly the interviews finished up on the women's pages. She seemed reluctant to talk about the missing years. 'If I'm a recluse I'm a very gay recluse,' she said, 'I can dance anyone off their feet.' To prove the point she startled reporters by leaping up and doing several spectacular high ballet kicks. 'I should really be called "Legs Batten" shouldn't I?' she laughed.

And so she diverted attention from the sensitive areas of her introverted life in which, for so long, she had been a prisoner of her mother, insulated from the stresses of the everyday world. She gave the impression of ideal happiness around her current eccentric way of life on Tenerife, painting a picture of an exotic and glamorous existence. To New Zealanders her legend was sacred; there was no one to challenge it and the sad reality was not to be laid bare for many years yet.

Behind what one newspaper called the 'bubbly extrovert' there lay a deeply insecure woman still badly missing the daily infusion of reassurance from her mother that had kept her afloat for nearly sixty years. In her memoirs she describes how at Mt Maunganui, in Tauranga, on one of her last days in New Zealand, she went alone to the beach where she had enjoyed those happy family holidays over half a century before. 'I spent the whole day lying in the sun and bathing,' she wrote. 'The peace and beauty of the scene seemed to kindle hope of a miracle. I felt that I had but to open my eyes to find mother sitting there beside me laughing and saying, "You little goose, to think that I would ever go away and leave you." But when I did look up there was no one to be seen – just the deserted beach and only the sound of the surf and the wind sighing through the golden tussocks.'

With Ellen gone there had been no one for a long time to supply the love she inwardly craved. However, she could at least find it in hungry, transient fashion. I was to meet only one of the lovers from whom now, at the age of sixty, she was to seek fleeting comfort in a surprisingly uninhibited demonstration of desire. It happened in Auckland. The man, whom I was not to meet until the very last weeks of my research, asked not to be named. Unmarried at the time, he was then manager of a well-known New Zealand company. He told me that Jean had astonished him by her forwardness and provocativeness during their brief liaison. 'I was quite amazed at her obvious experience,' he said. 'She really was an extraordinarily sensuous and stimulating woman. I was completely surprised by the speed with which our mutually agreeable affair developed. It began with her encouragement the first night we met.'

Later another prominent Auckland executive who had driven Jean to another town (on a much later visit to New Zealand in the 1970s) was to describe how she had come to his motel room and surprised him by insisting on cuddling and caressing him. 'It didn't go any further than that,' he said. 'But I can tell you that there was no doubt at all that, had I been willing, it would most assuredly have done so. What's more she was nearly seventy by then.' These revelations merely served to make more incomprehensible the barren and cloistered years Jean had sacrificed apparently willingly to her mother. They also deepened the mystery of the true nature of her sexuality, around which there had been persistent speculation throughout her life. Many of the men and women who had known her since adolescence had described her as cold, even prudish, sometimes actually recoiling with indignation even at the touch of a man's hand on her arm in conventional politeness. In her flying club days, during which large numbers of young men, finding her an irresistible challenge, had laid bets as to who would succeed in getting her into bed, she had apparently responded with such coldness and lack of interest some of them had suspected, somewhat simplistically, that she was lesbian. Her memoirs, written in her sixties, appear to endorse her mother's view that 'true freedom could only be obtained by training the mind to master the emotions, for to be governed by the body was to enslave oneself.'

Observers of her intimate relationship with Ellen had insisted that Jean had no need of emotional fulfilment beyond the love they shared, and for many of their years together this was undoubtedly true. But were they entirely right? Had there, perhaps, been grounds for Ellen's concern to keep her confined to her cabin on that long voyage to England? Out of Ellen's sight had she not found more normal satisfactions in her friend-ships with the men who had underwritten her fame? Were the rumours of her affair with a Swedish count perhaps well founded after all? Had the Swedish police been right in their broadminded assumptions about her disappearance with Carl Jacobson? Had she, out of Ellen's view, taken advantage of the casual opportunities that had presented themselves in Jamaica – and in wartime Britain, where she had met Richard? And had the wealthy men whom she claimed had wanted to marry her after Ellen's death been among the lovers it is clear she had?

Since she never revealed these matters to anyone, merely hinting mysteriously at them to a chosen few, we may never know the details. But the strong likelihood remains that Jean was, in truth, in inner rebellion against the repressive morality imposed on her by her authoritarian mother for the latter's own deep needs. And it adds weight to the belief of those of Jean's friends who insisted that Ellen, without doubt, destroyed her daughter's happiness.

'It is all wholly in character; it just further confirms our androgynous theory,' said Yvonne Edwards. 'Androgynous women have male sex drive with all its singlemindedness and intensity. Furthermore they develop a male ability to arrange their sex lives clandestinely, able to move easily from partner to partner in search of physical pleasure rather than emotional security, which Jean of course got for most of her life excessively from Ellen. Her mother probably would not have known of her highly secret affairs but one can't help wondering if their nomadic existence may not have owed something to moments of discovery – when Ellen perhaps decided to end a liaison with yet another swift move.

'Although Jean went to great lengths to represent herself in her writing and her actions as a highly moral, almost prudish person, that was almost certainly part of the cover, I'm convinced, for the fascinating duality of her personality. It also confirms her male qualities of ruthlessness, using the consider-able power of her physical charms either for pleasure or for professional advantage, or both. You only have to look at her at the age of fifteen in a bathing costume in those 1920s picnic pictures to see that here was someone with very early awareness of her body; someone who knew precisely what she was about. But it was all part of the unique person she was. If, back in 1909, Ellen had produced a biologically conventional daughter, then the world, quite simply, would not have had the remarkable Jean Batten.'

In April 1970 Jean left New Zealand and flew back to England. But, stimulated by the success of her reappearance, she was now reluctant to go home to Tenerife. Searching for more hospitality she astonished the 1920s pioneer, Sir Alan Cobham, whose air circus had once refused to give her a job, by getting in touch with him at his home on Guernsey in the Channel Islands. Sir Alan, who had founded one of Britain's most successful flight refuelling companies and, approaching seventy-six, had just retired, invited her to fly down and stay with him. She accepted with alacrity.

One is tempted to suggest that Cobham, one of the most eminent of the grand old men of pre-war British civil aviation, whose wife had died some years before (and from whom some warm and affectionate letters to Jean survive in her archive) might conceivably have been – after Oswald Girling – the second of the two men whom she frequently claimed in interviews had offered her marriage in the years immediately after Ellen's death. Her memoirs give no hint, merely referring to him as 'my old friend'. Sir Alan died only three years later, in 1973. The intimacy of his letters and the regularity with which he kept in touch through a series of elusive forwarding addresses, must qualify him at least as a candidate. Certainly his aviation eminence, his knighthood, and his business success with several homes scattered around the world, would have made him a highly agreeable proposition to Jean.

However, her 1970 visit to his Guernsey home was to be short. Two days after she arrived there was an unexpected phone call for her from Australia. It was an invitation from the fundraising organisers of the New South Wales Air Ambulance service to be a guest at a Sydney banquet in a few days' time. Qantas would fly her out for free. It was quite irresistible. Immediately cutting short her stay with Cobham, she flew to Australia for the second time in four months,

It was a thrilling moment for Nancy Bird Walton the day she went out to Kingsford-Smith Airport to meet Jean. Now fifty-four, she had married Charles Walton, a successful English businessman, and lived in a large comfortable home in the expensive north Sydney suburb of St Ives. As a nineteen-year-old student pilot she had once regarded Jean, she said, with awe and reverence, privileged even to be in her company. Over thirty years later she wasn't even sure whether she would recognise her.

But as Jean bounced jauntily off the aircraft looking amazingly younger than her sixty years, she spotted her instantly. 'She had mellowed a lot, I thought, and was a much more humble person than she'd been in the thirties,' said Nancy. 'I don't think any of us meant anything to her at all at that time. She was too famous to notice us.'

The hospitality from the Australian aviation community was unstinted and, as in the old days, she was delighted to find that she was not allowed to pay for a thing. In Melbourne, where she stayed with Freda Thompson, the pilot who had upstaged her at the Cootamundra ball back in 1934, she met Esther Mather again. Esther's husband had been killed in a motor accident in 1959, leaving her to support three children. She had a full-time job and wasn't able to put Jean up but she went with Freda to the airport to meet her. 'I was amazed,' said Esther. 'She hardly seemed to have aged at all. However, instead of bringing us up-to-date with her life she just talked about her famous flights. Her entire life seemed to have begun and ended in those years. I felt she was lonely and isolated in the past. Somehow she believed that the world still owed her a debt for what she had done for aviation.'

In Melbourne someone for whom Jean's fame was immortal now entered her life. Bob Miles was an Ansett Airlines captain who built radio-controlled model aircraft in his spare time. As a thirteen-year-old in 1934 he had been fascinated by her first flight to Australia and had determined one day to meet her. He had at last done so a few months earlier in Auckland where he had gone specially to see her with a proposal that he build her a quarter-scale model of the Gull. The plane, an impeccable replica with a wingspan of nearly eight feet, had now been completed and in Melbourne he flew it for her before a group of press photographers. Thus began a long friendship with Bob Miles and his wife Janette who were to provide her with much hospitality over the following years.

But the friendship was nearly to founder. It had been arranged that the model would go on public display at the RAF Museum in London. But when Captain Miles later wrote to Jean asking that its construction be acknowledged to him in a brief caption he was stunned by the rudeness of her reply. 'I have received your letter,' Jean wrote, 'and am astounded that you should now seek to impose conditions on my acceptance of the model and its display in the museum. I therefore hasten to write and let you know that under no circumstances would I be agreeable to your suggestions ... It occurs to me that, perhaps even subconsciously, you do not really want to part with it although you have written so repeatedly offering it to me. If this is the case, I am quite agreeable for you to keep it. In fact perhaps this is the best solution, in view of what you have written and I now think I would feel happier if you did so.'

Somewhat high-handedly — since the exquisitely detailed model, intended to commemorate her past, was costing her nothing — she concluded: 'I really do not care either way but, if you do want to go on with it, don't write to me, for this is definitely my last letter on the subject ... I will register this letter,' she added icily, 'so that you are sure to receive it and am also keeping a copy for reference.'

Bob Miles, who is a patient and gentle man, was deeply hurt. 'I almost told her to go to hell,' he said. 'But I kept my cool and the model went off to the museum. But it was very nearly the end of our friendship.'*

In her memoirs Jean wrote of that second 1970 visit to Australia that she flew extensively around the country as the guest of Ansett Airways. This was true, but she had gone to the

---

*Not only did the friendship survive but, later, Captain Miles built for Jean a model of her famous Moth, G-AARB. Today both models hang in the Museum of Transport and Technology in Auckland. And in their new habitat their creator is prominently acknowledged.

airline's chief, Sir Reginald Ansett, in Melbourne and asked for the tickets – one of which took her to Queensland to stay with another former friend, now President of the Queensland branch of the Australian Women Pilots' Association. Peg Kelman, whose husband Colin had died and who was now living in Brisbane, had reared five children since the 1930s. Although now sixty she was still an active pilot and offered to hire a club aircraft to fly Jean up to the Great Barrier Reef. They took a single-engined Piper Cherokee Arrow and followed the Queensland coast north to Rockhampton. The aircraft had dual controls and the two women sat side by side. 'I felt very honoured to have her with me and to be flying such a famous pilot,' Peg recalled. 'Halfway up to Rockie I said to her, "Now you have a go Jean."' The response was not what Peg had been expecting. 'She sort of froze and went rather rigid and drew away from the controls saying very firmly, "No, no, I don't want it." I must say I was very surprised because flying is like riding a bike. It's something you just don't forget. So a little further on I offered again. But she was quite emphatic. No way was she going to touch that control column and I didn't press her any more.'

The truth, according to former pilot colleagues of Jean's, was probably that she had lost confidence in her ability to fly well. 'She was such a paragon,' one of them said, 'that she would not have wanted to display anything less than perfect airmanship to the critical eyes of another pilot.' In fact Jean had always been reluctant to fly with other pilots, Nancy Bird Walton said, because she was sensitive to criticism. 'She flew as she lived her life – as a loner, preferring to have nobody watching. To her it was something intensely private.'

In the Cherokee, Peg Kelman flew Jean out to Great Keppel Island a few miles offshore from Rockhampton. 'To my amazement, since she was always such a prim and proper person, she stripped off and went skinny dipping,' said Peg. 'What's more she had a marvellous figure and could do it. I couldn't any more. And then she sat there eating oysters off the rocks. We even shared a room, which was unusual for Jean, and we talked a lot. She told me of the way her entire life had been dominated by her mother. She wasn't complaining or regretting it but it was clear that, despite her mother having made it to ninety, she believed that by the act of dying she had consciously chosen to desert her and leave her stranded in the world.

'Hearing all this for the first time I realised that Mrs Batten had affected the whole course of her life and had actually prevented her developing as a person. Instead of having her own husband and family and grandchildren here she was living this Greta Garbo existence on her island hideaway where she admitted she was virtually friendless. It all struck me as very, very sad.'

Later, in Cairns, Peg suggested they take a boat out to Green Island, another Barrier Reef resort. But when they tried to board it the boat was full. 'So she said to them, "Don't you know who I am?" and they said "No" and she said, "I'm Jean Batten." Well I don't think I'd better tell you what they said. But she didn't get on. And Jean was so angry she wanted to turn round then and there and go straight back to Brisbane.' But Peg talked her out of it and they went across to the island next day. 'She was like a spoilt child,' Peg said.

A visit to Australia that her hosts had intended to last a few weeks became protracted; Jean appeared reluctant to leave. She was passed from one group of women pilots to another all the way to Western Australia and back, and was given a side-trip to New Zealand – living and travelling for nearly three months entirely for free. At the end of it all, exhausted, she asked Qantas to fly her to Fiji so she could recover on a tropical beach.

Fortified, she flew on to America where she flung herself into a new round of heroine worship as the guest of the Ninety-Nines, an association of women pilots whose first president in 1929 had been Amelia Earhart. She got a brief taste of what the 1935 coast-to-coast tour would have been like had Ellen not vetoed it. When in October she finally got back to Tenerife she had been away from the island, continuously entertained and fêted, for ten months.

It was not easy to settle back into the secretive routine, the incognito life. She felt deflated and depressed. But the downside didn't last for long, for she had now well and truly opened Pandora's box. The news of her re-emergence was beginning to

get around. Within a few weeks she was in Paris as the guest of
the Old Tigers, a group of pioneer French aviators, and in
England revisiting Concorde. Learning that the whole Anglo-
French supersonic project was threatened by rising costs and
economic and environmental doubts she decided to launch a
one-woman campaign to save it. From Tenerife throughout
1971 she pounded out letter after letter on her portable typewriter, sending them in a steady stream to the London *Daily
Telegraph* which dutifully published them all. But not everybody believed in expensive supersonic air travel; from anti-
Concorde lobbyists she began to receive some bitter and abusive
letters.

Stimulated by the warmth of the response to her reappearance, she decided to create a shrine of her papers and memorabilia. She offered them to the RAF Museum at Hendon and
there she established the Jean Batten Archive, a collection of
press cuttings, photographs, maps, logbooks, trophies, medals,
passports, sketchbooks, items of clothing and correspondence.
She sorted and catalogued everything. Even the most mundane
items, she hoped, would be of public interest. And so, to a pair
of well-worn kid gloves, she attached a label inscribed in her
neat handwriting: 'The gloves Jean wore to Buckingham Palace
in 1936'. And on the bill for the coat she had bought from a
Tenerife boutique to launch her comeback she typed explicitly:
'Receipt for purchase of white kid coat with mink collar to wear
for visit to London on December 14 1969 for start of air race to
Sydney – the equivalent of £100! Well worth every peseta for it
gave me confidence and was greatly admired.'

But from her private correspondence she carefully removed
every letter that might have provided the slenderest evidence of
her true relationship with her father, her brothers, and the men
who had fallen in love with her. She sanitised the archive with
meticulous care and, to keep control of the papers, made it clear
to the museum that the material was merely on loan.

Anxious to remind people of her former glamour she began
attaching to her letters to old friends small photographs of
herself as she had looked in her heyday – always in white
helmet and goggles – saying, 'I thought you might like to have
the enclosed.' Esther Mather, who was one of the recipients,

said: 'She was a prisoner of her own image.'

By 1973 she had grown her hair long and dyed it auburn, and looked a great deal younger than her sixty-four years. She now began to write her memoirs. Throughout the 1970s she often alluded to them, raising expectations of startling revelations about her private life and 'scorching' references to famous people she had known.

Luck and the Record Breaker ran to nearly two hundred pages of close-typed narrative – much of it copied unchanged from her previous books – and spanning the years from her Rotorua childhood to the height of her comeback around 1976 when, for some unexplained reason, the narrative abruptly ended. As with her earlier books she wrote without professional help, confident that her fame would guarantee success despite her conspicuous lack of literary flair. It developed as a tediously disconnected, unrevealing chronicle, reflecting her egocentric and wondrously childlike view of a world that revolved around her. The emotional traumas that had seared her; the break-up of her family; her father's infidelities; the absolute dominance of her very being by her mother; the permanent rift with John; her enigmatic relationships with the series of men whose money had helped to make her famous – and others she had merely fancied; the stresses of success that had finally crumpled her: none of these central events could she bring herself to discuss, even though the memoirs were intended for posthumous publication. Just as she had sedulously crafted her living image, so she created for posterity a happy fairy-tale world, devoid of pain, guilt or ugliness. She wrote of herself as a paragon, the centre of her own universe; of a world in which the sun always seemed to be shining and the birds singing, dominated by fun and laughter, a world that knelt at her feet to applaud her and her deeds.

As they sat out on their balcony in their apartment on a lower floor of the Avenida building, Alan and Nollie Birch, an elderly retired bank manager and his wife, used to hear the typewriter clattering away above them. 'We never intruded into her life and she was not the sort of person who welcomed questions about herself,' Nollie recalled. 'She was a very private person. If you met her in the street she'd walk straight past you.

Very occasionally she invited us into her apartment. We were always struck by how few possessions she seemed to have. We didn't often manage to get her in here, but if we did and someone else arrived, she would immediately leap to her feet, make some excuse, and go.'

Alan Birch was struck by Jean's old-fashioned attitude to men. For his son in South Africa he tracked down a copy of one of her books and asked her to sign it. 'But she came running back a few minutes later clutching it and saying, "I can't possibly sign this – not for a man alone." We solved it by adding my son's daughter's name. That made it acceptable and she went ahead and signed. It was almost as if she had been risking some sort of scandal.'

In April 1977 Jean was back in New Zealand, this time as the guest of the Museum of Transport and Technology in Auckland to open a pavilion dedicated to the country's aviation pioneers. It was part of a memorial to Air Chief Marshal Sir Keith Park, the New Zealander who had distinguished himself as the commander of Fighter Command's illustrious 11 Group in the Battle of Britain.

Those who had met her on her visits seven years before were shocked by her hair, now spectacularly blonde. But, although she was sixty-eight, she had preserved her trim figure and her legs, still proudly displayed beneath very short dresses, were 'tanned and Dietrich-shaped', one reporter wrote.

But her skin, which the plastic surgery had smoothed, was beginning gently to wrinkle again and some people, noticing her pallor, thought she might be unwell. Newsfilm of the banquet that followed the opening ceremony shows her looking strained and gaunt, her normally fluent speech at times hesitant. People tried to persuade her to see a doctor, but she quite adamantly refused, saying it was merely a stomach upset and that she believed in conventional medicine only as a last resort. Instead she treated herself with some herbs she was carrying – a practice that had its roots in early childhood when Ellen had introduced her to traditional remedies, insisting that the expense of a doctor could be justified only for serious illness.

Her host was the museum's executive director, Ron Richardson, who had served in the RNZAF during the war as a flight engineer/gunner on Catalina flying boats in the Pacific. He and his wife, Estelle, invited Jean back to their home in Howick for a cup of tea. 'In the event she was feeling so rotten she stayed the night,' Ron said. 'But one night became several days and several days became three months.'

The Richardsons found her stimulating and amusing company but became privately alarmed that she might become a permanent fixture, threatening to rule their lives. As the weeks passed and she showed no inclination to leave, Ron began to wonder if she was in financial distress. She seemed to have so few possessions, was so chronically careful with money and appeared to own few clothes – some of them conspicuously well-worn. With her agreement he spoke to one of her great admirers, the Prime Minister. Robert Muldoon's response was swift. He raised the matter with his cabinet and it was agreed that Jean should be awarded an immediate state pension and given a grant of NZ$1,000. It was not a monumentally generous gesture, for the index-linked pension stood at only NZ$46 a week.

Whether she was genuinely hard up is another matter. In truth she was not exactly poor. Her assets, including her Tenerife apartment, the invested money from the prewar income, the RAF's compensation for the Gull and the profits from her Jamaican and Spanish property transactions, did, in 1977, represent a collective capital sum capable of yielding an income equal to that of a New Zealand mid-level professional salary. All this was to become evident after her death. But when, in 1977, people concerned for her welfare were rallying round needlessly to prop her up, her true financial state was cloaked in secrecy. Nonetheless, she accepted the government's gesture, believing sincerely that it was due recognition for her achievements of forty years before. Indeed there is evidence that she felt, privately, the government could have been more magnanimous. She told a friend in Auckland that what she had in mind had been a grace and favour house as a permanent home.

During that long 1977 winter holiday she went north again to visit her nephews and niece. Harold had died since her last visit and she stayed again in turn with Rick, Jim, and Isobel and their families on their farms. 'While she was here,' Jim Batten said, 'she made it clear that she didn't welcome visitors. Some very good friends of ours came in one day and afterwards she claimed they'd just come to see her. She described it as an intrusion and told us she didn't want to be treated like an exhibit.'

Back in Auckland, to her deep discomfort, there was to be yet another painful reminder of the contribution Fred Truman had made to her fame so long ago – even though he had now been dead for twenty years. His brother Reg, reading that Jean was in the country, decided he would like to meet her. 'It was so long after the events of the thirties and a lot of the sense of bitterness had faded so I thought it would be nice to hear how she had really felt about Fred,' Reg said. 'I heard that the Mayor of Auckland [Sir Dove Myer-Robinson] was holding a reception for her so I sent him a letter enclosing one to Jean asking if he would pass it on. When, after several weeks, I hadn't heard anything, I phoned Robbie to make sure she'd got my note. He told me, yes, he'd handed it to her and actually watched her open it. Apparently she'd taken one quick look and immediately screwed it up and thrown it on the floor. Clearly she didn't want to know us – the Trumans were too much of an embarrassment. I didn't try again.'

By the end of the northern summer of 1977 Jean was back once more in her lonely Tenerife world. The Birches only discovered she was home by chance, some time later; for there was never anyone to whom she felt close enough to call to say she was back. Nobody knew that, for the first time since Ellen's death on the island, Jean was seriously considering leaving Tenerife. It was over four hours' flying time to England, and as the frequency of her travels grew she began to wonder if she could afford to go on commuting to and from Europe with such abandon.

However, before she could address herself to the stressful implications of yet another upheaval, on the threshold of old age and without Ellen to guide and counsel her, a number of stimulating new events began to loom. She was to receive the Freedom of the City of London. She was invited to make a flight along the old Empire air route in Concorde. Her seventieth birthday was on the horizon. And from out of the blue came an exciting letter from a publisher in England: a proposal to republish *My Life*, her forty-year-old, long out-of-print book.

CHAPTER 23
The Rift that Refused to Heal
(1978–1980)

The publisher, Robert Pooley, was a prominent figure in the British aviation establishment. An energetic and enterprising man, then in his early forties, he headed a group of companies which produced navigation equipment and flight guides and published aviation books. Himself a pilot, he owned a light aircraft and several hot air balloons. He and his wife, Lyn, lived in a large and elegant medieval farmhouse at Felden near Hemel Hempstead in Hertfordshire. They were to play a major role in the remaining years of Jean's life.

'I was looking around for good aviation stories when I was amazed to read that the famous Jean Batten had resurfaced looking still surprisingly young and glamorous,' Bob recalled. 'It seemed a good publishing idea to try and persuade her to update and reissue her 1938 book, which had long been out of print and forgotten.' With some difficulty he managed to trace her; in 1978 he and Lyn flew to Tenerife to discuss the proposal.

'The tiny little apartment wasn't at all what we'd expected for such a famous person,' said Lyn. 'I just couldn't believe how small and bare it was, with literally nothing to provide a clue to

358

her fabulous past. I don't think there was a single personal item in it. She came across very much as a spinster and someone who was probably terribly, terribly lonely. Although it was ten years since she'd died, at the mere mention of her mother's name her eyes would moisten.'

Bob Pooley's mission was not a complete success. While Jean was willing to have her book reprinted she adamantly refused to update it. 'The problem,' said Bob, 'was that she had these memoirs she'd nearly finished and she wanted the full story of her life to be told in them – not as an addition to *My Life*.' Jean had so many misgivings about the wisdom of publishing what she saw – quite needlessly – as scandalous revelations, she was not prepared to show the Pooleys the manuscript she was incubating, or to discuss its publication. However, she happily signed a contract with Bob's Airlife Publishing Company to republish *My Life* almost exactly as it stood, ending abruptly in 1938 when she was still on the crest of the wave. She refused to add even a few lines to tell readers what had happened subsequently. In her view it would have created a sense of anticlimax.

Reluctantly Bob Pooley, who was to find Jean both demanding and somewhat intimidating, agreed. For he saw her as a significant survivor of aviation's colourful evolutionary years. 'She knew all the people I had only read about: Amy Johnson, Jim Mollison, Kingsford Smith – the greats of the 1930s. I think that by accepting her book as it stood I really hoped that she might later offer us her memoirs which, in theory, could have been a bestseller.'*

The book retitled *Alone in the Sky*, was not to appear for nearly two years during which protracted discussions ensued between Jean and the publisher, due to her hyper-fastidious concern about the jacket design and a series of drawings commissioned to illustrate her adventures. While the book was

---

*Disappointingly they were not. To make them a commercial publishing proposition they would have required extensive editing and interpretation. The nearest they are likely to get to publication is as a source of quotations and reference – as used, where relevant, in this biography.

being prepared for press a close personal friendship developed between her and the Pooleys. Bob, who was later to become its Master, invited Jean to become a freeman of the Guild of Air Pilots and Air Navigators, one of the City's livery companies. It led to the Freedom of the City of London and admission as one of the Guild's few women liverymen. For someone of nearly seventy who hadn't flown an aeroplane for nearly four decades it was a personal triumph, confirming her position as a formidable doyenne of pioneer aviation.

She had now become a constant visitor to Felden Grange, the Pooleys' home, set in its own parkland, twenty-five miles north-west of London – and when, in the spring of 1979, Lyn gave birth to a son, Sebastian, Jean was to become his godmother.

'She was, I felt, an old lady who really needed looking after,' Lyn Pooley said. 'But I had children and a home to manage and didn't have an awful lot of time to give her the devotion I felt she needed and wanted. She was enormously fastidious about her food. I used to take her breakfast in bed, and one day she looked at the tray and said, "That's very nice, but I'll need more toast than that." On another occasion the toast wasn't done the way she liked it. I had to go and make it again.

'Yet in a way I was very flattered that she wanted to come and stay with us, because after all she didn't really know us; it was merely that we were publishing her book. At first I found her very reserved. But this soon wore off and she began to talk and talk – always about herself and those few flying years. The sad thing was she'd really done nothing with her life since then. She only had her past. It was all she had to live for.'

Jean took the hospitality largely for granted, her gifts and contributions were minimal and when she left she wrote brief and rather conventional letters of thanks. In her heart she undoubtedly believed it was an honour for people to have her and usually this was precisely how most of them felt.

On 15 September 1979 Jean was seventy. The Pooleys decided that the occasion should be marked in some style. They held a spectacular birthday party for her on their huge lawn, bringing in people by helicopter. There were over one hundred guests who went for balloon rides and got through more than sixty bottles of champagne. Photographs show Jean, in a very short dress, at the controls of a helicopter, and cutting the cake with a sword. One of the guests who stayed on into the evening recalled that Jean was sparkling and vivacious, astonishing them all with her now familiar can-can style high kicks, and in tremendously expansive and witty form as she sat, holding court, surrounded by a group of modern aviators sipping brandy and remaining spellbound late into the night with her flying stories of long ago.

Delighted as they were to have her, the increasing frequency of Jean's visits began to put pressure on the Pooley household. In the autumn of 1979 it was arranged that, for lengthy stays, she would go to Bob's elderly mother, Hilda. Mrs Pooley, a widow, lived alone in a small modern second-floor flat, not far from Felden, in Boxmoor beside the Grand Union canal. She welcomed the companionship of someone of her own age. But she hadn't been expecting such an unorthodox personality.

'There were two Jeans,' Hilda said. 'One was happy and likeable, laughing and doing high kicks around the flat; the other was sad and secretive – the woman who would go to endless lengths to avoid the neighbours whenever we went out, pleading: "Please don't introduce me to anyone, Hilda."'

Jean's long stays with Hilda Pooley had other curious moments. Lyn described some of them. 'One would have expected that after a while she would have contributed something to the household, or perhaps occasionally brought in food for them both. Not a bit of it. She actually used to go out and shop for herself. She was very fond of steak and would buy herself a little fillet, cook it, eat it in front of Hilda, and then wash up her own dishes, carefully leaving Hilda's – often just a cup and saucer – untouched in the sink. I think that living on her own for so long had made her selfish. The classic occasion was the day she bought a punnet of strawberries. She came home, sat down, poured cream over them and began to eat them in front of Hilda. It was only when she had nearly finished and there were just a few left that she looked up and said, "Oh, Hilda, would you like one?" It was really very unkind.' However, such incidents were rare. Hilda was proud to have Jean there and most of the time she enjoyed her company.

In November 1979 Jean made her fourth visit to New Zealand since the start of her comeback. She went out to open a new branch of the National Bank which agreed to help her fulfil one of her greatest dreams: they paid for her to fly as far as Singapore in Concorde.

Nancy Bird Walton recalled that, later in Australia, Jean had described in a public speech her great excitement at flying supersonically. 'She told her audience, "I said to the passenger next to me, 'Aren't you thrilled to be going through Mach 2?' and he said, 'No, I'm much more thrilled to be sitting next to Jean Batten.'"' Nancy, who was in the audience, was aghast at her immodesty. 'I said to her, "It's a nice little story Jean but not really for *you* to say in public." But I don't think she quite understood my point.'

Jean spent Christmas 1979 with Ron and Estelle Richardson after which she became a guest of an Auckland businessman and his wife at their home in the city's smart eastern suburbs. In late 1988, after my documentary on Jean's life had gone out on Television New Zealand, I was invited to appear on a local talk-back radio show to discuss how the programme had been researched and made. Since the life of our national heroine, after her ephemeral fame, had remained a mystery to most New Zealanders until her public reappearance in 1970, there had been intense interest in the documentary and phone calls flooded in.

One came from the businessman's wife, who complained that my representation had not sufficiently stressed all the positive features of Jean's complex character. 'Your film was excellent but it neglected to say that she was also a warm and caring person,' she said with apparent resentment. 'People ought to know that she could be generous, that she loved children, that she was fond of animals and went regularly to church.' As her view of Jean appeared not wholly to coincide with the scores of opinions I had by then obtained from many other people around the world I invited her to elaborate on the six weeks Jean had spent in the granny-flat attached to their house.

She then admitted that Jean had not always been a model guest and that they had been witness to some strange and dramatic mood swings. 'She would sometimes sparkle when we had guests. I remember at one of our parties she was not only doing her famous high kicks but tried to copy a man who swung from the beams in our sitting room. She got stuck up there and someone had to lift her down. That was the fun side of her.

'But she could be naughty and petulant and then you had to be really firm. She once admitted: "I know some people think I'm a witch so I sometimes try it on just to see their reactions."'

The family found her unable to forgive or understand any break in routine. On one occasion her hostess took a telephone call at 11 o'clock in the morning. It delayed the serving of coffee by a few minutes. Jean was so put out she put on her coat and was about to stride out of the house in a huff when her friend hurriedly put the phone down and rushed to stop her.

Some time later the family invited a prominent American pilot and his wife to dinner. Jean had already met and liked the couple. 'But when she heard they were coming she was furious that we hadn't consulted her first. Yet we had invited them purely for her sake. Well, she was so angry she decided to punish us. She took a bottle of red wine, which was most unlike her, and disappeared into her room for the entire evening. She never emerged once, she refused to eat anything and the guests didn't meet her. It was the principle that her status demanded the courtesy, as she saw it, of consultation. It was a really dramatic performance; but then Jean was a superb actress.'

Invited to talk about the generosity she had found in Jean, her former hostess said, 'She noticed that we needed some garden furniture for our spa pool – so she very kindly offered to buy some as a present for having her so long. She went round the shops pricing stuff and discovered it would cost about $1,100. We were appalled when she told us and said on no account was she to spend that sort of money. We really had to be very tough.'

But the family succeeded. Jean did not buy a small present as a surprise instead. Other friends of Jean, hearing this story, were cynical. 'If she was not merely posturing she would have ordered the furniture with the option of changing it when the family saw it – or bought them something cheaper that was less embarrassing,' one of them said.

Lyn Pooley, who was well qualified to have a view on this, said, 'I think she was generous to the things that would promote her image. Also to the things to which she was devoted which was aviation – the biggest love and the greatest thing in her life. But to her friends I don't think I would have described her as a particularly generous person.'

However, despite Jean's occasional preposterous performances, her Auckland hosts grew fond of her, forgiving her sometimes monstrous conduct on the grounds that she was, as they saw her, a very great New Zealander whose deeds had earned her the right to behave badly if she wished. In fact they made Jean so welcome and comfortable in the flat that she began to hint that she might like to make it a more permanent arrangement. But the family did not pursue the idea.

Early in 1980 Jean embarked on a joint operation in New Zealand to promote *Alone in the Sky* and raise funds for the Museum of Transport and Technology. Its executive director, her friend Ron Richardson, arranged a lecture tour on which she spoke on her favourite subject to book and flying clubs. It was agreed that he would accompany her. 'We went in my car and stayed in motels,' he said. 'She was a fascinating phenomenon, a totally schizoid personality, charming and great fun to be with one moment and a prize bitch the next. There was something quite Jekyll and Hyde about her.'

'I'll never forget one morning when she was due to address over two hundred people who had come from miles around to hear her in Nelson. She just suddenly announced, without any good reason, that she wasn't going to appear and retreated to her room. I was dumbfounded and angry and wondered how on earth I was going to explain her rudeness to the organisers – I actually thought we might have to creep quietly out of town.

'However I went into her room and told her exactly what I thought of her and said I'd really had enough. Then I walked out and left her. To my amazement a few minutes later she came out dressed and ready, smiling and charming, saying "Let's go, Ron". And she went on like a pro, and gave one of the wittiest talks I ever heard her deliver.'

On the long journey around New Zealand Jean would sing to him in the car. 'She could also be very affectionate,' he said. 'She was great to dance with and could really hep it up with the best of them and in the motels she used to surprise me with her need for physical contact. She'd put her arms around me sometimes, wanting to be cuddled, in quite a sensual way that surprised me and on some of the long drives she'd put an arm round my shoulder and massage my neck in a highly physical and intimate fashion. It was really quite disconcerting. At other times she would remind me of a little girl. When she put her hair up she would look and behave just like one – then when she put it down again the impossible older side of her seemed to emerge. Yet despite it all there was something about her you couldn't help liking.'

Towards the end of the tour Jean and Ron Richardson arrived in her home town, Rotorua. Only a handful of people turned up at the aero club to meet her. Jean had accepted the position of patron of the New Zealand Airwomen's Association. Its president, Ena Monk, who drove out to the airport to meet her that dark, wet night got a chilling reception: 'We were late because we'd hit a dog on the way and had had to take it to the vet which was distressing in the extreme. But Jean wasn't at all sympathetic and made her intense displeasure very evident. I can still see her there. She had this enormous presence, this huge self-assurance. She turned to one of her old friends, Eva Warren, (who, as a young pilot of seventeen, had escorted her into Wanganui in 1934) and in her grand voice publicly reprimanded her: "You of *all* people should have been here to meet me."

'She then told us that she didn't like weekend pilots, which of course is just what we all were. And then proceeded to put me in my place. I had been calling her Miss Batten but when she addressed me as Ena I responded, thinking it would be friendly, by calling her Jean. But that didn't go down at all well. She winced and said witheringly, "Miss Batten, if you please."'

In Auckland a number of bookshops arranged prominent displays of *Alone in the Sky*. The manager of one was particularly proud of his layout -- until Jean arrived to inspect it. An Auckland woman with whom she was staying at the time said, 'He came to see me almost weeping. Apparently she'd gone in and swept all the books off the shelf. Just tipped them on to the floor. He begged me to get her out of the country quickly.'

Some compromise in the display was reached and Jean went along one day for a signing session. Her presence attracted a small crowd both in the shop and on the pavement outside. Among them, quite eerily, was her brother John.

Now seventy-seven he had been living in Essex in England since he had left New Zealand for good in 1968. Like his sister, he lived quietly and frugally on his own, surviving on his investments from more prosperous times. One of his pleasures was travel and as he feared and hated flying -- which may or may not have had some unconscious connection with his long-ago row with Jean -- he always went by sea. In the New Zealand autumn of early 1980 he was in Auckland for a few days, quite by chance, in the course of a round-the-world cruise. Walking up Queen Street one afternoon his curiosity was aroused by the crowd outside the bookshop. He crossed the street and joined them. To his utter amazement, since he thought she was in Tenerife, he saw from the window display that his sister was due to autograph copies of her book that very afternoon. And when he peeped inside there she was -- instantly recognisable despite the passage of nearly fifty years and her startling blonde hair. He was looking at Jean for the first time since 1931.

But the rift had festered for too long. He wanted to approach her, but he couldn't. Instead he stood inside the doorway, observing her for several minutes, torn between the wish to go forward and identify himself, and a fear of emotional consequences for them both. His courage failed him. He turned on his heel and walked away.

In 1987, at his home in Essex, he told me about the incident. 'I just stood there watching,' he said, 'thinking how lovely it would be to meet her. But it was not to be. You see, it would have meant barging in -- confronting her after half a century with her long-lost brother. It would really have been most inopportune; it would have looked as if I was trying to seek glory through Jean which was the last thing I wanted. After all, it was her moment, and heaven knows she'd earned it. I just didn't want to spoil it. So I quietly left the shop and went on my way. And, yes, I did feel rather sad.'

I asked John if he had later attempted to get in touch with Jean through the bookshop manager. He said that he had not. 'I don't think after so long I really had any feeling for her any more. We would have been virtual strangers.'

Jean's niece, Isobel, living near Whangarei in 1980, was surprised to get a phone call that evening from her uncle. He was staying ashore in Auckland, waiting for his ship which was making a side-trip to Sydney and back. 'John told me with some emotion that he'd seen Jean that day and didn't want to meet her. "Please don't give her my address or phone number," he pleaded. "I'm going to lie low until she's gone." The embarrassment was that Jean had already been up to see us all and, for the first time, had actually been expressing a wish to meet him again after all those years. She said she'd been trying to contact him without success all over the world. However, John very clearly preferred to leave things as they were and we had to respect his feelings. We didn't let her know he was in town.'

A sad and curious eerie twist to this story came from Jean's tour guide and host, Ron Richardson. 'She actually knew he was there in the bookshop that day,' he said. 'She told me so later. I could see that it had had quite a profound effect on her. I don't know how she recognised him after all those years; possibly the family had shown her pictures of him taken before he left New Zealand in the sixties. But Jean was sharp-eyed; she didn't miss much. She said she was hemmed in by the crowd round the table where she was signing the books. She wanted to get up and go to him, but before she could do so he'd gone. Anyway, that's what she told me. She explained about "the flaming row", as she called it, they'd had all those years ago. And she admitted she had been the aggressor. She believed her brother, who was quite a celebrity long before she was ever heard of, was jealous of her. But she did say that that day in the bookshop she deeply regretted not having made the gesture.'

And so, nearly fifty years after the row that had split brother and sister for so long, they were to stand briefly within sight of each other, neither quite able to summon the will to greet and forgive.

Swansong (1980–1982)

CHAPTER 24

Swansong (1980–1982)

In May 1980 Jean flew back to Tenerife. She was there for six months, resuming her lonely routines and going out of her way to avoid the few people she knew. In her absence the presence of the tourists seemed to have grown more oppressive; they now even swarmed into her once deserted swimming harbour at the bottom of her street. More than ever she determined to find a new home.

But again she delayed the final move and, in November, was back in Australia again – her fifth visit in ten years. She was the guest of honour at the sixtieth anniversary celebrations of Qantas who flew her out. Now seventy-one she was still bouncing with energy, frequently passing for a woman in her fifties.

While in Sydney there occurred an historic and deeply emotional event in her life. Her England–Australia solo speed record (for either sex) which had stood for forty-four years since she had flown it in the Gull in five days twenty-one hours in 1936, was broken by another woman pilot. Thirty-three-year-old Judith Chisholm, a former Heathrow air traffic controller and now an airline pilot flying HS125 executive jets around

Europe, arrived in Port Hedland, Western Australia, in three days eleven hours from England – almost cutting Jean's time in half. She flew in a small single-engined Cessna Turbo Centurion, a piston-engined aircraft, with costly radio and computerised navigation equipment of modern airliner sophistication, and cruised most of the way at between 20,000 and 30,000 feet, avoiding the worst of the weather. Jean had met Judith in England before going to Australia to wish her luck. Looking inside the Centurion she had been bewildered by the complexity of the navaids. 'It was equipped like a 747 – it must have had a million dollars' worth of gear,' she later told a friend in New Zealand. In fact the Centurion had all the necessary aids to be flown exactly like an airliner including, to Jean's fascination, an auto-pilot and an 'Omega' long-range radio-navigation system that provided a constant reading of latitude and longitude minute by minute on demand. It was a far cry from her own days of navigation by watch and simple magnetic compass and looking over the side to guess the degrees of her drift.

But Judith Chisholm, in the course of a round-the-world flight, was after more than just the England–Australia solo record. She intended also to shatter the most coveted of all Jean's records: her still standing time of eleven days and forty-five minutes for the England–New Zealand solo flight.

The absolute record had, in fact, been dramatically lowered only two years after she had set it. In 1938 a New Zealander, Flying Officer Arthur Clouston and his passenger, an English journalist, Victor Ricketts, in the same de Havilland Comet that had won the 1934 England–Australia air race, had flown from Gravesend in England to Blenheim, New Zealand, in only four days and eight hours. They hadn't crossed the Tasman with anything like Jean's navigational precision, having hit the New Zealand coast in Taranaki, sixty miles north off course. By the 1960s the big jets were flying from England to New Zealand routinely in under thirty hours. However, in 1980, although in practice it would not have been difficult, it so happened that no one had yet done it solo in any type of aircraft faster than Jean.

When Judith Chisholm passed through Sydney Jean went to

the airport to meet her and next day (25 November 1980) managed to persuade Qantas to give her a free ride to New Zealand in a 747 so that she could be in Auckland to greet her.

Shortly before she died tragically of cancer in her early forties, Judith Chisholm, in her cottage in Buckinghamshire, told me what happened next. 'I was somewhere in mid-Tasman between Sydney and Auckland and actually at that very moment thinking of Jean flying across all those years before so low she was picking up the sea spray. And then, amazingly, her distinctive, rather plummy voice came on the radio from the Qantas flight overtaking me above. She was actually on the flight-deck looking down at me and she said, "Hello Judith, you look tiny down there," and glancing up I could see the 747 contrailing against a blue sky far above me.'

It was an historic aviation moment and two hours later when Judith Chisholm landed in Auckland, there to congratulate her was the woman who had created the record eleven years before she had been born. Judith had cut Jean's time almost in half, arriving in only six days thirteen and a half hours from London.* Jean later told friends privately that she didn't consider it quite fair in view of the vastly greater sophistication of the Centurion compared with the rudimentary devices she had in the Gull. 'But I am sure,' Judith said, 'that I was just as frightened as she was. Flying over water on one engine is always frightening.'

Having witnessed the shattering of the most resistant of all her records, Jean found herself in New Zealand with nothing to do and nowhere to stay. She was rescued by Ron and Estelle Richardson whom she phoned and who invited her home for the night. Due to spend Christmas in Melbourne with Captain Miles and his family she now had time on her hands. To fill the intervening month she decided to go and stay with her nephews and niece in Northland. But when she rang Isobel she learnt, to her bitter disappointment – which she failed to conceal – that she was about to go into hospital in Whangarei. When she

---

*In 1982 the record was again to be broken, this time by a New Zealand pilot, Cliff Tait, celebrated for his long-distance delivery flights of light aircraft. He flew a single-engined Beech Bonanza from England to New Zealand in 4 days 7 hours.

called Rick and Margaret there was further disappointing news
– they were on the point of going to Australia on holiday. 'She
was rather put out by this,' Rick recalled, 'and in a bit of a huff
booked herself on a flight back to Australia next day.' Before
she left she phoned Jim Batten. He and Rhoda were not going
away and immediately invited her up to stay on the farm.
But Jean said it was too late to change her plans. The family
were left with the impression that somehow they had all
failed her.

In Melbourne she went to stay again with Esther Mather. 'I
felt,' said Esther, 'that her life had by then become very empty.
It seemed to be full of acquaintances with no real friends. This
was hardly surprising because in her seventies she was just as
cold and uninterested in other people as when she first came out
in the thirties.' After Christmas with Bob and Janette Miles,
Jean flew back to London. Of that last time they were ever to
see her Bob said, 'Her life was really a closed book. Yet there
was, somewhere inside her, a very soft spot; however she was
very selective when it came to revealing it.'

On the drive out to Melbourne airport Jean made one of her
rare references to Beverley Shepherd. She described to Bob
Miles the mental anguish she had endured when she had first
read that there had been two survivors of the Stinson crash.
'There was a long pause,' Bob recalled, 'then she said, very
quietly, "You know, he was the only man I really ever loved."'

By mid-January Jean was back in Tenerife. Although it lay in
balmy latitudes not far north of the Tropic of Cancer, Tenerife
could still feel the blast of late winter. 'Torrents of icy rain fell
on the coast and quite a lot of snow high up in the mountains,
with even the foothills covered,' she reported in a letter to
Hilda Pooley on the first day of March. 'I saw some swallows
during my walk this morning; and took a few crumbs for the
lizards who are timidly emerging from their hibernation to sun
themselves on the rocks. There are lots of wild flowers, too,
after the rain; the miracle of spring is once more taking place.'

1981 was to have been one of the most momentous years of
Jean's life. To celebrate the forty-fifth anniversary of her 1936
flight to New Zealand, Bob Pooley was organising a Concorde
charter flight from London to Auckland and back. It was sche-

duled to make the journey, with stops in Bahrain, Singapore and Melbourne, in just seventeen hours. It needed a hundred passengers each willing to write a cheque for the substantial sum of £3,450. It was a prestigious venture with the Duke of Edinburgh as its patron and a long list of distinguished vice-patrons drawn from the world of aviation and including Jean. The flight, profits from which were to go to the Guild of Air Pilots and Air Navigators, was due to leave in October on the anniversary of her 1936 journey and she was to be the guest of honour. So important to her was the flight she was the first to write a cheque to guarantee herself a seat on this ambitious adventure for which she became seized with excitement and which friends believed she intended to be her last-ever public appearance.

The publicity surrounding the charter thrust her briefly into public view again. She was invited by Britannia Airways to its headquarters at Luton in Bedfordshire to a ceremony in which the company named one of its 737 aircraft 'Jean Batten'. The airline was soon to play a key role in the most baffling mystery ever to surround her.

During the naming ceremony at Luton she was in sparkling form, waving to the television cameras and holding a group of airline pilots and engineers enthralled with her flying reminiscences. 'She had hard-bitten pilots riveted,' said the *Daily Telegraph*. 'She looked like a well-preserved movie star.'

Few people knew that her public performances were still a huge personal strain. Britannia Airways' Director of Customer Services, Bob Parker-Eaton, remembered that the day Jean had come to Luton she had arrived deliberately with a lot of time in hand. 'She asked if she could borrow my office to prepare herself. She seemed to need at least an hour of quiet and tranquillity to psyche herself up before she could go on stage. She was concerned that every detail of her dress and appearance should be exactly right and needed lots of reassurance. If we'd delayed the moment I think she might have gone to pieces. But we didn't and she was superb.'

In London Jean had now established a private base, somewhere to stay when friends couldn't put her up: the small and discreet Ebury Court Hotel in Belgravia. It was a caring family hotel in a former Regency house in Ebury Street, a little old-fashioned in the positive sense of devotion to its guests, many of whom returned again and again – the sort of place in which Miss Marple would have felt comfortable.

Mrs Diana Topham, who ran the hotel, remembers Jean as a model guest who kept to herself and communicated little. 'We were all very fond of her,' she said. 'The staff liked and respected her because she was always so charming and polite.' But it wasn't exactly cheap at the Ebury Court and Jean would stay only as a last resort. 'Sometimes she would pitch up in London with literally nowhere to go,' Muriel Tucker said. Muriel was a British Airways duty officer based at the airline's former Victoria Terminal. She was also a private pilot and during the 1970s got to know the reclusive celebrity as she commuted to and from her island home.

'I used to feel sorry for her,' Muriel added. 'She was always wearing this old navy serge suit. It had become so polished and threadbare I concluded she must be in severe financial straits. I remember one evening when I was on duty at the terminal, going down to the arrivals area. There was a woman there in a mac and a hat who looked very lost and forlorn. It turned out to be Jean, just arrived from Tenerife. She didn't seem to have anywhere to go. So I rescued her and took her home.'

During the summer of 1981 Jean became almost obsessively preoccupied with the forthcoming supersonic flight. She flew to London for a second face-lift, afterwards going to ground in Hilda Pooley's flat in Boxmoor to allow the disfiguring scars to heal and fade in private. It had been agreed that she would stay for six weeks. 'But,' said Hilda, 'six weeks became two months and then two months became three months.'

Sometime in August 1981 Jean went back to Tenerife to prepare for the New Zealand trip and to have her apartment redecorated for sale at last – although she had still not decided where she wanted to live. But all was not well with the charter: Bob Pooley was having difficulty selling the seats. Jean's letters throughout that summer, asking for news of sales, reflect her growing anxiety that the flight on which she had set her heart might be at risk. 'Hoping that the initial response for tickets is keeping up, and looking forward so much to hearing the good news when you at last have a full complement of passengers,' she wrote on 17 June.

By 24 August, when she next wrote, the organisers were having even more serious doubts about their ability to find enough customers for the supersonic luxury flight. 'I'm so glad that you are pressing on with renewed vigour to make a success of this venture,' she urged him, adding slightly threateningly, 'you really owe it to all the marvellous people who lent their names to support the project.'

With barely a week remaining to the flight's 16 October departure date and with many seats still unfilled, Jean was beginning to clutch at straws. 'How about trying to arrange some sort of tie-up with the organisers of the 1982 Brisbane Commonwealth Games,' she proposed somewhat desperately on 7 October. But her entreaties were in vain. Shortly afterwards the blow fell. Bob Pooley wrote with the sad news that the charter had been abandoned. It was stunningly traumatic news for Jean. The supersonic flight down her old Empire route was to have been the crowning event of her comeback. It was, friends were later to observe, the biggest most personal disaster of her life since the death of Ellen fifteen years before.

'She was absolutely devastated,' Lynn Pooley said. 'It was to have been her swansong of fame – her last grand appearance on the stage. And what's more, she seemed to blame Bob personally, although he'd worked day and night to try and get it off the ground. She never ever really forgave him.'

Jean's coolness to Bob Pooley is reflected in some of her subsequent letters to him. In a tart one on 22 October, ticking him off for having given her Tenerife phone number to a Thames Television producer, she wrote: 'Will you please note that I have now definitely retired!!' She concluded with the unhappy ultimatum: 'I have no intention of uttering another note until or unless the Concorde flight materialises!' In a PS she terminated the correspondence curtly: 'No need to reply.'

As Christmas loomed she broke her silence and in a brief letter stiffly signed 'Yours sincerely, Jean', wrote to him in terms which possibly implied a wish that the Pooleys might invite her to Felden for the festivities: 'I hope that you all have a wonderful time at Christmas; I will be thinking of you and the family on the Day.' However, Jean spent the Christmas of 1981 in the solitude of her apartment.

The few people who glimpsed her around the island that early winter of 1982 were convinced that she was growing more and more eccentric; her efforts to avoid human contact in the streets had become more bizarre: she would now cross the road to avoid eye contact and the need to speak to acquaintances.

For some time newspapers had been likening her to the world's most publicised and legendary recluse of all, the Swedish filmstar Greta Garbo (who died in New York on 16 April 1990 at the age of 83). The similarities in the two women's lives and personalities were striking.

Both had a rare and burning sense of destiny and greatness and were supremely successful in spectacular but short-lived careers. Jean's ended in 1937, Garbo's in Hollywood in 1941. Both lived most of their lives in retirement. Both possessed unforgettable beauty, and they were not dissimilar in appearance. Neither ever married (Garbo's affairs were widely publicised; Jean's conducted in deep secrecy). Both were obsessed with their health and the value of money. Both were abnormally frugal with possessions. Rootless and chronically unhappy they were constantly on the move living out of hotels, temporary apartments, and in self-imposed isolation in homes where few visitors were ever welcomed. Not many people ever got close to either of these androgynous women, and they shared, in their complex neuroses, the habit of concealing themselves from the intrusive world beneath floppy wide-brimmed hats.

In the spring of 1982 Jean at last made the move to leave Tenerife and recreate her simple lifestyle further north. Her preference, since she now spoke the language and was at ease within the culture, was for another Spanish territory.

She sold apartment 606, her home for more years than any other. It went to a Swedish couple for a modest sum – certainly not more than £10,000. She got rid of the few items of her very basic furniture and kitchen equipment and began to pack her suitcases. Into one of them, heavily battered from years of travel, she piled a mass of documents, papers and photographs, and her unfinished manuscript. She took the case to Britannia Airways and, together with a cloth carrier bag containing a painting palette and small plastic models of Concorde and the Harrier jump-jet, asked the local office of the airline to consign them personally (but unknown to him) to Bob Parker-Eaton at Luton to await her collection. And, significantly, to this assortment of her few remaining things she added her precious portable typewriter. Somehow the act of parting with her main instrument of communication seemed to signify the finality with which she viewed her retirement.

The last surviving letter she typed on it was to Bob Pooley on 27 April. It was to tell him that she had posted two plastic canary bird whistles to his son Sebastian (her godson) and daughter Samantha. 'I will probably be in London in mid-June,' she wrote, adding nostalgically, 'I often think of you all and the happy times we had together.'

She had already left suitcases, packed with winter clothes, with the Pooleys; and her golf clubs and a further suitcase containing photographs, jewellery and her paintings and sketches with the RAF Museum at Hendon.

Thus lightened of most of her worldly goods, and there were indeed very few, Jean now began a singularly curious series of departure rituals. Into an envelope she gathered a bunch of newspaper cuttings of stories about herself. She posted it to Annette Reid, virtually anonymously. 'I was greatly puzzled to receive them,' Annette, who lived only walking distance away, said. 'I looked to see if there was a note or a letter, but there was nothing – just all these clippings about Jean Batten. Then it occurred to me that perhaps it was her curious way of sending me an SOS, that something was wrong and she needed help. So I jumped into the car and drove quickly down to the Avenida Apartments. And there I was absolutely astonished to discover that she'd already sold the flat and left the island. None of us had the slightest idea she was planning to go. I suppose it was her sad way of saying farewell.'

Jean's neighbours, Alan and Nollie Birch, had a similar but rather more weird experience. 'I opened our front door one morning and there, dangling on the handle, was an old plastic bag,' said Nollie. 'Inside was a recent issue of the London *Daily Telegraph* and a copy of Britannia Airways' in-flight magazine. There was no note or anything but the magazine left us in no doubt who had left it – it featured an article about Jean Batten. Well, she'd done this sort of thing before and we thought she'd probably gone off for a couple of days to one of the other Canary Islands. It was not until several weeks later that we discovered she had sold up and gone for good. We probably knew her as well as anyone on Tenerife; so it was disappointing. But,' she added philosophically, 'we accepted that this was Jean's way.'

Whether Jean went to pay her final respects to Ellen nobody knows. But, in her last years on the island, as the stimulus of the comeback provided an antidote to grief, people noticed that less and less frequently was she entering the locked door in the wall of the British cemetery to renew the flowers in the niche below which she had once gone daily to shed her tears. When, sometime in June 1982, she took the bus on a long journey to Reina Sofia airport on the opposite side of the island and flew off for the last time, she had left Ellen's bones to rest in peace.

From here on Jean's movements become extremely difficult to plot and reconstruct. Her New Zealand passport, which I was eventually able to study – but which may not always have been stamped at Spanish airports – provides some vital clues. The most likely scenario is that she flew from Tenerife on an Iberia flight to Malaga in southern Spain from where she began to search for somewhere to live on the Costa del Sol. Since she didn't hire cars any more it is probable that she took the local commuter train from the station outside Malaga airport and travelled west through Torremolinos to Fuengirola then walked back to the place where she and Ellen had spent those happy years near the end of her mother's life. But Los Boliches was no longer the tiny fishing village she remembered. The once unspoilt coast was now, for mile after mile, one endless conurbation of closely packed tourist apartments, bars, marinas and villas, all swarming with foreign visitors. To someone who valued peace and seclusion above all else it was the ultimate nightmare.

It is likely that she went in search of La Paloma – by now no longer easily recognisable as the Sheherezade restaurant, flourishing in the shadow of a forest of tall buildings. She would have shuddered at the transformation of their once idyllic habitat, so chokingly full of memories of Ellen, and quickly moved on in search of a more peaceful location.

Travelling west, now by bus, she passed through Marbella and Estepona. But the avalanche of tourism had engulfed them both. Nowhere was there a tiny oasis among the sprawl of white concrete and terracotta. Along the coast road, that she and Ellen had so often followed on their journeys to the dentist and the bank, she went through San Roque and down the long hill through the palms and olive groves to the Spanish frontier with Gibraltar. But a dispute between Spain and Britain had temporarily closed the border and she couldn't immediately get into the Rock, which, she had told a number of people, she favoured as a final retirement home for its highly desirable blend of climate and colonial sense of security.

So anxious was she to investigate the place, however, she determined to circumvent the frontier. She went to the nearby Spanish port of Algeciras from where, her passport shows, she boarded the ferry for the two-and-a-half hour voyage to Tangier in Morocco on the opposite side of the Strait. She spent the night of 29 July there and next day recrossed the Strait direct to Gibraltar, either by ferry or hydrofoil.

She stayed in the colony, probably in a cheap hotel, for nearly three weeks. There is no record of what she did during this time but clearly she was pricing apartments and weighing up the pros and cons of a permanent life there. She established a temporary mail-drop at the local Barclays Bank, where once she had maintained an account, and it was to here that Bob Pooley wrote in the second week of August; concerned to know what had happened to her: 'We have not heard from you for some time, and we were hoping to see you in England last month. What are your plans? And have you now settled on the Rock? We are all very anxious to hear news from you.'

For some reason, which I was unable to establish, Jean decided against Gibraltar. However, with its London uniformed policemen and colonial governor, it had become, by the early 1980s, a claustrophobic and anachronistic little enclave of Britain – its limited landspace dominated by the towering rock, and with access to the Spain she loved a constant uncertainty. But the most probable reason why she eventually flew on to

England is that the colony had also become a tourist mecca and although the ebb and flow across the border from Spain had been temporarily stifled there was ample and depressing evidence that Gibraltar had also drastically changed, losing much of its colonial charm and character since she and Ellen had known it. It seemed that the whole coast of southern Spain had become one endless tourist colony.

It was probably at this moment, as she boarded the Gibraltar Airways plane for Gatwick on one of the few flights for which she ever paid for her own ticket, that she began to think of Majorca, the Spanish Mediterranean island with which, forty-six years before, she and Ellen had fallen in love.

She arrived back in London on 18 August 1982. The stamp confirming this, curiously, in view of her subsequent international travel, was to be the last entry in her passport.

Her stay in Britain lasted two months. It was the last time she was to set foot in the country. She spent some of those weeks of the late summer of 1982 with Hilda Pooley in her flat beside the canal and made some visits to Felden Grange. Bob and Lyn could no longer cope with her as a long-staying guest who expected hotel service and, in any case, were at that time too busy constantly to entertain her. Nor was it possible for her to prolong her visit to Hilda who was about to have one of her sons back from overseas, to stay.

There is no record of where she spent the time the Pooleys could not have her. The register there shows that she did not go, even for a night, to the Ebury Court. In truth, Jean had few remaining friends in England who could easily have coped with a long visit from her. It is likely that, to avoid the expense of a hotel, she found some low-budget accommodation in a less salubrious part of London – a small, eminently basic room somewhere of the sort she would have been wholly familiar and comfortable with in its transient anonymity.

What she did with her days nobody will ever know. She was now an extremely sad figure, at seventy-three just beginning again, despite the cosmetic surgery, to show her age, lonely despite her fierce spirit of independence, disillusioned and anxious about her future. After half a lifetime in warm climates she knew she couldn't survive, except in comfort she couldn't afford, in England any more. She would have walked the streets of central London, an upright figure moving with brisk stride for the exercise she demanded, eating frugally in small cafés, watching the pennies. The city, now with its startling admixture of the world's races, must have seemed as bewildering and as lonely as when, a beautiful young woman, she had paced the same streets over fifty years before, trying to raise money for the first of her epic flights.

Now she wanted only to leave the city on whose pavements the billboards had once proclaimed her feats and where the name JEAN had been enough to identify her to millions. She finally decided to go to Majorca.

Having booked her flight she went out to Felden Grange to say goodbye to the Pooleys. 'She came to lunch,' Lyn said. 'She was in an unusually gloomy and depressed frame of mind. She clearly still hadn't forgiven Bob for the Concorde charter failure. I think there was also some resentment that we hadn't had her to stay. So she was quite unusually subdued and uncommunicative and told us very little other than that she was about to go off to Majorca to find a new home. We gathered she wanted to buy a place from which she would commute to England from time to time and stay with people like us. I don't think by then there were any other friends.'

After the family lunch Lyn drove Jean down to Hemel Hempstead railway station. There in the forecourt they said goodbye. 'She was still rather grumpy,' said Lyn. 'The last thing she said was, "Well, I'm off and I'm going to ground. I'm just going to disappear and forget everything for a while. You won't see me."' As Jean walked away to the platform Lyn was in no doubt that they would be seeing her again at Felden within a few months.

Confirmation of her arrival in Majorca was in at least two letters, handwritten and brief, giving *lista de correos* (*poste restante*) in Palma as her address. One was to Bob Pooley; it was preoccupied with the sales and bookshop availability of *Alone in the Sky*. It was a brisk, routine and cheerful note. The second was addressed to Alistair Simpson, the managing director of the Pooley publishing company, Airlife, in Shrewsbury in Shropshire. It was a slightly peevish note, complaining about the deduction of tax from a royalty payment. It ended: 'I would be very grateful for an early reply – do please note the new address in Majorca. Kind regards, yours sincerely, Jean.'

The letter, written less than three weeks after she had arrived on the island, was dated 8 November, 1982. It was the last that any of her friends were ever to hear from her.

CHAPTER 25

The Aviator Vanishes (1982–1986)

The most extraordinary feature of Jean's disappearance, and a tragic commentary on the secretiveness of her life, was that it was to be more than two years before anyone did anything about it. There was literally nobody close enough to her to care sufficiently even to make casual enquiries. And when the first desultory steps to try and find her were finally taken it was to be another two years before anything like a serious search was to get under way.

When, at Christmas 1982, none of her friends and relatives received the customary card it didn't strike any of them as unusual. As Lyn Pooley put it: 'We knew there had been long periods in her life during which she had just gone to ground, and she had warned us when she left that it could be some time before we heard from her. So I think we just accepted that, for the time being, she had chosen to go out of circulation.'

However, when, in May 1983, Sebastian's fourth birthday had come and gone without the usual card from his godmother and Bob Pooley's publishing company had received not a single letter goading them into greater sales efforts for over six months, the Pooleys began to wonder if she was all right. 'She had never forgotten Sebastian's birthday before,' said Lyn, 'and never failed to answer Bob's letters.'

'I think I had concluded that she felt she'd begun to age too much and didn't want to be seen in public,' Bob said. 'And she'd so often threatened to disappear that I thought, well, this time maybe she really does mean it. And so we really did very little about it.'

Sadly, very few people felt any responsibility to try and locate her. Everyone was assuming that there was someone else closer to her to take the action they kept postponing. But there was nobody.

Her brother John, now eighty and living in Essex, did not even know she had disappeared. And if he had he would not have felt the need to make enquiries since there had been no relationship for more than fifty years. Even her three nephews, Colin in Australia, Rick and Jim, and their sister Isobel in New Zealand, were reluctant to do anything. 'I don't think we'd had a Christmas card since 1980 so, as far as the family in New Zealand was concerned, at that stage it was perfectly normal,' Rick Batten recalled.

But if family and friends were doing nothing the bureaucracy had been swift to respond. The New Zealand social welfare department had, in December, sent Jean a routine 'declaration of circumstances' form. Receiving no reply the special pension the cabinet had awarded her in 1977 had quietly been terminated in March 1983.

When Christmas of that year again brought no card to the Pooleys they still hesitated for, like everyone else in her life, they deeply respected her abnormal sensitivity over her right to privacy. But when her seventy-fifth birthday passed on 15 September 1984 and she had still not been in touch, Bob Pooley decided at last that there were grounds for serious concern. 'I'd just assumed,' he said, 'that having gone to ground for nearly two years she would emerge for the Big Seventy-Five.' But she didn't. Late in 1984 Bob phoned the public relations department at the New Zealand High Commission in London and set in motion the first formal enquiries.

The New Zealand government did not respond with much alacrity to the news that one of its most famous women was missing. It moved cautiously and diffidently and was to spend two years making intermittent and very limited enquiries through diplomatic channels. Had it involved Interpol, which it steadfastly refused to do, the mystery could have been solved within days.

The High Commission, from New Zealand House, its prominent square-looking building in London's Haymarket where Jean had last been seen as a lunch guest in 1981, began its leisurely investigation in January 1985. It took the logical first step of calling Jean's London bank, the 25 Charing Cross Road branch of Barclays, which was her latest mail depository. But this only served to deepen the mystery and heighten the concern: the manager said that Miss Batten had stopped using her accounts and that a large collection of mail had accumulated for her. They had not heard from her for more than two years and had no forwarding address. The manager agreed that, for a client who had been such a prolific communicator, the silence was worrying.

Bob Pooley also spoke to the bank manager. He was concerned that Jean might be in financial straits. He was relieved to be told that her accounts held 'substantial funds' – whatever that meant, for the bank's strict confidentiality rules did not permit more precise disclosure. In the absence of drawings, and with the flow of interest and dividends into her deposit account, the balance was slowly growing.

Having called the bank, the High Commission did nothing further. Unhappy at their seeming lack of interest Bob Pooley decided that it was time the High Commission got a prod from its overlords in New Zealand. In March 1985 he made a phone call to Auckland to a friend, John Jamieson, a property developer. The Jamiesons had had Jean to stay in their home in St Heliers in the eastern suburbs and had taken her for trips in their private Cessna; they had grown exceedingly fond of her and, like the Pooleys, had been concerned that they had received no Christmas card for three years running. John Jamieson promised to take the matter up immediately with his MP.

The MP for his electorate of Tamaki was a powerful figure in the New Zealand establishment who, until the previous year, had for nine years been prime minister. Sir Robert Muldoon, now an opposition back-bencher, was not only a statesmen well known around the world, he had met Jean on a number of occasions during the 1970s and was one of her genuine admirers. And back in the late 1940s, when his accounting firm had handled the dental practice's books, he had also known and liked Fred Batten. When he heard from John Jamieson that she was missing, Sir Robert acted with characteristic decisiveness. He got in touch with Mervyn Norrish, the Secretary for Foreign Affairs in Wellington, persuading him that more energetic diplomatic enquiries deserved to be made. As a consequence, in the English spring of 1985, the New Zealand High Commissioner in London, Bryce Harland, was asked to conduct a wider search.

Early in April the London diplomatic staff began more vigorous enquiries. But they were deliberately kept at a purely informal level. Later, Mervyn Norrish was to say in a letter to me: 'You will appreciate that the Government has no right to institute a formal enquiry – Jean Batten may have her own good reasons for keeping her whereabouts secret, and in such circumstances would quite correctly resent the Government intruding on her right to that privacy.'

Throughout the investigations which my wife, Caroline, and I were subsequently to make during our research for the documentary, the New Zealand Ministry of Foreign Affairs was consistently open and helpful and, in the belief that it might speed up the search, we were shown the admittedly limited record of the government's own informal enquiries. They confirmed the caution with which the ministry was proceeding in its deep concern not to intrude into Jean's private world.

The High Commission now began to alert some of the people they thought might be able to help. They spoke to Air New Zealand, the Bank of New Zealand, the National Bank of New Zealand, to the Royal Aero Club, to Airlife Publishing, Bob Pooley, the British Foreign and Commonwealth Office and the Spanish Embassy in London. None of them was able to throw much light on the mystery. However, it is now clear that whatever request was put to the Spanish Embassy it did not lead to the most obvious and simple step of all: a search of death records in all Spanish territories.

From the outset of their informal enquiries the High Commission was hampered by the unusual circumstances of Jean's life and the secretiveness with which she had insisted on surrounding it. Their attempts to find some recent residential addresses merely confirmed the trouble she took to live in anonymity. Bob Pooley had been able to provide the address of apartment 606 in Tenerife, but from there on the list developed as a succession of temporary mail-drops: lista de correos, Puerto de la Cruz; Airlife Publishing Company, Shrewsbury; c/o Barclays Bank, Gibraltar; c/o Barclays Bank, 25 Charing Cross Road; Feldon Grange, Feldon, Hertfordshire; and finally the inevitable *lista de correos*, Palma, Majorca.

This was sad enough; but even more tragic, the High Commission staff were now to find, was their inability to trace in Britain or Europe any meaningful friends, apart from the deeply concerned Pooleys. 'Is it possible,' a message to the Ministry in New Zealand said, 'that Miss Batten had a fear of ageing which may possibly have effected a personality change? We notice that publicity photographs taken in 1979 portray the image of a much younger woman sporting shoulder-length blonde hair.' And the telex, which the Ministry in Wellington showed me, added significantly: 'We are not aware of a close companion in her day-to-day life.'

And so, throughout 1985, the most helpful source of information and theories continued to be the Pooley family. But even they were now beginning to realise how little they really knew about Jean. Neither they nor the bank, when asked, could give the name or address of a single relative. Bob Pooley told the High Commission that he understood Jean had three brothers alive: two in New Zealand and one in England, but that he did not believe she had been on speaking terms with the latter, he said with some understatement, 'for some time'. The truth was that, of the two brothers, only John was still alive, but the High Commission was unable to confirm his existence let alone obtain his address – not that it would have helped in the least.

Strange as it may seem the informal government enquiries now under way made no attempt to establish if there were any relatives, caring or not, in New Zealand. It would not have taken long to find them and indeed, had thorough investigations been mounted through the British Foreign and Commonwealth Office, the High Commission would have learnt that one of the relatives had been named by Jean as her next-of-kin.

But in the spring of 1985 when the informal search from London was at its height the Batten family in New Zealand, not yet publicly linked to the missing aviator, were unaware that it was going on. Nor were they doing anything to find their aunt. 'People will always wonder why the family didn't act more quickly,' Rick Batten told me. 'Well there was a good reason. Back in the sixties, I think around 1967, not long after our grandmother Ellen died in Tenerife, Jean had ceased writing for a long time. My father (Harold) had become very concerned for her welfare and went to the New Zealand police. I can't remember precisely what steps they took but they did manage to trace her. She was alive and OK in Tenerife. But her anger at being traced was unbelievable. She wrote Dad a sizzling letter which we all read. She told him she was perfectly capable of looking after herself and never, ever was he to have the police look for her again. It was a really tough letter. It said that if he ever did so it would be the end of their relationship. He was flabbergasted. We all were. So now she'd apparently disappeared again none of us was willing to risk her wrath a second time. We had not the least doubt that she was alive and well somewhere and that when she was ready to emerge she would do so – in her own good time.'

Meanwhile in London the High Commission enquiries had moved abroad. Because she had spoken to the Pooleys of a friend with whom she sometimes stayed in Switzerland, the New Zealand Consulate General in Geneva was asked to check with the Swiss authorities if there was any record of her residence or indeed death there. And because of her friendships in Australia – about which virtually nothing was known to the Pooleys – the New Zealand High Commission in Canberra was also asked to make enquiries.

The Swiss connection was real enough. One of the homes of her former Jamaican neighbour, Lady Mitchell, was the Château de Bourdigny outside Geneva where Jean had last stayed for a few days in 1979. Neither the Pooleys nor the High

Commission knew who the friend was, but the Swiss Federal Office was able quickly to confirm that they had no record of Jean's presence in the country. What precise enquiries were made in Australia at this juncture I never discovered. They were obviously unfruitful.

Enquiries at the same time made in Spain produced an equally negative result. However, for some curious reason this second attempt to trace Jean in Spain was not pursued with much more vigour than the first. As New Zealand did not have an embassy in the country, diplomatic representation was conducted by the ambassador to France. On receipt of a telex from their colleagues in London the New Zealand Embassy staff in Paris approached the British Embassy in the French capital asking them to make enquiries through British diplomatic posts in Spain. This appears to have been efficiently done and it is probable that, in the process, not only the British Embassy in Madrid but the British Consuls in Malaga, Tenerife and Majorca were all asked to check the records they maintained of Spanish residence permits and deaths of British and New Zealand citizens in their territories. There was, however, one fatal flaw to these enquiries: they depended on Jean's having registered with one of the consulates since 1982 her intention to take up long-term residence, which she was by no means certain to have done. In the event that she had died they relied on the assumption that her death would have been reported to a British consulate. The belief that these far from methodical 1985 enquiries had been thorough and conclusive, and that the ground they had covered did not require further checking, was to prolong the search for Jean for another two and a half years.

When, in April, negative replies had come back from all these diplomatic sources in the relevant parts of Spain, it was assumed that there was a distinct possibility that Jean was alive or dead somewhere else in the world. And credence to this belief was lent by a startling piece of new information from the manager of her London bank. Subsequent re-examination of Jean's accounts, he now told the High Commission, had revealed that, sometime in November 1982 (the exact date was not recorded by the High Commission), Jean had been in London and at the Charing Cross Road branch had cashed a cheque for £50. As she had apparently flown to Majorca in October, these November London transactions could mean only one thing: that she had returned to England – and might still be in the country.

Yet nothing was ever done to check with the various United Kingdom authorities whether Jean had re-entered the country on her then still valid New Zealand passport, or whether she had registered for social security benefits. The only check made was a negative one: it was established that Jean's name did not appear in United Kingdom death records for the period from 1980 to 1984.

Until the autumn of 1985 her disappearance, which had now lasted nearly three years, had not made a line in the newspapers. At long last this was to change. In October of that year Bob Parker-Eaton, at Britannia Airways, wrote to the aviation magazine, *Flight International*, asking it to publish an appeal for information on her whereabouts so the airline could return the suitcase she had sent from Tenerife three years before. There was no response. However, although she had long since ceased to make news, the story was picked up by the London *Evening Standard* which briefly reported her disappearance. It was to be many months before any other British newspaper took the slightest interest in the mystery.

By the end of 1985, having satisfied itself that there was no record of Jean's presence or death in Switzerland or any relevant Spanish territory and that her New Zealand passport had finally expired in September 1984, the High Commission, with the agreement of the Ministry of Foreign Affairs in Wellington, abandoned the search. It had achieved very little. Sadly, its superficiality and lack of interest were to characterise the involvement of several cabinet ministers who, reluctantly, were dragged into the search over the next two years.

The first stories of Jean's disappearance did not appear in New Zealand and Australian newspapers until early 1986. In her homeland, where she was known to be a recluse, there was only academic public interest at first. As she would by now have been seventy-six it was assumed that she was probably dead. But, in Sydney, Nancy Bird Walton refused to believe this. And she certainly did not subscribe to a theory gaining ground that

Jean had taken her own life. She quoted one of the last letters she had received from her, written in Tenerife in September 1981, in which Jean had said: 'I cannot believe that my seventy-second birthday is only a week away. I am very fit at the moment and actually happier than I was at twenty-seven when there were so many worries and anxieties.'

Nancy wrote to Lord Acton who had lived on Majorca for fifteen years and had influence on the island. But he had not met her, nor had any of his friends or the British Consul. Nancy next wrote to the New Zealand Prime Minister, David Lange, asking him to institute an international search. He replied that 'efforts to locate Miss Batten will continue until the matter is, we hope, happily resolved'. But this was not to happen.

In April 1986 there was an event which, those who knew Jean were convinced, would have brought her out of hiding. It was the first Concorde flight from England to New Zealand – a charter which had succeeded where Bob Pooley's had failed. 'Her non-appearance finally convinced me something was seriously wrong,' Bob commented.

Nearly nine more months were to pass during which no further enquiries were made by anyone. The search had ground to a halt because, quite simply, there was no one in the world close enough to Jean to make the effort. At this point, towards the end of 1986, when she had been missing for just over four years, Caroline and I decided to make our own attempt to solve the mystery. Our motive was not affection for Jean, or personal concern for her fate, since we did not know her. To us she was much more than a missing celebrity: she was a major biographical challenge.

Early in December I wrote to her to introduce us and our credentials and to ask if she would be willing to co-operate in the production of a one-hour documentary film and a book about her life. I sent the letter to her London bank. But it merely joined the hundreds already in the bulging mail sack in Charing Cross Road. Early in 1987, when both the book and the documentary were about to be commissioned, we decided to proceed without her.

For the first time the search for Jean Batten was to become a full-time quest – a costly and protracted research operation to discover who she was, and where she was. We hoped that information from the first might just yield enough clues to help solve the second. However, we were realistic enough to believe that it probably wouldn't.

By now, amid growing public interest, newspaper, radio and television stories had begun to speculate on her fate. She was making news again in a way she hadn't done since her megastar years. People who hadn't been born when her name was a household word were learning about her in stories which recalled her courageous flights and printed pictures as she last looked – an elderly but still vivacious and attractive woman in her early seventies.

A large number of plausible theories were being canvassed:

1. She had gone to earth, like Garbo, to be alone* and would emerge to make one final grand entrance on the aviation stage.

2. She had hidden herself away to prevent the world seeing her grow old, and would never reappear.

3. She had converted to Catholicism and gone into a convent.

4. She had become ill (physically or mentally) and immobilised and was being cared for by friends.

5. She had become ill and immobilised and was being cared for in a hospital or by strangers who did *not* know who she was.

6. She had accidentally drowned in Majorca on one of her daily swims and her body washed out into the Mediterranean.

7. She had swum out to sea in Majorca and deliberately drowned herself.

---

*Contrary to legend, Greta Garbo's most quoted remark, 'I want to be alone', was, according to her biographers, never uttered. In fact what she said was, 'I want to be *left* alone'. At different times of her life it is clear that Jean wanted both.

8. She was not on Majorca at all but had gone to one of the other Balearic islands – Menorca, Ibiza or Formentera.

9. She was not even in the Balearics but in England, Spain, Gibraltar, Sweden, Jamaica, Australia – or even back in New Zealand.

10. She had changed her name and was living somewhere under an alias.

We worked for the first six months with our own slender resources, pouring personal money into the project until the first stage of script development funds arrived from Energy Source Television, the Wellington company who, with the help of funds from Television New Zealand, were eventually to commission the programme. Almost immediately it developed into a classic detective operation that was to prove, at every turn, depressingly frustrating and perplexing.

We did three things immediately. From Jean's next-of-kin, Rick Batten, we obtained (under his impressive Justice of the Peace seal) a written authority from the family to conduct the search on our joint behalves. We advertised around the world for information about her secret life. We set out to verify every single relevant fact that had been published about her disappearance. Almost immediately our efforts began to pay off.

CHAPTER 26

Mystery in Majorca (1986–1987)

The response, in the last months of 1986, to our appeals for information on Jean was overwhelming. From England, Australia and New Zealand people wrote and telephoned to express concern that she was missing. Letters poured in from the generation that had gone to airports to see and cheer her during her triumphant years. A retired air marshal wrote: 'Congratulations on your perseverance, patience and caring'; and an elderly Wellington man: 'All the people of New Zealand still love her.' Nineteen-thirties newspaper clippings, personal photographs of Jean with her Moth and Gull in distant box camera shots, reminiscences of meetings with her, and streams of Batten anecdotes began to arrive almost daily.

Although this huge correspondence produced helpful material for the elusive story of her life, however, it yielded few clues as to what had actually happened to her. However, we had now resolved that the documentary should not conclude with an unsatisfying unsolved mystery: from the beginning of 1987 we set out determinedly on the physical task of finding her.

Initially our path was strewn with rumours, wishful thinking and plain misinformation. Early on, an elderly Batten admirer,

Mrs Enid Blow, in Auckland, raised our hopes with the information that the manager of Barclays' New Zealand subsidiary had allegedly told her 'that Jean is alive but wishes to remain incommunicado'. When Caroline rang the manager for confirmation she was told, to her astonishment, that Jean's London bank accounts, which had not been operated for several years, 'had recently become active again'. If this were true it was an intensely dramatic development.

It was to be followed almost immediately by another: a letter from Jean's London bank manager, Mr P.R. Culverhouse, to Rick Batten in which he said: 'We understand there are personal friends in Auckland who do know your aunt's location and perhaps could confirm her current wellbeing, but we regret we have no names or addresses or means of contacting them ...'

Jean had lived her life in so many private compartments that the family knew little about the people with whom she stayed in Auckland on her 1970s visits, and did not know where to begin to find them. It left us all wondering if one of these families was not in fact hiding her at that very moment. Only much later were we to establish that both these pieces of information supplied by the bank had been based on gross misunderstandings.

Meanwhile the belief that Jean had gone to earth in New Zealand was suddenly to assume a fresh likelihood as reports of alleged sightings started to reach us. The first was from a young Air New Zealand 747 pilot who, having seen recent pictures of Jean in the newspapers, came to tell us he was convinced that he had met her at Auckland airport in 1985 – three years after her disappearance. He claimed that she had breezed uninvited into a navigation lecture room and astounded the pilots with her knowledge of flying. Later a niece of Rick Batten, who had actually met Jean in the 1970s, insisted that she had seen her in the Auckland suburb of Howick, but had been too much in awe of her great-aunt to approach her. Although events were to disprove both sightings they served at the time to increase our unease that Jean was alive and observing our now highly public efforts to probe her life. And increasingly, as we learnt more about her, we grew aware of a hitherto little-known darker side of her personality. Those who revealed it left us in no doubt that, if she were suddenly to emerge, she would not be amused by our efforts to unravel the truth about her life. As the uncertainties grew so did our nervousness.

In an attempt to bring matters to a head I wrote to the head of public relations at Barclays in London to ask outright if the bank was guarding the secret of her whereabouts. His reply was helpful. 'It is a fact,' he wrote back, 'that no banking transactions have been carried out by Jean Batten with Barclays in London since her disappearance. Nor indeed have we heard anything from her. It would be wrong therefore to make the assumption that we have any more knowledge of this lady than anybody else.' In a subsequent letter he confirmed also that no one was working her account for her. This meant that, if Jean were alive, she was surviving independently of her principal bank funds. But then we didn't know what money, if any, she kept in accounts in other parts of the world. Much later we were to discover that there were several.

More out of curiosity than belief in a swift solution we turned to parapsychology: to clairvoyants. We went to see two local psychics, a mother and daughter team who had enjoyed some success in helping the New Zealand police find missing people.

Anne Older and her daughter, Megan, lived on Auckland's North Shore. We were instantly struck by their gentleness and elegance. An aura of tranquillity and a slightly hard to define luminous quality surrounded them. Anne knew of Jean but Megan, in common with many New Zealanders of her generation, had never heard of her. Working without picture or sound-tape reference they sat down together and, in an impressive and intimidatingly intense process of concentration, began to communicate with sources they each referred to as 'my people'.

Jean was emphatically alive, they soon declared. Both claimed to see her 'sitting, quite passive, with a very barren feeling – sitting quite tranquilly in a place which feels sparse, not poor. The surroundings are whitewashed ... it is a warm climate ... she is being well cared for ... but they do not know who she is.'

Our faith in these visions was increased immeasurably when

Anne and Megan Older went on, with what seemed like supernatural insight, to describe things that were then far from common knowledge: the past dominance of Ellen, her determination that her daughter should never desert her for marriage, and the relationship they saw 'in which both women believed they were immortal, that they were above other people and just walked over them'.

If the revelation were true where was this place the clairvoyants had been told about? It sounded like the Mediterranean. But what about the November 1982 cheque that Jean was supposed to have cashed in London? Was it before or after she wrote her last letter on the 8th? The precise date now seemed important. But the bank ignored the family's letters asking for the information. We therefore drafted for Rick Batten a letter to Barclays' Chairman, Sir Timothy Bevan. It produced a prompt response. The crucial transaction had been on 13 October 1982 – not in November as the bank had told the New Zealand High Commission. It seemed that Jean had not gone back to England after all.

The mystery was shortly to be further compounded by news of an alleged sighting in Australia. A Wellington truck driver, Bill Borrows, and a Lancashire-born hospital worker living in New Zealand, Mary McGeachin, told *The Dominion* newspaper that they had met and talked to Jean Batten on Sydney railway station during a visit to Australia around Easter 1984. Their disclosure was prompted by news stories of her disappearance.

Walking up the station approach ramp they had overtaken an elderly woman with blonde hair struggling with a heavy suitcase. When Bill Borrows offered to carry it for her she recognised his New Zealand accent and said: 'Do you know who I am? I'm Jean Batten.' She had then proceeded to tell him that she had flown small aeroplanes across the world back in the 1930s.

Later, in Auckland, I met Bill Borrows. I showed him recent photographs of Jean and played some tapes of her voice. He was convinced that it was the woman he had met. If it wasn't the real Jean had it been a look-alike, a clone in appearance and speech who for her own troubled reasons had decided to adopt and flaunt Jean's persona? We were not to learn the truth for

many more months, but until then Australia was to assume a
new priority among the countries on our list.

For some weeks early in 1987 we had been aware from our
enquiries that we were not alone in our search. The London
Sunday Times, we discovered, was also investigating her disappearance. In February its Madrid-based reporter, Tim
McGirk, published his story, attractively presented as the lead
in the paper's widely read magazine section.* It was a thorough
and perceptively written piece, the first serious attempt to track
Jean down in the Spanish islands where many people were
convinced she had gone into retreat. But it left the mystery
unsolved.

McGirk had gone to Majorca where he did something so
obvious it was astonishing no one had taken the trouble to do it
sooner. He went to the headquarters in Palma of both the
Guardia Civil, responsible for rural areas, and to the National
Police. In the files of the seventy thousand foreigners who lived
permanently on the island there was no record, he claimed, of
Jean as a registered visitor, or as a death statistic. Nor was there
at the British Consulate. No one recognised her photograph at
the Palma post office. Or in the monastery village of Valldemosa which had so enchanted Jean and Ellen on their 1936
Spanish holiday. He also drew a blank in Tenerife.   ·

The failure of the *Sunday Times*, with all its vigour and
resources, seemed to us only to make the mystery more intract-
able. We were not to know then that the investigation, despite
its obvious logic and apparent thoroughness, had failed to look
hard enough under the stones it had lifted.

Our own story, meanwhile, despite its Agatha Christie
quality, had begun to look as if it might never acquire a satisfactory ending either. Bombarded day and night by phone calls
from the media, from concerned strangers, from well-meaning
people with irrelevant scraps of information, and from a
growing number of eccentrics with bizarre theories, Rick Batten
decided the time had come to involve Interpol. Surprisingly,
since it had all the facilities to do so, the New Zealand government, in its enquiries prompted by the former Prime Minister,

Jean Batten is Missing: Sunday Times Magazine, 1 February 1987.

had made no effort to enlist the help of the international police organisation, one of whose secondary functions is publicly stated as the tracing of missing persons; indeed a blue-cornered circular is in use by police forces throughout the world specially for the purpose.

In September 1986 New Zealand's Minister of Police, Mrs Ann Hercus, had, in reply to a parliamentary question, said: 'Unless reasons exist indicating fears are held for the safety of persons over twenty years, police do not normally make enquiries.' However, police headquarters in Wellington later said that if a request were made Interpol would be called in 'but that hasn't happened'.

Encouraged by this potential for help and assuming that a four-year disappearance constituted ample ground for concern, Rick Batten decided to act. He drove from Ruakaka to his area police headquarters in nearby Whangarei. Asking to see the area commander he was shown into the office of Superintendent Brian Wells. 'I introduced myself as a representative of Jean Batten's family,' Rick said. 'I explained the history of the search, the continuing frustration and our now very deep concern for our aunt's safety. I asked if it would be possible for the New Zealand police to initiate a missing person's enquiry through Interpol.'

In the belief that the grounds were demonstrable and now wide public knowledge, and that an Interpol search would be a mere formality, Rick was taken aback by the Superintendent's response: 'He was not in the least sympathetic or interested. Interpol's job was the pursuit of criminals, not missing people, he said. He flatly refused to deal with it. I was flabbergasted. I went home almost feeling guilty that I had wasted his time.' On the drive back to Ruakaka, Rick Batten, now quietly seething with resentment, determined that he would not let the matter rest. That night, before his anger had subsided, he wrote a letter to the Minister of Police in Wellington.

It was nearly three months before Mrs Hercus replied. 'Unless genuine fears are held for the safety of the person concerned,' she repeated yet again, it was not a police matter. Washing her hands of the entire business, she suggested the family try the Salvation Army Missing Persons Bureau and the

New Zealand Red Cross.

It was now clear that if Jean Batten was to be found it would be without the help of her own government. In fact the Minister of Police had been badly advised by a police bureaucracy that knew full well that Interpol could be used for this purpose and that genuine fears did exist. The request was being stubbornly refused for quite the wrong reason – from a reluctance born of a history of failed Interpol searches for New Zealanders vanishing abroad. Had the Minister insisted that Jean's photographs and particulars be circulated through the international channels that had long existed for this purpose, she would have been located before the month was out.

Somehow it all came back to the bleak fact that, because of the isolation with which Jean had become neurotically obsessed, nobody really cared. But Nancy Bird Walton insisted: 'People actually did care. It may sound a terrible thing but we all, I'm afraid, were inhibited by the fear that she would resent our intrusion.'

The Justice Minister's letter to Rick Batten was further confirmation that the New Zealand government wanted as little as possible to do with the whole affair — and the police likewise. It was clear that if Jean's fate were to be established there would have to be a major private investment in systematic, basic detective work. Had anyone, for instance, bothered to check conclusively whether she had come home to live incognito in New Zealand – perhaps in one of the beach cottages that had once taken her fancy – or to die? Had anyone checked the status of her passport; indeed, whether she held more than one? Had anyone checked the country's immigration records, whether she had changed her name, was drawing social welfare benefits, or had even died under her own or another name in New Zealand? Although these questions seemed quite fundamental it appeared that no one had tried to get answers to any of them.

We set out to do so. We drew up a list of aliases we thought she might have used, creating permutations of her mother's name, Blackmore, her middle name, Gardner, and her birth name Jane. And, just in case, we added Ellen and Shepherd for good measure.

Most of the answers were not difficult to get. The Minister of Internal Affairs, Peter Tapsell, confirmed that she had not changed her name by deed poll and that her New Zealand passport had expired in September 1984. Despite persistent press reports that she also held a United Kingdom passport the British Consulate General in Auckland quickly established through the Home Office in London that she didn't. And although individual passenger landing cards were only kept by the immigration statistics people for six months, unofficial but reliable enquiries showed that Jean's death under her own, or other possible names had not been reported. Nor, we discovered, was she drawing any social welfare benefits.

By now our home had acquired something of the atmosphere of a private enquiry agency, the volume of our mail had grown dramatically and our two answerphones were overloaded with calls whenever we were out.

As the months went by our biggest hope was that we might find somewhere in the world a true lifelong friend of Jean's to guide and advise us – someone to whom she had felt able to confide her innermost burdens and hopes. But it soon became clear that such a person probably did not exist, and never had. However, the dossier grew and with it our knowledge of her strengths and susceptibilities, her foibles and bewildering contradictions of character, her many idiosyncrasies and eccentricities and, increasingly intriguingly, her little-known private face. Her name began to dominate our conversation; her presence, in an eerie and pervasive way, seemed to permeate our home; we even began to dream about her.

Our greatest nightmare was that Jean would emerge, a formidable figure, outraged at the now irreversible process we had begun. The trauma of her wrath would be on our own heads, we were frequently warned by a small core of elderly people who believed that the flaws in her character, emerging for the first time, should remain buried, her fairy-princess image left untarnished.

At first, out of fear and respect, many of those who had known her regarded the intimate details of her life as too sacred to discuss – they saw it as disloyal and a betrayal. However, as time went on and fears for her safety grew, inhibitions began to melt, assessments to become more frank and honest.

The ripples from our international advertising had some surprising consequences. One evening on the phone from Melbourne an Antipodean voice introduced himself as Barry Jones, the Australian Federal Minister for Science. He began to ask a lot of questions about the search. The relevance of his interest at first seemed so unlikely that I concluded immediately that it was a New Zealand friend engaged in one of our country's traditional pastimes of leg-pulling. I was guarded and unhelpful, trying hard to identify the voice. But as he continued talking about Jean's flights which he remembered from his childhood and about her Australian contemporaries, Melrose and Broadbent, it began to dawn on me that it was indeed the Australian Minister for Science. One of his country's most colourful politicians who had played a leading role in the post-war revival of the Australian film industry, he had rung to ask if he could help. I said he could certainly do so if he could persuade his ministerial colleagues to help the Batten family discover whether Jean was alive or dead in Australia. He promised he would. But in the event the Australian bureaucracy was to prove as reluctant as its New Zealand counterpart to conduct any meaningful investigation.

When we arrived in Australia, in April 1987, it was with the strong conviction, following the possible Sydney railway station meeting, that Jean might easily be living there. We met for the first time the three veteran pilots, Nancy Bird Walton, Peg Kelman and Esther Mather. Between them, and another woman pilot, Layne Glanville Williams, in Sydney, and Captain Bob Miles in Melbourne, we had soon met all the significant surviving Australians with whom Jean had formed friendships and in whose homes she had stayed in the years of her come-back. They all found it unthinkable that she could have returned to Australia and made contact with none of them.

'The last time we met I felt that something had died within her,' Esther Mather said. 'She had lost all her animation. I'm convinced she's committed suicide. She had nothing any more to live for. I suspect that all she wanted was to join her mother.' We weren't convinced. We thought it not impossible that she might, in her inner loneliness, have been drawn back to the locations of her happiest memories. Gone perhaps to visit the grave of the only man she had ever really loved?

Although we knew it was a long shot we decided to try and find out. From Brisbane we drove south to the MacPherson Ranges on the northern New South Wales border. The narrow gravel road wound steeply and sharply up through eucalypt and sub-tropical rainforest into the cool uplands of the Lamington Plateau, 3,000 feet above sea level. There, in lonely isolation, at the road end, was the guesthouse from which Bernard O'Reilly had set out on his heroic trek through the mountain jungle fifty years before. It was now a modern lodge catering for a steady stream of tourists come to walk the bush tracks and view the wildlife. The manager was Bernard O'Reilly's nephew, Peter, who regularly described his uncle's 1937 rescue of the Stinson survivors in evening slide lectures.

The remains of the Stinson could still be reached in a two-day trek across the ranges. So enduring was the legend that persisted around the rescue that, only a few weeks before our visit, there had been a re-enactment of it and a reunion of some of the members of the rescue party with the last remaining survivor of the crash, seventy-nine-year-old Sir John Proud.

Ten minutes' walk through the rainforest we found that a memorial plaque had been bolted to a large rock. Beverley Shepherd's name was among the five dead. 'As long as it stands this rock will tell of man's courage, mateship, endurance and self-sacrifice,' the inscription said.

By great coincidence, staying at the guesthouse that night was an elderly but still amazingly active woman, Nell Cavell, who had lived in a valley below the ranges all her life. She told us she remembered the Stinson going over, under scudding cloud and deluging rain, on the afternoon of the crash. 'I looked up and thought, gosh, it's never come over that low before,' she recalled.

We learned that a major Australian television drama was at that moment in production to tell the story of the disaster. One of the characters was Jean Batten, who would be seen searching for the Stinson day after day. But the real Jean had never been seen at O'Reilly's.

In Canberra, thanks to Science Minister Barry Jones, we met

an official of the Department of Immigration and Ethnic Affairs. The department operated a highly efficient computerised system which held records of everyone who arrived in or left Australia by normal means. It would have confirmed whether or not the woman encountered in Sydney could possibly have been the real Miss Batten. But despite our ministerial introduction the official told us that the information could only be supplied to the New Zealand police. Since the latter had refused to be involved it was to be the first of many Catch 22 impasses that were to plague the search. Indeed we began to wonder quite seriously how any missing person was ever found.

In England, for the first time we met Jean's brother, John, who had just turned eighty-four. Because he prefers to live without a telephone our several visits to his tiny terraced house in Colchester in Essex had to be arranged time-consumingly by a flurry of letters. But, eventually, one afternoon in the spring of 1987, we drove down there and knocked on his door. With much charm and old-world courtesy he welcomed us into his reclusive domain. Its simply furnished frugality struck us immediately by the way it seemed to mirror the austerity in which Jean also had lived much of her life.

The only pictures we had seen of John had been in publicity stills from the film studios of the 1920s, which portrayed him as a handsome young actor. Sixty years later, though bald and grown smaller, he was still strikingly goodlooking and his features – he had Jean's high forehead and cheekbones – were ruddy pink from four daily miles of exercise and a careful, strictly vegetarian diet. His background as an actor showed in the care of his speech and in theatrical gestures.

Over a pot of nettle tea made from the leaves he picked with gloves on long brisk walks along the nearby River Colne, he began to talk with apparent pride of his celebrated sister. It was only when my questions became detailed that his replies grew so vague he had to confess the astounding truth that he hadn't spoken to her since 1931. But he described the long silence in matter-of-fact terms that suggested he had few regrets – that it had been just one of those things.

But now that she had disappeared, missing for five years, what were his feelings? He had read about it in the newspapers, he said, but frankly didn't understand what all the fuss was about. 'She said she wanted to go to earth for a few years, didn't she? I suspect she's enjoying it so much she wants to prolong it – like Garbo.'

We were struck by the great sadness that showed in John's face in repose. We thought of the accounts we had been given of the deep rift between this once well-known actor and his famous sister and, although he did not wish to speak of the things that had come between them, we couldn't help wondering whether perhaps he now harboured some private regrets which he was reluctant to admit.

We were to grow fond of John Batten, to meet him on a number of occasions and to maintain a warm correspondence. I was to film an interview in which he candidly described the bookshop incident and rationalised the true feelings for Jean he could not bring himself to reveal. And so, in this story of her life, so extraordinarily resistant to the most determined research, I have been unable to do more than record, as he elected to explain it, his own version of the relationship, which others, competent to comment, had observed across the years with great sadness.

At the RAF Museum in Hendon no one had seen Jean since around 1980 but there, in the archive she had devotedly arranged, I saw for the first time the big collection of her memorabilia – her cuttings, photographs, and aircraft logbooks, her trophies and medals, the watch and the protractor with which she had navigated, her flying helmet and the Union Jack and New Zealand flags she had worn as scarves. There was also an immense amount of assorted trivia – the ephemera of her life: things like airline menu cards, in-flight magazines and invitations to events at which she had been guest of honour. There was even the door key to her Percival Gull, neatly labelled in her handwriting.

Much more revealing were the contents of the locked suitcase she had left at the museum merely for safekeeping. The staff had never opened it, but now, in the hope that it might yield up a tiny helpful clue, they unlocked it for me. Among an assortment of minor possessions, there were Jean's original A and B pilot's licences, Ellen's last United Kingdom passport with all the frontier evidence of their seven-year nomadic zig-zagging across Europe in the 1950s, and Jean's original New Zealand passport issued in Wellington early in 1930.

Handling these documents and artifacts, nor sure whether their owner was alive or dead, gave us both an awkward and slightly guilty feeling of intruding into crevices of her world she had intended no one ever to probe. And the feeling grew stronger as we handled her sketchbooks and paintings. Two which puzzled us and gave us a strange feeling were bizarre, surrealistic paintings of an almost identical Jamaican scene: a view of the Caribbean observed through palm trees and a profusion of tropical foliage. When she had first painted it, in the late 1950s, the scene was dominated by three human arms rising up from the vegetation as if beseeching for support. Curiously they were painted as three left hands growing out of one arm. Years later she had recreated the scene but with only two arms, one left, one right. The paintings fascinated us. Had they been a suppressed cry for help? Why had she painted the pleading hands again after an interval of ten years? The only clue was the wistful caption: 'In memory of Blue Horizon'. Those outstretched hands were to haunt us through the months of our search. And curiously we were to be reminded of their distressing undertones a few days later when we had a call from the manager of a London security company who had read one of our appeals for information and claimed to have met Jean in 1969. This in itself was of little relevance, but the circumstances were.

At the time, the man said, he had been serving in London with the Royal Canadian Mounted Police and had been allocated duties to guard a senior Canadian government official who had been a patient at Bowden House Clinic, an alcohol and drug rehabilitation hospital at Harrow-on-the-Hill. 'One of the other patients,' he said, 'was a woman in her sixties who was being treated for alcoholism. One day I had a long chat with her. She told me she was a New Zealander, that she had once flown little biplanes across the world and that she had made a flight from England to New Zealand. One of the things she said stuck in my mind: "I used to have the world at my feet. Now look at me – nobody cares." I didn't actually ask her name. But

I later realised it must have been Jean Batten.'

Rick Batten wrote to the clinic. The reply said that Jean had never been a patient – not under her own name nor any of our now standard range of permutations of Jean, Jane and Ellen; Gardner, Blackmore and Shepherd. It was not a great surprise because all the evidence had suggested that Jean, despite the constant risks she had faced during the years of her fame had, with the help of Ellen's firm hand, always treated alcohol with extreme caution. But later, back in New Zealand, I was to learn, from one of the friends in whose home she had stayed for many weeks during the 1970s, that she had once, in an unusual rush of confidence, admitted that, during her deep depression in the wake of Ellen's death, turned heavily to the bottle for comfort. Her ritual daily quarter bottle of champagne which she was fond of referring to in interviews, had sometimes become several bottles. Indeed enough to drink herself into a stupor. This would have been in the second half of the 1960s when she had sat for week after week alone and in despair in her Tenerife apartment, not caring whether she lived or died. Had she used the opportunity of her secret trip to London to prepare herself for the 1969 BP air race with a face-lift to have herself dried out at the same time? And had she deliberately chosen a clinic on Harrow Hill with a view across the grey hazy suburban sprawl that covered the long-since obliterated site of Stag Lane aerodrome? If so she must have used a false name.

Or had our informant got it all wrong? Was it perhaps another famous woman aviator he had met, one whose life had been lived in much more hard-drinking circles than Jean's? Could it have been Beryl Markham from Kenya, whose name regularly cropped up during my search, offered by helpful people who did not know she had died in Nairobi in August 1986? Whoever she was, the Bowden House patient who claimed in her youth to have flown from England to New Zealand was to remain a mystery.

If by any chance this sad woman had been Jean, then the treatment must have been successful. For there is no evidence at all that, in the active years of her comeback that followed, she ever drank other than in moderation.

At Felden in Hertfordshire we met the family who had done

more than anyone else to befriend Jean during her renaissance, and had made the biggest efforts to have her traced. By the spring of 1987 she had been missing for four and a half years and the Pooleys had privately long given up hope of ever seeing her again. In the corner of a spare room in their rambling old farmhouse we saw the two suitcases and two smaller bags Jean had left in their safekeeping until she found a new home in the sun. Bob and Lyn had long ago opened them in the hope that they might contain some clue to her whereabouts. But there had been none; they held mainly clothes and books. However, they did find a small address book. It contained the names of many prominent aviation personalities well known to the Pooleys whom they already knew could not help. But it also contained scores of other names and addresses of people around the world whom they did not know. As they had not attempted to get in touch with any of them we offered to do so. We photocopied the tiny pages and took them back to London to study more closely.

On the first page of the address book was a quotation which she had many times copied out during her life:

I pass through this world but once
If there is any kindness I can do let me do it now
Let me not defer it for
I pass this way but once.*

Searching for someone who might provide her with a secret bolt-hole, we alighted on the name of Mary Mitchell whose Bermuda house and Geneva château addresses were listed. Although we did not then know it Lady Mitchell, of all the people she knew, had the great wealth and international connections, had she chosen to do so, to provide Jean with a permanent, comfortable retreat out of sight of the world. But, when I wrote, Mary Mitchell replied expressing the now familiar concern that she hadn't heard from Jean for many years. We

---

*Adaptation of a quotation usually attributed to Stephen Grellet (1773–1855), but there are other claimants to its authorship.

did just wonder whether Lady Mitchell was putting out a smokescreen to cover the fact that she was harbouring her old friend at one of her homes in Boston, Rio, Bermuda, Jamaica or Switzerland. For we had now quite irrationally grown suspicious of much of the information we were getting, largely, I think, because we were still subconsciously trapped in the belief that the clairvoyants might be right. But later, when I was able to speak to Mary Mitchell on the phone in Bermuda, it was obvious from the depth of her concern that she had no idea where Jean was.

Nor did Sir Peter Masefield, then Deputy Chairman of British Caledonian Airways, whose name was also there. Sir Peter, who was later to make a major contribution to the narrative of the documentary, had not met her since 1978. 'She had then become a tragic and lonely figure,' he said, 'still searching for something she was never to find – the pot of gold at the end of the rainbow. She'd been so remote that, when the Christmas cards stopped, one didn't think it was the end, but just a further retreat into darkness.'

Caroline wrote to every person whose name appeared in the address book. Many had since died or moved away. None of those who replied had heard from her since 1982. Furthermore, most of the names turned out not to be friends so much as acquaintances, and officials in various aviation bodies.

However, one of the names to which our attention had been instantly drawn – by the prominent box inked around it – was that of Rosemary Madoc. Caroline had earlier discovered in Australia that Beverley Shepherd had a sister Rosemary. Wondering if it could be the same person, she traced Mrs Madoc to her home in Hampshire. The widow of a Royal Marines general, she turned out indeed to be Beverley's sister. But at the time of Jean's friendship with her brother and his death in 1937 she had been living out of Australia, she said. She had met her for the first time when Jean had tracked her down at her husband's London club during the 1970s. She thought that the gesture and the initiative after so many years confirmed the enduring romantic attachment in her heart with the Shepherd family. 'I know my mother had very much hoped they would marry,' she said.

Rosemary Madoc had no idea where Jean now was. 'But that morning we had coffee with her at the club she told me she was sick of social life and of being a permanent object of public interest and curiosity wherever she went. She intended, she told us, to get away from it all and find some secluded part of the world in which to live in peace on her own.'

The address book revealed the existence of three bank accounts of which we had not been aware: with the Banco Hispano Americano in Tenerife, the National Bank of New Zealand in Auckland and the Bank of New South Wales in Sydney. We wrote to them all. They replied in identical terms: Miss Batten had not operated her account since 1982. In each account, we were much later to learn, there were modest funds.

Meanwhile, at her principal bank, Barclays in Charing Cross Road, a lot more money had accumulated and her mail now filled two large sacks. It occurred to us that, among the hundreds of letters, there might be some clues that could introduce us to hitherto unrevealed corners of her life. But when Rick Batten wrote asking that the family be allowed to examine the mail, the manager refused. The bank, taking the view that Jean must be assumed to be alive until proved dead, was determined to protect her interests.

One of our last hopes now was the airline that had named one of its aircraft after her in the early 1980s and still held one of her suitcases. I drove to Britannia Airways headquarters at Luton airport in Bedfordshire where a public relations officer showed me the suitcase: it had clearly seen better days, and was now covered in dust in a storeroom. It was the last of the possessions of which Jean had divested herself, and it sat there as a sad and shabby testimony to a life lived largely out of suitcases. But the airline was unwilling to open it, still regarding her, as did her bank, as a customer whose privacy must be respected.

I was about to leave Luton when someone suggested I meet Britannia's administration officer, Bob Hutchinson. It was to prove in one respect a highly rewarding encounter.

Until now no one had known when, or even on what airline, she had made the fateful journey to Majorca. Bob Hutchinson, who had been customer relations manager at the time, turned out to have been one of the last English people ever to have spoken to Jean. 'She came to us sometime towards the end of 1982,' he said, 'and asked if we could fix her a free flight to Majorca. Well, as we were only operating charters into Palma at the time we had to get special dispensation for her, which we did.'

I asked him if he could remember the date. 'I doubt it,' he said, 'not after all this time.' I explained how important the date was to the tracing of Jean's journey into oblivion.

'Hang on,' he said, 'it might just be in my 1982 diary – if I've kept it.' He had, and searched through the pages. A meticulous man, he had actually scribbled down a note of the flight number and the date. Britannia had flown her from Gatwick to Palma, Majorca, on charter flight BY001A on Friday 15 October 1982. And it was by no means, I was now startled to learn, the last that the airline had heard from her.

'A few weeks later,' Bob Hutchinson said, 'she began to write and telephone with a demand that, free of charge, we fly out to her a large consignment of books. She wanted several hundred copies of *Alone in the Sky* put on one of our charters. The idea was that she would meet the flight at Palma, sit in the airport building and autograph them all, and then the same aircraft would bring them back to England. But I'm afraid it just wasn't on. We didn't have the spare cargo capacity and we don't hang around on the ground in Palma. The whole thing was quite impractical.'

From where, I asked him, was Jean writing and phoning. 'I actually had her Palma address and phone number,' he said, as my heart skipped a beat. 'I might just still have them.' But although he searched his diaries the vital information was not there. It was not for many months that I was to learn just how close I had come that afternoon to solving the mystery of Jean's disappearance.

CHAPTER 27

The Spanish Document (1987)

In Tenerife, although Jean's distinctive figure would soon have made her conspicuous there, we went to the capital, Santa Cruz, to check the records of expatriates registered with the British Consul. It was not a conclusive enquiry because registration is not mandatory.

The files, which disclosed that she had entered the name of her nephew Rick, as her next-of-kin, showed that she had not bothered to register her residence on the island after 1974 – although she would have been required regularly to renew her Spanish *residencia* permits with the Tenerife police. (We were to discover subsequently that her last renewal, made in Puerto de la Cruz, had extended her right to live anywhere in Spain or its island territories until 22 September 1983, long after the date of her disappearance.)

In Spain we went to Malaga to retrace the journey she had made in the summer of 1982 along the Costa del Sol through Torremolinos, back to Los Boliches and the now delapidated villa La Paloma. Along the playa we walked, calling at villas and restaurants, showing photographs of Jean as she had looked in her early seventies. But always the response was a solemn headshake. Even residents there since the early 1960s, when Jean and Ellen had been part of the small fishing community, showed no glimmer of recognition. Wherever they had paused in their travels it seemed that they left no trace of themselves.

In Marbella we went on radio and gave interviews to local newspapers. Our appeals produced no one who could help or had ever met the Battens. So we drove on to Gibraltar. There at the Bristol Hotel her picture was not recognised; nor did an appeal in the *Gibraltar Chronicle* bring any response.

We left until last the island of Majorca. So impressed had we been by the apparent thoroughness of the *Sunday Times*, with its reputation for tenacity, that we had somehow accepted its conclusion that Jean's last letter posted there might even have been intended deliberately to mislead her friends. So we arrived in Palma, early in May 1987, by no means convinced that she was any longer there. Yet our instincts told us that having come so far it might be prudent to repeat the enquiries. From a small hotel in one of the harbour yacht basins we set out to do so — with funds for just a five-day stay on the island.

We began with the British Consul in his office overlooking one of Palma's central squares, the Plaza Mayor. Michael McLoughlin, an efficient man whose precise manner suggested he might once have commanded a ship in the Royal Navy, said that he had already built up a small file on the missing aviator but had no record whatsoever of her presence on Majorca. 'She never registered with us which is the customary thing for British expatriates to do,' he told us. 'Nor have we been notified by the Spanish authorities of her death or injury or illness.' He had made numerous enquiries within the British community which formed a large part of the permanently resident colony of foreigners. None of them had seen her.

We located the Britannia Airways representative, a genial and helpful Majorcan, Tony Estella Salom. But on 15 October 1982, the day Britannia had flown Jean in to Palma international airport, he had not been asked by the airline's head office either to meet her or to extend any courtesies. Nor had he any knowledge of her subsequent requests to the company to fly in a consignment of books. He therefore had no record of her address.

We also drew a blank at the British-American Club. And the warden of the Anglican Church said no one answering Jean's description had ever attended a service. We arranged to be interviewed on the English language radio station: it brought no news of her.

Again we turned to the newspapers, this time to both the English and Spanish language press. We were interviewed by a reporter, Josemaria Rodriguez, of the daily *El Día de Baleares* who, two months earlier, on his own initiative, inspired by the *Sunday Times* story, had conducted his own investigation. He told us that he had been to the National Police and the Guardia Civil and had also checked the island's death register, all without success. Our own pictures and stories proclaiming us as investigative television journalists from New Zealand were given generous prominence, for Jean's beauty and bravery and the sadness of her disappearance were things which readily touched the Spanish heart. Within forty-eight hours of our arrival few Majorcans could have been unaware that an aviation celebrity had dropped out of sight in their midst. But not a single person wrote or telephoned with even the most irrelevant clue.

The depth to which we were taking our Majorcan enquiries was so demanding of Caroline's basic Spanish we now engaged an interpreter. We put her to work immediately making, from the lobby phone in our hotel, a stream of calls around the hospitals. The big psychiatric one in Palma said that Jean was not among their English patients; nor was she in any of the old people's homes we called.

The immigration authorities at the airport, through which nine million visitors poured every year, told us that the landing cards of arriving passengers were only held for six months. There was no way of discovering whether she had arrived and subsequently left.

On her last visit to Felden Grange Jean had spoken of Menorca, one of the smaller Balearic islands to the north-east of Majorca. Its remoteness had apparently appealed to her as a new haven. As a result of phone calls we made to some prominent members of the expatriate community on the island the Spanish governor was persuaded to have a full official search made by the Menorca police. It found no trace of Jean.

So we stuck to Majorca, a large sun-blessed island of spectacular beauty, its plains dotted with big conical-towered windmills and mountains cloaked in olive groves and Aleppo pine. If the message the clairvoyants had received was to be relied upon then, somewhere here, in hiding, possibly unwell, was Jean Batten.

Double-checking the enquiries of the *Sunday Times*, we drove up into the northern mountains through almond and olive groves carpeted with brilliant red poppies. Up here, where the air had a champagne quality, we found the village of Valldemosa and the ancient monastery that had so captivated Jean and Ellen fifty years before. It was now a museum with Chopin, and the French woman writer Georges Sand, with whom he had been living, commemorated in lifelike waxworks. In the narrow streets of the village we stopped a number of elderly nuns from a local convent. But our pictures of Jean meant nothing to them.

As the most persistent and romantic theory had her in a Majorcan convent, we decided to enlist the help of the Catholic Church. At its headquarters in an ancient stone building beside Palma Cathedral we were solemnly received by a senior dignitary, Padre Mas, in his modern and efficient-looking office. Through our interpreter he explained that, to have become a sister in one of the orders, Jean must have converted to Catholicism and entered as a novitiate. However, as most of the convents were serving the community, running such institutions as schools, hospitals and geriatric homes, she would have had to demonstrate some productive skill.

There was no central staff register as the convents were autonomous; to search them all would be a formidable task, the priest explained. A computer print-out he gave us showed that there were a phenomenal 192 on the island. We called upon a few, but soon gave up in favour of a new line of enquiry.

From time to time, we had learnt, foreign celebrities came to Majorca to bury themselves away in small villages up in the northern mountains. The English poet and author, Robert Graves, had been one of them. He had chosen the picturesque village of Deia, on the high northern slopes where the mountains dropped abruptly away to sea cliffs and sandy coves. We went there, following the narrow winding road through woods of mountain oak. But no one in Deia betrayed a flicker of recognition at the pictures. However, by now we were so convinced of a carefully executed plan to conceal her that, when we left, it was with the conviction that we may not have been told the truth.

On our last day in Palma, although it had purportedly already been done by the New Zealand government, by the *Sunday Times* and by the Balearic newspaper, we decided to make our own approach to the Majorcan authorities. I went with our interpreter first to the *Juzgados*, the Ministry of Justice, in central Palma. Here were held the death records for the whole island. But the clerk shook his head; it was not permitted to search the register. To do so required the special authority of the President of the *Juzgados* – the Chief Justice of the Balearics no less. The procedure would be slow and complicated.

But as I turned to leave, the clerk spoke again to my interpreter. 'He says you are permitted to make one enquiry for one date, if you wish,' she said. Jean's last letter had been dated 8 November 1982. Despite the alleged sightings in New Zealand and Australia I had become convinced that whatever had happened to her must have occurred swiftly. For her principal activity, the compulsive outpouring of letters, to have ceased so abruptly was, I felt, out of character and ominous.

So, wildly guessing, I added an improbable two days to the crucial date. 'The 10th of November 1982,' I said. The clerk went to a long row of large leather-bound volumes on shelves behind him. He pulled one down and laid it on the counter, rapidly turning the pages. On that date twelve deaths had been registered. Jean Batten's was not one of them.

At National Police headquarters I met the detective inspector responsible for foreigners on the island. Inspector Francisco Oliver listened attentively as my mission was explained. The pictures of Jean as a young pilot he studied admiringly, commenting on her beauty. He turned to the prints of her as she would have looked around the time she had arrived in Palma and went away briefly to check a file. There was no record of her as a registered resident foreigner, he said. But we didn't then know that Jean had arrived in Majorca with the valid Spanish *residencia* she had taken out in Tenerife and would not have needed to register again for several months.

I asked the inspector, on behalf of the Batten family, if he would search the death register and have formal enquiries made around the island. But he said that he could only act at the request of the New Zealand police through Interpol. For them he would immediately arrange for a full formal investigation. 'If the señora is alive on the island we can soon find her,' he said. 'She could not hide here successfully for very long.'

'Why,' he added, 'have your police not contacted us? We could soon end the mystery for them.' The reason was so inadequate it defied rational explanation.

It left only the cemetery. Even though the *Sunday Times* and *El Día de Baleares* had claimed to have checked it out, as they had also said they had the death register, we decided the effort was worth duplicating. Palma city cemetery is on the northwestern outskirts, a vast white mosaic of headstones stretching into the far distance. It not only went outwards; to save space it went up as well. In what we first took to be multi-storey car parks, thousands of coffins had been set in tiers into the white concrete walls.

At the reception desk a custodian told us it would be a simple matter to peruse the burial register. The records were in the office upstairs, conveniently arranged alphabetically. We had not expected it to be so quick and easy. There was only one difficulty. It was ten past two in the afternoon. The office had closed for the day at two o'clock. For a few minutes we debated what to do. We were scheduled to fly out of Majorca at seven o'clock next morning. There wouldn't be time to come back to the cemetery. Should we postpone our departure to make this final apparently simple check? But the quest had been so hopeless, so utterly devoid of even the tiniest trace of Jean that we were convinced the burial records would merely add to the catalogue of disappointment. We stuck to our plans and flew out the next morning.

Back in New Zealand in the middle of 1987 we had to accept that there was probably only one way Jean's fate would ever be established. Our own government would have to be persuaded to overcome its curious reluctance to involve Interpol. We decided that the time had come to approach the Prime Minister,

David Lange. Early in June I persuaded Rick Batten to write to him.

To the family's disappointment and incredulity Mr Lange replied that 'there is in fact very little we can do in addition to what has already been done to locate Miss Batten'. As some of the most obvious routine checks had not yet been made it struck the family as an extraordinary response. Rick Batten's considerable patience had now run out. He approached his member of parliament, Dr Lockwood Smith. A member of the opposition National Party he readily agreed to pursue the matter and wrote immediately to the Prime Minister. His letter produced a noticeably more helpful response. It prompted at last a letter from the Minister of Police agreeing to consider pursuing the search through Interpol if a practical 'starting point' for an investigation could be established. For the first time since Bob Pooley had taken his concern to New Zealand House two and a half years earlier there seemed a possibility that something meaningful might at least be done by Jean's own country.

To help the momentum I too wrote to the Prime Minister offering to make available to the police all the information we had collected. I said that the Majorca police needed only a simple formal request from the New Zealand police to undertake the full physical search they had never been asked to do.

But although the Prime Minister may now have been willing to help, the police bureaucracy was not. Astonishingly they were now to fight a determined rearguard action. It began with a phone call to our office from the detective senior sergeant in charge of the Interpol section of police headquarters in Wellington. He wanted to know what helpful evidence we had. I summarized it for him and relayed, yet again, the offer from the Majorca police. The Interpol man sounded deeply cynical. His lack of enthusiasm, born, he said, of long and bitter experience, came dispiritingly over the phone. Interpol apparently had rarely succeeded in finding New Zealanders missing in Europe. He felt that to approach the Majorca police would be sheer waste of time.

To our knowledge they were never asked to look.

During our many meetings and phone discussions with Rick

Batten in these intensely frustrating weeks, we were tempted to believe that there was, unthinkable as it seemed, an active plot within the Beehive (the ministerial offices in Wellington) to inhibit the search. But the truth was much less sinister. It was, I was to conclude, simply massive bumbledom, inertia and lack of interest.

It certainly said something about the regard in which Jean Batten was now held by the country whose leaders had once worshipped her, and been so proud to be identified with her brave feats. We couldn't help wondering if, had it been a famous All Black who had gone missing, our sport-obsessed nation might have responded with more official interest and alacrity.

As a last resort we tried to influence public opinion. Where we and the Batten family had failed could perhaps the media, that had once made her so famous, succeed? The *New Zealand Herald* agreed to send a reporter to hear the story of ministerial impotence and bureaucratic apathy. But after we had spelt out the sombre facts she said it sounded like 'a political story' and a parliamentary journalist would have to tackle it. The story was never written.

At this moment, for the first time, we began to lose faith. It seemed that only Jean's family and two film makers actually cared about her fate any more. And the omens were not encouraging. Even the clairvoyants were now getting less optimistic messages. Where originally they had seen Jean alive but immobilised, now they saw only darkness.

I wrote a treatment for the documentary which poignantly concluded with unsolved mystery. I had little doubt that it would remain that way. In any case our research funds were almost spent.

We couldn't, however, quite bring ourselves to accept defeat. It had become such an obsessive mission it could not easily be abandoned. Besides we had ignited concern and helpfulness in so many quarters around the world that a major correspondence was still in full spate. We decided to do nothing to terminate it.

Throughout the New Zealand winter of 1987 Caroline had drafted and typed a large number of letters for Rick Batten's signature. They had gone to the Salvation Army and the

International Red Cross; to the Australian Federal Police and the Australian ministers of immigration and social welfare; to the Governor of Gibraltar; to the ministries of justice, immigration and the interior in Madrid, Malaga, Tenerife and Majorca, as well as to the provincial governors in the two Spanish islands. The letters to Spain had been carefully written in Spanish. None was ever to be acknowledged – with one triumphant exception.

On Wednesday 23 September 1987 among Rick Batten's morning mail at his home in Ruakaka was a letter from Palma, Majorca. In fact it wasn't strictly a letter, but a small compliments slip from the *Administración de Justicia* with a scribbled note in Spanish. Attached to it was a document, also in Spanish. It was a response to a routine letter Caroline had drafted and typed for Rick several weeks earlier. Unable to understand it, but sensing it was important, he phoned us immediately, and spoke to Caroline. She asked him to read the Spanish but his pronunciation did not make the text clear. All that he could identify was the name 'Señora Jean Gardner Batten'. So it was agreed that he would drive the thirty miles to Whangarei airport and ship the documents down to us on that afternoon's flight. With mixed emotions of excitement and curiosity I went to collect it. I tore the envelope open and struggled to interpret the contents. But my Spanish is no better than Rick Batten's. All that I could identify was Jean's name and her birthplace; Rotorua, New Zealand. It looked decidedly ominous. I hurried back to Mt Eden with it.

Caroline translated the handwritten note: 'Attached is the document you requested.' For a few seconds she studied the enclosure carefully. But somehow we both knew what it was.

'*Certificacion en extracto de inscripcion de defuncio,*' she read aloud. 'It's a copy of her death certificate. She's actually been dead for nearly five years.'

The certificate recorded that Jean had died in Palma on 22 November 1982 – just five and a half weeks after she had arrived on the island. It gave no indication of the cause of death, where it had occurred, or where she was buried.

We should have felt great sadness. But that was to come later when the full reality had sunk in. For the moment the only emotion was a bewildering numbness. We rang Rick to tell him. He had already guessed. He said he would immediately tell Jim and Isobel and the rest of the family. We discussed how the world should hear. But first there was the mystery of why and how she had died and where she was buried. And why, if the Spanish authorities had a record of her death nearly five years before, no one had been told.

That evening we arranged a triangular conference call between Auckland, Ruakaka and Majorca. Rick, Caroline and I spoke to the British Consul, Michael McLoughlin, and gave him the news. He was puzzled that the consulate had not been routinely informed and agreed to seek immediately from the court in Palma copies of any police and post-mortem reports that might explain the circumstances.

When she had left the Pooleys the month before her death, although moody and somewhat withdrawn, Jean had been in physically robust health. One mystery had now been replaced by another.

As the information from the Majorcan court would take some days to obtain, the family agreed that the news of her death should be made public as soon as possible. To reach the largest possible audience quickly we decided that I would break the story with a simple announcement to Television New Zealand. By the time I phoned the network newsroom in Auckland the main evening news was already going to air. There was only fifteen minutes remaining for a late item to be dropped into the bulletin.

Suddenly I was to know why such monumental apathy had allowed the tragedy to pass unnoticed for five long years. I was put through to the duty sub-editor in the news control room. He listened politely as I gave him the stark facts. There was a pregnant pause. He said: 'Sorry, you'll have to explain who she is.'

CHAPTER 28

Final Loneliness (1987)

For forty-eight hours our phones rang incessantly. Calls came from newspapers, radio stations, television networks and Batten admirers. They came from Australia and even from Fleet Street as the story broke across the world, putting Jean's name in the headlines for the last time.

Pictures recalling her finest hour, as she stood on the wing of the Gull waving bouquets to the crowd, told millions who had never heard of her of the beauty and fame she had once enjoyed. THE FINAL LONELINESS OF THE LONG-DISTANCE AVIATOR, said one of the papers. *The Times* paid tribute to her daring and her fame in a major obituary that would have pleased her. First on our doorstep early that sad evening was a reporter from the *New Zealand Herald*. She rapidly put the country's aviation hero into current perspective when, looking anxiously at her watch, she announced briskly: 'We'll need to be quick to meet our deadline – it'll have to be once-over-lightly I'm afraid.' It would not have been like that fifty years ago.

Stunned by the news, people were demanding to know how someone so famous could die in obscurity without anyone knowing for five years. What was the cause of death and where was she buried? Why hadn't the Spanish authorities, who had recorded on her death certificate that she was born in Rotorua, New Zealand, not informed the government of her native land? For several days these questions remained unanswered. It was only when the *New Zealand Herald* sent a reporter, Tim Murphy, and a photographer, Michael Tubberty (both of whom happened to be on holiday in London) to Majorca to investigate, that the truth began to emerge.

Arriving on the island Murphy and Tubberty hired an interpreter; an expatriate freelance journalist, a blunt-spoken Geordie from Newcastle-upon-Tyne, now nearing retirement. Bert Horsfall had lived in Majorca for over twenty-five years, filing local stories to the London newspapers. He knew his way around the island and spoke effective Spanish with a heavy accent. Murphy had already phoned from England to give him the details of the death certificate which the *Herald* had wired through to London. With this information Horsfall had gone to the Palma death registry, and unlike myself a few months earlier had, within minutes, been shown Jean's entry in the register. The date, ironically, was only 12 days later than the one I had blindly stabbed at that morning. The register also revealed where she had died: at a hotel called the Vista Porto Pi in Palma. And how she had died: from natural causes – from an infection of the lung which had led to a pulmonary abscess.

At the cemetery where we had come within ten minutes of unlocking the truth, the *Herald* men asked to see the burial records. With the help of the death reference number which Bert Horsfall had obtained from the *Juzgados*, the staff quickly confirmed that she was indeed there; buried on 22 January 1983, exactly two months after the date of her death. Her body had lain in the cemetery morgue during which time no one had come forward to claim her.

Her name was, in fact, in two separate cemetery record systems: one alphabetical, the other chronological. In the latter her name was conspicuously entered in red ink to signify the involvement of the judiciary and the necessity for a postmortem. 'Jean Gardner Batten' was all it said. Unlike the other names listed on the page no address was given. Just her burial number: 146.

In the alphabetical register they could not find her name under B. Under Spanish custom, by which people are known by their middle names, she had been listed under G for Gardner. It explained possibly why two earlier searches of the cemetery records had failed.

Murphy and Tubberty asked if they could photograph her grave. The assistant manager took them to see it. They had been expecting a simple, lonely and possibly neglected plot with its own headstone. They were certainly not prepared for the reality: for the truly appalling and ignominious circumstances of her burial.

They were led to a corner of the cemetery in the shadow of a high wall. A concrete walkway ran down an arid slope on which, in a series of terraces, a number of barren plots had been excavated. These bleak rectangles of parched earth, each about ten yards long and two yards wide, were contained within concrete walls adorned by iron railings. They were paupers' graves and in one of them, Fosa Comun No. 7, Jean had been buried. It looked uncommonly like a bear pit at a zoo.

She had been consigned there, they were told, because nobody had bothered to find out who she was. Her last resting place was a communal grave into which over 150 people had been packed. For most of them, for whom this anonymous fate had been forced upon the relatives by poverty, there was nothing to indicate who they were. The only exceptions to judicial oblivion were two of the dead whose presence was marked by small mobile plaques which got casually moved about the pit by staff who came regularly to rake the weeds from the salmon-pink earth. It was also too apparent that no one had known of her significance. Yet the death certificate recognition of her place of birth meant that her New Zealand passport must have been found and that her relatives could have been traced. Why then had no one done so?

The *Herald* men went with Bert Horsfall to the address from which, five years earlier, Jean had been taken to the morgue. The Edificio Vista Porto Pi turned out to be a small modern apartment building. It stood on a hill in a seedy quarter of Palma's southern outskirts with a distant view of the harbour across a wasteland of dusty brown grass, studded with abandoned, rusting motor cars. Close by were the docks of a Spanish naval base. It was an unpeaceful place beside a busy main road, the Calle Miro Juan, ceaselessly roaring with traffic. In 1982 the apartment block (now owned by Taylor Woodrow) had been a hotel. Jean had died in a small room on the fifth floor. But none of the people who now lived in the block had ever heard of her and all the former hotel staff had long since gone.

However the newspapermen learnt that a man called Ramon Morales, who had worked at the former hotel, was now at another hotel not far away. When they caught up with him he said immediately that he well remembered 'the beautiful woman who used to sit for hours every day on her balcony'. Morales did not know her name or anything about her. On the day of her death he had arrived at work to find his tearful colleagues helping to remove her body to a Justice Ministry ambulance. A maid had found her dead in her room, fully clothed. He remembered very clearly that the hotel manager had notified the British Consulate in Palma. However any record of this was subsequently emphatically denied by the Consul, Michael McLoughlin, who had arrived in Majorca some years after Jean's death. A great deal of the Consulate's work was involved with the problems of British and Commonwealth visitors to the island and all incidents, regardless of the way they were reported, had always been carefully logged, he said. Checking back on the records for the relevant week in November 1982 his staff had found no reference to Miss Batten.

Tim Murphy's story, with its revelation of Jean's anonymous death, was picked up by the Spanish press who promptly attacked what they saw as the inefficiency and callousness of their government. The national Spanish newspaper *El Pais* decided to investigate. It quickly discovered the unforgiveable truth, which it revealed under the emotive headline *Sola en el cielo y en la tierra* – Alone in the sky and in the earth.

From the Justice Ministry in Palma the newspaper learnt that, within a few days of Jean's death, there had in fact been an attempt by the *Juzgados* to inform her government. It had sent a formal notification to the New Zealand Embassy in Madrid. This would have been helpful if New Zealand had ever had an embassy in Spain which it hadn't. At that time diplomatic relations with Spain were handled from the New Zealand Embassy in Paris; by 1987 they had been switched to the country's ambassador in Rome. The result of this bureaucratic bungle was that the notification, undelivered in Madrid, had been returned by post to the *Juzgados* in Majorca. There, unbelievably, it had merely been filed away in the archives and no attempt ever made to advise the Spanish Foreign Office, the British Consul in Palma, the New Zealand government in Wellington, its embassy in Paris – or the Batten family.

In New Zealand the relative ease with which we had finally established her fate was hailed as a triumph of persistence – and an indictment of the government. But its ineffectual role was now water under the bridge. Of much more urgent concern to the family was to know what had actually happened to their aunt during those last five weeks of her life. Rick Batten made a personal call to the Foreign Affairs Minister, Russell Marshall, demanding that his ministry approach the Spanish government to find out. It was to prove a protracted and, initially, an unfruitful process.

Early in October 1987 we went to England to make arrangements to shoot the documentary. Although the story now had a conclusion, unsatisfactory shreds of mystery persisted. We refused to believe that somebody capable of being traced had not been with Jean at the end.

Some of the answers were now provided in the report of her death which the British Consulate in Majorca had obtained from the Spanish Justice Ministry. It revealed that she had been found dead at 12.50 in the early afternoon in apartment 505 at the Hotel Vista Porto Pi. Her body had been taken to the morgue at Palma cemetery where a post-mortem had established the pulmonary abscess cause of death: her right lung had been found to be extensively inflamed and deeply infected. How had someone who had always put such a high price on her health allowed herself to die of what sounded like a treatable infection? It seemed incredible and wholly out of character. In whose care had she been allowed to let her life ebb away as her lungs were overwhelmed by what the autopsy report described as purulent infection? I decided to fly to Majorca to find out.

While I was preparing to go we had a call in London from the executors of Jean's estate. She had left a will, dated September 1974, prepared by Barclays Bank and, with it, a personally typed and much amended note. In it she had made a request: 'In the event of my death ... my body is to be flown to London for cremation ... After cremation the urn, which I would like made of alabaster, is to be flown to New Zealand in a Concorde supersonic airliner (if possible) and placed on or near the Auckland International airport where I landed on 16 October 1936 on the conclusion of my solo flight, the first in history, from England to that city.'

Subsequently, in a handwritten alteration, she had crossed out the Concorde stipulation and opted for the less grandiose 'an airliner of Air New Zealand'. But whether or not her remains could be identified after five years was another matter. Rick Batten, learning of these wishes, asked me if I would look into the feasibility of disinterment during my visit to Majorca.

Meanwhile, Britannia Airways offered to show us for the first time the contents of the suitcase she had left with them early in 1982. No longer in need of clues to her whereabouts, we drove up to Luton not expecting much of interest. But we were wrong. When Bob Parker-Eaton opened the old, battered case that had lain in the company storeroom for five years, we were to find, in a crumpled buff envelope, the 200 pages of her close-typed secret manuscript, *Luck and the Record Breaker*. It was over 120,000 words long.

We flicked through the pages with a thrill of excitement. For, the day we had left New Zealand to fly to London, one of Jean's Auckland friends had revealed in a newspaper interview* that her memoirs 'would tell all'. Audrey Jamieson (whose husband John had gone to Sir Robert Muldoon to expedite the search for Jean) was reported to have said that when she had stayed with them in 1980 she claimed to have completed a book 'that would shock the international world. It was about her private life and lovers: she said she had left nothing untold,' Mrs Jamieson told the newspaper. 'She had been deliberating for years whether she would release the book during her lifetime.'

*Auckland *Sun*, 3 October 1987

Clearly Jean had thought better of it. But appetite whetted and curiosity aroused, I began hopefully to dip into this apparently hot property on my flight down to Majorca next day.

As quotations from her manuscript earlier in this biography have shown, the book proved a major disappointment in its revelations. Not a hint of the more intimate side of her life was anywhere revealed. Nor, surprisingly, were her memoirs to add much to the sum of knowledge we had by then amassed on the main events of her life. It was, however, valuable to know that, quite independently of her own heavily censored written record, we had got most of it right. Indeed we now knew that we had uncovered far more information, much of it deeply revealing of her character, than she would ever have brought herself to disclose.

What did emerge from the memoirs was a powerful sense of her belief in her own indestructibility. And of this, ironically, I was soon to be reminded on the ground in Majorca when I was to learn the true and tragic way in which her life had ended.

In Palma I was fortunate to recruit the man who had smoothed the way of the *New Zealand Herald* team a few weeks earlier. Now familiar with the story, Bert Horsfall drove me straight to the Vista Porto Pi in the shabby southern suburbs. The former hotel rooms had been converted into self-contained apartments and No. 505 had been sold, by coincidence, the previous day. Inside it looked immediately familiar – almost identical in specification to apartment 606 in Tenerife, where Jean had spent over a fifth of her life. Here was another small, rectangular, aseptically white bedsitter, another sparsely furnished retreat, typical of the inexpensive, anonymous places in which she felt comfortable.

Her balcony above the noisy street, trembling with the passage of heavy trucks, may once have enjoyed a distant view of the harbour. But the vista was now largely obscured by new apartments that had reared up among a forest of construction cranes and ugly pylons. What thoughts had occupied her as she had sat out here on her white wrought-iron chair in the winter sun during those last weeks, as infection destroyed her? Surely someone must have observed her slow descent into death? Now that I was actually standing in the room in which her life had ended it seemed more important than ever to try and find them.

Bert Horsfall took me to a nearby tourist hotel, the Los Pinos, where the waiter worked who had seen Jean's body removed from the Vista Porto Pi. But he had returned to mainland Spain for the winter. We were given the names of other staff who had once worked at the hotel, but when we got to their new work places all their hotels were closed until spring.

However, at the Hotel Zenith, in a steep and narrow street above the harbour, we at last found someone who remembered Jean from his days as a night clerk at the Porto Pi. Although he personally could tell us little about her, he was able to direct us, in our first real breakthrough, to the hotel's former manager, Gabriel Colom Ramis, who now ran a travel agency. Its office was, by coincidence, back in the Vista Porto Pi building and Gabriel Colom, a sympathetic man with greying hair and a permanent warm and broad smile, remembered the elderly senora as well. In limited but descriptive English he described how she had arrived one day in the middle of October 1982 'for to rent an estudio for the winter'. She spoke good Spanish, paid her rent regularly in advance and was much liked by the staff. She kept to herself and was what he called 'a very activity lady' who went out every day for long walks on her own. Sadly, before any of them could get to know her better, she had unexpectedly died.

Gabriel Colom said that when he came on duty that morning he was told that the Englishwoman was ill. He had immediately gone up to see her. She had been lying, fully clothed, on her bed. He offered to call a doctor; the hotel had two on call for emergencies. But Miss Batten, he said, had indicated emphatically that he was not to do so. As she appeared unwell, but not seriously ill, he decided to abide by her wishes and went back to his office. Some hours later a chambermaid came to report that she was dead.

'Immediately we called the *Juzgados*,' he said. 'They take pictures and take the body to the cemetery.' Among Jean's few possessions, which the *Juzgados* officials took away, was her New Zealand passport. 'In Majorca we don't know where was the consulate of New Zealand,' Gabriel Colom said. 'But then somebody told us it was the British Consulate so we called them.' He insisted that, as a result, someone from the Consulate had later that day come round to the hotel. (The Consulate remained adamant that no such visit was made.)

To Colom Jean had been just another elderly foreign woman who had come south to spend a lonely winter in the sun. He was amazed when, later, he read in the papers that she had once been an international celebrity. During her time at the hotel she had never spoken of her flying career.

Just as we were leaving, Gabriel suddenly remembered something. 'The chambermaid who found her this day, Maria Alcaraz, she is still in Palma, I think.' He had no idea where, but believed that Maria's daughter worked in a grocer's shop a few hundred metres down the street. We immediately went there. The daughter told us that her mother now did office cleaning work in the city. She telephoned her and Maria Alcarez agreed to meet me at her apartment in central Palma after work that evening.

That morning a camera crew had flown in from Madrid to join me. They were to shoot the final sequence of the documentary at the communal grave. I decided to have them come with me to record my interview with what sounded like the last person ever to have spoken to Jean.

Maria Alcarez was plump and pretty, in her mid-forties, and lived with her husband in a small prosperously furnished apartment on the fourth floor of one of the city's older buildings among a honeycomb of narrow, cobbled streets a few minutes' drive from the centre. We sat her down in front of the camera and Bert Horsfall translated my questions and the cameraman her replies.

Almost immediately she revealed the startling fact that the infection that had killed Jean had come from a dog bite.

Maria's account of it that follows is a translation from her interview transcript: 'I looked after her and saw her every day when I went into her room to clean it. I did not know she was famous. I did not even know her name. But I thought what a solitary lonely person she was, although she did not seem unhappy and she often told me how much she was enjoying Majorca.

'I noticed that she had very few possessions. They all fitted into a little valise. This, and a leather handbag, was all she seemed to own. She never wore any jewellery and dressed very simply. I thought she probably didn't have much money.

'She spent her time reading English and Spanish newspapers which she would go out to buy every day from the kiosk down the street. She would also go shopping down there for her food – things like fillet steak which she would cook in her room, yoghurt, fruit and mineral water.

'Every day she would go for a long walk. I don't think she ever went swimming, not in the sea or in the hotel pool. She would talk to the other guests but didn't really mix with them or become friendly with anyone. But she was always very polite and we all liked her.

'On her walks she would sometimes go up into the woods behind the hotel and pick flowers to bring back to her room. One day up there she told me she had been bitten in the leg by a dog. I saw the wound, just below the knee; it was quite a small puncture made by the dog's teeth. She had put some ointment on it and covered it with a bandage.'

Although there is no rabies in Majorca, Maria was sufficiently concerned to try and persuade Jean to see one of the doctors on call to the hotel.

'But she would not agree. No way did she want a doctor to come near her. She said, "It is nothing, Maria. It will soon heal up by itself." But it didn't. It got worse and her leg became more and more red and more and more swollen until she couldn't use it any more and took to her bed.

'Soon she stopped eating. All I ever saw her take was water; she began to drink glass after glass. It went on like this for about two weeks. Every morning I would ask if I should get the doctor and she would always say no very firmly. She said she didn't have a fever, just a very dry mouth. She didn't look ill during these days and I certainly had no idea she was dying.'

The morning of 22 November 1982 Maria told me she would never forget. When she came in as usual Jean was dressed and lying on the bed. 'She had been drinking so much water she had wet the bed. She asked me to forgive her and said would I get her some soda water. It took all my strength to lift her out of bed and sit her in a chair. I then went downstairs to the bar and got her a bottle of soda. I poured some into a glass and left her there in the chair while I went to get clean bed-linen.'

At that moment something startling happened. For the first time Jean addressed Maria in English. 'I didn't understand a word but I knew later that she might suddenly have been calling for help, probably for a doctor. I think, for the first time, she knew she was very, very ill, and for the first time I really saw that she was. Looking back now to that day I think that she may have realised, at that moment, that she was dying. All of a sudden I felt very frightened. I hurried out to get the clean sheets. When I came back, just a few minutes later, I saw that she had let the glass of soda water drop on to the floor. Her head had fallen to one side. She was dead.

'It was a very rapid death,' Maria added. 'She didn't have time to suffer. Her face did not carry a look of suffering.' Maria said she wanted to send a message to Jean's family: 'Tell them they must not be sad that she died so far away in Spain, uncared for. On the contrary she was well looked after. Everyone in the hotel was kind to her because she was such an agreeable, undemanding person. She died with love around her.'

But she had also died quite needlessly. The virulent infection that travelled from her leg to her lungs could have been stemmed quite simply. Antibiotics would have saved her. Why had she rejected the doctors? Did she still, at seventy-three, naively believe Ellen's fundamentalist teachings that all illness could be cured by vigorous exercise, plain food, fresh air, lots of fluid – and sheer willpower? Or had she subconsciously decided that life had nothing left for her?

The psychologists Michael and Yvonne Edwards, who had spent so long at my behest attempting to understand the things that influenced and drove her, were convinced that Jean was, by 1982, possessed of a death wish.

'To some extent I believe she suicided,' Michael said. 'Of course it wasn't deliberate or conscious. But I think the dog bite was fortuitous. Without it she would have gone on a bit longer, lost and rudderless, along the downward slope. She could have had herself quickly treated. But she had actually stopped living many years back – probably around the time of her mother's death. She was trapped in the past and out of phase with the present. I don't think that living had much point for her any more.'

Yvonne Edwards agreed. 'I had the sense that she was tidying up her life as people do, preparing for the end in her meticulous fashion: carefully labelling her memorabilia at the museum for posterity, divesting herself of possessions, leaving suitcases all over the place. As Michael says, it wasn't a consciously premeditated thing. Of course at the time she intended to collect all that stuff one day. But was she ever going to find that new permanent home she was ostensibly looking for? I don't honestly think so. Once that subconscious dying mode took over it was almost as if she saw the inevitability – and didn't fight.'

Now that we knew how she had died there remained only the delicate matter of her possible disinterment and reburial in New Zealand. I went back to Palma cemetery with an interpreter to discuss it with the manager. In rapid Majorcan Spanish he explained that it was no longer a desirable option. He pulled a large sheet of paper from his drawer and proceeded to illustrate the technical difficulty.

He sketched a cross-section of the communal grave in which Jean's body had lain for five years. The simple black wooden coffins in which the paupers were buried – not, he said, in plastic bags as several newspapers had claimed – were laid in the fifteen-foot deep pit in rows only a few inches apart. There were dozens in each row and as those at the lower levels disintegrated, so more people were buried on top. 'It is a never ending process,' he explained. 'The communal graves are regularly being topped up. It is for economy of space.'

It was apparent that Jean's body now lay beneath as many as fifty other coffins. In theory, he said, with forensic help, it might just be possible to find her body which would have no personal identification, and her bones could now be mixed up with other people's. The only reference would be her burial number, 146, stamped on a metal plate attached to her coffin. But as the wood may have rotted away the numbered plate might no longer be close to her remains and might even have sunk to a lower level. It would be a harrowing grave-digging operation, he added, that could only be sanctioned on exceptional grounds such as the need for evidence of murder.

Clearly no case existed to attempt such a macabre exercise. There was also another persuasive reason for leaving Jean to rest in peace. Before trying to retrieve her body the relatives, where they could be traced, of the scores of others lying in communal grave No. 7 would, as a courtesy, have to be consulted. The process could take years. Furthermore, I was warned that it might create a public outcry for still yet another reason: Jean was not the only celebrity buried there.

In the same grave was the body of a famous Spanish singer, Jorge Sepulveda. He had not, in fact, died in poverty but he had wanted to be cremated. Knowing that the Catholic Church would refuse this and not wanting his grave to become a shrine, he had instructed his wife to arrange for his burial anonymously. He had followed Jean into the grave in 1983 a few months later.

The Batten family in New Zealand were to agree that, distressing as the circumstances of her burial were, it would be insensitive to disturb the grave. I went to visit it for the last time with the camera crew. The shot we got that I liked best showed something Jean would have approved of. It was a tall clump of pampas grass, its soft, silver-white fronds shivering in the breeze on their slender canes. Jean would have recognised one of her own country's most prolific botanical symbols – the New Zealand *toetoe*. Two years later, in 1989, beneath its feathery blooms, a simple plaque with her familiar helmeted features in bronze relief, and an inscription in English and Spanish, was attached permanently to the concrete wall of the grave by the New Zealand government.

It took over six months for the Batten family to learn officially why they had not been notified of her death. When his appeal to Foreign Affairs Minister Russell Marshall produced no result Rick went to his solicitor in Whangarei. The latter's pressure on the ministry was more successful. But it was not until April 1988 that a formal explanation was to arrive in New Zealand from the Spanish Foreign Ministry in Madrid.

In a letter to the family solicitor a New Zealand Foreign Affairs official wrote: 'The Head of the Consular Division at the Spanish Foreign Affairs Ministry has told us that usually the Spanish authorities in the place of death notify the Spanish

Foreign Ministry who inform the relevant embassy. He said in this case the system had quite unusually gone wrong. But, he added, it was rare in Spain for a foreigner to be living virtually alone and without any communication whatsoever with relatives abroad ... We have accepted the Spanish authorities' assurances that such cases are few and far between, and are satisfied that the question should be left with the New Zealand government having registered concern that the Spanish authorities failed in this instance.'

The pursuit of Jean's passport and possessions took longer. The former was eventually returned to the family and proved helpful in identifying her movements in her last years. But all attempts to trace the few things she had taken to Majorca in her handbag and valise failed. The lengthy search for them was eventually the subject of a long, detailed report by the Regional Information Brigade of the Palma Police. A translation of the report reached the family in May 1988.

On first reading we were astounded at the accurate and definitive summary it gave of Jean's movements in the Spanish territories after her return to Europe from Jamaica in 1953 – even down to her addresses and some of her *residencia* permit numbers and dates. We were filled with admiration for Spanish police thoroughness. But something bothered us about this precise catalogue; in the manner and order of its presentation it looked uncommonly familiar. Suddenly the truth dawned: it was an immaculate regurgitation of all the information we had collected so painfully over the twelve months of our own detective operation and which Caroline had translated into Spanish and sent on behalf of the family to the Spanish Ministry of the Interior and Police. That it now came back to us in the guise of original Spanish police work we found charmingly ironical.

The police report described the extensive search for Jean's possessions. They had even approached Lord Acton, the Palma post office, the local branch of Barclays Bank, the cemetery and Britannia Airways. At Court No. 3 at the Ministry of Justice in Palma, where a judge had ordered her burial, there was no record of the personal effects which the Hotel Vista Porto Pi staff claimed to have handed to the ministry's officials. The family finally gave up, concluding that the possessions had either been destroyed at the time of her burial, or stolen.

Although she ended her life in a pauper's grave, Jean was not poor. Her extreme caution with money – except where aviation causes were concerned – led many people to believe she had fallen on hard times, but when probate was finally obtained on her estate late in 1988 her total worth was disclosed to be very close to £100,000.

She left it to aviation organisations, to her nephews Rick and Jim, and to her nieces Isobel and Penny – the latter the daughter of her brother John, who got nothing. Yet he was probably the only surviving person who had helped her tangibly with money during her lean years. When she had been stranded and penniless in New Zealand early in 1931 he had paid her boat fare back to London, and given her a roof over her head. When she was distraught with grief after Ellen's death he had extended the olive branch and offered her a home in Auckland.

I went down to Colchester to meet him again after the news of her death. I had wondered, now that he knew Jean was dead, whether he might feel free to speak at last of the matters that had brought fifty years of silence between them. But he did not; and I did not press him.

In England that early winter of late 1987 I found one of the few remaining airworthy Gipsy Moths in the world. Temporarily we attached to its wings and fuselage the registration letters of the almost identical aeroplane which, in 1934, had taken Jean to fame – G-AARB. On a bleak and freezing day in December its owner, Michael Vaisey, who had earlier introduced us to the Dorée family, bravely flew it for us in the dense, oppressive grey haze that shrouded Bedfordshire while we filmed it through the open door of a Cessna 172. In close formation we rose through a thick blanket of low cloud and broke out into a tunnel of watery yellow sunlight amid the tendrils of another threatening cloud mass above.

Here was the imagery the documentary needed of the fragile silhouette of her biplane crossing the world. The Moth had no radio. We couldn't talk to its pilot. But we sensed his loneliness. As he twitched along beside us, in a mind-numbing air temperature of −15°C, we knew briefly the utter vulnerability and just a little of the fear that had been Jean's constant companions.

Back in New Zealand the horror people felt at the news of her appalling end was shortlived. There was talk of a memorial to commemorate her; at the end of 1989, the government sent a cabinet minister to Majorca to unveil a plaque on the wall above the communal grave. And, eighteen months later, in Tenerife, the mayor of Puerto de la Cruz (whose town had begun, pridefully, to identify itself with the famous pilot who had lived there so anonymously) unveiled another plaque. It was put up in a prominent place in the entrance hall of the Avenida apartment building. The place has become a kind of shrine, now actively promoted by the local tourist board.

Many people believed that, in the way that permanent honour had been done in Sydney to Australia's flying hero, Sir Charles Kingsford Smith, Auckland's airport, where she had concluded the best remembered of all her flights and where she had wanted to be buried, should be named after her. But the airport's administrators lacked the courage and vision of their Sydney counterparts. They quibbled that it would create confusion to spring a new name on the airlines. So they took the easy option: they named just the international terminal after her. (It was left to the initiative of the mayor of Manukau City, in which the airport lies, to launch a public subscription to pay for a statue.) The terminal is seldom referred to by her name; passengers are largely unaware of its existence. But the less than adequate gesture seemed in keeping with the reluctance her country's government had shown when asked to look for her.

Yet she had, in her golden years, brought immense honour and lustre to New Zealand. And though it was not perhaps widely appreciated at the time, she became the finest woman pilot of the era, eminently superior in her navigation and airmanship and the consistency of her feats, to her more celebrated and better remembered colleagues, Amy Johnson and Amelia Earhart. Although she lived in their shadow Jean Batten was a greater perfectionist, a more brilliant organiser and a great deal more professional in her attitude to flying, creating more long-distance records than either of them. And where they both eventually killed themselves, Jean's ruthlessly high standards, and her messianic determination, kept her alive.

But although she survived, it was for a life of deep inner

loneliness. She chose for much of it to isolate herself from others and to sublimate her being in total fusion with a powerful and jealous mother. Ellen, some people said, had taken possession of her daughter's soul. Yet what Jean achieved, there is no question, she could not have accomplished without her. Her ultimate, brilliantly managed fame was a triumph for the symbiosis of their relationship.

That it was also at the expense of Jean's personal happiness, despite her brave and bold façade, there can be little doubt. The demands of the image of awesome perfection that she and Ellen decided to create led in turn to the web of deception and the covert existence so skilfully exercised and so resistant to research.

I came to distrust the verdicts of many of those who claimed to have known her best for, in truth, she revealed only a tiny part of herself to any of them. When Annette Reid had said in Tenerife, 'I don't believe she had a single intimate friend in the world – not one real friend,' I had not at the time believed it was possible. But, on the day I stood in Palma cemetery, staring in disbelief at the bleak, parched earth of communal grave No. 7, I knew I was confronting the tragic reality of it.

I also knew that, despite the years of the search, tracing her footprints across the world, the full explanation of the many contradictory features of her character that made her a unique phenomenon, had probably, in the end, eluded me.

The revelations that slowly exposed the true woman behind the fairy-princess image stirred many emotions, but, most persistently, deep sadness. Sadness that such resounding fame had yielded so little personal fulfilment and happiness; that her disappearance could produce such monumental indifference from friends, family and the government of her native land; that the ultimate tragedy had been descent into totally needless death.

But through that last bizarre, defiant gesture, Jean was spectacularly and ironically to remind the world of her heroic legend – guaranteeing her immortality as one of history's truly great aviators.

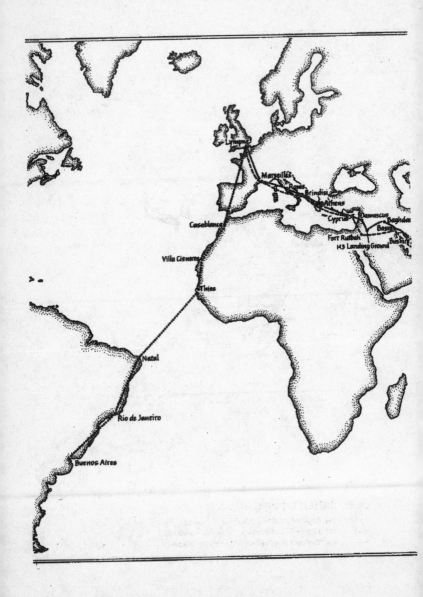

London

Marseilles
Rome
Brindisi
Athens
Cyprus   Damascus
                        Baghdad
Casablanca   Basra
                Fort Rutbah Bushire
                H3 Landing Ground

Villa Cisneros

Thies

Natal

Rio de Janeiro

Buenos Aires

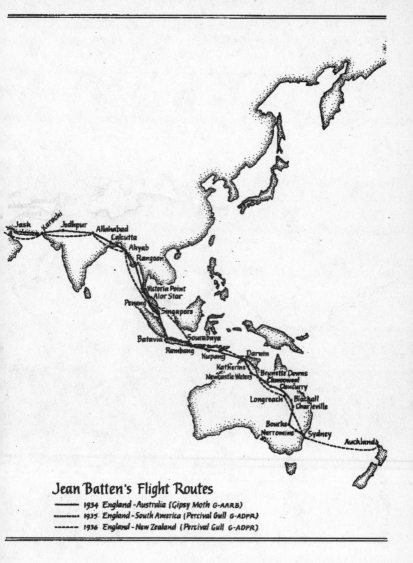

Jean Batten's Flight Routes

——— 1934 England – Australia (Gipsy Moth G-AARB)
·········· 1935 England – South America (Percival Gull G-ADPR)
------- 1936 England – New Zealand (Percival Gull G-ADPR)

Jask
Karachi
Jodhpur
Allahabad
Calcutta
Akyab
Rangoon
Victoria Point
Alor Star
Penang
Singapore
Batavia
Rambang
Kupang
Sourabaya
Darwin
Katherine
Newcastle Waters
Brunette Downs
Camoowal
Cloncurry
Longreach
Blackall
Charleville
Bourke
Narromine
Sydney
Auchlands

APPENDIX 1

Jean Batten's Principal Flights

1933 (9–16 April) England–Karachi. De Havilland Gipsy M Moth with Gipsy II engine (G-AALG). After series of forced landings crashed following engine failure on approach to Karachi, thus ending first attempt to fly to Australia.

1934 (21 April) England–Rome. De Havilland Gipsy M Moth with Gipsy I engine (G-AARB). This second Australia attempt ended when she ran out of fuel and crashed in rain and dark in the middle of the San Paolo wireless station in Rome. After major repairs to the aircraft she flew it back to Brooklands on 5–6 May for a third attempt.

1934 (8–23 May) England–Australia. Women's solo record of 14 days 22 hours 30 minutes from Lympne to Darwin beating Amy Johnson's 1930 time by over 4 days for the 10,500-mile flight. Reached Sydney 30 May.
 Route: Lympne – Marseilles – Rome – Brindisi – Athens – Cyprus – Damascus – Rutbah Wells – Baghdad – Basra – Bushire – Jask – Karachi – Jodhpur – Allahabad – Calcutta – Akyab – Rangoon – Victoria Point – Alor Star – Singapore –

Batavia – Surabaya – Lombok Island – Kupang – Darwin – Katherine – Newcastle Waters – Brunette Downs – Camooweal – Cloncurry – Blackall – Charleville – Bourke – Narromine – Sydney.

1935 (8–29 April) Australia–England. Gipsy Moth (G-AARB). Time from Darwin to Lympne 17 days 16 hours 15 minutes was women's solo record. Jean thus became the first woman to fly solo from England to Australia and back.

Route: Sydney – Bourke – Longreach – Winton – Cloncurry – Camooweal – Newcastle Waters – Darwin – Kupang – Lombok Island – Surabaya – Batavia – Singapore – Alor Star – Victoria Point – Rangoon – Akyab – Calcutta – Allahabad – Jhansi – Jodphur – Karachi – Jask – Basra – Baghdad – Damascus – Cyprus – Athens – Foggia – Rome – Marseilles – Lyons – Dijon – Abbeville – Croydon.

1935 (11–13 November) England–Brazil. Percival Gull 6 with Gipsy Six engine (G-ADPR). World absolute records (for pilots of either sex in any type of aircraft) of 2 days 13 hours 15 minutes for the 5,000-mile flight from Lympne to Natal and of 13 hours 15 minutes for the 1,900-mile South Atlantic crossing from Thies in Senegal to Natal in Brazil. First woman to fly herself from England to South America.

Route: Lympne – Casablanca – Villa Cisneros – Thies – Natal – Araruama (forced landing on beach compelled by fuel leak) – Rio de Janeiro – Pando – Buenos Aires – Montevideo – Buenos Aires.

1936 (5–16 October) England–New Zealand. Percival Gull 6 (G-ADPR). World absolute record: 14,224 miles in 11 days 45 minutes total elapsed time which included 2½ days stopover in Sydney. First direct flight from England to New Zealand and world absolute record for flight from Australia to New Zealand (Sydney–Auckland in 10½ hours). Also broke England–Australia solo record (for either sex) with Lympne–Darwin time of 5 days 21 hours.

Route: Lympne – Marseilles – Brindisi – Cyprus – H3 landing ground (Syrian Desert) – Basra – Karachi – Allahabad – Akyab

– Penang – Singapore – Rambang – Kupang – Darwin –
Brunette Downs – Longreach – Charleville – Sydney –
Auckland.

1937 (19–24 October) Australia–England. Percival Gull 6 (G-
ADPR). Solo record (for either sex) of 5 days 18 hours 15
minutes becoming first person to hold both England–Australia
out and back solo records simultaneously.

Route: Sydney – Charleville – Winton – Camooweal –
Newcastle Waters – Daly Waters – Darwin – Rambang –
Batavia – Alor Star – Rangoon – Allahabad – Karachi – Basra
– Damascus – Athens – Naples – Marseilles – Lympne –
Croydon.

APPENDIX 2

Jean Batten's Honours

Decorations

1935 *Brazil*: Officer of the Order of the Southern Cross.

1936 *France*: Chevalier of the Legion of Honour.

1936 *Britain*: Commander of the Order of the British Empire (CBE).

Trophies

Britannia Trophy, awarded by the Royal Aero Club for the most meritorious flight of the year by a British subject in 1935 and 1936.

Segrave Trophy, awarded for the most outstanding demonstration of the possibilities of transport on land, water or in the air, 1936.

Johnston Memorial Air Navigation Trophy, awarded by the Guild of Air Pilots and Air Navigators, London, 1936.

Harmon International Trophy (USA), awarded for the most outstanding flight by a woman in 1935 (jointly with Amelia Earhart) and outright in 1936 and 1937.

Challenge Trophy, awarded for outstanding flying achievements by the Women's International Association of Aeronautics (USA) in 1934, 1935 and 1936.

Coupe de Sibour, 1937.

Medals

Fédération Aéronautique Internationale (Awarded 1938 on the vote of twenty-two member countries. First time awarded to a woman aviator.)

Royal Aero Club of Great Britain

Academie des Sports (France)

Danish Royal Aeronautical Society

Aero Club de France

Swedish Royal Aero Club

Ligue Internationale des Aviateurs

Aero Club of Argentina

Aero Club of Finland

Royal Aero Club of Norway

BIBLIOGRAPHY

Babington Smith, Constance: *Amy Johnson* (Collins, 1967)

Batten, Jean: *Solo Flight* (Jackson & O'Sullivan, 1934); *My Life* (Harrap, 1938): reissued as *Alone in the Sky* (Airlife, 1979)

Boase, Wendy: *The Sky's the Limit: Women Pioneers in Aviation* (Osprey, 1979)

Chichester, Francis: *Solo to Sydney* (Conway Maritime Press, 1982)

Churchill, Sarah: *Keep on Dancing* (Weidenfeld & Nicolson, 1981)

Curtis, Lettice: *The Forgotten Pilots* (G.T. Foulis, 1971)

Davis, Pedr: *Charles Kingsford-Smith* (Landsdowne Press, 1985)

Ewing, Ross (and Ross MacPherson): *The History of New Zealand Aviation* (Heinemann, 1986)

Frater, Alexander: *Beyond the Blue Horizon* (Heinemann, 1986)

Hudson, Kenneth (and Julian Pettifer): *Diamonds in the Sky* (The Bodley Head/BBC Publications, 1979)

Jillet, Leslie: *Wings Across the Tasman* (A.H. & A.W. Reed, 1953)

Johnson, Howard: *Wings over Brooklands* (Whittet Books, 1981)

Joy, William: *The Aviators* (Rigby, 1965)

Lomax, Judy: *Women of the Air* (John Murray, 1986)

Lovell, Mary: *Straight on Till Morning: The Biography of Beryl Markham* (Hutchinson, 1987)

MacKenzie, Roy: *Solo: The Bert Hinkler Story* (Jacaranda Press, 1962)

Mitchell, Harold: *The Spice of Life* (The Bodley Head, 1974)

Moolman, Valerie: *Women Aloft* (Time-Life Books, 1981)

Parker, John: *King of Fools* (Macdonald, 1988)

Payne, L.G.S.: *Air Dates* (Heinemann, 1957)

Penrose, Harald: *Wings Across the World* (Cassell, 1980)

Sands, Frederick (and Sven Broman) *The Divine Garbo* (Sidgwick & Jackson, 1979)

Sharp, C. Martin: *DH: A History of de Havilland* (Airlife, 1982)

Swinson, Arthur: *The Great Air Race* (Cassell, 1968)

Taylor, Sir Gordon: *The Sky Beyond* (Cassell, 1963)

Taylor, Michael J.H. (and David Mondey): *Milestones of Flight* (Janes, 1983)

Taylor, John W.R. (and Kenneth Munson): *History of Aviation* (New English Library, 1975)

Walker, Alexander: *Garbo: A Portrait* (Weidenfeld & Nicolson, 1980)

White, Leo: *Wingspread* (Unity Press, 1941)

Wixted, Edward P.: *The North-West Aerial Frontier 1919–1934* (Boolarong Publications, 1985)

ACKNOWLEDGEMENTS

I wish to express much gratitude to the following people and organisations who helped me establish the story of Jean Batten's life and aided my efforts to understand the person she was:

Australia

Nell Cavell, Jack Chapman, Angela Darling, Sue Duval, Rita Fozzard, Layne Glanville Williams, Ivy Graves, Dorothy Herbert, Tom Hollinrake, the Rt Hon Barry Jones, Peg Kelman, Beverley Leech, Esther Mather, Bob and Janette Miles, Jim McDougall, Peter O'Reilly, Senja Robey, Bruce Shaxson, Arch Steinbeck, Kath Sunderland, Nancy Bird Walton, Ted Wixted, Brian B. Whitton.

Organisations in Australia

Bureau of Air Safety (Department of Aviation, Canberra), Department of Aviation, Queensland, The Longreach Leader.

Britain

Lord Balfour of Inchrye, Dr Glyn Bennet (University of Bristol), Edna Bianchi, Captain Brian Calvert, Zena Carus, the late Judith Chisholm, Gavin Cochrane, Doreen Courtney, the late Victor Dorée, Grace Dorée, Mary Dorée, Eva Fitzpatrick, Alex Henshaw, Deborah Hulme, Bob Hutchinson, Percy Jayes, Norman Jones, Rosemary Madoc, Margaret Mackay, Stewart Mackay, Penny Messer, Elizabeth Millar, Chris Morris (Shuttleworth Collection), the Earl of Onslow, Ron Paine, Bob Parker-Eaton, Bob and Lyn Pooley, Hilda Pooley, Air Commodore Henry Probert, Nicolas Sangines, Ian Scott-Hill, Laurel Stewart (now Lady Armstrong), John Stroud, Peter Symes (Shuttleworth Collection), Diana and Romer Topham, Muriel Tucker, Reginald Turnill, Michael Vaisey, Squadron Leader Malcolm Willey, Dr Glenn Wilson (Institute of Psychiatry), J.R.C. Young.

Organisations in Britain

Air Historical Branch (RAF), Barclays Bank Trust Co Ltd, Barclays Bank plc, Bowden House Clinic, Britannia Airways, British Aerospace (Hatfield), BBC Written Archives Centre (Caversham), British Council, British Library (Colindale), British Women Pilots' Association, Brooklands Museum, Burmah-Castrol Group, City of London Guildhall Library, Civil Aviation Authority, Thomas Cook & Sons, Croydon Airport Society, Daily Express, Guild of Air Pilots and Air Navigators, Hunting Engineering Ltd, Interpol Section – New Scotland Yard, Ministry of Defence, National Army Museum Archives, National Savings Bank, New Zealand High Commission (London), Public Record Office (Kew), Royal Aero Club, Royal Aeronautical Society, Shuttleworth Collection, Spanish National Tourist Office, the Stock Exchange, The Times Newspaper Archives, the staff of the Aviation Records section of the Royal Air Force Museum.

Jamaica

C.D. 'Bobby' Alexander, Blanche Blackwell, Morris Cargill, Fiona and John Edwards, Beth Jacobs, Anne Keighly, Lady Mitchell, Ertis Morrison, Anne-Marie Muirhead, T.A.D. Smith, Hurley and Dorothea Whitehorn.

New Zealand

Don Batten, Glen Batten, Jim and Rhoda Batten, Rick and Margaret Batten, Karlye Baynes, Gwen Blott, Muriel Bradshaw, Frank Brittain, Joyce Burch, Alice Carrick-Robertson, Pam and Ces Collins, Dr Alvin de Berry, Gloria Deighton, Carole and Don Denison, Frank and Aileen Drewitt, Dr Ruth Flashoff, Connie Foubister, Oscar Garden, Lucy Goodison, Ramai Hayward, Frances Herdson, Hermione Heywood, Cyril Hilliard, Clare Higham, Zena Ireland, John and Audrey Jamieson, Susie Johnson, David Kelly, Puti Kingdon, the late Captain Fred Ladd, Alan Carlisle, Mary Lee-Richards, Yvonne Loader, Willow Macky, Kathy Martin, Zelda McCracken, Ola McCullogh, Ena Monk, Sir Robert Muldoon, Tim Murphy, Lionel Murray, Mary Nathan, Mervyn Norrish, Anne and Megan Older, Bill Oliver, Connie Parker, Eric Patterson, Hayden Patterson, Ron and Estelle Richardson, Clare Robinson, Isobel Scott-Davidson, Bill Sexton, Betty Sharman, Bob and Doris Smillie, Noya Smith, Ted Smith, Eleanor Spragg, Freda Stark, Isabel Stokes, Michael Tubberty, Reg Truman, the late Rose Truman, Shirley-Anne Truman, Betty Walker, Eva Warren, Keith Watson, G.N. Wells, E. White, Lorraine Wilson (Museum of Transport and Technology), Douglas Wood, Joe Wright, Julia Yates.

Organisations in New Zealand

Alexander Turnbull Library, Auckland Public Library, Auckland Museum, Department of Internal Affairs, Department of Justice, Department of Social Welfare, Invercargill City Library,

Jean Batten School (Mangere), Ministry of Defence, Ministry of Foreign Affairs, Museum of Transport and Technology, NZ Airwomen's Association, *New Zealand Herald*, NZ Military Historical Society, Rotorua City Council Museum, Wanganui City Council Library.

Spain

Costa del Sol: Lewis and Trudi Benjamin, Mayor and staff, Municipality of Fuengirola.

Majorca: Maria Alcarez, Gabriel Colom Ramis, Tony Estella Salom, Ray Fleming, Bert Horsfall, Padre Mas, Michael McLoughlin (British Consul), Inspector Francisco Oliver (Spanish National Police).

Tenerife: Señor Baez, Banco Hispano Americano, Alan and Nollie Birch, Hermione Chadwick, Irene Davies, Keith Hazel (British Vice-Consul), Mary Ireland, Señor and Señora Jose-Maria, Noel and Annette Reid.

Other

Denise Almao (NZ Embassy Rome), Marie de Beauregarde (French Women Pilots' Association), Natasha Chernikova (NZ Embassy Rome), Sven Hugosson (Royal Swedish Aero Club), Stig Kernell (Royal Swedish Aero Club), Mila Meuser (Switzerland), Romano Nodari (RAI Italian Television), Graham Payn (Switzerland).

Extract Acknowledgements

I am grateful to Curtis Brown on behalf of the estate of Lady Audley for permission to quote from Sarah Churchill's autobiography *Keep on Dancing*.

Crown copyright material quoted in the Whitehall correspondence about the award of Jean's CBE is reproduced by permission of the Controller of Her Majesty's Stationery Office.

Photographic Acknowledgements

For her perfectionist photocopying work, restoring many priceless pictures in the Batten family collection, I owe special thanks to Auckland photographer Anne Carpenter.

INDEX

WARNER BOOKS

WARNER BOOKS
Cash Sales Department, P.O. Box 11, Falmouth, Cornwall, TR10 9EN
Tel: +44(0) 1326 372400. Fax +44 (0) 1326 374888
Email: books@barni.avel.co.uk

POST and PACKAGING:
Payments can be made as follows: cheque, postal order (payable to Warner Books)
or by credit cards. Do not send cash or currency.

| U.K. Orders | FREE OF CHARGE |
| E.E.C. & Overseas | 25% of order value |

Name (Block Letters) _____

Address _____

_____

Post/zip code: _____

☐ Please keep me in touch with future Warner publications

☐ I enclose my remittance £ _____

☐ I wish to pay by Visa/Access/Mastercard/Eurocard

Card Expiry Date

| | | | | | | | | | | | | | | | | |

_____